The Syntax of Volitives in Biblical Hebrew and Amarna Canaanite Prose

Linguistic Studies in Ancient West Semitic

edited by

Cynthia L. Miller-Naudé and Jacobus Naudé

The series Linguistic Studies in Ancient West Semitic is devoted to the ancient West Semitic languages, including Hebrew, Aramaic, Ugaritic, and their near congeners. It includes monographs, collections of essays, and text editions informed by the approaches of linguistic science. The material studied will span from the earliest texts to the rise of Islam.

1. *The Verbless Clause in Biblical Hebrew: Linguistic Approaches*, edited by Cynthia L. Miller
2. *Phonology and Morphology of Biblical Hebrew: An Introduction*, by Joshua Blau
3. *A Manual of Ugaritic*, by Pierre Bordreuil and Dennis Pardee
4. *Word Order in the Biblical Hebrew Finite Clause: A Syntactic and Pragmatic Analysis of Preposing*, by Adina Moshavi
5. *Oath Formulas in Biblical Hebrew*, by Blane Conklin
6. *Biblical Hebrew Grammar Visualized*, by Francis I. Andersen and A. Dean Forbes
7. *Time and the Biblical Hebrew Verb: The Expression of Tense, Aspect, and Modality in Biblical Hebrew*, by John A. Cook
8. *Diachrony in Biblical Hebrew*, edited by Cynthia L. Miller-Naudé and Ziony Zevit
9. *The Syntax of Volitives in Biblical Hebrew and Amarna Canaanite Prose*, by Hélène Dallaire

The Syntax of Volitives in Biblical Hebrew and Amarna Canaanite Prose

Hélène Dallaire

Winona Lake, Indiana
Eisenbrauns
2014

www.eisenbrauns.com

Library of Congress Cataloging-in-Publication Data

Dallaire, Hélène.
The syntax of volitives in biblical Hebrew and Amarna Canaanite prose / Hélène Dallaire.
pages cm.—(Linguistic studies in Ancient West Semitic ; 9)
Includes bibliographical references and indexes.
ISBN 978-1-57506-307-2 (hardback : alk. paper)
1. Hebrew language—Grammar, Comparative—Canaanite language. 2. Hebrew language—Verb. 3. Canaanite language—Verb. 4. Tell el-Amarna tablets. I. Title.
PJ4564.D35 2014
492.45—dc23
2014033733

The paper used in this publication meets the minimum requirements of the American National Standard for Information Sciences—Permanence of Paper for Printed Library Materials. ANSI Z39.48-1984.⊗™

Contents

Acknowledgments

It gives me great pleasure to acknowledge those who have been instrumental in stimulating my interest in the topic of this book and have provided support throughout this academic project. First, I wish to thank my doctoral adviser, Stephen A. Kaufman, who freely shared his expertise in Comparative Semitics and stretched my abilities to comprehend better the peoples and languages of the ancient Near East. I could not have accomplished this task without his continual support and professional guidance. I also thank my second reader, Nili Fox, whose support and rich suggestions contributed to the fine-tuning of this manuscript. I am indebted to the late Anson F. Rainey, whose endless inspiration and generous contribution energized me to complete this work. Sincere thanks to Annalisa Azzoni, who spent countless hours reading my drafts, making recommendations, and proofreading every part of the manuscript.

I am deeply grateful to Cynthia L. Miller-Naudé and the late Michael P. O'Connor, who provided invaluable recommendations when I submitted the manuscript for publication in the LSAWS series. Their investment of time and scholarly expertise contributed significantly to the improvement of the original manuscript. To Jim Eisenbraun and the Eisenbrauns staff, especially my editor Beverly McCoy, whose support I value highly, I am extremely thankful.

I thank my friends in Canada, the U.S., Israel, the Philippines, and elsewhere around the world who have been sources of strength along the way. I honor, respect, and thank my family, especially my late mother, who continually provided humorous words of encouragement, inspiration, and faithful support, even in her times of grave illness. And most of all, to my Creator, whose constant presence provided meaning for the entire project: to Him be the glory!

Abbreviations

General

ASV	American Standard Version
BH	Biblical Hebrew
c.	common
coh.	cohortative
CS	Central Semitic
EA	El Amarna
f.	feminine
impv(s).	imperative(s)
JPS	Jewish Publication Society Version
juss.	jussive
KJV	King James Version
m.	masculine
n(n).	note(s)
NIV	New International Version
NJPS	New Jewish Publication Society Version
NRSV	New Revised Standard Version
p/pl.	plural
pron.	pronoun/pronominal
PS	Proto-Semitic
s/sg.	singular
WTT	William Tyndale Translation of the Bible

Reference Works

AcOr	*Acta Orientalia*
AfO	*Archiv für Orientforschung*
ANET	*Ancient Near Eastern Texts Relating to the Old Testament.* Edited by J. B. Pritchard. 3rd ed. Princeton, 1969
AnOr	Analecta Orientalia
AO	*Der Alte Orient*
AOAT	Alter Orient und Altes Testament
AOS	American Oriental Series
ArOr	*Archiv Orientální*
AuOr	*Aula Orientalis*
BAR	*Biblical Archaeology Review*
BASOR	*Bulletin of the American Schools of Oriental Research*
BASS	*Beiträge zur Assyriologie und semitischen Sprachwissenschaft*

BDB	F. Brown, S. R. Driver, and C. A. Briggs, editors. *A Hebrew and English Lexicon of the Old Testament with an Appendix Containing the Biblical Aramaic*. Oxford, 1996
BeO	*Bibbia e Oriente*
BHL	*Bibliotheca Hagiographica Latina Antiquae et Mediae Aetatis*. 2 vols. Brussels, 1898–1901
Bib	*Biblica*
BiOr	*Bibliotheca Orientalis*
BSOAS	*Bulletin of the School of Oriental and African Studies*
CAT	A. F. Rainey. *Canaanite in the Amarna Tablets: A Linguistic Analysis of the Mixed Dialect Used by the Scribes from Canaan*. 4 vols. Leiden, 1996
CBQ	*Catholic Biblical Quarterly*
FO	*Folia Orientalia*
GKC	*Gesenius' Hebrew Grammar*. Edited by E. Kautzsch. Translated by A. E. Cowley. 2nd ed. Oxford, 1910
HAR	*Hebrew Annual Review*
HO	Handbuch der Orientalistik
HS	*Hebrew Studies*
HSM	Harvard Semitic Monographs
HSS	Harvard Semitic Studies
HUCA	*Hebrew Union College Annual*
IEJ	*Israel Exploration Journal*
IOS	Israel Oriental Studies
JAAR	*Journal of the American Academy of Religion*
JANES	*Journal of the Ancient Near Eastern Society*
JAOS	*Journal of the American Oriental Society*
JBL	*Journal of Biblical Literature*
JCS	*Journal of Cuneiform Studies*
JHS	*Journal of Hebrew Studies*
JNES	*Journal of Near Eastern Studies*
JNSL	*Journal of Northwest Semitic Languages*
JQR	*Jewish Quarterly Review*
JSem	*Journal of Semitics*
JSOT	*Journal for the Study of the Old Testament*
JSOTSup	Journal for the Study of the Old Testament: Supplement Series
JSS	*Journal of Semitic Studies*
JTS	*Journal of Theological Studies*
LASBF	*Liber Annuus Studii Biblici Franciscani*
MUSJ	*Mélanges de l'Université Saint-Joseph*
OLA	Orientalia Lovaniensia Analecta
Or	*Orientalia* (n.s.)
RB	*Revue Biblique*
SBFLA	*Studii Biblici Franciscani Liber Annus*
Sem	*Semitica*
UF	*Ugarit-Forschungen*
VT	*Vetus Testamentum*

VTSup	Vetus Testamentum Supplements
WTJ	*Westminster Theological Journal*
ZA	*Zeitschrift für Assyriologie*
ZAH	*Zeitschrift für Althebräistik*
ZAW	*Zeitschrift für die alttestamentliche Wissenschaft*

Chapter 1
Introduction

1.1. Introduction

Over the last century, numerous books and articles have been published on the verbal system of the Semitic languages. Thanks to the discovery of Ugaritic texts, libraries of Akkadian tablets, Canaanite letters found at Tell el-Amarna in Egypt, Hebrew and Aramaic inscriptions, and the Dead Sea Scrolls, our understanding of the phonology, morphology, and syntax of the Semitic languages has increased greatly.

My interest in the verbal system, more specifically in the syntactic relationships of volitives,[1] emerged while I was studying Semitic languages and teaching Biblical Hebrew to students of various backgrounds. I observed that the morphology of individual verbs was overemphasized while the syntax of each form in context was understated. As a result, students often failed to understand the author's intended message expressed through the intricacies of the language.

Over the past decades, linguists have examined the syntax of languages from a number of perspectives.[2] I believe, as do text-linguists, that a text

1. In Semitic studies, volitives are verbal forms (e.g., cohortative, imperative, jussive) marked for wishes, requests, petitions, and commands. They belong to the world of direct volitives in the subsystem of *irrealis* mood (J. A. Cook, *Time and the Biblical Hebrew Verb: The Expression of Tense, Aspect, and Modality in Biblical Hebrew* [LSAWS 7; Winona Lake, IN: Eisenbrauns, 2012] 237). In the world of linguistics, volitives belong to the category of deontic modality, a subjective system in which the speaker wishes to influence a future act or event ("wish, desire, volition"). The speaker's utterance is considered an illocutionary act. In deontic modality, the desired event always refers to the future (D. P. Ziegeler, "Mood and Modality in Grammar," in *Encyclopedia of Language and Linguistics* [ed. K. Brown; 14 vols.; 2nd ed.; Oxford: Elsevier, 2006] 8:259–67; K. Allan, "Mood, Clause Types, and Illocutionary Force," *Encyclopedia of Language and Linguistics*, 8:267–71).

2. Syntax "refers to the organization of the words in a sentence and to the set of rules or constraints that organize words into sentences" (J.-P. Koenig, "Syntax-Semantics Interface," *Encyclopedia of Language and Linguistics*, 12:427). Linguists recognize that the study of syntax is complex and at times subjective. According to Bloomfield, "[D]etails of syntax are often complicated and hard to describe . . . obscured . . . in most treatises, by the use of philosophical instead of formal definitions of constructions and form-classes" (L. Bloomfield, *Language* [New York: Holt, Rinehart & Winston, 1963] 201). On the other hand, "young children developing language typically acquire their system with relative ease and, for some aspects of syntax, in a relatively short time period. Children demonstrate some

cannot be studied outside its context or macrostructure, where the overall purpose of the discourse is found. Therefore, I have chosen to examine the volitives of the Northwest Semitic (NWSemitic) languages,[3] not only as individual morphemes of modality, but as linguistic elements within the larger framework of syntax. I will comment on the following elements:

1. Morphology[4]
2. Degree of markedness for volitional nuances
3. Types of clauses with volitives
4. Word order in clauses with volitives
5. Verbal sequences
6. Sociolinguistic elements (e.g., speaker/listener relationships)

A study of this magnitude must acknowledge its challenges. The biblical corpus is a multiauthored and multilayered text that represents scribal traditions from multiple dialects ranging from north to south Canaan (and no doubt beyond), with various layers of editing, completed over centuries.[5] Consequently, any attempt to describe one paradigm for the modal system of volitives presents its challenges. Thus, I have chosen to limit my research to the prose texts mentioned below (see §1.4. Corpus).

In Semitic languages, verbal systems of modality include the following forms: jussives, precatives, cohortatives,[6] imperatives, and subjunctives. Other

knowledge of the syntax of their language when they combine words productively, that is, they use combinations that are new, not just imitations, or when they show understanding of different combinations" (E. L. Bavin, "Syntactic Development," *Encyclopedia of Language and Linguistics*, 12:383). For a detailed discussion on Linguistics theories related to Semitic studies, see Cook, *Time and the Biblical Hebrew Verb*, 1–76. Cook surveys major linguistic theories on Tense (e.g., "Universal Tense" theory of Jespersen; "R-Point" theories of Reichenbach, Hornstein, Bull, Comrie, Decklerck, Klein, Olsen) and Aspect (e.g., Situational, Phasal, and Viewpoint). In his article on the place of linguists in biblical studies, Bodine provides a survey of the history of the study of syntax from the fifth century to the early 1990s (W. Bodine, "How Linguists Study Syntax," in *Linguistics and Biblical Hebrew* [ed. W. R. Bodine; Winona Lake, IN: Eisenbrauns, 1992] 89–107). He describes the approaches of grammarians and linguists, beginning with Protagoras, Priscian, and Helias, followed by the Renaissance years when, according to him, "[T]he study of syntax did not notably advance" (p. 93) and continuing with a brief explanation of the following methods: the syntagmatic and paradigmatic approaches of de Saussure, the Bloomfield school, glossematics (Hjelmslev), functionalism (Trubetzkoy and Jakobson), systemic-functional linguistics (Halliday), tagmemics (Pike and Longacre), stratificational grammar (Lamb and Lockwood), transformation-generative grammar (Chomsky), among others.

3. The NWSemitic languages are the languages of Syria–Palestine.

4. Only where directly relevant to our study.

5. According to Ohad Cohen, "[I]t is almost certain that more than a few linguistic changes occurred over the ages" (Ohad Cohen, *The Verbal Tense System in Late Biblical Hebrew Prose* [HSS 63; Winona Lake, IN: Eisenbrauns, 2013] 10).

6. Jussives are also called "optatives" (Tali Bar, "Optative Expressions," in *Encyclopedia of Hebrew Language and Linguistics* [ed. Geoffrey Kahn; Leiden: Brill, 2013] 3:716). Cohortatives are also called "hortatives."

verbal forms such as the *yiqtol*, *weqatal*, and the infinitive absolute, though not normally included in the category of volitives, adopt modal functions under specific conditions, especially where they are syntactically connected to volitives.

In this book, I will focus primarily on NWSemitic prose in which "wishes," "desires," "requests," and "commands" are expressed through the verbal forms mentioned above. Volitional concepts are found in every language, expressed through specific verbal morphemes, syntagmas, intonation,[7] syntax, and/or through other linguistic means. The Semites of the ancient Near East (ANE) undoubtedly expressed modality in more ways than those to which we have access (e.g., through intonation, body language, volume level).[8] My research must accept its limitations and depend solely on literary evidence in order to reach its conclusions.

Through an examination of the NWSemitic prose texts, especially the prose of Biblical Hebrew and Amarna Canaanite, I will attempt to answer the following questions: Do volitives function in a similar way from language to language in the NWS corpus? Where and why are there overlaps in morphology and syntax among the various languages? What morphological and syntactical differences exist among the languages? In attempting to answer these questions, I will keep in mind that, within each of the languages, scribes from different areas used, to a greater or lesser extent, specific dialectal and scribal traditions (e.g., northern vs. southern, peripheral vs. central). Therefore, one language may show a variety of nuances represented by the same verbal form. These nuances depend on the geographical provenance of the document and/or the scribal tradition used in its composition.

1.2. Assumptions

My study of the volitives in Biblical Hebrew and Amarna Canaanite (EA) is based on the assumptions that: (1) it is possible to recognize modality in

7. E. Couper-Kuhlen speaks of at least three viewpoints on the linguistic approach to the study of "intonation": (1) intonation is a grammatical component of modality; (2) intonation is expressed in the information flow connected to the movement of ideas ("the information that is in the speaker's focus of consciousness at a given moment"); and (3) intonation as a contextualized linguistic sign, meaning that interpretation of intonation must be done within its context in order to be interpreted accurately. These three proposals are interconnected and rarely function independently from each other. In addition, the register, register shifts, timing, and rhythm of the intonation contribute to the level of modality in a discourse (W. Couper-Kuhlen, "Intonation and Discourse: Current Views from Within," in *The Handbook of Discourse Analysis* [ed. D. Shriffrin, D. Tannen, and H. E. Hamilton; Malden, MA: Blackwell, 2001] 14–16). Although access to "intonation" as a linguistic marker in ancient Semitic languages is lost to us, we can assume that it functioned as an element of the modal system nonetheless.

8. F. R. Palmer mentions that, through these "paralinguistic features of language," a great deal of the meaning of a message can be contained (F. R. Palmer, *Semantics* [Cambridge: Cambridge University Press, 1981] 39).

the direct discourse of NWSemitic languages through morphemes marked for modality (verbal and nonverbal), syntax, and word order; and (2) the modal system of Biblical Hebrew includes a *yaqtula* subjunctive that corresponds to that of the Ugaritic and EA modal forms. Due to the loss of final short vowels in Hebrew, the *yaqtula* can only be ascertained in the III-*he*, *biconsonantal*, and Hiphil of *strong* verbs under specific conditions.[9]

1.3. Methodology

The introductory chapter provides a basic definition of *modality* from the perspectives of linguistics and Semitic studies, and describes methods used to express modality in Semitic and non-Semitic languages.[10] The following two chapters (chap. 2: Biblical Hebrew [BH]; chap. 3: El-Amarna Canaanite [EA]) will describe and compare:

1. marked and unmarked verbal forms used to express nuances of wishes, commands, requests, deliberations (auto-suggestions), and other volitional ideas in dependent and independent clauses
2. sociolinguistic features and speech patterns in three main social contexts: (a) greater to lesser; (b) lesser to greater; and (c) between equals
3. syntactical features of volitives in multiclause sentences in which volitives are governing or are governed by other verbs (e.g., Imperative *followed by waw*-Jussive; Cohortative *followed by waw*-Jussive)
4. types of clauses with volitives (e.g., main, purpose/result)
5. the modal system (paradigm) of the language

---

9. The *yaqtula* is evident in the vocalized NWSemitic languages, in EA texts, and in Ugaritic where the verb is marked with a final *ʾalep*. See J. Huehnergard, *An Introduction to Ugaritic* (Peabody, MA: Hendrickson, 2012) 57; P. Bordreuil and D. Pardee, *A Manual of Ugaritic* (LSAWS 3; Winona Lake, IN: Eisenbrauns, 2009) 47–50; D. Pardee, "Ugaritic," in *The Ancient Languages of Syria–Palestine and Arabia* (ed. R. D. Woodard; Cambridge: Cambridge University Press, 2008) 21–23; idem, "Ugaritic," in *The Semitic Languages* (ed. R. Hetzron; New York: Routledge, 1997) 139; D. Sivan, *A Grammar of the Ugaritic Language* (Leiden: Brill, 2001) 103–7; J. Tropper, *Ugaritische Grammatik* (AOAT 273; Münster: Ugarit-Verlag, 2000) 455–57; A. F. Rainey, *Canaanite in the Amarna Tablets: A Linguistic Analysis of the Mixed Dialect Used by the Scribes from Canaan*, vol. 2: *Morphosyntactic Analysis of the Verbal System* (Leiden: Brill, 1996) 254–64; idem, "The Ancient Hebrew Prefix Conjugation in the Light of Amarnah Canaanite," *HS* 27 (1986) 4–19; H. Fleisch, "Yaqtula cananéen et subjonctif arabe," in *Studia Orientalia in Memoriam Caroli Brockelmann* (ed. Manfred Fleishhammer; Wissenschaftliche Zeitschrift der Martin Luther-Universität Halle-Wittenberg / Gesellschafts- und sprachwissenschaftliche Reihe 17/2–3; Halle: Martin Luther-Universität, 1968) 65–76; W. L. Moran, "Early Canaanite *yaqtula*," *Or* 29 (1960) 1–19.

10. The main focus will be placed on the evidence in Biblical Hebrew prose and in the correspondence of EA Canaanite, with additional examples taken from Ugaritic, Phoenician, Hebrew inscriptions, and Arabic, where they contribute directly to the discussion on the modal systems studied in this book.

The concluding chapter will present a summary of the findings and include a comparison of the volitional system in Biblical Hebrew and Amarna Canaanite, in light of the evidence found in other Semitic languages (e.g., Ugaritic and Arabic).

1.4. Corpus of Texts

The *primary* texts include:

1. *Biblical Hebrew*: prose texts from Genesis through 2 Kings, 1–2 Chronicles, Ruth, Esther, and Nehemiah[11]
2. *EA Canaanite*: EA 1–14 (Babylonia); 19–23 and 25–30 (Mittani); 33–40 (Alashia); 68–96 (Byblos–Rib-Haddi), 101–35 (Byblos); 267–71, 297–300, 378 (Gezer); 286–90 (Jerusalem); 362–67 (various rulers)

but treating all of these as a single corpus can be problematic!

The *secondary* texts include:[12]

1. *Ugaritic*:[13] all prose texts published — *so no epic texts? verbal discourse would be same! and they are narrative.*
2. *Phoenician*: Aḥiram, Yeḥimilk, and Šhipiṭbaʿal (Old Byblian); Kilamuwa and Azitawada (North Phoenician); Yeḥaumilk, Tabnit, and Ešmunazar (Middle Phoenician); Umm El-Amed, Piraeus, and Pirgy (Late Phoenician)
3. *Moabite, Ammonite, Edomite*: all texts published
4. *Hebrew inscriptions*: all texts published

---

11. Where directly relevant to our study, additional examples will be provided from the prophets and wisdom literature.

12. I will refer to the modal system of these NWSemitic languages only where they contribute significantly to our study.

13. The taxonomy of Ugaritic among the Semitic languages has been debated since the discovery of the tablets at Ras Shamra in 1929. According to J. F. Brent,

> [E]ach scholar places emphasis upon his own selection of isoglossae and draws his own conclusions from them. Even if two different scholars choose the same group of isoglossae they are likely to draw two different conclusions from the data. In addition, some place great weight on seemingly insignificant isoglossae while others intend first to "weigh" the isoglossic evidence and to choose those which seem to be the most important. (J. F. Brent, "The Problem of the Placement of Ugaritic among the Semitic Languages," *WTJ* 41 [1978] 84)

Consequently, Ugaritic has been identified with (1) the NWSemitic corpus or Northern Canaanite (e.g., D. Pardee, "Canaanite Dialects," in *The Ancient Languages of Syria–Palestine and Arabia* [ed. R. D. Woodard; Cambridge: Cambridge University Press, 2008] 103; Z. Harris, *Development of the Canaanite Dialects. An Investigation in Linguistic History* [repr., New Haven, CT: Yale University Press, 1967] 10–11); (2) the Central Semitic corpus (e.g., R. M. Voigt, "The Classification of Central Semitic," *JSS* 32 [1987] 1–21); and (3) the northern dialects (e.g., E. Lipiński, *Semitic Languages: Outline of a Comparative Grammar* [OLA 80; Leuven: Peeters, 2001] 50, 55, 59). I chose to include Ugaritic (when directly related to BH and EA) for its West Semitic features (e.g., morphology of the prefix conjugation) and for its affinities with the language of the EA Canaanite correspondence.

At the beginning of the research, I had planned on incorporating an Aramaic component into the book, but as the work progressed and the modal system became clearer through a study of the NWSemitic languages listed above, I opted to omit Aramaic. The Aramaic language is situated at one end of the dialectal continuum, while the Canaanite languages (e.g., Hebrew, Phoenician, Moabite, Edomite, and Ammonite) are clustered at the opposite end. The isoglosses that help identify the taxonomy of the Canaanite languages distance Aramaic from the Canaanite languages (e.g., the Canaanite shift is not a feature of Aramaic).[14] Consequently, I decided to limit my research to the NWSemitic (Canaanite) texts listed above.[15]

---

14. Rebecca Hasselbach, "Canaanite and Hebrew," in *Encyclopedia of Hebrew Language and Linguistics* (ed. Goeffrey Kahn; Leiden: Brill, 2013) 1:607; H. Gzella, "Northwest Semitic Languages and Hebrew," in *Encyclopedia of Hebrew Language and Linguistics* 2:852–63.

15. For information on the dialectal continuum, see W. R. Garr, *Dialect Geography of Syria–Palestine, 1000–586 B.C.E.* (repr., Winona Lake, IN: Eisenbrauns, 2004) 1–21. The taxonomy of Semitic languages is still debated by scholars. What was once presented as a three-branch system (*East Semitic*: Akkadian; *NW Semitic*: Canaanite, Ugaritic, Amorite, and Aramaic; and *South Semitic*: Arabic and Ethiopic) was challenged after the discovery of Semitic texts in other dialects/languages (e.g., Ebla, Mari, Tell Beydar). The similarities between the verbal system of Ugaritic and Arabic added to the complexity of the classification issue since Ugaritic was thought to belong to the NW Semitic branch and Arabic to the South Semitic category. The West Semitic group was eventually divided into two groups: Canaanite and Aramaic. Proponents of the Central Semitic hypothesis lumped into the same category Ugaritic, Hebrew, Aramaic, and Arabic, based on shared innovations. For scholarly discussions on the taxonomy of Semitic languages, see John Huehnergard, "Phyla and Waves: Models of Classification of the Semitic Languages," in *The Semitic Languages: An International Handbook* (ed. S. Weninger; Handbooks of Linguistics and Communication Science 36; Berlin: de Gruyter, 2011) 259–78; Jo Ann Hackett and N. Pat-El, "On Canaanite and Historical Linguistics: Rejoinder to Anson Rainey," *MAARAV* 17 (2010) 173–88; A. Rainey, "The Northwest Semitic Literary Repertoire and Its Acquaintance by Judean Writers," *MAARAV* 15 (2008) 193–205; idem, "Redefining Hebrew: A Transjordanian Language," *MAARAV* 14 (2007) 67–81; idem, "Whence Came the Israelites and Their Language," *IEJ* 57 (2007) 41–64; A. Rubin, "The Subgrouping of the Semitic Languages," in *Language and Linguistics Compass* 2 (2008) 79–102; Huehnergard, "Features of Central Semitic," 163; S. Izre'el, ed., *Semitic Linguistics: The State of the Art at the Turn of the Twenty-First Century* (Oriental Studies 20; Winona Lake, IN: Eisenbrauns, 2002); Lipiński, *Semitic Languages*, 48–90; A. Faber, "Genetic Subgrouping of the Semitic Languages," in *The Semitic Languages* (ed. R. Hetzron; New York: Routledge, 1997) 3–15; J. Huehnergard, "Remarks on the Classification of the Northwest Semitic Languages," in *The Balaam Text from Deir ʿAlla Re-Evaluated: Proceedings of the International Symposium Held at Leiden, 21–24 August 1989* (ed. J. Hoftijzer and G. van der Kooij; Leiden: Brill, 1991) 282–93; S. A. Kaufman, "The Classification of the North West Semitic Dialects of the Biblical Period and Some Implications Thereof," in *Proceedings of the Ninth World Congress of Jewish Studies. Panel Sessions: Hebrew and Aramaic Languages* (ed. M. Goshen-Gottstein; Jerusalem: Magnes, 1988) 41–57; R. Hetzron, "La division des languages sémitiques," in *Actes du premier congrès international de linguistique sémitique et chamito-sémitique* (ed. A. Caquot and D. Cohen; Berlin: de Gruyter, 1974) 181–94. For relationships between Uga-

Although the verbal systems of poetry and prose have much in common, the syntax of the verb in poetry differs significantly from that in prose. As stated by Douglas Gropp, "[T]here is much overlap in the functioning of the finite verb between poetry and prose, but the great bulk of the most *peculiar usages* [italics mine] of the finite verb forms is to be found in poetry."[16] For this reason, I decided to distance myself from the *peculiar usages* of the verbal forms in poetic texts and chose to limit my research solely to the prose texts of the corpus mentioned above.

1.5. Definition of Terms

1.5.1. Modality

Finding a single and simple definition for *modality* is challenging. Linguists have broached the subject "from different vantage points: philosophical, semantic, diachronic-typological, and formal synchronic-typological."[17] In his early work on discourse, Grimes highlighted the complexities of defining *mood* and *modality*. He noted:

> Mood borders on being a catchall term for a variety of systems that are not mutually exclusive with each other. One suspects that we might get farther toward understanding modal phenomena if we did not put them under the terminological umbrella of modal phenomena or mood—themselves terms that some linguists distinguish and others do not. Nevertheless, quite a few things that have to do with communication options, logical status, and attitude of the speaker toward the content of the message, are customarily stirred into this pot, and until we get a really clear idea of what the differences are they are likely to remain fixed in our minds as mood.[18]

In the first edition of *Mood and Modality* (1986), F. R. Palmer agreed with Grimes's statement, noting that "the notion of modality . . . is . . . vague and leaves open a number of possible definitions, though something along the lines of Lyons's 'opinion or attitude' of the speaker seems promising."[19] In the second edition (2001), Palmer describes *modality* as "the status of the proposition

ritic and Arabic, see A. Avanzini, "Origin and Classification of the Ancient South Arabian Languages," *JSS* 54 (2009) 205–20; A. S. Kaye, "Does Ugaritic Go with Arabic in Semitic Genealogical Sub-Classification?" *FO* 28 (1991) 115–28; Gzella, "Northwest Semitic Languages and Hebrew."

16. D. Gropp, "The Function of the Finite Verb in Classical Biblical Hebrew," *HAR* 13 (1991) 46.

17. E. Cohen, *Modal System of Old Babylonian*, 40.

18. Joseph E. Grimes, *The Thread of Discourse* (Janua Linguarum Series Minor 207; The Hague: Mouton, 1975) 234–35.

19. F. R. Palmer, *Mood and Modality* (Cambridge: Cambridge University Press, 1986) 2. See also J. Lyons, *Semantics* (Cambridge: Cambridge University Press. 1977) 2:452.

that describes the event"[20] and adopts the binary categories of *Realis* (e.g., nonmodal, declarative, indicative, factual, and assertion) and *Irrealis* (e.g., modal, nondeclarative, subjunctive, nonfactual, nonassertion) as the basis for his taxonomy of modality.[21]

On the grammatical level, Palmer remarks that categories for "mood" and "modal systems" are not evident in all languages. In some languages, a grammatical distinction exists between the system of modal verbs (e.g., specific verb forms) and the category of mood (e.g., indicative, subjunctive). In other languages, one of these two categories—"mood" and "verbal modal system"—seems to be more salient than the other. This is evident in languages where certain grammatical forms have mostly fallen into disuse or have disappeared altogether (e.g., the English subjunctive).[22] Palmer defines *mood* as "the grammaticalization of speakers' (subjective) attitudes and opinions."[23] He groups grammatical markers of modality under three headings: (1) individual suffixes, clitics, and particles; (2) inflection; and (3) modal verbs.[24]

Palmer highlights the binary distinction that exists between real and unreal propositions.[25] He states that, "typically with mood, all or most clauses are either Realis [e.g., indicative; nonmodal, declarative, factual] or Irrealis [e.g., subjunctive; modal, nondeclarative, nonfactual]: the system is basically ('prototypically') binary."[26] A second pair of features discussed by Palmer are the notions of *speculation* (epistemic modality) and *permission* (deontic modality):

20. F. R. Palmer, *Mood and Modality* (2nd ed.; Cambridge Textbooks in Linguistics; Cambridge: Cambridge University Press, 2001) 1.

21. Ibid., 1–3. Palmer refers to the work of Marianne Mithun who identifies *realis* modality with actualized situations (having occurred or occurring) and *irrealis* with situations that belong to the realm of thought (M. Mithun, *The Languages of Native North America* [Cambridge: Cambridge University Press, 1999] 173). Palmer treats the binary modal system of indicative/subjunctive in chapter 5 and the concepts of Realis/Irrealis in chapter 6. He states that this division is "to some degree a decision based more on practical considerations than on a clear set of criteria for the distinction" (*Mood and Modality* [2001], 5) but adds that "there are sufficient differences to warrant discussion of them in a separate chapter" (ibid.,145). Jan Joosten echoes Palmer and states that, "in the classical languages, the indicative mood expresses *realis*, while the other personal moods—subjunctive, optative, imperative—express *irrealis*. . . . the cohortative-imperative-jussive group clearly belongs to the realm of *irrealis*: the forms express commands, wishes, and contingent events, i.e., processes that have not yet come about" (*The Verbal System of Biblical Hebrew* [Jerusalem: Simor, 2013] 31–32).

22. Palmer, *Mood and Modality* (2001), 4.

23. Pamer, *Mood and Modality* (1986), 16.

24. Palmer, *Mood and Modality* (2001), 19.

25. Ibid., 1.

26. Ibid., 4; see also discussion on the use of the terms *realis* and *irrealis* vs. *indicative* and *subjunctive* on pp. 142–143.

1. *Epistemic* modality (propositional), which is linked to the degree of certainty a speaker expresses toward the potential realization of the proposition (e.g., he *must* find the location). In *epistemic modality*, a proposition is examined for its "possible" or "necessary" truth. This category also identifies the degree of commitment by the speaker toward his proposition (e.g., speculation, deduction, heard about, for the sake of appearance). Epistemic modality treats a proposition as information based on the knowledge and belief of a speaker.[27]
2. *Deontic* modality (event), which is linked to the degree of desire or wish (illocutionary force) the speaker employs to attempt to make the proposition become a reality (e.g., *Find* the location!).[28] In *deontic modality*, the proposition is examined for the degree of "obligation" or "permission" it contains; it points to the subject's desire to have the object perform a certain action ("directives").[29] This category includes the elements that indicate volition on the part of the speaker and deal with possible actions rather than with facts. This category includes elements of will and not only knowledge as fact. The volitives (e.g., jussive, imperative, cohortative) communicate *deontic* modality since the speaker expresses a desire and is concerned with the response of the hearer.[30]

In his study of the semantic theories of modality, Portner defines *modality* as "the linguistic phenomenon whereby grammar allows one to say things about, or on the basis of, situations which need not be real."[31] This definition was formulated based on his research into the modal features present in "sentential," "subsentential," and "discourse modality." At sentence level (sentential), Portner examines modal auxiliaries (e.g., must, can, might), modal verbs (e.g., need to, ought to), modal adverbs (e.g., maybe, probably, possibly), generics, habituals and individual-level predicates, tense and aspect, conditionals, covert modality, and disjunction. At the clause level (subsentential), he surveys modal adjectives (e.g., necessary, certain), propositional attitude verbs and adjectives (e.g., believe, hope, remember), verbal mood (especially the indicative and subjunctive), infinitives, dependent modals, and negative polarity items. At the

27. Ibid., 135; Palmer, *Mood and Modality* (2001), 24–35.
28. Ibid., 70–76.
29. Ibid., 70.
30. Ibid., 80–82; S. N. Callahan, *Modality and the Biblical Hebrew Infinitive Absolute* (Abhandlungen für die Kunde des Morgenlandes 71; Wiesbaden: Harrassowitz, 2010) 35; A. Shulman, "The Function of the 'Jussive' and 'Indicative' Imperfect Forms in Biblical Hebrew Prose," *ZAH* 13 (2000) 169, 180.
31. Paul Portner, *Modality* (Oxford: Oxford University Press, 2009) 1.

discourse level, Portner highlights evidentiality, clause types, performativity of sentential modals, and modality in discourse semantics.[32]

In his volume on tense, aspect, and modality in Biblical Hebrew, Cook examines briefly the grammatical categories of mood (attitude of mind of speaker), modal logic (worlds of necessity and possibility to which an utterance may be related), and speech act theory (related to "locutionary," "illocutionary," and "perlocutionary" acts) and concludes that *modality* can be defined "in terms of the temporal *existence* of an event or with respect to alternative situations."[33] As Cook states, "[T]he lack of strong uniformity across languages renders it difficult to draw firm conclusions"[34] on a unified system. Echoing Portner, Cook states that only through a close examination of the features of each language—in our case, the NWSemitic languages—can a system of modality be defined accurately.[35]

The following properties have traditionally been the focus of studies on modality: attitudes and opinions, speech acts, objectivity/subjectivity of the speaker, factuality/nonfactuality of propositions, possibility and necessity of truth within the proposition.[36] Palmer suggests that modality is the "grammaticalization of the speaker's (subjective) attitudes and opinions"[37] and that "modality in language is . . . concerned with the subjective characteristics of an utterance, and it could even be further argued that subjectivity is an essential criterion for modality."[38]

English modals such as *can, should, must, may*, and others are not easily translatable into other languages. Other languages employ their own unique systems to express "ability/permission" (*can*), "suggestion" (*should*), "obligation" (*must*), and "possibility" (*may*). At times, these concepts are expressed through verbal inflection while, at other times, word order, particles, and other linguistic features provide the mood of the sentence.[39] For example, in the Korean language, modal ideas are not indicated with auxiliaries but, instead, with various suffixes added to the verb stem. H. H. B. Lee refers to these types of verb forms as "presumptive tenses," through which permission (*can*), suggestion (*should*), obligation (*must*), and possibility (*may*) are expressed. The suffixes differ slightly from past (-àsgès) to present/future (-gès).[40]

32. Ibid., 4–8.

33. Cook, *Time and the Biblical Hebrew Verb*, 70.

34. Ibid., 54.

35. Ibid., 55; Portner, *Modality*, 1.

36. Palmer, *Mood and Modality* (1986), 4.

37. Ibid., 16.

38. Ibid.

39. Palmer, *Mood and Modality* (2001), 92–98, 101–3.

40. H. H. B. Lee, *Korean Grammar* (Oxford: Oxford University Press, 1994) 92–94; e.g., *halmaniga god osigèsda* 'Granny might come soon'; *jaŋgugilo ogo ìsgèsda* '[He] may be on his way to England'; *jagnjane boàsgès ɨbnida* '[You] might have seen it last year'.

The Tagalog system provides equivalent concepts in two ways: (1) with the *maka-* prefix on a verb to indicate ability/permission (*can*),[41] and (2) with independent morphemes indicating possibility (*maaari'* 'may'), obligation (*dapat* and *kailangan* 'must'), and suggestion (*dapat* 'should') before an infinitive.[42] Greek (Classical and *Koiné*) also uses verbal forms and independent morphemes to express this sort of modality. The indicative form of the verb "may be used alone where in English we employ an auxiliary verb."[43] The indicative imperfect of impersonal expressions may indicate such modal ideas, especially when accompanied by an infinitive (e.g., δεῖ).[44] The optative with ἄν ("potential optative"[45]) is used for "future possibility, propriety, or likelihood, as an *opinion* of the speaker; and may be translated by *may, might, can* (especially with a negative), *must, would, should* (rarely *will, shall*)."[46] Some of the functions of the Greek subjunctive include the idea of "possibility" (*might*).[47] Greek also uses independent morphemes to fulfill similar modal ideas: e.g., χρή,[48] ἔξεστιν.[49]

Although most languages have an identifiable linguistic structure designed to express modality, the elements in the system may have more than one function; they may extend their meanings to more than one semantic domain. Through her study of modal auxiliaries in English, A. Wierzbicka demonstrates that linguistic economy in most languages dictates that markers serve

41. T. V. Ramos and R. M. Cena, *Modern Tagalog* (Honolulu: University of Hawaii Press, 1990) 93; T. V. Ramos, *Tagalog Dictionary* (Honolulu: University of Hawaii Press, 1971) 177.

42. These include: "*maaári'*—'to make something possible; may; possibly.' *Maaari kang magtagumpay*—'You might become successful'" (Ramos, *Tagalog Dictionary*, 177); "*dapat* and *kailangan*—'to express obligation; must'; *Dapat gawin*—'This ought to be done'" (p. 96); "*kailangan*—'need; ought; must; necessary; indispensable'" (p. 65).

43. H. W. Smyth, *Greek Grammar* (Cambridge: Harvard University Press, 1956) 401. πιστεύων [δὲ θεοῖς πῶς οὐκ εἶναι θεούς ἐνόμιζεν 'Since he trusted in the gods how could (or should) he believe there were no gods?' (Xenophon, *Memorabilia* 1.1.5); ὀλίγου εἷλον τὴν πόλιν 'a little more and they would have taken the city' (Thucydides 8.35; Smyth, *Greek Grammar*, 401).

44. ταῦτα δὲ ἔδει ποιῆσαι 'You ought to do these things' (Matt 23:23).

45. Smyth, *Greek Grammar*, 407.

46. Ibid. γνοίς δ' ἂν ὅτι τοῦθ οὕτως ἕξει 'you may see that this is so' (Xenophon, *Cyropaedia*, 1.6.21); ἅπαντες ἂν ὁμολογήσειαν 'all would agree' (Isocrates 11.5; Smyth, *Greek Grammar*, 407).

47. "Possibility": οὐ γὰρ ἀπέστειλεν ὁ θεὸς τὸν υἱὸν εἰς τὸν κόσμον ἵνα κρίνῃ τὸν κόσμον, ἀλλ' ἵνα σωθῇ ὁ κόσμος δι' αὐτοῦ 'For God did not send the Son into the world in order to condemn the world, but so that through Him the world might be saved' (John 3:17).

48. οὐ χρή, ἀδελφοί μου, ταῦτα οὕτως γίνεσθαι 'This, my brothers, should not happen' (Jas 3:10).

49. οἱ μαθηταί σου ποιοῦσιν ὃ οὐκ ἔξεστιν ποιεῖν ἐν σαββάτῳ 'Your disciples are doing what they ought not to do on the Sabbath' (Matt 12:2).

multiple functions.[50] For example, the word *can* is used to express ability (e.g., "Our team *can* beat your team") and permission (e.g., "You *can* go now!"). The word *shall* also carries several meanings or expresses several moods, depending on the context in which it is found. For example, *shall* expresses strong volition in the following statement: "You *shall* obey my orders!" In the sentence: "I *shall* write a letter tomorrow," it expresses "intermediate volition," while in: "Good dog, you *shall* have a bone later," *shall* expresses "weak volition."[51] Thus, in English, one modal element can carry several meanings. I expect this to be true in other languages as well, where one verbal form marked for modality or one independent morpheme can express various degrees of modality depending on the context in which it it found.

According to S. N. Callahan, "[I]n general, 'modality' addresses the possibility, necessity, or desirability of a state of affairs."[52] These can be identified through linguistic elements (sometimes called "attitudinal operators") that include morphemes, syntax, and word order. In general, the linguistic approach determines modality by examining the attitude, wish, and intent of the speaker revealed through "attitudinal operators," such as:

1. modal auxiliaries (e.g., English: *can, must, should*; Chinese: *yīnggāi, yīngdang, gāi* 'ought to, should')
2. verbal inflections (e.g., EA Canaanite: *yaqtula, yaqtul* jussive)
3. modal adverbials (e.g., German: *ja, doch, denn* 'truly, though, evidently')
4. modal particles (e.g., Hebrew: אַל ,נָא)
5. parenthetical verbs (e.g., French: *pouvoir, devoir, vouloir* 'be able to, have to, want to'; Chinese: *huì, néng* 'be able to, have permission')

According to F. Kiefer, where no "attitudinal operators" are present, the sentence is by default "declarative" or "indicative" and reveals an unmarked state.[53] This is not always the case, however, since many languages use similar types of "operators" in order to indicate the "declarative" state.[54] As noted by Palmer, modality is not "necessarily marked in the verbal element, nor is there any obvious reason why it should be, apart from the fact that the verb is the most central part of the sentence. . . . Since modality is not confined to verbal

50. A. Wierzbicka, "The Semantics of Modality," *Folia Linguistica: Acta Societatis Linguisticae Europaeae* 21 (1987) 25–43.

51. Ibid., 25–43.

52. Callahan, *Modality and the Biblical Hebrew Infinitive Absolute,* 17; idem, "Mood and Modality: Biblical Hebrew," in *Encyclopedia of Hebrew Language and Linguistics* (ed. Geoffrey Khan; Leiden: Brill, 2013) 2:687.

53. F. Kiefer, "On Defining Modality," *Folia Linguistica: Acta Societatis Linguisticae Europaeae* 21 (1987) 67–94.

54. T. Shopen, *Language Typology and Syntactic Description*, vol. 1: *Clause Structure* (3 vols.; Cambridge: Cambridge University Press, 1984) 1:166.

features, quite independent 'modal' particles can also be considered."[55] In addition to the few auxiliary verbs (e.g., יָכֹל) and verbs that convey desirative ideas in Hebrew (e.g., קָוָה, שָׁאַל), modal particles such as אַל and נָא contribute to the modality of an utterance.[56]

Discourse analysts advocate that modality relates, not merely to one element but, rather, to the whole sentence and, at times, to the greater context in which the statement is found. This contradicts the traditional view of many prominent grammarians, who limit their analysis of a language to the sentence level.[57] Discourse analysis highlights the relationship of the sentence and other smaller units to the larger context. In their study of Biblical Hebrew, F. I. Andersen and A. D. Forbes adopt a discourse analysis approach, stating that they see "grammar as extending above and below the sentence into discourse."[58] They present eight aspects that serve as the basis for their approach to discourse analysis: (1) interface with syntax using the *unified* approach (in contrast to the *disjoint* approach); (2) text types (exposition, narration, indirect speech, dialogue); (3) primary foci (information structure and discourse cohesion, structure, and semantics); (4) basic units of analysis (phrases and clauses); (5) dimensions/levels of discourse (informational, intentional, textual, exchange); (6) representation(s) (text description, phrase markers, labeled graphs, discourse representation structures); (7) analytic procedures (expertise, directives/protocol, symtactic/semantic/pragmatic rules, evidence fusion); and (8) rule and knowledge bases (information on clause syntax and semantics, semantic networks, cognitive models, and world knowledge).[59]

Michael O'Connor highlights three main areas of study in discourse linguistics: (1) language in social interaction; (2) language structure beyond the clause level; and (3) language in specific text types.[60] His article focuses on the first two areas. Regarding (1) "language in social interaction," two major sources drive the discussion: the philosophical (e.g., why people say what they say) and the social-psychological (e.g., how people express themselves in their

55. Palmer, *Mood and Modality* (1986), 45. See also Callahan, *Modality and the Biblical Hebrew Infinitive Absolute,* 36–37; idem, "Mood and Modality: Biblical Hebrew," 2:687–89.

56. Callahan, *Modality and the Biblical Hebrew Infinitive Absolute*, 36–37.

57. Bloomfield described the sentence as "an independent form, not included in any larger (complex) linguistic form" (Bloomfield, *Language*, 170). Benveniste agrees with this description and states: "Une phrase ne peut donc pas servir d'intégrant à un autre type d'unité" (E. Benveniste, *Problèmes de linguistique générale* [Paris: Gallimard, 1966] 128). In Martinet's view, "[R]ien ne se trouve dans le discours qui ne soit déjà dans la phrase" (André Martinet, *La linguistique synchronique, études et recherches* [3rd ed.; Paris: Presses universitaires de France, 1970] 223).

58. F. I. Andersen and A. D. Forbes, *Biblical Hebrew Grammar Visualized* (LSAWS 6; Winona Lake, IN: Eisenbrauns, 2012) 7.

59. Ibid., 313.

60. M. O'Connor, "Discourse Linguistics and the Study of Biblical Hebrew," in *Congress Volume: Basel 2001* (ed. A. Lemaire; VTSup 92; Leiden: Brill, 2002) 21.

own context; sociolinguistic approach). Both the coded language of deferential addresses (e.g., expressions of politeness, honor, vocatives) and the shape of conversations (e.g., interdependent adjacent pairs) belong to the study of social discourse and can be identified in Biblical Hebrew through morphological and/or syntactical features.[61] Regarding (2) "language structure beyond the clause level," O'Connor highlights two models in recent scholarship: the "global model," in which text-linguists attempt to identify a fixed hierarchy between the discourse and larger context, and the "local model," which examines interclausal relationships in the text.[62]

According to Longacre's "global" method of analysis (originally Pike's "tagmemics"), the text cannot be studied outside its macrostructure. Longacre identifies a series of types of discourse found in languages and examines the verbal system according to the function of each verbal form within each type of discourse. He states:

> Traditionally, within a grammar of a given language all the uses of each tense/aspect or mode of a language are listed and described en bloque in the same section of the grammar. Thus, for Biblical Hebrew the Gesenius-Kautzsch-Cowley grammar (1910) devotes five pages to the use of the perfect, six pages to the use of the imperfect, a page or two each to the cohortative and jussive, then nine pages to the imperative, some four pages to the imperfect with the *waw*-consecutive, and finally further pages to the infinitives and participles. . . . I posit here that (*a*) every language has a system of discourse types (e.g., narrative, predictive, hortatory, procedural, expository, and others); (*b*) each discourse type has its own characteristic constellation of verb forms that figure in that type; (*c*) the uses of given tense/aspect/mood form are most surely and concretely described in relation to a given discourse type. . . . The constellation of verb forms that figure in a given discourse type are structured so that one or more privileged forms constitute the mainline or backbone of each type, while other forms can be shown to encode progressive degrees of departure from the mainline. . . . Applying (*a*), (*b*), and (*c*) above to Biblical Hebrew, one can construct the following argument: (1) For Biblical Hebrew, we must (at least) distinguish narrative (N), predictive/procedural (P), hortatory (H), and expository (E) texts and paragraphs. (2) Within each of these types the verb forms/clauses used in that type can be arranged on a scale from the most relevant (mainline) in that discourse type, down to the type of verb/clause that is least relevant.[63]

In Longacre's view, the *hortatory discourse* in Biblical Hebrew uses mainly the volitives (jussive, imperative, cohortative) in order to provide the primary line of exhortation. These types of verbs, marked for modality, function at various levels. Longacre distinguishes between the unmitigated type of horta-

61. Ibid., 24–25.

62. Ibid., 26–27.

63. Robert Longacre, *Joseph: A Story of Divine Providence—A Text Theoretical and Textlinguistic Analysis of Genesis* 37 and 39–48 (Winona Lake, IN: Eisenbrauns, 1989) 59–60.

tory discourse, the partially mitigated, the wholly mitigated, and the deferential hortatory discourse, where the imperative form of the verb is avoided altogether to give place to the jussive. The choice of verb is closely related to the status of the speaker (e.g., equal to equal, superior to inferior, inferior to superior). Longacre notes that the modal imperfect and the perfect consecutive are also common in hortatory discourse.[64] Roy Heller adds that,

> the inherent aspectual sense of the two forms as non-punctilliar and their parallel usage in Predictive Discourse cause them to be natural continuative forms for Hortatory Discourse. While their sense in Predictive Discourse is simply declarative future, in Hortatory Discourse the foundational forms lend their volitional force to the accompanying *(We)YIQTOL* and *WeQATAL* CLAUSES. In all cases, the accompanying forms also take on hortatory force very similar, if not identical, to their imperative, cohortative, and jussive counterparts.[65]

1.5.2. Volitive

The term *volitive*[66] refers to morphemes or syntagmas the main functions of which are to express wish, desire, petition, and command. These ideas can be expressed at all levels of volition, from "weak" desire to "strong" command.[67] Hebraists have focused their study of modality on the three volitives—Imperative, Jussive, Cohortative. But as we will discuss below and as has long been recognized by Hebraists, the modal system of Hebrew comprises these three verbal forms along with the *yiqtol*, *qatal*, *weqatal*, and *infinitive absolute*. Volitives may be considered "direct" or "indirect." "Direct" volitives appear in main clauses and may or may not be preceded by a conjunctive element, while indirect volitives are normally preceded by a conjunctive element and function in subordinate clauses.[68] Although volitives are not marked for tense, they involve an element of futurity in that they all refer to an action that has not occurred and may potentially occur either in the near or distant future.

64. Ibid., 57.

65. Roy L. Heller, *Narrative Structure and Discourse Constellations: An Analysis of Clause Function in Biblical Hebrew Prose* (HSS 55; Winona Lake, IN: Eisenbrauns, 2004) 469.

66. Volitives are also referred to as "modals" (E. J. Revell, *The Designation of the Individual: Expressive Usage in Biblical Narrative* [Kampen: Kok Pharos, 1996] 276).

67. Since languages do not normally include morphemes or syntagmas for each possible volitional nuance, I anticipate that, in all the NWSemitic languages treated in this book, individual morphemes will express a variety of nuances.

68. See Paul Joüon, *A Grammar of Biblical Hebrew* (Subsidia Biblica 14; 2 vols.; rev. ed.; trans. T. Muraoka ; Rome: Pontifical Biblical Institute, 2006) 373. Joüon states that the "direct" volitives "may be used without a Waw, or with a Waw which has the purely juxtaposing value of *and*" (§114a). He then describes the "indirect" volitives as verbal forms "used with a Waw which logically has subordinating (final, i.e., indicating a purpose, or consecutive) value, e.g., *and* (*consequently*)" (§114a).

1.5.3. "Marked" versus "Unmarked"

According to modern linguistics, the concept of *markedness* is applicable to several features of a language (e.g., phonology, grammar, syntax).[69] The notion of "markedness" involves two opposite elements in relationship with each other. According to C. Miller-Naudé,

> the marked construction may have one of two relationships to the unmarked one—the nature of the markedness opposition may be *privative*, where the presence of a feature at one pole signals the absence of the feature at the opposite pole, or *equipollent*, where the presence of a feature at one pole signals the logical opposite of that feature at the other pole.[70]

Scholars agree that an element (e.g., morpheme, word order) used in its most general sense is considered "unmarked."[71] Major studies have demonstrated that "unmarked" elements "appear more frequently cross-linguistically" than "marked" elements.[72] According to Korchin, "[C]ore grammar is unmarked in opposition to peripheral grammar, which constitutes a marked accretion to the

69. This distinction between "marked" and "unmarked" in the area of phonology was first presented by the Prague school of linguistics. Subsequently, the concept was applied to other aspects of linguistics. J. H. Greenberg. *Language Universals* (The Hague: Mouton, 1966) 10, 14. For a summary of the development of scholarship on "markedness" during the last century (e.g., de Saussure's structural linguistics; Jakobson's Prague Linguistic Circle; Russian Formalism; Trubetzkoy's binary opposition for "markedness"; Chomsky's generative linguistics and universal grammar; Prince and Smolensky's Optimality Theory), see P. D. Korchin, *Markedness in Canaanite and Hebrew Verbs* (HSS 58; Winona Lake, IN: Eisenbrauns, 2008) 1–45. See also B. Comrie, *Aspect: An Introduction to the Study of Verbal Aspect and Related Problems* (Cambridge: Cambridge University Press, 1976) 111–22.

70. C. L. Miller-Naudé, *The Representation of Speech in Biblical Narrative: A Linguistic Analysis* (HSM 55; Atlanta: Scholars Press, 1996) 309. The concept of binary opposition for "markedness" was originally proposed as a normative paradigmatic system by Nikolai S. Trubetzkoy in his article "Die phonologischen Systeme," *Travaux du Cercle Linguistique de Prague* 4 (1931) 96–116. The system was further developed by Roman Jakobson during the following decades and included binary opposition in nouns, verbs, cases, and other linguistic features (for a complete list of Jakobson's works, see the bibliography in Korchin, *Markedness in Canaanite and Hebrew Verbs*, 351–53). See also T. Yishai, "Markedness," in *Encyclopedia of Hebrew Language and Linguistics* (ed. Goeffrey Kahn; Leiden: Brill, 2013) 2:578–79.

71. J. A. Hawkins states that "grammars will select the unmarked and more highly valued options before they resort to the more marked and less valued ones. These latter will be selected only when there is some compelling reason for doing so, and only when the more highly valued options in that set have already been chosen" (John A. Hawkins, "Explaining Language Universals," in *Explaining Language Universals* [ed. J. A. Hawkins; New York: Blackwell, 1988] 5); Miller-Naudé, *Representation of Speech in Biblical Narrative,* 309–18.

72. See also M. Lee, "Language, Perception and the World," in *Explaining Language Universals* (ed. J. A. Hawkins. New York: Blackwell, 1988) 215; W. Croft, "Typology and Grammar," *Concise Encyclopedia of Syntactic Theories* (ed. K. Brown and J. Miller; New York: Pergamon, 1996) 346.

default setting encompassed by the core."[73] Where an element expresses nuances other than its basic idea, the element is said to be "marked" for specific semantic use. Comrie states that an element is marked "to show that it does not correspond to the normal direction of flow of information."[74] In contrast to "unmarked" elements representing a "simple" or "common" meaning, the "marked" form corresponds to a "marked" meaning.[75]

In his study of markedness in Canaanite and Biblical Hebrew, Korchin examines the binary oppositions in two main categories: (1) within the semiotic *locales* of "synchronic and diachronic" temporality, "paradigmatic and syntagmatic" spaciality, and "signified and signifier" morphemic oppositions; and (2) within the semiotic *dynamics* of "hierarchy and inclusion," a consistent dichotomous "binary" relationship, and the "privative" (presence vs. absence) nature of a given property.[76]

The "markedness" of an element may vary according to the context in which it is found. For example, in Biblical Hebrew, the long imperative is "marked" for politeness in prose, while it is "unmarked" for politeness in poetry (especially in Psalms), since it is commonly used in passages where one addresses God in prayer, thus making the long imperative an "unmarked" form in prayers to God.[77]

Moods can also be "marked" or "unmarked." With relationship to English *moods*, Grimes states that "the declarative is without doubt the unmarked mode."[78] In other words, in the absence of specific indicators of modality, a sentence is by default in the indicative mood. *Word order* can be "marked" or "unmarked." In a study of 63 languages from Asia, Africa, Europe, North and South America, and Australia, Susan Steele concluded that there are 6 basic word orders that represent the word order of the main clause of most languages (in order of frequency): SOV, SVO, VSO, VOS, OVS, and OSV.[79] The first two (SOV and SVO) are the most common. None of the languages examined by Steele uses only one type of word order for main clauses. The "unmarked"

73. Korchin, *Markedness in Canaanite and Hebrew Verbs*, 38.

74. B. Comrie, *Language Universals and Linguistic Typology* (Chicago: University of Chicago Press, 1981) 121.

75. J. Haiman, "Iconicity," in *Concise Encyclopedia of Syntactic Theories* (ed. K. Brown and J. Miller; New York: Pergamon, 1996) 199.

76. Korchin, *Markedness in Canaanite and Hebrew Verbs*, 63–64.

77. According to Tsevat, a comparison of the prose texts and the Psalms reveals that the long imperative is proportionately eight times more common in the book of Psalms than it is in the prose portions of the Hebrew Bible (M. Tsevat, *A Study of the Language of the Biblical Psalms* [JBL Monograph Series 9; Philadelphia: Society of Biblical Literature, 1955] 25).

78. Grimes, *Thread of Discourse*, 325.

79. SOV examples: Turkish, Somali, Japanese, Burmese, Navajo.
SVO examples: English, Albanian, Czeck, Mandarin, Indonesian.
VSO examples: Tahitian, Squamish, Narinjari (Australia).
VOS examples: Tagalog, Tongan (Oceanic), Kapampangan.

word order predominates, and the "marked" construction occurs as needed for specific nuances.

Most scholars of Biblical Hebrew advocate that, in prose, the "normal" or "unmarked" word order is VSO.[80] When a clause or sentence has SVO or OVS word order or begins with another element, such as אֲשֶׁר, כִּי, or a negative particle, it is usually marked for disjunction and conditioned by interclausal relationships or marked to indicate emphasis.[81] A minority of scholars present a different view: that SVO is considered the "normal" word order both for verbal and nominal clauses.[82]

1.6. Sociolinguistic Issues

One aspect of our research focuses on the social interactions represented in the discourse of narrative prose (e.g., between individuals of equal status; between an individual and a group of people; in monologues). As stated by W. M. Schniedewind, "[L]anguage is constrained by its role as a communication device. . . . A language is conditioned by the ebb and flow of social life."[83] Different social contexts require that utterances include identifiable linguistic markers to indicate the type of relationship that exists between the speaker(s) and the audience (e.g., greater to lesser, lesser to greater), and to indicate the attitude with which the speaker delivers his message (e.g., politeness, respect).

For OSV, see Susan Steele, "Word Order Variation: A Typological Study," in *Universals of Human Language*, vol. 4: *Syntax* (ed. G. H. Greenberg; Stanford: Stanford University Press, 1978) 588.

80. V = *verb*; S = *subject*; O = *object*. T. O. Lambdin, *Introduction to Biblical Hebrew* (London: Darton, Longman & Todd, 1991) 39; Emil Kautzsch, ed., *Gesenius' Hebrew Grammar* (ed. E. Kautzsch; trans. A. E. Cowley; Mineola, NY: Dover, 2006) 456; B. K. Waltke and M. O'Connor, *An Introduction to Biblical Hebrew Syntax* (Winona Lake, IN: Eisenbrauns, 1990) 129; T. Muraoka, *Emphatic Words and Structures in Biblical Hebrew* (Jerusalem: Magnes, 1985) 28; R. J. Williams, *Hebrew Syntax: An Outline* (2nd ed.; Toronto: University of Toronto Press, 1976) 96; B. L. Bandstra, "Word Order and Emphasis in Biblical Hebrew Narrative: Syntactic Observations on Genesis 22 from a Discourse Perspective," in *Linguistics and Biblical Hebrew* (ed. W. R. Bodine; Winona Lake, IN: Eisenbrauns, 1992) 123; Y. Endo, *The Verbal System of Classical Hebrew in the Joseph Story: An Approach from Discourse Analysis* (Studia Semitica Neerlandica; Assen: Van Gorcum, 1996) 35; A. B. Davidson, *Hebrew Syntax* (3rd ed.; Edinburgh: T. & T. Clark, 1989) 146; R. Buth, "Word Order Differences between Narrative and Non-Narrative Material in Biblical Hebrew," in *Proceedings of the Tenth World Congress of Jewish Studies* (Jerusalem: World Union of Jewish Studies, 1990) 11.

81. See Lambdin, *Introduction to Biblical Hebrew*, 39; GKC, 455; Muraoka, *Emphatic Words and Structures*, 32ff.; Williams, *Hebrew Syntax*, 96; Bandstra, "Word Order and Emphasis," 123.

82. Joüon, *A Grammar of Biblical Hebrew*, 474; Eldon Clem, *Unmarked Subject-Verb Position* (M.A. Thesis, Trinity Evangelical Divinity School, 1987) 114.

83. W. M. Schniedewind, "Prolegomena for the Sociolinguistics of Classical Hebrew," *JHS* 5 (2004), http://www.jhsonline.org/Articles/article_36.htm [accessed July 5, 2013].

Scholars agree that language reflects sociolinguistic dynamics determined by the social identity of the speaker and listener. As stated by J. P. Gee, "[E]ach social language has its own distinctive grammar. However, two different sorts of grammars are important to social languages": (1) the first one being the set of grammatical units (e.g., nouns, verbs, phrases, clauses) and (2) the second being the "rules" by which one creates patterns (collocational patterns) that correspond to one's social identity.[84]

J. Lyons speaks of six areas of speech in which participants demonstrate "contextually appropriate utterances" and "communicative competence": (1) participants must know their *social roles* within the cultural setting (e.g., standing in the community, age, sex); (2) participants must know the *space and time* when they speak (e.g., situational appropriateness); (3) participants must recognize the *degree of formality* appropriate for the context; (4) participants must choose an *appropriate medium* specific to the context (e.g., judges declare verdicts in formulaic language); (5) participants must consider the *subject matter* in their choice of vocabulary; and (6) participants understand *rules of behavior* in specific domains (e.g., with superior, with family).[85]

Determining the social status of the participants of a conversation involves many factors. Linguists speak of the need to understand the "frame of reference" of the speaker—contextualization—in order to interpret accurately the sociolinguistic dynamics of a discourse.[86] M. Heller speaks of

> the notion of a *communicative repertoire*, as well as the concept of *speech situation* or *speech event*. All these concepts, central to the ethnography of communication, are based on the assumption that people use language in ways which vary systematically in co-occurrence with other dimensions of their social relations. . . . Individuals possess sets of linguistic resources which vary according to their access to the communicative situations in their community.[87]

O'Connor points out the fact that social dynamics in discourse require contextualization. He notes that speakers choose deferential language such as markers of politeness, honorific (e.g., "my lord"), deprecatory terms (e.g., "your servant"), and other face-saving expressions in order to identify social distinctions. In his view, when an inferior addresses a superior with deferential language, he or she seeks "to deflect attention from himself and to avoid encroaching on his superior or threatening his superior's social status, his 'face.'"[88]

---

84. James P. Gee, *How to Do Discourse Analysis: A Toolkit* (New York: Routledge, 2011) 156–58.

85. Lyons, *Semantics*, 574–91.

86. M. Heller, "Discourse and Interaction," in *The Handbook of Discourse Analysis* (ed. D. Schiffrin, D. Tannen, and H. E. Hamilton; Malden, MA: Blackwell, 2001) 258.

87. Ibid., 259.

88. O'Connor, "Discourse Linguistics and the Study of Biblical Hebrew," 23.

In a description of Javanese respectful behavior, Clifford Geertz mentions that:

> status is determined by many things—wealth, descent, education, occupation, age, kinship, and nationality, among others, but the important point is that the choice of linguistic forms as well as speech style is in every case partly determined by the relative status (or familiarity) of the conversers.[89]

Geertz speaks of "etiquette patterns" in which an emotional setting is established by the speaker in order to express politeness and put the listener at ease before a conversation can proceed further. These types of patterns are used by the speaker in order to

> surround the other with a wall of behavioral (*lair*) formality which protects the stability of his inner life (*batin*). . . . [The speaker] may choose to build such a wall for one of two reasons. He and the other person are at least approximate status equals and not intimate friends; and so he responds to the other's politeness to him with an equal politeness. Or the other is clearly his superior, in which case he will, in deference to the other's greater spiritual refinement, build him a wall without any demand or expectation that you reciprocate.[90]

Geertz adds that,

> in Javanese it is nearly impossible to say anything without indicating the social relationship between the speaker and the listener in terms of status and familiarity. . . . A number of words (and some affixes) are made to carry in addition to their normal linguistic meaning what might be called a "status meaning."[91]

We find similar expressions of politeness in many modern languages. Recognition of social differences can be expressed through the choice of personal pronouns. For example, in French (*tu*/*vous*), German (*du*/*Ihr*), Italian (*tu*/*lei*), and Spanish (*tu*/*vos*), there are still two active second-person pronouns: (1) one used in informal addresses, and (2) one for expressing politeness.[92]

---

89. Clifford Geertz, "Linguistic Etiquette," in *Readings in the Sociology of Language* (ed. Joshua A. Fishman; New York: Mouton, 1977) 282.

90. Ibid., 289–90.

91. Ibid., 283.

92. In their article on the sociolinguistic function of pronouns, Brown and Gilman speak of the pronoun of "intimacy" and the pronoun of "formality" (R. Brown and A. Gilman, "The Pronouns of Power and Solidarity," in *Style in Language* [ed. T. A. Sebeok; Cambridge, MA: MIT Press, 1960] 256). The authors recognize that the pronoun of "formality" can be used between equals simply to express respect, without distinguishing the social status of the speaker and listener. In today's French communities, this distinction ("tu" vs. "vous") is slowly disappearing. The younger generation is increasingly using the second-person singular pronoun ("tu" common form) to address elders, a concept that was considered impolite with previous generations. Revell comments on this choice designation in French (*Designation of the Individual*, 17).

In the Korean language, we find a complex system, in which the speaker always identifies himself/herself as "greater than," "lesser than," or "equal to" the listener, by including particles or suffixes or infixes on the verb, based on the following five categories of speech: (1) low plain;[93] (2) low formal;[94] (3) medium style;[95] (4) high plain;[96] and (5) high formal.[97] Each of these categories uses different markers to indicate the declarative, interrogative, imperative, and optative (propositive) moods.[98] In addition, the Korean language includes "honorific" verbs, "honorific suffixes" on regular verbs, and "humble suffixes" on regular verbs.[99] This type of system provides specific speech patterns for all possible social settings.

In Tagalog—the official language of the Philippines—the particle *po* is added at the end of a phrase or sentence by a speaker whose social status is lower than that of the addressee. This marker indicates that the speaker officially recognizes his social position and the social status of his listener. This particle can be compared to *sir* or *ma'am* in English.[100] It is accompanied by the second-person plural pronoun (*kayo*) or by the third person (*sila*), when it is necessary to express even greater respect.[101]

Many Asians add physical expressions of politeness to the appropriate linguistic elements of respect. For example, in Japan, where rank and social status are of utmost importance, the greeting "determines the quality of the ensuing conversation. . . . One's manner of greeting is a reflection of one's family and educational background."[102] An important part of the greeting is found in the

93. The "low plain" style of language "is the lowest style of speech in Korean, used by adults to children, between children, between intimate friends, male or female, and it is also the standard style of written Korean" (H. H. B. Lee, *Korean Grammar*, 102).

94. The "low formal" style is used "between equals and by elders to younger" (ibid., 100).

95. This style is "used by elders to those younger where the high plain is felt to be a little too high and the low plain style a little too low. It can be used between equals whose relationship is not so intimate as to require the low plain style" (ibid., 104).

96. This style is "lower and less polite than the low formal style, and is used by older people to younger, and by people of higher social status to those of lower one" (ibid., 101).

97. This style is "the most polite form of speech whereby the speaker expresses respect toward the addressee(s). It is used on formal occasions, in conversations between strangers, by younger people to their elders, and by people of lower social status to those of a higher one" (ibid., 98).

98. Ibid., 98–106.

99. Ibid., 44, 92–94.

100. "*Po* is significantly absent from the speech of older people and superiors and in interchanges between equals" (R. V. Ramos. *Conversational Tagalog* [Honolulu: University of Hawaii Press, 1985] 2).

101. Ibid., 3.

102. K. Hijirida and M. Yoshikawa, *Japanese Language and Culture for Business and Travel* (Honolulu: University of Hawaii Press, 1987) 12.

bow, an expression used to indicate respect. The bow "plays an important role in achieving good human relations. . . . A proper and beautiful bow is said to ideally convey the resonance of a sincere heart . . . and may determine the course of the developing relationship."[103]

In ancient Semitic languages as in modern languages, markers of respect were used by speakers when speakers and hearers belonged to different social classes.[104] As stated by O'Connor, in speech, "the demands of deference between speakers lead to patterns of particular complexity, far exceeding those usually grouped under the meek heading of politeness."[105] These complex features are indicated in a number of ways: (1) with linguistic markers;[106] (2) with expressions indexed for social deference;[107] (3) through syntactical structures;[108] and/or (4) with physical expressions, such as bowing before a king.[109] Miller-Naudé identifies two primary strategies that index the social relations of inequality between speaker and listener in Biblical Hebrew: (1) *terms of address* (e.g., socially distant: אֲדֹנִי 'my lord', אִישׁ הָאֱלֹהִים 'man of God', בְּרוּךְ יְהוָה 'blessed of the Lord'; socially intimate: אָבִי 'my father', אִמִּי 'my mother', בְּנִי 'my son'); and (2) *deferential forms* (e.g., עַבְדְּךָ 'your servant', אֲמָתֶךָ 'your maidservant').[110] Terms of address and deferential expressions are frequent in Biblical Hebrew. In both cases, they identify an inferior addressing a superior

103. Ibid., 26–27.

104. E. J. Bridge discusses expressions of politeness (e.g., address in jussive) and deference (e.g., use of עבדך, אדון) in the Lachish letters ("Polite Language in the Lachish Letters," *VT* 60 [2010] 518–34); E. J. Revell, "Address, Forms of," in *Encyclopedia of Hebrew Language and Linguistics* (ed. Goeffrey Kahn: Leiden: Brill, 2013) 1:32–33. D. Pardee notes that, "in Ugaritic practice, the social superior was always mentioned first, which . . . was not a feature of first-millennium epistolography. Thus, if the social repationship of the correspondents was to be expressed explicitly in a letter from the later period, it had to be by epithet" (D. Pardee, "Epistolary Formulae: Biblical Period," in *Encyclopedia of Hebrew Language and Linguistics* [ed. Goeffrey Kahn: Leiden: Brill, 2013] :852).

105. O'Connor, "Discourse Linguistics and the Study of Biblical Hebrew," 20.

106. B. Christiansen, "A Linguistic Analysis of the Biblical Hebrew Particle *na*ʾ: A Test Case," *VT* 59 (2009) 379–93; T. L. Wilt, "A Sociolinguistic Analysis of *Na*ʾ," *VT* 46 (1996) 237–55; S. A. Kaufman, "An Emphatic Plea for Please," *MAARAV* 7 (1991) 195–98.

107. Miller-Naudé, *Representation of Speech in Biblical Narrative*, 269–71.

108. As will be demonstrated through a study of the syntax of volitives.

109. Bodily expressions of politeness were found in ancient Near Eastern contexts whenever one of lower social status approached a ruler. This type of behavior is described in the greeting formula of many of the EA Canaanite letters: "At your feet, seven times I fall . . ." (e.g., EA 45, 49, 51, 52, 68, 73, etc.) and is also depicted in many paintings and reliefs of the first and second millennium B.C.E. See J. B. Pritchard, ed., *The Ancient Near East in Pictures*, vol. 1 (Princeton: Princeton University Press, 1958): #5 (Syrians presenting gifts to Amen-em-heb at Thebes), #5 (foreigners bow down before a royal servant on a relief from Hor-em-heb's tomb at Memphis), #45 (foreigners presenting gifts to Men-Kheper-Reseneb), #47 (wall painting of tomb 63 at Thebes, on which tribute bearers bow before the ruler), #371 (townspeople bow before Sennacherib as he receives the booty from Lachish).

110. Miller-Naudé, *Representation of Speech in Biblical Narrative*, 269–71.

with whom he or she has an official relationship, and with whom he or she wishes to minimize the possibility of displeasing the listener.[111] When social relations indicate intimacy, familial terms are the norm.

While terms of address point to the addressee (e.g.,אֲדֹנִי 'my lord'), terms of deference draw attention either to the speaker (e.g., עַבְדְּךָ 'your servant': "addressee-based" deference) or to the addressee (e.g., אֲדֹנִי הַמֶּלֶךְ 'my lord, the king': "speaker-based" deference). [112] In deferential language, the relationship of inequality typically identifies an inferior as addressing a superior. According to Revell, "[S]uch third person reference avoids the appearance of intimacy produced by the use of first and second person forms, obviating the assumption that the speaker and addressee are equal. It . . . distances speaker from addressee."[113]

Miller-Naudé maintains that, "in considering deferential language, two caveats are in order. First, deferential language indexes the social relationships of participants within a conversation. Within narrative, however, the ideology of the narrator, rather than the putative social relationships of the characters, ultimately controls the use of the deferential language."[114]

In order to identify expressions of deference in the texts of the NWSemitic corpus, it is necessary for us to establish a list of speakers/listeners involved in discourse. As noted by Revell, it is impossible to group the participants of all narratives and to determine with absolute certainty the dynamics of every discourse without a certain level of subjectivity.[115] The views of the author no doubt contribute to the interpretation of the data, but the breadth of the corpus of texts ensures that the analysis and results are as objective as possible.

A society comprises numerous social groupings (e.g., gender, occupation, social position, familial designation, and age group).[116] Social dynamics in discourse occur between individuals of the same group and between individuals of different groups. The following list represents the possible *speakers* and *listeners* implicated in the direct discourse of the corpus under study. The individuals listed in each group may belong to more than one category (e.g., a king is also a husband, a son, and a father):[117]

111. Revell, *Designation of the Individual*, 269–70.

112. Miller-Naudé, *Representation of Speech in Biblical Narrative*, 272; idem, "Direct and Indirect Speech: Biblical Hebrew," in *Encyclopedia of Hebrew Language and Linguistics* (ed. Geoffrey Khan; Leiden: Brill, 2013] 1:740–42).

113. Revell, *Designation of the Individual*, 267.

114. Ibid., 280.

115. Ibid., 27.

116. Revell lists individuals under "general categorization" (e.g., man, woman, child), "relationship" (e.g., familial, kinship by marriage, master-servant), "occupation" (e.g., king, priest, prophet), and "status" (ibid., 29–44).

117. "Speakers" and "Listeners" are also called "Senders" and "Receivers" (Susan M. Ervin-Tripp, "Interaction of Language, Topic and Listener," in *Readings in the Sociology of*

1. *God*: this category includes all the Hebrew words and expressions that are used to refer to the God of the Hebrews (e.g., אֱלֹהִים, יְהוָה).
2. *Celestial beings*: as messengers of God, angels exercise authority over the individuals with whom they interact (e.g., מַלְאָכִים).
3. *King/queen*: Egyptian Pharaoh, Hebrew kings, kings of foreign nations, queens (e.g., מֶלֶךְ,מַלְכָּה).
4. *Prophet*: Hebrew prophets, false prophets, prophetesses (e.g., נָבִיא, נְבִיאָה).
5. *Priest*: high priest, priests, Levites (e.g., כֹּהֵן, בְּנֵי לֵוִי).
6. *Official*: rulers/leaders of the community (e.g., Moses, Aaron, David before he was anointed king, future kings), judges, officers in the service of the king, political rulers over small and large communities, elders (e.g., שֹׁפֵט, נָדִיב, נָשִׂיא, זָקֵן).
7. *Family member*: father,[118] mother, husband,[119] wife, father-in-law, son-in-law, daughter-in-law, son, daughter, brother, sister (e.g., אֵם, בַּעַל, אָב, אִשָּׁה, חָם, חֹתֶנֶת, חָתָן, בֵּן, בַּת, אָח, אָחוֹת, אִישׁ).
8. *People*: male or female commoners, children (e.g., נַעַר, אִישׁ, אִשָּׁה, יֶלֶד).[120]
9. *Servant*: may be a servant of the king, of a prophet, of an official, of a commoner; concubine, prostitute (e.g., עֶבֶד, שִׁפְחָה, מְשָׁרֵת, זֹנָה, פִּילֶגֶשׁ).

When two individuals of the same category are interacting, they may be of "equal," "greater-to-lesser," or "lesser-to-greater" status, depending on the context of the discourse. When an individual is speaking to himself, the default category I choose is that of "equal status." There are times when the king's position supersedes the authority of the prophet, while at other times, the prophet is in a position of authority over the king, as a messenger sent by God. The sta-

Language [ed. Joshua A. Fishman; New York: Mouton, 1977] 194) or "Speakers" and "Addressees" (Miller-Naudé, *Representation of Speech in Biblical Narrative*, 269–81).

118. The term "father" may refer to one's *personal* designation as one who has sired children or to one's *role* or *status* as patriarch of a certain clan or society (Floyd G. Lounsbury, "Linguistics and Psychology," in *Readings in the Sociology of Language* [ed. Joshua A. Fishman; New York: Mouton, 1977] 57). Several biblical stories present a father as someone who could become subordinate to a member of his own family, especially when the latter acquired a position of leadership in the community (e.g., Joseph as ruler of Egypt with Jacob, his father).

119. Although patriarchal societies of biblical times placed the man in a place of authority over the woman, social dynamics between a husband and his wife/wives differ from biblical story to biblical story. Several accounts compromise the established hierarchy of the times and hint that a wife could exercise authority over her husband. For example, in 1 Kings 21, Jezebel controls the situation, dictates actions in the name of her husband (who lets them all happen without intervening), and brings about her own desired results.

120. This category includes unspecified audiences/listeners (e.g., "whoever . . ."). Curses and blessings often address generic audiences and affect not only immediate hearers but also generations to come.

tus of the prophets, priests, and officials may be on "equal," "greater-to-lesser," or "lesser-to-greater" standing, depending on the context of the utterance.

This hierarchy of speakers/listeners does not represent the same value for all the languages studied here. By this I mean that, in Biblical Hebrew, direct discourse involves a much greater variety of individuals than texts from EA Canaanite involve. Phoenician and Hebrew inscriptions differ in purpose and include only a limited number of speakers. These differences will be considered in the final comparison.

1.7. Modality in Sign Language

Sign language has its own physical code for expressing modality.[121] Specific signs exist for the following modal auxiliaries: *can/could, must, should, will/would*. None exists for the word *may*. The idea of permission indicated by this auxiliary (*may*) is included in the sign for the verb, where the hands perform a tilting motion back and forth in contrast to a direct sign for the indicative mood. In order to indicate the intensity of modality in a sentence, signs may be accompanied by a concert of elements such as facial expressions, forward tilting of the body, raised eyebrows, tilting of the head and other bodily postures. In addition, the interpreter may distinguish between a mild and a sharp statement by adjusting the sharpness of the sign presented to the recipient of the message or by adjusting the speed at which the sign is given.

Where modals are needed (e.g., *can, should, must, will, would*), sentences can be expressed in three ways: (1) with the modal sign at the end of the sentence; (2) with the modal sign preceding the verb; and (3) with the modal sign preceding the verb and repeated at the end of the sentence.[122] When someone signs a command or a statement in the imperative mood, the second-person pronoun is usually omitted. The verb is expressed with the signer looking intently at the addressee, with the verb accompanied by a sharp, tense movement of the hands and/or the head according to the intensity required by the situation.[123] Where emphasis needs to be placed on the action, the modal sign for *must* may

121. Two main systems of signing are used in North America: ASL (American Sign Language) and the English based system. In the ASL system, the interpreter signs only what is relevant and is not concerned with the grammar and syntax of the message. Key words are accompanied by bodily movements which carry special codes. The English based system is more concerned with the accuracy of details as represented by the morphology and syntax of the language interpreted. Modality is present in both systems, represented more specifically in the English based style of interpretation than in the ASL method (Diane Lillo-Martin, "Where Are All the Modality Effects?" in *Modality and Structure in Signed and Spoken Languages* [ed. R. P. Meier, K. Cormier, and D. Quinto-Pozos; Cambridge: Cambridge University Press, 2009] 241–62; David Quinto-Pozos, "Deictic Points in the Visual-Gestural and Tactile-Gestural Modalities," in ibid., 442–67).

122. T. Humphries, C. Padden, and T. J. O'Rourke, *A Basic Course in American Sign Language* (Silver Spring, MD: T.J. Publishers, 1982) 98.

123. Ibid., 68.

accompany the verb, the distance between the speaker and interpreter may be reduced, and the facial expression may indicate urgency. In the case of a mitigated command, the signs are accompanied by very little movement of the head or body.

At times, implied commands are given through a description of the situation, rather than through a sign representing a verb. For example, a mother may tell her child to go and wash simply by giving the sign for "Dirty!" The command of washing is understood and does not need to be expressed with a verb meaning 'to wash'. In a case when permission is asked (related to the Hebrew jussive or cohortative), the interpreter uses a sign specifically designed to mean "Let . . ." followed by the verb.

Word order is not emphasized in sign language, except in cases where the stress needs to be placed on the subject or the object of the sentence. In such cases, the sign for the emphasized element may or may not come first in the sentence. Rather than using word order, interpreters will often accentuate an element or statement by using space (close or distant) or as mentioned above, with various bodily postures. In contrast to spoken and written languages, sign language for the deaf is less concerned with morphology and syntax for the transmission of an accurate message. Space and the body are instruments of "silent intonation" and can transmit a message quite accurately within a complex system of modality.

1.8. Three-Person System of Volitives

1.8.1. First-Person Volitive

The first-person volitive, often referred to as the "hortative" mood (BH cohortative), is placed in the same modal category as the imperative, since it expresses a desired result and not the observation of a specific action.[124] Its basic function is to express wishes and requests for permission. The identifying marker of the first-person volitive is not always morphologically depicted within the verb form itself but may be identified by an accompanying modal element (verb or auxiliary) or by a special construction. For example, in Biblical Hebrew, one of the first-person volitives (the cohortative) includes an identifying marker of modality—a final, long *-a*—while in French, the same type of request uses the imperative form of the verb followed by an object pronoun.

Laissez nous partir! (French) נֵלְכָה Let us go! (Hebrew)

In Greek, the subjunctive can express a wish or request. It such cases, it "compensates for the absence of an imperative of the first person."[125]

124. For Biblical Hebrew, see Lambdin, *Introduction to Biblical Hebrew*, 118; E. J. Revell, "The System of the Verb in Standard Biblical Prose," *HUCA* 60 (1989) 32; Longacre, *Joseph*, 119.

125. Smyth, *Greek Grammar*, 404.

νῦν ἴωμεν καὶ ἀκούσωμεν τοῦ ἀνθρώπος
Let us go now and hear the man. (Plato, *Protagoras* 314b)

1.8.2. Second-Person Volitive

Grammarians describe the *imperative* as a verbal form, the function of which is to issue "orders, commands, demands, and requests." Linguists add to this list of functions: "threats, exhortations, permissions, concessions, warnings, advice."[126] Lyons prefers the word "mand" over "command" since the latter "is often used rather confusingly to refer to requests and entreaties as well as commands or orders in the narrow sense."[127]

The imperative mood can be expressed on several levels: strong or emphatic, polite, delayed, immediate, and so on. Palmer notes that the imperative form of the verb does not necessarily express a command stronger than *must*. From his perspective, the force of the statement is left to the interpretation of the hearer and not necessarily determined by the speaker.[128] For example, if a commander in an army speaks to his subordinates and says, "Sit here!" the command is undoubtedly interpreted by its hearers as emphatic or even absolute. If the same statement ("Sit here!") comes from a parent to a child, the reaction to the instruction may cause different results. The statement "Come in!" is often equated to "You may come in!" and, although the imperative form of the verb is used, the directive is weaker than in the previous example.

Austin speaks of the various degrees of modality that can be expressed by the same verbal command:[129]

"Shut it!"	=	"I order you to shut it."
"Shut it, if you like"	=	"I permit you to shut it."
"Very well then, shut it!"	=	"I consent to your shutting it."
"Shut it if you dare."	=	"I dare you to shut it."
"You must shut it."	=	"I order you to shut it."
"You ought to shut it."	=	"I advise you to shut it."

Some languages use imperatives and/or nonimperatival verb forms to express commands. In Hebrew, both the imperative and the second-person imperfect are used for this purpose.

שֵׁב or תֵּשֵׁב	קוּם or תָּקוּם
Sit down!	Stand up!

126. Martin Huntley makes a contrast between "declarative" and "nondeclarative" sentences, whereby indicative corresponds to "declarative," while imperative corresponds to "nondeclarative" (M. Huntley, "The Semantics of English Imperatives," *Linguistics and Philosophy* 7 [1984] 103–33).

127. Palmer, *Mood and Modality*, 23–24.

128. Ibid., 108.

129. J. L. Austin, *How To Do Things with Words* (London: Oxford University Press, 1962) 73–74.

In Modern Hebrew, the imperfect is the most common form used to express a command. In Biblical Hebrew, the imperative is used for requests that require immediate results, while the imperfect and the infinitive absolute occur when the fulfillment of the command affects long-term response (e.g., the Ten Commandments).[130]

In Tagalog, there is no imperative form of the verb. Ramos and Cena note that a command is expressed by the infinitive with the second-person personal pronoun.[131]

Maglinis ka / kayo ng bahay.	(You) clean the house.
Kunin mo / ninyo ang sapatos.	(You) wash the shoes.

Although it is impossible to prove, there is little doubt that intonation and body language were also means used for expressing commands in the languages of the ancient Near East. Unfortunately, distance in time limits our accessibility to this sort of information.

1.8.2.1 Negative Command

Some languages express a negative command with a negative particle and imperative, while other languages use different verbal constructions. For example, in French, the imperative form of the verb appears both in a positive and a negative command:[132]

French:	*Mangez!* (impv.)	*Ne mangez pas!* (impv.)
	Eat!	Do not eat!

Other languages use a negative particle with the imperative and/or the negative particle followed by another form of the verb. For example, in order to express different nuances of negative commands, Greek uses the aorist subjunctive or the present imperative with μη, depending on the context and desired results:[133]

μὴ θαύμαζε (impv.)	Don't be astonished! (Plato, *Gorgias*, 482 a)
μηδὲ θαυμάσης τόδε (subj.)	And do not wonder at this! (Aeschylus, *Agamemnon*, 879)

130. L. Glinert, *The Grammar of Modern Hebrew* (Cambridge: Cambridge University Press, 1989) 285. In several dialects of colloquial Arabic (Syrian, Egyptian, etc.), the imperfect replaces the imperative for (1) politeness, (2) after *ma*, (3) in commands with *ya* . . . *ya* . . . , and (4) in negative commands (D. D. De Lacy O'Leary, *Colloquial Arabic* [London: Routledge & Kegan Paul, 1963] 114–15).

131. Ramos and Cena, *Modern Tagalog*, 88. Some Filipino authors present the lack of a "command" form as a reflection of Filipino society, where passivity is seen to prevail.

132. R. F. Comean, F. L. Bustin, and N. J. Lamoureux, *Grammaire: An Integrated Approach to French* (3rd ed.; New York: Holt, Rinehart and Winston, 1986) 29.

133. Smyth, *Greek Grammar*, 409.

In *Koiné* Greek, in cases in which a negative command is given to stop an action that is already in progress, the imperative construction is used; but when a command is given "to forbid the occurrence of an act that is not in progress," the aorist subjunctive is the verb of choice.[134] According to Hewett, the idea of the negative subjunctive "is future in its orientation, so, quite naturally, this is an ingressive type of activity."[135]

μὴ φοβοῦ, μόνον πίστευσον (impv.)
Do not fear (anymore), only believe! (Luke 8:50)

μὴ οὖν ἐπαισχυνθῇς τὸ μαρτύριον τοῦ κυρίου (subj.)
Do not be ashamed to testify of our Lord! (2 Tim 1:8)

As in other Semitic languages, Classical Arabic uses a negative particle followed by the jussive to express a negative command. Wright states that "no negative particle can be placed before the imperative. Consequently, when a prohibition is uttered, the jussive must be used."[136]

Modern Hebrew (MH) uses the negative particle אַל with the second-person imperfect, or the negative particle לֹא with the infinitive (in indirect commands). In Biblical Hebrew (BH), the negative particle אַל precedes the jussive, while the particle לֹא precedes the imperfect:

אל תַּעֲשֶׂה את זה	Do not do this! (MH)
תגיד לו לא לעשׂות את זה	Tell him not to do this! (MH)
אל־תעשׂ אותו	Do not do it! (BH)
לֹא תעשׂה	Do not do (it)! (BH)

Tagalog uses the infinitive for positive and negative commands (see above). In the negative, the particle *huwag* appears before the verb:[137]

Huwag kang tumayo.	Do not stand.
Huwag mong inumin ang gatas.	Do not drink the milk.

In some languages, a *general* prohibition or negative command may be expressed by a nonfinite form. For example, in English, a prohibition on smoking is indicated with a negative particle plus a participle:

No smoking! (participle)

134. J. A. Hewett, *New Testament Greek: A Beginning and Intermediate Grammar* (Peabody, MA: Hendrickson, 1986) 192–93.

135. Ibid., 193.

136. W. Wright, *A Grammar of the Arabic Language* (3rd ed.; 2 vols.; Cambridge: Cambridge University Press, 1991) 2:43.

137. Ramos and Cena, *Modern Tagalog*, 89.

Modern Hebrew and French indicate *general* prohibitions with a negative particle plus an infinitive:[138]

לֹא תגרד	No scratching!
אסור להיכנס	It is forbidden to enter!
Ne pas entrer!	Do not enter!

1.8.3. Third-Person Volitive

The third-person volitive is often placed in the same modal category as the imperative, since it speaks of a potential action to be performed in the near or distant future, usually by a third party. Called the "jussive" or "optative," its basic functions reflect those of the cohortative and include wishes and requests for permission. Depending on the language, the distinguishing marker of the jussive may not be part of the verbal form itself but may be present in the form of a modal auxillary, another verb serving a modal function, or a special construction. For example, in French, the jussive mood is expressed by the imperative with a third-person object pronoun and infinitive.

Laissez le parler! (French: imperative + pronoun + infinitive)

In English, on the other hand, the first verb of the construction is in the present tense, followed by the object pronoun and the infinitive.

Let him shovel! (English: present + infinitive)

Hebrew distinguishes between the indicative mood and the jussive mood by using two different morphemes. The jussive form of the verb is often referred to as a short form of the indicative, since it displays a short theme vowel corresponding to the theme vowel of the indicative, and a loss of a final weak consonant (see discussion in §2.3.1). But this description of the morphology of the jussive is inaccurate since we now know that the origin of the imperfect is *yaqtulu* and that of the jussive is *yaqtul*.

יָקֵם אֶת הַהֵיכָל Let him erect the Temple! (Hebrew: jussive)

1.9. Modality in Semitic Languages

In modality in Semitic languages, the focus goes primarily on the verbal forms that can be identified as volitives based on their morphological features and the primary function of which is to express volition. Additional verb forms normally included in the indicative system may be translated with modal nuances, depending on the context in which they are found (e.g., imperfect, perfect consecutive).

138. Glinert, *Grammar of Modern Hebrew*, 296.

Major grammars of the Semitic languages devote only short sections to discussions on modality.[139] Issues related to modality in Semitic languages are also discussed in a number of scholarly articles.[140]

---

139. For Akkadian, see J. Huehnergard, *A Grammar of Akkadian* (HSS 45; 3rd ed.; Winona Lake, IN: Eisenbrauns, 2011) 142–47; E. Cohen, *The Modal System of Old Babylonian* (HSS 56; Winona Lake, IN: Eisenbrauns, 2005); A. Ungnad, *Akkadian Grammar* (trans. H. A. Hoffner Jr.; rev. L. Matouš; Atlanta: Scholars Press, 1992) 66–68; W. von Soden, *Grundriss der Akkadischen Grammatik* (AnOr 32; Rome: Pontifical Biblical Institute, 1952) 131–36; G. Buccellati, *A Structural Grammar of Babylonian* (Wiesbaden: Harrassowitz, 1996) 178–93. For Arabic, see Wright, *Grammar of the Arabic Language*, 1:51–62; 2:24–44; A. F. L. Beeston, *A Descriptive Grammar of Epigraphic South Arabian* (London: Luzac, 1962) 25–26. For Ugaritic, see Bordreuil and Pardee, *Manual of Ugaritic*, 47–50; Sivan, *Grammar of the Ugaritic Language*, 103–7; Tropper, *Ugaritische Grammatik*, 719–34; S. Segert, *A Basic Grammar of the Ugaritic Language* (Los Angeles: University of California Press, 1984) 56, 90–92; C. Gordon, *Ugaritic Textbook* (AnOr 38; Rome: Pontifical Biblical Institute, 1965) 71–73, 115–18; H. Cazelles, "Précis de grammaire ugaritique," *BeO* 21 (1979) 253–65; E. Hammershaimb, *Das Verbum im Dialekt von Ras Schamra: Eine morphologische und syntaktische Untersuchung des Verbums in den alphabetischen Keilschrifttexten aus dem alten Ugarit* (Copenhagen: Hammershaimb, 1941) 98–104, 124–27; E. D. Mallon, *The Ugaritic Verb in the Letters and Administrative Documents* (Ph.D. diss., Catholic University of America, 1982) 73–94; D. Sivan, *A Grammar of the Ugaritic Language* (HO 28; Leiden: Brill, 1997) 99–108; E. Vereet, *Modi ugaritici: Eine morpho-syntaktische Abhandlung über das Modalsystem im Ugaritischen* (Leuven: Peeters, 1988). For EA Canaanite, see W. L. Moran, *Amarna Studies: Collected Writings* (ed. J. Huehnergard and S. Izre'el; Winona Lake, IN: Eisenbrauns, 2003) 47–53, 179–95; Rainey, *Canaanite in the Amarna Tablets*, 2:244–72. For Phoenician, see C. R. Krahmalkov, *A Phoenician-Punic Grammar* (Handbook of Oriental Studies, Section 1: The Near and Middle East 54; Leiden: Brill, 2001) 151–54; Z. Harris, *A Grammar of the Phoenician Language* (AOS 8; repr.; New Haven, CT: American Oriental Society, 1990) 40–41; J. Friedrich and W. Röllig, *Phönizisch-punische Grammatik* (AnOr 46; Rome: Pontifical Biblical Institute, 1970) 190–91; A. van den Branden, *Grammaire phénicienne* (Beirut: Librairie du Liban, 1969) 109–10. For Epigraphic Hebrew, see S. Landis Gogel, *A Grammar of Epigraphic Hebrew* (Atlanta: Scholars Press, 1999) 78, 90–102, 255–68. For Biblical Hebrew, see Joüon, *A Grammar of Biblical Hebrew*, 125, 138–43, 373–86; C. H. J. van der Merwe, J. A. Naudé, and J. H. Kroeze, *A Biblical Hebrew Reference Grammar* (Sheffield: Sheffield Academic Press, 1999) 71, 150–53, 171–72; A. Shulman, *The Use of Modal Verb Forms in Biblical Hebrew Prose* (Ph.D. diss., University of Toronto, 1996); Waltke and O'Connor, *Introduction*, 564–79; GKC, 124–32, 316–26; Lambdin, *Introduction to Biblical Hebrew*, 100, 118–19.

140. For Proto-Semitic, see E. A. Bar-Asher, "The Imperative Forms of Proto-Semitic and a New Perspective on Barth's Law," *JAOS* 128 (2008) 233–55; For Akkadian, see D. O. Edzard, "Die Modi beim älteren akkadischen Verbum," *Or* 42 (Festschrift I. J. Gelb; 1973) 121–31; W. von Soden, "Der akkadische Subordinativ-Subjunctiv," *ZA* 63 (1973) 56–58; idem, "Tempus und Modus im älteren Semitische," in *Babylonien und Israel: Historische, religiöse und sprachliche Beziehungen* (ed. H.-P. Müller; Darmstadt: Wissenschaftliche Buchgesellschaft, 1991) 463–93. For Ugaritic, see J. Cantineau, "La langue de Ras Shamra," *Semitica* 3 (1950) 21–34; L. Delekat, "Zum ugaritischen Verbum," *UF* 4 (1972) 11–26; T. L. Fenton, "Command and Fulfillment in Ugaritic —*tqtl:yqtl* and *qtl:qtl*," *JSS* 14 (1969) 34–38; M. E. J. Richardson, "Tense, Aspect and Mood in Ugaritic *YQTL*," in *Proceedings of the Fifth International Hamito-Semitic Congress 1987* (ed. Hans G. Mukarovsky; 2 vols.;

The categories of modal forms that concern us include verbs that express "wish, petition, and command"—in other words, verbs that express a desire that the hearer and/or speaker of the utterance behave in a certain way. Since the morphology and syntax of the volitives in the NWSemitic corpus are connected to the use of modal forms in the languages of other regions, I will present here a brief survey of the modal systems of East (Akkadian–Old Babylonian) and South (Classical Arabic, Classical Ethiopic–Geʿez) Semitic languages. Where needed, these languages will be used for comparison in the conclusion of the book.

1.9.1. East Semitic – Akkadian (Old Babylonian)

Buccellati speaks of a threefold division of moods in Old Babylonian. The first category (*primary moods*) includes moods marked by internal inflection (indicative, imperative). The second group (*secondary moods*) includes moods marked by external inflection (desiderative, subjunctive, ventive). The verbal forms of the third category (*periphrastic moods*) are identified as modals by the presence of an adverbial particle (asseverative, prohibitive).[141] Our discussion will be restricted to the following categories, excluding the negative correlative of these basic moods (prohibitive, vetitive):

Indicative (preterite, perfect, present)	*iprus / iptaras / iparras*
Imperative	*purus*
Desiderative / Precative	*liprus*
Subjunctive	*iprusu*

The indicative mood includes the preterite, perfect/durative, and the present. These forms are used to describe facts. The imperative expresses a command. As in other Semitic languages, the imperative is not used to express a negative

Beiträge zur Afrikanistik 40–41; Vienna: Afro-Pub., 1990–91) 2:283–89; D. Sivan, "The Use of *QTL* and *YQTL* forms in the Ugaritic Verbal System," in *Past Links: Studies in the Languages and Cultures of the Ancient Near East Dedicated to Professor Anson F. Rainey* (ed. S. Izre'el, I. Singer, and R. Zadok; IOS 18; Winona Lake, IN: Eisenbrauns, 1998) 89–103; J. Tropper, "Das ugaritische Verbalsystem," *UF* 24 (1992) 313–37. For Phoenician, see Philip C. Schmitz, "Phoenician-Punic Grammar and Lexicography in the New Millennium," *JAOS* 124.3 (2004) 539–41. For EA Canaanite, see Moran, "Early Canaanite *yaqtula*," 1–19; P. E. Dhorme, "La langue de Canaan," *RB* n.s. 10 (1913) 369–93; Fleisch, "Yaqtula cananéen et subjonctif arabe," 65–76; W. L. Moran. "New Evidence on Canaanite *taqtul(na)*," *JCS* 5 (1951) 33–35; Rainey, "Ancient Hebrew Prefix Conjugation," 4–19. For Biblical Hebrew, see J. Huehnergard, "The Early Hebrew Prefix-Conjugation," *HS* 29 (1988) 19–23; Kaufman, "An Emphatic Plea for Please," 195–98; T. H. Meek, "Result and Purpose Clauses in Hebrew," *JQR* 46 (1955) 40–43; H. M. Orlinsky, "On the Cohortative and Jussive after an Imperative or Interjection in Biblical Hebrew," *JQR* 31 (1940–41) 371–82; and 32 (1941–42) 191–205, 273–77; A. F. Rainey, "Further Remarks on the Hebrew Verbal System," *HS* 29 (1988) 35–42; E. Talstra, "Tense, Mood, Aspect and Clause Connections in Biblical Hebrew: A Textual Approach," *JNSL* 23 (1997) 81–103.

141. Buccellati, *Structural Grammar of Babylonian*, 178.

command. The prohibitive consists of the negative particle *lā* followed by the present. The vetitive is formed by adding the prefixes *ayy-* and *ē-* to the preterite. The precative is marked by a *l(ū)-* prefix in the third person (sg. and pl.) and first-common-singular forms, with the first-common-plural form marked by the preposed particle *i-*. In Assyrian, the first-person plural also appears with the particle *lū*. When accompanied by a negative particle, this mood is called vetitive.

liškun	let him/her place (3m/f sg)	or: may he/she place
lišbā	let them dwell (3f pl)	or: may they dwell
luškun	let me place (1c sg)	or: may I place
i niškun	let us place (1c pl)	or: may we place

The first-common-singular precative occurs in interrogative sentences:

am-mīnim ana bīt abīya lullik
Why should I go to my father's house?

The subjunctive appears in subordinate clauses and is distinguished by its *-u* ending, except in cases where the verb has a vocalic or ventive ending.[142]

1.9.2. South Semitic – Classical Arabic

Grammarians of Classical Arabic discuss five moods: the Indicative, Subjunctive, Jussive (or Conditional),[143] Imperative, and Energic:

Indicative	*yaqtulu/qatala*
Subjunctive	*yaqtula*
Jussive	*yaqtul*
Imperative	*uqtul*[144]
Energic	*yaqtulan(na)*

The indicative mood indicating "fact" or "state" is common with the perfect and imperfect. Under specific circumstances, these two verb forms also fulfill modal functions such as expressing wishes and requests. The *Subjunctive* mood occurs only in subordinate clauses and is governed by a number of particles, such as: *ān* ('that, in order that'), *li* ('that, in order that'), *ḥattā* ('until, until that, that, in order that'), *fa* following a clause that contains an imperative and indicates a result, *wa* when the action of the subordinate clause is simultaneous with that of the previous clause, *āw* ('unless that'), *īḏan* or *īḏḏan*

142. Huehnergard treats this feature in a discussion on verbs with the "subordination marker -*u*" rather than treating it as the subjunctive mood. His discussion includes examples in which the marker -*u* appears on the preterite, the durative, and the perfect (Huehnergard, *Grammar of Akkadian*, 183–84). See also B. Kienast, *Historische Semitische Sprachwissenschaft* (Wiesbaden: Harrassowitz, 2001) 263–92.

143. According to Wright, *Grammar of the Arabic Language*, 51

144. *qatul > *qutul > uqtul (Bar-Asher, "Imperative Forms of Proto-Semitic," 236).

('in that case, well then') when the context expresses the future result of a previous statement. These particles are not restricted to the subjunctive but may also be accompanied by other forms of the verb (e.g., perfect, imperfect).

The jussive expresses the idea of request or wish and is found in main clauses and in the protasis (with *īn*) or apodosis of conditional clauses. The jussive may be accompanied by various particles such as: *li-* (proclitic) and the negative particle *lā*. The imperative expresses a command and is formed from the jussive by dropping the prefix of the second-person singular.[145] As in other Semitic languages, the imperative does not take a negative particle but expresses a negative command with a negative particle with second-person jussive. The imperative may appear with the same endings as the energic, *-an(na)*.

The so-called energic mood is formed by adding the ending *-an(na)* to the jussive form of the verb.[146] According to Tamar Zewi, this modal element expresses subjective nuances such as: promises, self-encouragement, wishes, threats and warnings, commands, consequences, affirmations, prohibitions, rhetorical questions.[147] She concludes that the modal form with *-an(na)* ending "is not a distinct mood but an enforcement of the indicative, or in other words an addition of a modal nuance to the indicative."[148] This modal form may be preceded by the particle of emphasis *la* (proclitic) with the idea of 'truly, surely'. It can also appear in the apodosis of conditional clauses when both the the protasis and apodosis are introduced by the particle *la*.

1.9.3. South Semitic – Classical Ethiopic (Geʿez)

Dillman contends that there are only two moods in Geʿez: the Subjunctive and the Imperative.[149] Lambdin's modal paradigm includes the Indicative, the Subjunctive, and the Imperative moods,[150] while Chaine adds the Infinitive and the Gerundive to Lambdin's three categories.[151]

145. Wright, *Grammar of the Arabic Language*, 61.

146. This modal ending appears on the first-, second-, and third-person jussive. There are rare occurrences with the imperative. For a study of the so-called energic forms in Classical Arabic, see Tamar Zewi, *A Syntactical Study of Verbal Forms Affixed by -n(n) Endings in Classical Arabic, Biblical Hebrew, El-Amarna Akkadian and Ugaritic* (AOAT 260; Münster: Ugarit-Verlag, 1999) 13–63.

147. Ibid., 16.

148. Ibid.

149. Dillmann begins his discussion on moods by emphasizing these two groups. When discussing the Imperfect, he introduces the idea of a new mood, the Indicative/Imperfect, formed as a secondary development of the Subjunctive (p. 176). August Dillmann, *Ethiopic Grammar* (ed. Karl Bezold; trans. James Crichton; London: Williams & Norgate, 1907) 173.

150. Thomas O. Lambdin, *Introduction to Classical Ethiopic* (Atlanta: Scholars Press, 1978); B. Kienast, *Historische Semitische Sprachwissenschaft*, 263–92.

151. Marius Chaine, *Grammaire éthiopienne* (Beirut: Imprimerie catholique, 1938) 27.

Indicative	*yeqattel* / *qat(a)la*
Subjunctive/jussive	*yeqtel*
Imperative	*qetel* [152]

The indicative mood is expressed by the perfect or imperfect, although these two verbal forms may also express other modal nuances. The subjunctive, when found in main clauses, expresses volitional ideas of wish, exhortation, or request (cohortative, jussive). In certain cases, the verb is preceded by the particle *la-*. Whenever a second-person subjunctive is preceded by *ʾi-* , it expresses a negative command. In dependent clauses, the subjunctive expresses purpose or result and may or may not be preceded by the conjunction *kama*. This construction for purpose/result clauses is more common than the infinitive with prefix *la-*. The subjunctive occurs after verbs of "willing," "wishing," "begging," "commanding," "permitting," "promising," and "beginning." The imperative is formed by removing the preformative of the subjunctive and adding the vowel *-e-* between the first two radicals of the root. It occurs only in independent clauses. The imperative is used to express positive commands and is not found accompanied by a negative particle. The subjunctive is used for negative commands.

152. **qatul* > **qutul* > **qətəl* (Bar-Asher, "Imperative Forms of Proto-Semitic," 242).

Chapter 2
Biblical Hebrew

2.1. Introduction

An enormous number of scholarly publications on the verbal system of Biblical Hebrew have appeared on the market during the last century, especially during the last three decades.[1] Consequently, a taxonomy of modal and non-modal verbs has appeared throughout the literature in a variety of paradigms. A study of the Hebrew verbal system is complex and not devoid of problems, because (1) our distance in time from the languages we attempt to describe is great; (2) the variety of dialects and discourse types found in the Hebrew text is numerous (e.g., from Classical to Late Hebrew, from narrative to prophetic discourse); (3) diachronic changes that occur within the language are multi-layered; and (4) the influence of other languages on Hebrew is evident in the literature. As stated by Joosten,

> A major problem with grammatical studies on biblical Hebrew is that the language of the Bible is not a unity. What presents itself today as one book is in reality a small library of writings originating in different periods, areas and social milieus. Moreover, the individual books of the Bible are scarcely more homogeneous than the collection as a whole. Scholars claim to detect, with varying degrees of certitude, different literary layers even within single books. No con-

1. Ohad Cohen, *The Verbal Tense System in Late Biblical Hebrew Prose* (HSS 63; Winona Lake, IN: Eisenbrauns, 2013); Jan Joosten, *The Verbal System of Biblical Hebrew: A New Synthesis Elaborated on the Basis of Classical Prose* (Jerusalem: Simor, 2012); F. I. Andersen and A. D. Forbes, *Biblical Hebrew Grammar Visualized* (LSAWS 6; Winona Lake, IN: Eisenbrauns, 2012); R. D. Holmstedt, "The Typological Classification of the Hebrew of Genesis: Subject-Verb or Verb-Subject," *JHS* 11 (2011) 2–39; Adina Moshavi, *Word Order in the Biblical Hebrew Finite Clause: A Syntactic and Pragmatic Analysis of Preposing* (LSAWS 4; Winona Lake, IN: Eisenbrauns, 2010); S. Izre'el, ed., *Semitic Linguistics: The State of the Art at the Turn of the Twenty-First Century* (Oriental Studies 20. Winona Lake, IN : Eisenbrauns, 2002); R. D. Holmstedt, *The Relative Clause in Biblical Hebrew: a Linguistic Analysis* (Ph.D. diss., University of Wisconsin–Madison, 2002); G. Hatav, *The Semantics of Aspect and Modality: Evidence from English and Biblical Hebrew* (Amsterdam: John Benjamins, 1997); P. Gentry, "The System of the Finite Verb in Classical Biblical Hebrew," *HS* 39 (1998) 7–41; A. Shulman, *The Use of Modal Verb Forms in Biblical Hebrew Prose* (Ph.D. diss., University of Toronto, 1996); V. DeCaen, *On the Placement and Interpretation of the Verbs in Standard Biblical Hebrew Prose* (Ph.D. diss., University of Toronto, 1995); Revell, "The System of the Verb in Standard Biblical Prose," 1–37; E. Talstra, "Text Grammar and Hebrew Bible II: Syntax and Semantics," *BiOr* 39 (1982) 26–38.

> sensus exists as to the dating of most of the texts. All that is widely accepted is the variegation of biblical Hebrew.[2]

My study focuses primarily on the historical development of the modal/volitive verbal forms and on their pragmatics in prosaic texts. I expect these to differ in different types of discourse and to show that language is not stagnant but changing under the influence of time and space.[3]

Due to the long, intricate process of transmission, unintentional and interpretive scribal variations appear in the MT. Where textual errors and changes are directly related to my research, I first consider the internal witness of the MT and, then, I give consideration to the variant readings suggested by the ancient versions traditionally used for textual criticism.[4] This process will enable us to gain insight into the ancient scribes' understanding of the verbal system and to recover the earliest and possibly the most accurate rendering of the text.

Due to their basic morphological features, the Biblical Hebrew volitives (cohortative, imperative, jussive) have traditionally been linked to modified forms of the imperfect, a main verb of the "indicative" modal system. Therefore, in most grammars, the treatment of volitives is found in the same section as the imperfect.[5] The volitives rarely occur with stative verbs, especially where the imperative is concerned.[6] Lambdin addresses the three volitives as three forms of the imperative, one being a "direct imperative" (the imperative), while the other two are identified as "indirect imperatives" (the jussive and the cohortative).[7] Many Biblical Hebrew grammarians elaborate on the syntax of "direct volitives" in main clauses in contrast to the use of "indirect volitives" with *waw* found in subordinate clauses (e.g., purpose and result clauses).[8] As

2. Joosten, *Verbal System of Biblical Hebrew*, 7–8.

3. For a collection of studies on diachrony in Biblical Hebrew, see *Diachrony in Biblical Hebrew* (ed. Cynthia Miller-Naudé and Ziony Zevit; LSAWS 8; Winona Lake, IN: Eisenbrauns, 2012); Dong-Hyuk Kim, *Early Biblical Hebrew, Late Biblical Hebrew, and Linguistic Variability: A Sociolinguistic Evaluation of the Linguistic Dating of Biblical Texts* (VTSup 156; Leiden: Brill, 2012); Ian Young and Robert Rezetko, *Linguistic Dating of Biblical Texts* (2 vols.; London: Equinox, 2008).

4. For example, Qumran; LXX and other Greek versions; Aramaic and Syriac versions; Vulgate.

5. GKC, §48; J. Blau, *A Grammar of Biblical Hebrew* (2nd ed.; Porta Linguarum Orientalium n.s. 12; Wiesbaden: Harrasowitz, 1993) §20.4; P. Joüon, *A Grammar of Biblical Hebrew* (trans. and rev. T. Muraoka; Subsidia Biblica 14; Rome: Pontifical Biblical Institute, 2006) 135–39, 365–86. See also D. Gropp, "The Function of the Finite Verb in Classical Biblical Hebrew," *HAR* 13 (1991) 45–62.

6. Joosten, *Verbal System of Biblical Hebrew*, 94.

7. T. O. Lambdin, *Introduction to Biblical Hebrew* (London, Longman & Todd, 1991) 118.

8. This distinction is found in Joüon, *A Grammar of Biblical Hebrew*, 365–86; Blau, *Grammar of Biblical Hebrew*, 64; idem, "Studies in Hebrew Verb Formation," *HUCA* 42 (1971) 133–46.

a rule, modal (nonindicative) prefix conjugations—jussives, cohortatives, imperfects—appear at the head of clauses.[9] Revell notes that

> a second person modal is used to ask the addressee to act. A first person modal presents an action which the speaker hopes or intends to perform. Where the addressee is superior to the speaker, the action indicated by a first person modal requires the authorization of the addressee, and sometimes also some action to enable the speaker to act as intended. In this situation, then, a first person modal also presents a form of request. A third person modal with subject representing either addressee or speaker, may be used to avoid direct reference in asking the former to act, or to authorize action by the latter. . . . Thus all modal forms used in deferential speech can be said to present a request to the addressee.[10]

Joosten echoes this sentiment, stating that "the meaning of the three forms is practically the same.[11] According to Joosten, "[T]he first person cohortative, second person imperative and third person jussive make up a single suppletive paradigm of affirmative volitive forms."[12] In her dissertation on the modal forms in Biblical Hebrew, A. Shulman includes the imperative, the "'jussive,' a shortened form of the indicative imperfect, and 'cohortative,' a lengthened form of the indicative imperfect" in her system of modality in Biblical Hebrew.[13] Her description of the Hebrew volitives seems to disregard the possibility that the origins of the jussive and cohortative may be different from the origin of the imperfect.[14]

Y. Endo and A. Niccacci both present an analysis of the verb forms from the perspective of discourse analysis and emphasize the functions of each volitive based on its relationship to other verbs found in the wider context.[15] According to R. Longacre, the three volitives carry the main line of the story in what he characterizes as "hortatory discourse."[16] In his view, these three main verbal forms carry a wide range of nuances, all intended to "cause the hearer to behave in a certain way." These nuances vary from context to context, depending

9. Revell, "System of the Verb in Standard Biblical Prose," 1–37; Shulman, *Use of Modal Verb Forms.*

10. E. J. Revell, *The Designation of the Individual: Expressive Usage in Biblical Narrative* (Kampen: Kok Pharos, 1996) 276.

11. Joosten, *Verbal System of Biblical Hebrew*, 18.

12. Ibid., 313.

13. Shulman, *Use of Modal Verb Forms*, 1.

14. As will be noted below, the jussive issues from a *yaqtul* verbal form and not from the *yaqtulu*, while the cohortative is a relative of the *yaqtulan(na)* modal verb found in other NWSemitic languages.

15. Y. Endo, *The Verbal System of Classical Hebrew in the Joseph Story: An Approach from Discourse Analysis* (Studia Semitica Neerlandica; Assen: Van Gorcum, 1996) 191–231; A. Niccacci, *The Syntax of the Verb in Classical Hebrew Prose* (trans. W. G. E. Watson; JSOTSup 86; Sheffield: JSOT Press, 1990) 78–81.

16. R. Longacre, *Joseph: A Story of Divine Providence—A Text Theoretical and Textlinguistic Analysis of Genesis* 37 and 39–48 (Winona Lake, IN: Eisenbrauns, 1989) 119–21.

on the social status of the individuals involved and depending on the intention of the speaker.

Before proceeding further in our discussion, we must distinguish between "volitives" (jussive, imperative, cohortative) and "nonvolitive modals" (*yiqtol* imperfect, *weqatal*). Volitives—cohortative, imperative, jussive—include a limited number of morphemes that express ideas of "volition, wish" and "desire" from the point of view of the speaker. When speaking of "nonvolitive modals" (e.g., *yiqtol*, *weqatal*), one must extend the system to verbal forms that go beyond the ideas of "wish" and "desire" and include ideas of "potentiality," "possibility," and "uncertainty." I have chosen to include in my study these sorts of verbal forms, which are not normally found under the rubric of "volitives" but function in a similar way under specific conditions.[17]

This expanded concept for the modal system of Hebrew has been studied by P. Gentry, J. Joosten, G. Hatav, and others. These scholars challenge the view that the imperfect (*yaqtulu*) is the principal verb of the indicative system, since the imperfect fulfills regular modal functions and cannot be treated simply as an "indicative" or "declarative" at the expense of recognizing its modal functions.[18] According to Gentry's paradigm of the verbal system, the imperfect, together with the jussive and cohortative, is included in the "projective" category of modals, in which the speaker's wish or decision about a certain action is expressed through the verb, whether it be an imperfect or a morphologically distinguished volitive. Gentry determines the major functions of the jussive and cohortative primarily through the position of the verb in the clause.

Joosten goes beyond Gentry's proposition and not only removes the long *yiqtol* (*yaqtulu*) from the indicative paradigm of Biblical Hebrew verbs but states that "*weqatal* is basically modal."[19] In the conclusion of his study, Joosten states:

17. For a full treatment of the *yiqtol* imperfect and the *weqatal* as modal forms in Biblical Hebrew, see Joosten, *Verbal System of Biblical Hebrew*, 261–312; Hatav, *The Semantics of Aspect and Modality*; idem, "The Long Form of the Prefix Conjugation Referring to the Past in Biblical Hebrew Prose," *HS* 40 (1999) 15–26; idem, "The Indicative System of the Biblical Hebrew Verb and Its Literary Exploitation," in *Narrative Syntax and the Hebrew Bible* (ed. Ellen van Wolde; Leiden: Brill, 1997) 51–71; R. S. Hendel, "In the Margins of the Hebrew Verbal System: Situation, Tense, Aspect, Mood," *ZAH* 9 (1996) 152–74; Gentry, "The System of the Finite Verb in Classical Biblical Hebrew"; Niccacci, *The Syntax of the Verb*, 88; Revell, "The System of the Verb," 1–37, esp. §13; Shulman, *Use of Modal Verb Forms*; Alexander Andrason, "The Panchronic *Yiqtol*: Functionally Consistent and Cognitively Pausible," *JHS* 10 (2010) 2–63. In addition to a discussion of the modal functions of the imperfect and perfect consecutive, my study also includes a discussion on the infinitive absolute when it functions as a command.

18. Gentry, "The System of the Finite Verb in Classical Biblical Hebrew"; Joosten, "The Indicative System," 51–71; Hatav, *The Semantics of Aspect and Modality,* 142–61.

19. Joosten, "The Indicative System," 58 n. 27.

> In light of all this, *yiqtol* should be pulled out of the indicative system and set on one side, together with the other modal verb forms of Biblical Hebrew: the imperative, the jussive, the cohortative, and *weqatal*. These forms constitute a modal subsystem opposed *en bloc* to the indicative system.[20]

Joosten proposes the following paradigm, in which the *yiqtol* and *weqatal* participate freely in the Hebrew system of modality:[21]

Indicative	***Modal***
qatal, wayyiqtol, participle	juss., impv., coh. (volitives)
yiqtol, weqatal (nonvolitive)	

Hatav takes Joosten's system a step further and proposes that the *yiqtol* and *weqatal* are the two major modal forms of the BH verbal system, while the jussive, imperative, and cohortative are restricted in their modal expressions.[22] Hatav compares the modal functions of the *yiqtol* and *weqatal* with the primary functions of the volitives (imperative, jussive, cohortative) and concludes that the *yiqtol* and *weqatal* not only fulfill all the nuances of modality expressed by the volitives (jussive, cohortative, imperative) but that they are commonly found in other nonfactual contexts such as conditions, interrogative sentences, and other types of situations involving potentiality and possibility. In her opinion, the *imperative*, *jussive*, and *cohortative* belong to a subsystem of modality, rather than to the primary line of the paradigm.[23] She supports her argument by noting that the volitives are all morphologically linked to the *yiqtol* (therefore, a secondary development of the main modal verb) and that the three forms are marked for specific types of modality. Hatav states:

> It is well acknowledged by Hebraists, e.g., Qimron (1980), that they [the jussive, cohortative, and imperative] form a suppletive paradigm of directives . . . , according to the person inflection. That is, they all function to utter some directive, and the choice of one of them is determined by the person in question. If the sentence expressing the directive is in second person the imperative (and sometimes the jussive) is used, if it is in first person it is in cohortative and if it is in the third person it is in jussive. As a result of this, each form "specializes" in a certain directive.[24]

According to Hatav, the *yiqtol* and *weqatal* have greater flexibility than the volitives and can be included in the alethic, epistemic, and deontic categories

20. Ibid., 58.
21. Joosten's paradigm omits the infinitive absolute, a form used to express commands (Joosten, "The Long Form of the Prefix Conjugation," 16; idem, *The Verbal System of Biblical Hebrew*, 19, 39–40, 65–67, 266–76, 295–301).
22. Hatav, *The Semantics of Aspect and Modality*, 142–61.
23. Ibid., 198.
24. Ibid., 151.

of modality.[25] On the other hand, the *imperative, jussive*, and *cohortative* are limited to the deontic category of modals.[26] Hendel follows Hatav's idea and states that the imperfect "has tended to obscure the distinction between deontic and epistemic modality in descriptions of Hebrew."[27]

In his study of markedness in the verbal systems of Canaanite and Biblical Hebrew, Paul Korchin proposes that, in the *formal structure* paradigm, the *yqtl-u* and *yqtl-a* are viewed as equipollent binary oppositions "with respect to the primary associational matrix underlying the system (*y-qtl-*)."[28] This distinction is "characterized by the differential presence vs. presence of specific morphemic marks (*-u* / *-a*) or marks (*-e-* + *-n-*)."[29] He proposes the following paradigms for the *formal structure* of the prefix conjugations:

Formal Structure

yqtl-Ø
(unmarked)

yqtl-u (singly marked) | *yqtl-a* (singly marked)

yqtl-e-n
(doubly marked)

Regarding the *functional structure* paradigm, Korchin proposes that the binary opposites *yqtl-u* and *yqtl-a* exhibit functions that are more specific and restricted than the unmarked *yqtl-Ø*.[30] The *yqtl-u* (realis—marked nonanterior) functions in temporal opposition to *yqtl-Ø* (unmarked ant/nonanterior and ind/nonindicative), while the *yqtl-a* (irrealis—marked nonindicative) functions in modal opposition to the *yqtl-Ø*.[31] The lack of *-u* in the *yqtl-Ø* "signifies functional neutrality with respect to nonanteriority" and the lack of *-a* "signifies functional neutrality with respect to nonindicative modality."[32] The prefix conjugation with *-e-n* ending is not considered intrinsic to the Hebrew verbal system. Rather, it is interpreted by Korchin as a prefix conjugation with

25. For Ronald Hendel, *deontic* modality "involves the speaker's will, as in statements of wish, command, permission, or obligation. These kinds of utterances express the speaker's desire or decision concerning an action"; and *epistemic* modality "involves the speaker's opinion or knowledge about a proposition, as in statements of doubt, belief, or other shades of expectation or opinion. Epistemic utterances related to the speaker's state of knowledge, rather than to the speaker's will" (Hendel, "In the Margins of the Hebrew Verbal System," 169).

26. Hatav, *The Semantics of Aspect and Modality*, 142.

27. Hendel, "In the Margins of the Hebrew Verbal System," 170.

28. Paul Korchin, *Markedness in the Canaanite and Hebrew Verbs* (HSS 58; Winona Lake, IN: Eisenbrauns, 2008) 327–28.

29. Ibid., 327.

30. Ibid., 328.

31. Ibid.

32. Ibid.

an enclitic particle "appended to temporally marked *yqtl-u-* and to modally marked *yqtl-a-*."[33]

Functional Structure

yqtl-∅
(Ant/non-Ant) (Ind/non-Ind)
(unmarked)

yqtl-u	*yqtl-a*
(non-Ant)	**(non-Ind)**
(singly marked)	(singly marked)

yqtl-e-n
(+Cont)

In his study of the *waw*-prefixed verb forms, Cook proposes the following paradigm:[34]

Indicative Function:	Perfect (*qatal*)
	Narrative Preterite (*wayyiqtol* < *yaqtul*)
	Imperfect (*yiqtol* < *yaqtulu*)
Modal Functions:	Modal Perfect (*weqatal*)
	Modal Imperfect (*yiqtol* < *yaqtulu*?)
	Jussive (*yiqtol*)
	Imperative (*qĕtol*)

For the purpose of this book, the main focus will remain on the three main volitives, followed by a discussion of the other verbal forms that function as modals under specific circumstances (*yiqtol*, *weqatal*, infinitive absolute). It is important to remember that each verb form carries several nuances, is used in several types of discourse, and may overlap in function with other closely related forms.

Verbs often appear in "meaningful syntactical sequences." When this occurs, the first verb of the sequence fulfills its basic roles, while the verbs that follow express subordination and belong to one of the following categories:

1. *Sequentiality*: the fulfillment of events must occur in the order in which they are stated (e.g., imperative + *weqatal*). In order to determine temporal and logical sequentiality, the clauses are tested for irreversibility. Where the events are reversible, they are not sequential.[35]

33. Ibid., 328.

34. J. A. Cook, "The *Vav*-Prefix Verb Forms in Elementary Hebrew Grammar," *JHS* 8 (2008) 11.

35. In his discussion of temporal succession and *ordo naturalis* in discourse, Cook notes that the order in which clauses appear in a text is not only syntactically significant, it is also semantically noteworthy. Irreversability must take into consideration the necessity that the clauses be asymmetrical—not simply joined by the conjunctive marker "and"; it must

2. *Conjunctivity*: the events can occur in any order without changing the logical outcome (e.g., imperative + *waw*-imperative). Such events are reversible and, therefore, not marked for sequentiality.
3. *Parallel/Hendiadys*: two or more verbs represent a single event (e.g., וַיַּעַן וַיֹּאמֶר). In these cases, the verbs are reversible and do not represent sequence.
4. *Purpose/Result*: the purpose or result stated in the subordinate clause (the *consequent*) depends on the fulfillment of the event of the main clause (the *antecedent*).[36] These verb sequences primarily indicate subordination of one event to another and are secondarily logically sequential (e.g., *Go* [antecedent] *to the king in order to inform* [consequent] *him of the defeat of his armies*). Sentences with purpose or result clauses are tested against a negative condition: IF the *antecedent* (main clause event) does not take place, then, the *consequent* (the purpose or result) cannot occur.[37]

2.2. The Imperative

The Hebrew language includes a variety of verbal forms through which direct and indirect commands are expressed. These include: the regular imperative, the regular imperative with נָא, the long imperative, the long imperative with נָא, the infinitive absolute, the imperfect, the perfect consecutive, the jussive, and the jussive with נָא. The regular imperative is the unmarked form for commands or requests for action. Other verb forms and syntagmas express a wide range of nuances, from soft polite requests to strong commands. My study of the imperative will include a short section on morphology, followed by a survey of the various syntactic functions played by the imperative, either in contexts where it functions independently from other verbs, or in contexts where it is syntactically related to other volitives and nonvolitives. The following constructions and verb sequences will be taken into consideration in the process of research:

Imperative	
Imperative	*as interjection*
Imperative	*as adverb*
Imperative	*with ethical dative*
Regular Imperative	*with* נָא
Long Imperative	

indicate linguistically the irreversible-sequential idea of "and then" (John A. Cook, "The Semantics of Verbal Pragmatics: Clarifying the Roles of *Wayyiqtol* and *Weqatal* in Biblical Hebrew Prose," *JSS* 49 [2004] 251). See also Tarsee Li, *The Expression of Sequence and Non Sequence* (Ph.D. dissertation, Hebrew Union College–Jewish Institute of Religion, 1999) 10.

36. J. H. Grimes, *The Thread of Discourse* (Lanua Linguarum Series Minor 207; The Hague: Mouton, 1975) 223.

37. Joosten, *Verbal System of Biblical Hebrew*, 140, 144–56.

Long Imperative	*with* נָא	
Imperative	*followed by*	Imperative
Imperative	*followed by*	Cohortative
Imperative	*followed by*	Jussive
Imperative	*followed by*	*yaqtul*
Imperative	*followed by*	Perfect
Imperative	*followed by*	Infinitive Absolute
Negative Imperative		

In order to determine whether certain patterns of speech involving imperatives are particular in specific social classes, I examine the relationships between speakers and listeners and group the utterances into the following categories:

1. from greater to lesser
2. from lesser to greater
3. between individuals of equal social status[38]

Finally, comments will be made both on the significance of word order in clauses with imperatives, and on the types of clauses which include imperatives.

2.2.1. Regular Imperatives

The Hebrew imperative[39] occurs in the second-person masculine and feminine, in the singular and plural. The sufformatives, which identify the difference in gender or number, are the same as those of the imperfect, giving us the following basic paradigm:[40]

	singular	*plural*
masculine	שְׁמֹר	שִׁמְרוּ
feminine	שִׁמְרִי	שְׁמֹרְנָה

When imperfect verb forms appear with *a* as the theme vowel (statives, III-guttural), the imperative retains the *a* as the theme vowel (e.g., שְׁכַב, לְבַשׁ). When the imperative is followed by a *maqqep*, the theme vowel reduces from *ḥolem* to *qameṣ ḥaṭup* (e.g., שְׁמָר־לְךָ).[41]

38. In the introduction, I proposed a basic paradigm for categorizing the individuals involved in the discourse passages. This list is used to determine the social dynamics between speaker(s) and audience—from "greater to lesser," from "lesser to greater," and between "equals."

39. According to Joosten, the imperative functions in commands, requests, invitations, permissions, concessions, blessings, and predictions (*Verbal System of Biblical Hebrew*, 121).

40. E. A. Bar-Asher noted that Proto-Semitic included several imperative forms, for example, the *qatil*, *qatul*, and *qital* forms ("The Imperative Forms of Proto-Semitic and a New Perspective on Bath's Law," *JAOS* 128 [2008] 233.)

41. I assume that other Canaanite languages such as Phoenician and Moabite had the same morphological features, but the lack of vocalization prevents us from highlighting clear evidence. In Phoenician, the imperative expresses commands but, since there is no morpho-

1. *Command.* The general idea of the imperative is, more often than not, that of a direct *command* that requires immediate attention.[42] According to Joosten, “The speaker wants the addressee(s) to enter into the process designated by the verbal form.”[43]

קַדֶּשׁ־לִי כָל־בְּכוֹר
Consecrate to me all the firstborn (Exod 13:2)[44]

הִתְיַצֵּב כֹּה עַל־עֹלָתֶךָ וְאָנֹכִי אִקָּרֶה כֹּה
Stand here by your burnt offering while I go inquire over there (Num 23:15)

הָסִירִי אֶת־יֵינֵךְ מֵעָלָיִךְ
Put away your wine from you (1 Sam 1:14)

2. *Request* or *mitigated command.* In addition, the imperative may also represent a *request* or a *mitigated command*, especially in the context of prayer, and in passages where one of “lesser” social status is addressing one of “higher” status.

מְשָׁל־בָּנוּ גַּם־אַתָּה גַּם־בִּנְךָ גַּם בֶּן־בְּנֶךָ
Rule over us, you and your son and your grandson (Judg 8:22)

וְעַתָּה יְהוָה אֱלֹהֵי יִשְׂרָאֵל שְׁמֹר לְעַבְדְּךָ דָוִד אָבִי אֵת אֲשֶׁר דִּבַּרְתָּ לוֹ
Now, O Lord God of Israel, *fulfill* for your servant David, my father, that which you spoke to him (1 Kgs 8:25)

2.2.1.1. Imperative as Interjection

Some Hebrew imperatives function as interjections. Rather than expressing commands or requests, they provide a sense of exclamation and bring attention to the statement that follows. They are “used in ways approaching that of discourse markers without lexical content.”[45] According to Joosten, (1) where these imperatives are isolated, and simply connected to the preceding clause by a conjunction, they function as interjections; (2) where the meaning of the imperatives seems unrelated to the context, they also function as interjections.[46] Such verbs are syntactically related to no other verbs in the context.

---

logical difference between the imperative and the infinitive absolute, it is possible that in some cases commands are given with infinitives rather than with imperatives.

42. From a sample of 118 passages, we find 87 examples of “commands.”

43. Joosten, *Verbal System of Biblical Hebrew*, 326.

44. In this volume, all translations of Scripture are mine, unless otherwise indicated.

45. Ibid., 332.

46. Ibid.

1. The imperative of רָאָה does not always represent the idea of 'seeing' or 'looking at' something but is often used to draw attention to a specific matter, with a sense similar to that of הִנֵּה.[47]

רְאוּ כִּי־יְהוָה נָתַן לָכֶם הַשַּׁבָּת
See! The Lord has given you the Sabbath (Exod 16:29)

רְאֵה נָתַתִּי לִפְנֵיכֶם אֶת־הָאָרֶץ
Look! I have put this land before you (Deut 1:8)

רְאֵה נָתַתִּי בְיָדְךָ אֶת־סִיחֹן מֶלֶךְ־חֶשְׁבּוֹן
See! I have given Sihon the king of Heshbon into your hands (Deut 2:24)

2. The verb שָׁמַר, when used in the Niphal imperative with ethical dative, can be considered as an *interjection* carrying out the idea of a *warning* against performing a certain action. In most cases, this warning can be introduced by "make sure that you do not!'

הִשָּׁמְרוּ לָכֶם עֲלוֹת בָּהָר וּנְגֹעַ בְּקָצֵהוּ כָּל־הַנֹּגֵעַ בָּהָר מוֹת יוּמָת
Make sure that you do not go up and touch the edge of the mountain; anyone who touches it will surely die (Exod 19:12)

הִשָּׁמֶר לְךָ פֶּן־תִּכְרֹת בְּרִית לְיוֹשֵׁב הָאָרֶץ אֲשֶׁר אַתָּה בָּא עָלֶיהָ פֶּן־יִהְיֶה לְמוֹקֵשׁ בְּקִרְבֶּךָ
Make sure you do not make a covenant with the inhabitants of the land which you are entering, lest it becomes a snare for you (Exod 34:12)

הִשָּׁמְרוּ לָכֶם פֶּן־תִּשְׁכְּחוּ אֶת־בְּרִית יְהוָה אֱלֹהֵיכֶם אֲשֶׁר כָּרַת עִמָּכֶם
Make sure that you do not forget the covenant of the Lord your God which He has established with you (Deut 4:23)

3. The Hiphil imperative of יָהַב does not imply an action to be performed by the hearer but places emphasis on the *suggestion* made by the following cohortative:

הָבָה נִלְבְּנָה לְבֵנִים וְנִשְׂרְפָה לִשְׂרֵפָה
Let us make bricks and let us fire (them) (Gen 11:3)

---

47. Also רְאֵה אַתָּה אֹמֵר אֵלַי 'See! You have said to me' (Exod 33:12); רְאֵה נָתַן יְהוָה אֱלֹהֶיךָ לְפָנֶיךָ אֶת־הָאָרֶץ 'Look! The Lord your God has provided this land before you' (Deut 1:21); רְאֵה הַחִלֹּתִי תֵּת לְפָנֶיךָ אֶת־סִיחֹן 'See! I have begun to deliver Sihon before you' (Deut 2:31).

הָבָה נֵרְדָה וְנָבְלָה שָׁם שְׂפָתָם
Let us go down and confuse their language (Gen 11:7)

הָבָה נִתְחַכְּמָה לוֹ פֶּן־יִרְבֶּה
Let us deal wisely (with them) lest they multiply (Exod 1:10)

4. The Hiphil imperative הוֹאֶל often carries the idea of *politeness* and *respect* toward the addressee.

וְעַתָּה הוֹאֵל וּבָרֵךְ אֶת־בֵּית עַבְדְּךָ לִהְיוֹת לְעוֹלָם לְפָנֶיךָ
So now, *please bless* the house of your servant so that it may last forever before you (2 Sam 7:29)

וַיֹּאמֶר נַעֲמָן הוֹאֵל קַח כִּכָּרָיִם
Naaman said: *Please take* two talents (2 Kgs 5:23)

וַיֹּאמֶר הָאֶחָד הוֹאֶל נָא וְלֵךְ אֶת־עֲבָדֶיךָ
Then one said: *Please come* with your servants (2 Kgs 6:3)

2.2.1.2. Imperative as Adverb

In Biblical Hebrew prose, where the imperative is followed immediately by another imperative, or by a cohortative (with or without connecting *waw*), the first verb often functions adverbially. In such cases, the imperative describes the *manner* in which the action of the second verb is to take place. Some have suggested that these imperatives function as interjections rather than as adverbs, but since most of the imperatives found in such verb sequences are verbs of motion, I prefer interpreting them as adverbs of manner.[48] In my opinion, they are not simply "attention-getters," but they imply movement (e.g., going, arising, coming, going up, going down; see discussion below). Interjections do not require the performance of an action but only demand the attention of the listener(s).

Lambdin treats this type of construction in his section on "verbal hendiadys and related idioms" but states that "in meaning the first [verb] serves to qualify the second and is best translated adverbially in English."[49] In this type of verb sequence, the two verbs always agree in gender[50] but do not always agree in

48. GKC identifies some of these verbs as interjections rather than as adverbs and state that "imperatives as קוּמוּ, קוּם, לְכוּ, לֵךְ, when immediately preceding a second imperative, are for the most part only equivalent to the interjections, *Come! Up!*" (GKC §110h).

49. Lambdin, *Introduction to Biblical Hebrew*, 238.

50. For example, קוּמִי שְׂאִי (Gen 21:18); לֵךְ קַח (Gen 27:13); קוּמוּ שׁוּבוּ (Gen 43:13); לְכוּ עִבְדוּ (Exod 10:24); קוּם רֵד (Deut 9:12); לְכִי שַׁאֲלִי (2 Kgs 4:3); לֵכְנָה שֹּׁבְנָה (Ruth 1:8).

Table 2.1. Verbs That Follow Some Adverbial Imperatives

Verb	*Followed by Verb of*	*List of Verbs That Follow the Adverbial Imperative*
הָלַךְ	motion	הָלַךְ, יָרַד, שׁוּב, בּוֹא
	other	שָׁקַה, שָׁכַב, כָּרַת, קָרַב, נָפַל, יָעַד, לָקַח, רָעָה, דָּרַשׁ, סוּר, עָשָׂה, כּוֹן, זָעַק, אָכַל, מָצָא, עָבַר, בָּרַח, אָהַב, נָבָא, כָּנַס, פָּרָה, עָבַד, אוּר, קָבָה, אָמַר, שָׁאַל, רָאָה, סָתַר, דִּבֵּר
קוּם	motion	יָצָא, בָּרַח, רָדַף, יָרַד ,עָבַר, עָלָה, הָלַךְ
	other	יָשַׁב, לָקַח, נָשָׂא, אָכַל, קָרָא, בֵּרַךְ, עָשָׂה, בָּנָה
בּוֹא	motion	-
	other	שָׁכַב, דִּבֵּר, עָשָׂה, לָקַח, סָגַר
יָרַד	motion	-
	other	עוּד
רוּץ	motion	-
	other	מָצָא, דִּבֵּר
נָגַשׁ	motion	-
	other	בּוֹא, פָּגַע
סָבַב	motion	-
	other	יָצַב
עָלָה	motion	-
	other	נָשָׂא

person and number since, in some instances, a singular imperative is followed by a plural (never singular) cohortative.[51]

לְכָה וְנָשׁוּבָה פֶּן־יֶחְדַּל אָבִי מִן־הָאֲתֹנוֹת וְדָאַג לָנוּ

Let us go back, or my father will stop worrying about the asses and will worry about us (1 Sam 9:5)
(singular imperative + plural cohortative)

לְכוּ וְנָבֹאָה וְנַגִּידָה בֵּית הַמֶּלֶךְ

Let us go and tell the king's household (2 Kgs 7:9)
(plural imperative + plural cohortative)

51. E.g., לְכָה נַשְׁקֶה (Gen 19:32); לְכוּ וְנִפְּלָה (2 Kgs 7:4); לְכוּ וְנַפִּילָה (Jonah 1:7); חֲזַק וְנִתְחַזְּקָה (1 Chr 19:13).

The most common verbs with adverbial functions are שׁוּב, עָלָה, בּוֹא, קוּם, הָלַךְ, מָהַר, and נָשָׂא.[52] The following verbs fulfill this role only once or twice in our corpus: רוּץ, יָרַד, הוֹאִיל, שָׁלַח, and סוּר. The verbs in this category include active verbs and stative verbs. Table 2.1 lists the verbs that follow some of the adverbial imperatives mentioned above, as found in the prose sections of the Hebrew Bible.

The verbs הָלַךְ and קוּם appear in constructions of this sort more frequently than any other verb. One of the main differences between these two verbs is in the type of verb that follows them. Most verbs that follow the imperative of קוּם are verbs of motion. The opposite is true of the verb הָלַךְ. Most verbs that follow the imperative of הָלַךְ are not verbs of motion. The verb הָלַךְ is often followed by verbs of 'speaking' such as אָרַר, שָׁאַל, נָבָא, דִּבֶּר, אָמַר, and קָבַב. When this combination occurs, the verb הָלַךְ is never connected to the verb of 'speaking' by a *waw*. The verb הָלַךְ is the most flexible in this type of construction and operates as an adverb with the greatest number of possibilities.[53] Its distribution is found in four categories:

a. Imperative	*followed by*	Imperative[54]
b. Imperative	*followed by*	*waw*-Imperative[55]
c. Imperative	*followed by*	Cohortative[56]
d. Imperative	*followed by*	*waw*-Cohortative[57]

One would expect that in an economical language such as Hebrew, where a limited number of forms express a great number of ideas, different verbal constructions would differ in meaning. We find that some nuances expressed by the Hebrew language are difficult to translate into English. The meaning of an asyndetic construction such as an "Imperative *followed by* Imperative" often seems to be the same as its equivalent syndetic construction "Imperative *followed by waw*-Imperative." A distinction in meaning between *a* and *b*, and between *c* and *d* should be evident, by the simple fact that the syntagmas differ. Yet in many cases, when imperatives function as adverbs, the meaning is the same in constructions with *waw* and without *waw*, especially when both verbs express movement.

52. S. Fassberg, "Sequences of Positive Commands in Biblical Hebrew: הָלוֹךְ וְאָמַרְתָּ, לֵךְ וְאָמַרְתָּ, לֵךְ אֱמֹר," in *Biblical Hebrew in Its Northwest Semitic Setting: Typological and Historical Perspectives* (ed. S. E. Fassberg and A. Hurvitz; Jerusalem: Magnes / Winona Lake, IN: Eisenbrauns, 2006) 51–64.

53. We find one occurrence of the verb הָלַךְ with adverbial functions in Moabite: לך אחז את נבה 'Go take Nebo' (line 14).

54. E.g., Gen 27:13, 42:19, 45:17, 29:7; Exod 12:31, 19:24; Num 22:6, 11, 17; Deut 5:30; 1 Sam 20:21, 9:3, 15:6; 2 Sam 14:21, 7:3; 2 Kgs 4:3; 1 Chr 21:2; 2 Chr 34:21, 16:3; Neh 8:10; Ruth 1:8.

55. E.g., Josh 18:8; Judg 10:14; 2 Sam 14:30, 15:22; 1 Kgs 1:13; 2 Kgs 6:13.

56. E.g., Gen 19:32, 31:44; 1 Sam 9:10.

57. E.g., Judg 19:11, 13; 1 Sam 9:5, 14:1; 2 Kgs 7:4, 9; Neh 6:2, 7; Jonah 1:7.

In the cases in which an imperative of הָלַךְ precedes another imperative, the majority of the syntagmas are asyndetic (without *waw*). From the 48 occurrences found in Genesis to 2 Kings, Ruth, Esther, and Chronicles, 43 appear without the *waw*.[58] In the 5 syndetic constructions (with *waw*),[59] the passage indicates one of two possibilities: (1) the second imperative introduces a purpose clause; or (2) dittography (the *waw* between the two imperatives is immediately preceded by a *waw* or a *yod*, an indication that the scribe erroneously duplicated the sign for *waw/yod* (see examples below).

זֹאת עֲשׂוּ טַעֲנוּ אֶת־בְּעִירְכֶם וּלְכוּ־בֹאוּ אַרְצָה כְּנָעַן
Do this! Load your animals and *go* into the land of Canaan (Gen 45:17)

versus:

לְכִי וּבֹאִי אֶל־הַמֶּלֶךְ דָּוִד וְאָמַרְתְּ אֵלָיו
Go to King David and say to him (1 Kgs 1:13—possible dittography)

לְכוּ רְאוּ אֶת־הָאָרֶץ וְאֶת־יְרִיחוֹ
Go see the land and Jericho (Josh 2:1)

versus:

וַיֹּאמֶר לְכוּ וּרְאוּ אֵיכֹה הוּא
Then he said: *Go see* where he is (2 Kgs 6:13—dittography or purpose clause)

לְכוּ וְזַעֲקוּ אֶל־הָאֱלֹהִים אֲשֶׁר בְּחַרְתֶּם בָּם
Go cry out to the gods whom you have chosen (Judg 10:14—dittography or purpose clause)

versus:

לְכִי אִמְרִי לְיָרָבְעָם כֹּה־אָמַר יְהוָה אֱלֹהֵי יִשְׂרָאֵל
Go say to Jeroboam: Thus says the Lord God of Israel (1 Kgs 14:7)

וַיֹּאמֶר אֲלֵהֶם לְכוּ דִרְשׁוּ בְּבַעַל זְבוּב אֱלֹהֵי עֶקְרוֹן
Then he said: *Go inquire* with Baalzebub, the god of the Ekronites (2 Kgs 1:2)

versus:

58. Gen 27:13, 29:7, 42:19, 45:17; Exod 5:18, 8:21, 10:8, 24, 12:31, 19:24, 32:7, 33:1; Josh 2:1; Judg 18:2; 1 Sam 3:9; 15:6; 20:21, 40; 26:19; 2 Sam 3:6, 7:3, 14:21, 18:21, 24:1; 1 Kgs 2:29; 14:7; 15:19; 18:1, 8, 11, 14; 19:15, 20; 20:22; 2 Kgs 1:2, 6; 4:3, 7; 5:5; 8:10; 22:13; Ruth 1:8; Esth 4:16; 2 Chr 16:3.

59. Judg 10:14; 2 Sam 15:22; 1 Kgs 1:13; 2 Kgs 6:13, 7:14.

> וַיִּשְׁלַח הַמֶּלֶךְ אַחֲרֵי מַחֲנֵה־אֲרָם לֵאמֹר לְכוּ וּרְאוּ
>
> The king sent (them) after the Aramean army saying: *Go see* (2 Kgs 7:14—dittography or purpose)

The imperative of קוּם, commonly used as an adverb, has been studied for its special use as an *inchoative* (also referred to as an *ingressive* or *inceptive*), in which the verb focuses on the onset of the main action expressed by the following verb.[60] According to Lambdin, when קוּם serves an adverbial function, it "seems to do little more than give a slight emphasis to the fact that some activity is about to begin . . . ; the imperative often corresponds to 'come, come now, so.'"[61]

In most cases in which the imperative of קוּם is followed by another imperative, the construction is asyndetic (without *waw*).[62] When the construction is syndetic (with connecting *waw*), the *waw* is preceded by another *waw* or by a *yod*, evidence of dittography. This phenomenon is also attested with the verb הָלַךְ. The following examples compare asyndetic and syndetic syntagmas with קוּם:

> וְעַתָּה קוּם עֲבֹר אֶת־הַיַּרְדֵּן הַזֶּה אַתָּה וְכָל־הָעָם הַזֶּה
>
> Now, *cross over* this Jordan, you and all this people (Josh 1:2)

versus:

> וַיֹּאמְרוּ אֶל־דָּוִד קוּמוּ וְעִבְרוּ מְהֵרָה אֶת־הַמַּיִם כִּי־כָכָה יָעַץ עֲלֵיכֶם אֲחִיתֹפֶל
>
> Then they said to David: *Go cross over* the water quickly because Ahitophel is scheming against you (2 Sam 17:21—dittography or purpose)

> וַיֹּאמֶר יְהוָה אֵלַי קוּם לֵךְ לְמַסַּע לִפְנֵי הָעָם וְיָבֹאוּ וְיִירְשׁוּ אֶת־הָאָרֶץ
>
> Then the Lord said to me: *Go* on the journey before the people, so that they may enter and inherit the land (Deut 10:11)

versus:

> קוּמִי וּלְכִי אַתְּ וּבֵיתֵךְ וְגוּרִי בַּאֲשֶׁר תָּגוּרִי
>
> *Get going,* you and your household, and settle where you can settle (2 Kgs 8:1—dittography)

---

60. BDB mentions this use of קוּם in terms of "arising out of inaction," "starting" and "making a move" (F. Brown, S. R. Driver, and C. A. Briggs, eds., *A Hebrew and English Lexicon of the Old Testament with an Appendix Containing the Biblical Aramaic* [Oxford: Clarendon, 1996] 878; 6b, c). F. W. Dobbs-Allsopp, "Ingressive *qwm* in Biblical Hebrew," *ZAH* 8 (1995) 31–54.

61. Lambdin, *Introduction to Biblical Hebrew*, 239.

62. Gen 13:17; 19:14, 15; 21:18; 27:19, 43; 28:2; 31:13; 35:1; 43:13; 44:4; Exod 12:31, 32:1; Num 22:20; Deut 2:24, 9:12, 10:11; Josh 1:2, 7:13, 8:1; Judg 7:9, 8:20; 1 Sam 9:3, 16:12, 23:4; 2 Sam 13:15, 19:8; 1 Kgs 14:12; 17:9; 19:5, 7; 21:7, 15, 18; 2 Kgs 1:3; Neh 9:5.

In addition to the most common verbs, הָלַךְ and קוּם, imperatives with adverbial function include the following verbs:

שׁוּב for *repetition*:

שֻׁבוּ שִׁבְרוּ־לָנוּ מְעַט־אֹכֶל

Go again to get a little grain for the famine (Gen 43:2)

שׁוּב שְׁכָב

Go back to bed (1 Sam 3:5–6)

שָׁלַח for *causation*:   *why not just Hiphil of second verb?*

וְעַתָּה שְׁלַח הָעֵז אֶת־מִקְנְךָ

Now, *have someone bring* your livestock (Exod 9:19)

וְעַתָּה שְׁלַח קְבֹץ אֵלַי אֶת־כָּל־יִשְׂרָאֵל

Now, *have (them) gather* all the Israelites to me (1 Kgs 18:19)

Instances in which the adverbial imperative is of the same root as the following verb are quite rare. In these cases, the adverbial imperative reinforces the idea of the following verb.

and

לְכוּ וְהִתְהַלְּכוּ בָאָרֶץ וְכִתְבוּ אוֹתָהּ וְשׁוּבוּ אֵלַי

Go patrol the land and write it, then return to me (Josh 18:8)

d. Hography?

וַיֹּאמֶר שָׁאוּל לְנַעֲרוֹ טוֹב דְּבָרְךָ לְכָה נֵלֵכָה

Saul said to his servant: Your suggestion is good. *Let us go!* (1 Sam 9:10)

חֲזַק וְנִתְחַזְּקָה בְּעַד־עַמֵּנוּ

Let us strengthen ourselves on account of our people (1 Chr 19:13)

standard/ classical

Verb sequences involving adverbial imperatives are found mostly in preexilic Hebrew.[63] Of the limited number of cases in which the sequence is found in exilic and postexilic Hebrew, most instances appear with the verb הָלַךְ. This shows that the regular use of this root in Hebrew was retained throughout the centuries with little change in function.

---

63. Genesis (22×), Exodus (16×), Numbers (5×), Deuteronomy (5×), Joshua (4×), Judges (4×), 1 Samuel (13×), 2 Samuel (11×), 1 Kings (24×), 2 Kings (11×), Ruth (2×), Esther (2×), Nehemiah (2×), 1 Chronicles (1×), 2 Chronicles (2×).

2.2.1.3. Regular Imperatives with נָא

The imperative is often accompanied by the particle נָא.[64] This particle originates from a Semitic verbal form traditionally called "energic" or "emphatic"—from *yaqtulanna*.[65] Over time, the *-anna* ending became a separate particle, often appearing with a *dagesh forte* in the *nun*, especially after a long imperative or cohortative. Gottlieb states that the modal particle נָא, which appeared for the first time as a separate particle in Ugaritic, developed into an independent morpheme in Hebrew, leaving the modal verb with a final *-a*, an ending that is present on the Biblical Hebrew long imperative and cohortative.[66] Gottlieb writes:

> Due to this word dividing we are able to ascertain a tendency in the Ugaritic linguistic instinct to conceive the energetic element *n* or *nn* as an independent word. . . . It is my opinion that this beginning development towards an independence of the energetic element, which we find in Ugaritic, and which was expressed also in the language of the Amarna letters . . . was continued in Hebrew where we recognize the element in the enclitic particle נָא.[67]

The particle נָא occurs mostly with the jussive, cohortative, and imperative (long and regular imperative with or without pronominal suffixes).[68] It also follows

64. The distribution of imperatives with נָא in the Hebrew Bible is as follows: Genesis (38×), Exodus (8×), Numbers (12×), Deuteronomy (1×), Joshua (2×), Judges (17×), Samuel (37×), Kings (33×), Nehemiah (3×), Chronicles (3×). The book of Job includes 18 occurrences of the imperative with נָא, substantially more than any other poetic book in the Hebrew Bible. These passages would deserve attention in a study of "volitives" in poetry.

65. The "energic" label was introduced in Hebrew grammars more than a century ago, and remained the accepted term for a form that does not indicate "emphasis" but expresses various levels of modality (e.g., petition, question, doubt). For *yaqtulanna* as the origin of the particle נָא, see Paul Haupt, "The Hebrew Particle *-nâ*," *Johns Hopkins University Circulars* 13 (1894) 109; Kaufman, "An Emphatic Plea for Please," 198; H. Gottlieb, "The Hebrew Particle *nâ*," *AcOr* 33 (1971) 47–54; C. Gordon, *Ugaritic Textbook* (AnOr 38; Rome: Pontifical Biblical Institute, 1965) 72 n. 2; B. Christiansen, "A Linguistic Analysis of the Biblical Hebrew Particle *na*ʾ: A Test Case," *VT* 59 (2009) 381.

66. Gottlieb, "The Hebrew Particle *nâ*," 51.

67. Ibid., 51–52.

68. The particle נָא is found more often with the regular imperative than with the long imperative. It occurs with a perfect consecutive only once, in Gen 40:14, in the apodosis of a conditional clause. The context is that of a man (a prisoner, Joseph) making a "polite" request from his equal (another prisoner, the cupbearer). When perfect consecutives carry the imperative mood of a previous imperative (always a regular imperative), the particle נָא does not follow the perfect consecutive but always follows the imperative (e.g., Gen 6:21, 47:29, 19:2; 1 Sam 19:2; 2 Sam 14:2). When two imperatives appear in sequence, in most cases, the particle נָא accompanies the first imperative of the sequence (e.g., Gen 15:5; 27:3, 26; 1 Sam 14:17, 15:25, 17:17; 1 Kgs 20:7; 2 Kgs 4:26, 5:7), and on a few occasions, it accompanies both imperatives (e.g., 2 Sam 14:2; Neh 1:11). It is never the case that only the second imperative of the sequence is followed by the particle נָא.

adverbial particles such as אִם, אַיֵּה, and הִנֵּה or accompanies the negative particle אַל. It comes as no surprise that it never occurs with the negative particle of prohibition לֹא, since נָא and אַל are morphemes marked for modality, while לֹא belongs to the indicative system. As expected, the particle נָא occurs in direct speech (never in indirect speech[69]).

Over the years, several interpretations have been suggested for the particle נָא. In his article on the particle נָא,[70] M. Bar-Magen compares *Targumim Onqelos* and *Jonathan* with the MT and surveys rabbinic literature and Bible commentaries in order to determine the earlier understandings of the particle. Bar-Magen lists three traditional interpretations:

1. the idea of politeness, meaning "please," following the rabbinic tradition:[71] אין נא אלא לשון בקשה
2. the temporal idea "now"[72]
3. the speaker-centered nature of the request, highlighting the desire for a personal favor[73]
4. the word is left untranslated when neither "please" nor "now" fits the context

Modern commentators and grammarians follow interpretations similar to those offered by rabbinic and medieval commentators, with additional suggestions. GKC treats the particle in two seemingly contradictory ways:

1. as a particle that is "used to emphasize a demand, warning, or entreaty,"[74] frequently strengthening a cohortative, jussive, or imperative;[75]
2. as a particle that is often added to the imperative and jussive "to soften down a command, or to make a request in a more courteous form."[76]

---

69. Lina Petersson, "The Syntactic Pattern Imperfect *w-yiqtol* and the Expression of Indirect Command in Biblical Hebrew" (paper presented at the World Congress of Jewish Studies, Jerusalem, 28 July 2013).

70. M. Bar-Magen, "המלה 'נא' במקרא," *Beit Miqra* 25 (1989) 163–71.

71. Bar-Magen mentions that Rashi interprets נָא both as a particle of politeness and as the temporal, meaning 'now' (ibid., 163–71).

72. E.g., *Targum Onqelos*, Saadia Gaon, Ibn Ezra, Ramban, Rashbam, Kimchi, Radaq. Ramban distinguishes between occurrences with נָא after a verb (meaning 'now') and נָא after another particle (meaning 'please'). He also adds that, not only is the particle נָא related to לשון בקשה (language of politeness) and to עתה (temporal "now"), but it is also related to the לשון תחינה (language of supplication). Ibn Ezra adds a nuance to the meaning of the particle, indicating that the action is to be performed ככה ('in this manner'), in other words, in a specific way, for example: דַּבֶּר־נָא בְּאָזְנֵי הָעָם 'Speak to the people in this way' (Exod 11:2; ibid., 166).

73. Joosten, *The Verbal System of Biblical Hebrew*, 122.

74. GKC, 308.

75. Ibid., 319 and 321.

76. Ibid., 324.

Gottlieb identifies נָא with an "energetic" mood, and calls it an "optative particle."[77] He states that:

> the tendency to apply the energetic mood in expressions of command, exhortation or wish . . . was continued in Hebrew where the particle נָא is nearly always used in such expressions. . . . In its primary application, where the particle is used to "intensify" an immediately preceding voluntative, jussive or imperative, it is applied exactly analogously with the independent energetic element in Ugaritic.[78]

Joüon, referring to נָא as a particle of "entreaty," states that in most passages the morpheme adds a weakening nuance roughly equivalent to "please!"[79] Joüon also speaks of three additional usages:

1. the idea of begging for favor or mercy (e.g., "I plead, I beg of you")
2. an emphasis on the command when used with an imperative (e.g., "Do come!")
3. a forceful nuance on the wish of the speaker when occurring with a cohortative (e.g., "I wish/would really like to go forward").[80]

According to Lambdin, when the particle נָא appears, "[T]he command in question is a logical consequence either of an immediately preceding statement or of the general situation in which it is uttered."[81] Fassberg agrees with this interpretation and notes that נָא functions in an appeal or a plea only where it is accompanied by the particle אָנָּא.[82] This view is adopted by Waltke and O'Connor, who also refer to נָא as a "particle of entreaty" and a "precative particle."[83] Kaufman disagrees with Lambdin's view and treats נָא as a particle of "politeness" the meaning of which includes all nuances of "please!"[84] Shulman interprets נָא as a particle of entreaty "used to mark an utterance as a polite, personal, or emotional request of the addressee."[85] When it occurs with an imperative, according to Shulman, the speaker uses נָא to avoid the appearance of giving a forceful command to the addressee.[86] Christiansen expands on Shulman's interpretation and adds that the particle נָא plays two main roles: (1) it is a propositive particle that marks politeness especially with the imperative; and

77. Gottlieb, "The Hebrew Particle *nâ*," 53.

78. Ibid., 52–53.

79. Joüon, *A Grammar of Biblical Hebrew*, 350.

80. Ibid., 350. B. K. Waltke and M. O'Connor refer to this type of first-person volitive as a "cohortative of resolve" (*An Introduction to Biblical Hebrew Syntax* [Winona Lake, IN: Eisenbrauns, 1990] 579).

81. Lambdin, *Introduction to Biblical Hebrew*, 170.

82. S. E. Fassberg, *Studies in Biblical Syntax* (Jerusalem: Magnes, 1994) 71 [Hebrew].

83. Waltke and O'Connor, *Introduction to Biblical Hebrew Syntax*, 579.

84. Kaufman, "An Emphatic Plea for Please," 197–98.

85. A. Shulman, "The Particle נָא in Biblical Hebrew Prose," *HS* 40 (1999) 57.

86. Ibid., 67.

(2) it signals a proposed course of action with the cohortative and jussive.[87] In her study on parenthetical words and phrases in Hebrew, Tamar Zewi notes that the particles אָנָּא and נָא express deontic modality of appeal and plea.[88]

In his study of נָא, Thomas Finley focuses on the relationship between speaker and listener and states that:

> the post-positive *n*ʾ and the pre-positive *ʾn*ʾ either deflect attention from the authority of the speaker if the listener is subordinate, or stress submissiveness if the listener has greater authority. . . . When the speaker has greater authority, the particle *n*ʾ perhaps indicates close identification with the listener, almost in an empathetic sense.[89]

Since the Hebrew particle נָא has become an independent particle of respect and politeness, whenever a speaker includes it in a discourse, he/she expresses "directive illocutionary force."[90] The following examples present various types of situations in which the imperative appears with נָא in prose:

1. *Pleas of desperation.* The situation is one of life and death:

וְאִם־אַיִן מְחֵנִי נָא מִסִּפְרְךָ אֲשֶׁר כָּתָבְתָּ
But if not, *please blot me out* of the book which you have written (Exod 32:32)

וַיֹּאמֶר אֵלַי עֲמָד־נָא עָלַי וּמֹתְתֵנִי
Then he said to me: "*Please stand* over me and kill me for agony has seized me" (2 Sam 1:9)

2. *Urgency.* The request must be fulfilled immediately, without delay:

עַתָּה רוּץ־נָא לִקְרָאתָהּ וֶאֱמָר־לָהּ
Please, run now to her and say to her (2 Kgs 4:26)

3. *Nonurgent request.* The request is neither a matter of life and death, nor one of urgency but requires attention in the near future:

שָׂא נָא עֵינֶיךָ וּרְאֵה מִן־הַמָּקוֹם אֲשֶׁר־אַתָּה שָׁם
Now lift up your eyes and look from where you are (Gen 13:14)

הָבֵא־נָא יָדְךָ בְּחֵיקֶךָ
Now put your hand in your bosom (Exod 4:6)

---

87. Christiansen, "Linguistic Analysis of the Biblical Hebrew Particle *na*ʾ," 391.
88. Tamar Zewi, *Parenthesis in Biblical Hebrew* (Leiden: Brill 2007) 153.
89. T. J. Finley, "The Proposal in Biblical Hebrew: Preliminary Studies Using a Deep Structure Model," *ZAH* 2 (1989) 10.
90. Marco Di Giulio, "Discourse Marker: Biblical Hebrew," in *Encyclopedia of Hebrew Language and Linguistics* (ed. Geoffrey Khan; Brill, 2013) 1:757.

קַח־נָא אִתְּךָ אֶת־אַחַד מֵהַנְּעָרִים וְקוּם לֵךְ בַּקֵּשׁ אֶת־הָאֲתֹנֹת

Take now with you one of the young men and go look for the asses (1 Sam 9:3)

4. *Politeness.* The speaker expresses respect toward the listener:

קוּם־נָא שְׁבָה וְאָכְלָה מִצֵּידִי

Please sit and eat of my game (Gen 27:19)

הַגִּידָה־נָּא לִי מָה־אָמַר לָכֶם שְׁמוּאֵל

Please tell me what Samuel said to you (1 Sam 10:15)

וְעַתָּה קַח־נָא בְרָכָה מֵאֵת עַבְדֶּךָ

Please accept now a gift from your servant (2 Kgs 5:15)

5. *Strong petition.* The seriousness of the matter at hand is clearly expressed by the speaker's request:

וְעַתָּה הִשָּׁבְעוּ־נָא לִי בַּיהוָה

Swear to me now by the Lord (Josh 2:12)

אֲדֹנָי יֱהוִֹה זָכְרֵנִי נָא וְחַזְּקֵנִי נָא אַךְ הַפַּעַם הַזֶּה הָאֱלֹהִים

O Lord God, *please remember me and strengthen me* just this one time O God (Judg 16:28)

Occurrences of imperative with נָא are common in narratives but noticeably absent from "legal" material. Although the Pentateuch includes major sections of instructions and laws, the volitives used in the legal material are never accompanied by the particle נָא. Since the purpose of the legal material is basically to describe the desired life-style and behavior of the Israelite community in a more general sense, it is understandable that a particle used in direct discourse to express immediate emotional nuances would be absent. The description of laws does not involve emotional implications, as do a number of other contexts (e.g., prayer, politically oriented requests, pleas of desperation).[91]

Social dynamics: The imperative with נָא appears regularly at every level of society and is almost as popular with speakers of lower status as it is with those of higher status. According to the findings in this study, the use of נָא with the

91. Prophetic literature includes numerous passages in which divine speech uses נָא with a cohortative in a self-address or when addressing individuals. In such cases, it can hardly be said that God is attempting to be polite or courteous. For example: לְכוּ־נָא אֶל־מְקוֹמִי אֲשֶׁר בְּשִׁילוֹ אֲשֶׁר שִׁכַּנְתִּי שְׁמִי שָׁם 'Go to my place in Shiloh where I have established my name' (Jer 7:12); וְעַתָּה אֱמָר־נָא אֶל־אִישׁ־יְהוּדָה וְעַל־יוֹשְׁבֵי יְרוּשָׁלַם 'Speak now to the men of Judah and to the inhabitants of Jerusalem' (Jer 18:11); אֱמָר־נָא לְבֵית הַמֶּרִי 'Say now to this rebellious house' (Ezek 17:12).

imperative is far from being restricted to specific social groups or to specific situations. It is used freely in all types of conversations, in a great variety of settings, and at every level of society.

2.2.1.4. Imperative with Ethical Dative

Many imperatives are accompanied by an *ethical dative* construction formed with the preposition ל + a second-person pronominal suffix (agrees in number with the verb).[92] The dative in Hebrew appears primarily in this type of construction in which "the suffixed pronoun . . . refers to the subject of the sentence (that is, it is reflexive or co-referential with the subject), and the subject indicates the agent of the event."[93] According to GKC, the most frequent use of the *ethical dative* is with the imperative, and it is used "in order to give emphasis to the significance of the occurrence in question *for* a particular subject."[94] Muraoka speaks of the *centripetal lamed* and states that the construction brings focus on the actor who "establishes his own identity, recovering or finding his own place by determinedly dissociating himself from his familiar surrounding. Notions of isolation, loneliness, parting, seclusion, or withdrawal are often recognizable."[95] According to Muraoka, this would involve not only a verbal idea but also an emotional aspect through which the attitude of mind of the actor is perceived.[96]

Joüon, BDB, and König link the *ethical dative* construction to the "reflexive voice," whereby the actor does the action to himself.[97] Waltke and O'Connor treat the "reflexive" and the "centripetal" ideas separately and translate passages representing the former idea by "—self" and leave the latter idea untranslated.[98] Kaufman suggests that the *ethical dative* may possibly be linked to the middle voice, since "its increasing frequency is tied to the gradual disappearance of other lexical and grammatical means of expressing 'middle voice' in Semitics."[99]

92. This term has won general recognition and will be used here, even though it is not an exact representation of the classical *ethical dative*.

93. J. A. Naudé, "David: Biblical Hebrew," in *Encyclopedia of Hebrew Language and Linguistics* (ed. Goeffrey Kahn; Leiden: Brill 2013) 3:274–75.

94. GKC, §119s.

95. T. Muraoka, "The So-Called *Dativus Ethicus* in Biblical Hebrew," *JTS* n.s. 29 (1978) 495–98.

96. Ibid., 497.

97. Joüon, *A Grammar of Biblical Hebrew*, 488; E. König, *Historisch-komparative Syntax der hebräischen Sprache* (Leipzig: Hinrichs, 1897) §35.

98. Waltke and O'Connor, *Introduction to Biblical Hebrew Syntax,* 208.

99. R. Fradkin defines *middle voice* as a verbal construction in which "the subject of the verb performs the action 'for her or his own benefit' " (Robert Fradkin, *Stalking the Wild Verb Phrase* [Lanham, MD: University Press of America, 1991] 104). Smyth defines the middle voice as a syntagm whose function is to show "that the action is performed with special reference to the subject" (H. W. Smyth, *Greek Grammar* [Repr.; Cambridge: Harvard University Press, 1956] 390). Smyth then distinguishes between the "direct reflexive middle," which

Although the *ethical dative* occurs more frequently with the imperative than with any other verb form, it is also found with the cohortative,[100] jussive,[101] imperfect consecutive,[102] imperfect (2nd and 3rd persons),[103] perfect (consecutive),[104] and participle.[105] Stative,[106] transitive,[107] and intransitive[108] verbs can be accompanied by an *ethical dative*. In this section, my observations include only transitive and intransitive verbs, since the stative verbs are never found in the "imperative with *ethical dative*" construction. My examination of 65 passage with imperative + *ethical dative* reveals that the construction expresses the "middle reflexive" voice, with various nuances:

1. *Middle/Reflexive*. The actor is requested to perform the action "on himself, for himself, with reference to himself, or with something belonging to himself."[109] Focus is placed on the actor(s) of the imperative.

"represents the subject as acting directly *on himself*," and the "indirect reflexive middle," by which the subject is acting "*for himself, with reference to himself,* or *with something belonging to himself*" (p. 391). According to Boyd's definition of *middle voice*, "the subject is both in control of and affected by the action of the verb" (S. Boyd, *A Synchronic Analysis of the Medio-Passive-Reflexive in Biblical Hebrew* [Ph.D. diss., Hebrew Union College–Jewish Institute of Religion, 1993] 26). S. Kaufman, in his review of M. Sokoloff's "Scholar's Dictionary of Jewish Palestinian Aramaic," *JAOS* 114 (1994) 245 n. 9. For studies on the *ethical dative* in Aramaic, see M. Sokoloff, "The Hebrew of Bereshit Rabba according to MS. Vat. Ebr. 30" *Lešonenu* 38 (1968–69) 270–79 [Hebrew]; Jan Joosten, "The Function of the So-Called *Dativus Ethicus* in Classical Syriac," *Or* 58 (1989) 473–92; T. Muraoka and B. Porten, *A Grammar of Egyptian Aramaic* (Leiden: Brill, 1998) 273. Sokoloff (influenced by H. J. Polotsky and E. Y. Kutscher) advocates that the *ethical dative* indicates ingressivity ("The Hebrew of Bereshit Rabba," 270–72).

100. E.g., Num 22:34; Josh 22:26; 1 Sam 26:11; 2 Sam 19:27; 2 Kgs 6:2.

101. E.g., Judg 6:31; Gen 38:23; 2 Kgs 12:6.

102. E.g., Gen 4:19, 3:7, 13:11, 6:2, 21:16, 30:37, 33:17; Exod 18:27; Josh 5:3; 1 Sam 13:1; 2 Kgs 17:9.

103. E.g., Gen 7:2, 34:9; Exod 20:4, 23; 20:23; 34:17; Deut 5:8; 16:21, 22; 19:2, 3, 7; Josh 8:2; 1 Sam 21:10.

104. E.g., Lev 23:15; Num 34:10; Deut 4:16, 9:16, 10:1, 27:2; Josh 17:15, 24:22; 1 Sam 8:18, 22:5; 2 Sam 7:23, 12:9; 1 Kgs 3:11; 2 Kgs 18:21.

105. E.g., Gen 13:15.

106. In verbal constructions with the *ethical dative*, statives function as true "middle"-voice verbs. E.g., חָרָה (Gen 4:6; 2 Sam 13:21, 20:7; 2 Sam 22:8), חָסֵר (Deut 15:8).

107. E.g., אָחַז (2 Sam 2:21); בָּנָה (Num 32:24; 1 Kgs 2:36); בָּרַח (Josh 24:15; 2 Sam 24:12; 1 Kgs 18:25); יָהַב (Deut 1:13; Josh 18:4; Judg 20:7); כון (Josh 1:11); כָּתַב (Exod 34:27; Deut 31:19); לָקַח (Gen 14:21, 28:2, 45:19; Exod 9:8; 12:21; 30:23, 34; Num 16:6, 27:18; Josh 3:12, 4:2); פָּסַל (Exod 34:1; Deut 10:1); קָנָה (Ruth 4:8); שָׁאַל (2 Kgs 4:3); שָׁלַח (Num 13:2); שִׂים (Josh 8:2; Judg 19:30).

108. E.g., הָלַךְ (Gen 12:1, 22:2; Josh 22:4); חָדַל (2 Chr 25:16, 35:21); נָסַע (Num 14:25; Deut 1:7); סור (2 Sam 2:22); עָלָה (Josh 17:15); קום (Lev 26:1, Deut 16:22); שׁוּב (Deut 5:30).

109. This definition of the *middle reflexive* voice is taken from Smyth's *Greek Grammar*, 390–91.

וַיֹּאמֶר מֶלֶךְ־סְדֹם אֶל־אַבְרָם תֶּן־לִי הַנֶּפֶשׁ וְהָרְכֻשׁ קַח־לָךְ

The king of Sodom said to Abram: Give me my life but take the goods *for yourself* (Gen 14:21)

קוּם לֵךְ פַּדֶּנָה אֲרָם בֵּיתָה בְתוּאֵל אֲבִי אִמֶּךָ וְקַח־לְךָ מִשָּׁם אִשָּׁה מִבְּנוֹת לָבָן אֲחִי
אִמֶּךָ

Go to Padan Aram, to the house of Bethuel, my mother's brother and take (*for yourself*) a wife from there, from the daughters of Laban, my mother's brother (Gen 28:2)

שְׁמָר־לְךָ אֵת אֲשֶׁר אָנֹכִי מְצַוְּךָ הַיּוֹם הִנְנִי גֹרֵשׁ מִפָּנֶיךָ אֶת־הָאֱמֹרִי וְהַכְּנַעֲנִי וְהַחִתִּי
וְהַפְּרִזִּי וְהַחִוִּי וְהַיְבוּסִי

Observe (*for your own benefit*) that which I command you this day; I am about to drive out from before you the Amorites, the Canaanites, the Hittites, the Perizzites, the Hivites and the Jebusites (Exod 34:11)

בְּנוּ־לָכֶם עָרִים לְטַפְּכֶם וּגְדֵרֹת לְצֹנַאֲכֶם וְהַיֹּצֵא מִפִּיכֶם תַּעֲשׂוּ

Build cities *for yourselves,* for your children, and enclosures for your flocks, but do what you promised (Num 32:24)

הָלוֹךְ וְדִבַּרְתָּ אֶל־דָּוִד כֹּה אָמַר יְהוָה שָׁלֹשׁ אָנֹכִי נוֹטֵל עָלֶיךָ בְּחַר־לְךָ אַחַת־מֵהֶם
וְאֶעֱשֶׂה־לָּךְ

Go say to David: Thus says the Lord: I lay upon you three things; choose one (*the one you prefer*) of them and I will do it for you (2 Sam 24:12 // 1 Chr 21:16)

וַיֹּאמֶר אֵלִיָּהוּ לִנְבִיאֵי הַבַּעַל בַּחֲרוּ לָכֶם הַפָּר הָאֶחָד וַעֲשׂוּ רִאשֹׁנָה כִּי אַתֶּם הָרַבִּים
וְקִרְאוּ בְּשֵׁם אֱלֹהֵיכֶם וְאֵשׁ לֹא תָשִׂימוּ

Elijah said to the prophets of Baal: Choose (*for yourselves*) one bull and prepare it first since you are many, then call upon the name of your gods, but do not light the fire (1 Kgs 18:25)

וַיֹּאמֶר הַגֹּאֵל לֹא אוּכַל לִגְאָל־לִי פֶּן־אַשְׁחִית אֶת־נַחֲלָתִי גְּאַל־לְךָ אַתָּה אֶת־גְּאֻלָּתִי
כִּי לֹא־אוּכַל לִגְאֹל

The kinsman redeemer said: I cannot redeem lest I endanger my own estate; so take (*for yourself*) my right of redemption because I am not able to redeem it (Ruth 4:6)

2. *Focus on "individuals" or "selected groups"* by means of which the command or request is directed to *each individual* within the group, or to *each tribe* within a larger community. This is often the case when the imperative occurs in the plural.

לֵךְ אֱמֹר לָהֶם שׁוּבוּ לָכֶם לְאָהֳלֵיכֶם
Go say to them: Return (*each one of you*) to your own tents (Deut 5:30)

וְעַתָּה קְחוּ לָכֶם שְׁנֵי עָשָׂר אִישׁ מִשִּׁבְטֵי יִשְׂרָאֵל אִישׁ־אֶחָד אִישׁ־אֶחָד לַשָּׁבֶט
Now select twelve men from among the Israelites, a man per tribe (each tribe was to make an independent choice–Josh 3:12; also 4:2)

וְעַתָּה הֵנִיחַ יְהוָה אֱלֹהֵיכֶם לַאֲחֵיכֶם כַּאֲשֶׁר דִּבֶּר לָהֶם וְעַתָּה פְּנוּ וּלְכוּ לָכֶם
לְאָהֳלֵיכֶם אֶל־אֶרֶץ אֲחֻזַּתְכֶם אֲשֶׁר נָתַן לָכֶם מֹשֶׁה עֶבֶד יְהוָה בְּעֵבֶר הַיַּרְדֵּן
Now the Lord your God has given your brothers rest just as He had said to them; so now, go back (*each one of you*) to your own tents, to the land that you possess, which Moses, the servant of the Lord, gave to you while on the other side of the Jordan (Josh 22:4)

וְאִם רַע בְּעֵינֵיכֶם לַעֲבֹד אֶת־יְהוָה בַּחֲרוּ לָכֶם הַיּוֹם אֶת־מִי תַעֲבֹדוּן אִם אֶת־אֱלֹהִים
אֲשֶׁר־עָבְדוּ אֲבוֹתֵיכֶם אֲשֶׁר מֵעֵבֶר הַנָּהָר וְאִם אֶת־אֱלֹהֵי הָאֱמֹרִי אֲשֶׁר אַתֶּם יֹשְׁבִים
בְּאַרְצָם וְאָנֹכִי וּבֵיתִי נַעֲבֹד אֶת־יְהוָה
And if it displeases you to serve the Lord, choose (*each one of you*) this day whom you will serve; whether the gods which your forefathers served across the river or the gods of the Amorites in whose land you are dwelling; but as for ME AND MY HOUSE, we will serve the Lord (Josh 24:15)

3. *Separation or setting apart.* The fulfillment of the command requires that the actor(s) separate himself (themselves) from the rest of the group.

וַיֹּאמֶר יְהוָה אֶל־אַבְרָם לֶךְ־לְךָ מֵאַרְצְךָ וּמִמּוֹלַדְתְּךָ וּמִבֵּית אָבִיךָ אֶל־הָאָרֶץ אֲשֶׁר
אַרְאֶךָּ
The Lord said to Abram: Leave (*separate yourself from*) your country and your relatives and the house of your father, for a land which I will show you (Gen 12:1)

וַיֹּאמֶר קַח־נָא אֶת־בִּנְךָ אֶת־יְחִידְךָ אֲשֶׁר־אָהַבְתָּ אֶת־יִצְחָק וְלֶךְ־לְךָ אֶל־אֶרֶץ הַמֹּרִיָּה
Then He said: Now take your only son whom you love, Isaac, and go to the land of Moriah (*separate yourself from the community*) (Gen 22:2)

וַיֹּאמֶר אַבְרָהָם אֶל־נְעָרָיו שְׁבוּ־לָכֶם פֹּה עִם־הַחֲמוֹר וַאֲנִי וְהַנַּעַר נֵלְכָה עַד־כֹּה
Then Abraham said to his servants: Stay here (*by yourselves*) with the asses while I and the boy go up there (Gen 22:5)

וְעַתָּה בְנִי שְׁמַע בְּקֹלִי וְקוּם בְּרַח־לְךָ אֶל־לָבָן אָחִי חָרָנָה
Now my son, listen to me; flee (*by yourself*) to Laban my brother, to Haran (Gen 27:43)

4. *Contrastive.* The action to be performed by the actor is in contrast to the action performed by another (other) actor(s). Exod 32:16 states that God made the first set of stone tablets and wrote the text on them. The contrast between the making of the two sets of tablets ("I made the first set; now you carve the second set") is seen through the use of the *ethical dative* in Exod 34:1 (also Deut 10:1).

וְהַלֻּחֹת מַעֲשֵׂה אֱלֹהִים הֵמָּה וְהַמִּכְתָּב מִכְתַּב אֱלֹהִים הוּא חָרוּת עַל־הַלֻּחֹת
Now, the tablets were made *by God,* and the writing was the writing of God, engraved upon the tablets (Exod 32:16)

versus:

וַיֹּאמֶר יְהוָה אֶל־מֹשֶׁה פְּסָל־לְךָ שְׁנֵי־לֻחֹת אֲבָנִים כָּרִאשֹׁנִים וְכָתַבְתִּי עַל־הַלֻּחֹת
אֶת־הַדְּבָרִים אֲשֶׁר הָיוּ עַל־הַלֻּחֹת הָרִאשֹׁנִים אֲשֶׁר שִׁבַּרְתָּ
The Lord said to Moses: (*You,*) carve two stone tablets similar to the first ones, and I will write upon the tablets the words which were upon the first tablets that you broke (Exod 34:1)

5. *Idiomatic expressions.* Hebrew uses a verbal construction with *ethical dative* in order to express a warning ("Beware!" "Be careful!" "Stop it!"):[110]

וַיֹּאמֶר אֵלָיו אַבְרָהָם הִשָּׁמֶר לְךָ פֶּן־תָּשִׁיב אֶת־בְּנִי שָׁמָּה
Abraham said to him: *Be careful* not to take my son back there (Gen 24:6)

הִשָּׁמֶר לְךָ פֶּן־תִּכְרֹת בְּרִית לְיוֹשֵׁב הָאָרֶץ אֲשֶׁר אַתָּה בָּא עָלֶיהָ פֶּן־יִהְיֶה לְמוֹקֵשׁ
בְּקִרְבֶּךָ
Be careful not to cut a covenant with the people of the land where you are going lest it becomes a snare in your midst (Exod 34:12)

וַיֹּאמֶר לוֹ הַלְיוֹעֵץ לַמֶּלֶךְ נְתַנּוּךָ חֲדַל־לְךָ לָמָּה יַכּוּךָ וַיֶּחְדַּל הַנָּבִיא
When he spoke to him he said: Have we placed you as a counselor for the king? *Stop it!* Why should they strike you down? Then the prophet stopped (2 Chr 25:16)

In the majority of cases, the text provides no information regarding the fulfillment of the imperative. Some passages include the fulfillment of the command and use the same verb as the imperative without the *ethical dative*. A minority of cases include the fulfillment using the same verb as the imperative with the

110. This expression is found only in the Pentateuch. See also Exod 19:12, 34:12; Deut 4:9; 6:12; 8:11; 12:13, 19, 30; 15:9.

ethical dative. When the command is given, and the speaker wishes to indicate that focus is on the actor, the *ethical dative* is present. When the narrator continues recounting the events of the story, he has the need to express interest in neither the speaker nor the addressee. Therefore the *ethical dative* is no longer needed, unless it expresses one of the nuances stated above (e.g., "separation," "contrast").

The following question can be addressed here: Why do we only find the regular imperative and not the long imperative with an "ethical dative"? My study of the long imperative (see §5.2.2 below) reveals that the long imperative is used mainly for polite requests, the fulfillment of which is for the benefit or interest of the speaker. The imperative with *ethical dative*, on the other hand, demands that an action be performed for the benefit or interest of the addressee. It is therefore understandable that the long imperative and the regular imperative with *ethical dative* appear in different contexts. The long imperative and the imperative with *ethical dative* are syntagmas that are opposed in function, the former focusing on the speaker(s) of the utterance and the latter focusing on the recipient(s) of the command.

2.2.2. Long Imperatives

A lengthened form of the imperative with final ָה occurs in the masculine singular (e.g., שְׁמֹר/שָׁמְרָה). This long form is theoretically present in the other forms of the verb, but gender/number markers and pronominal suffixes prevent the identification of the final ָה in our consonantal text.

2.2.2.1. Theories on the Origin of the Long Imperative

Scholars have proposed three different origins for the long imperative:

1. the *yaqtulan(na)* modal verb[111]
2. the *yaqtula* Canaanite injunctive[112]
3. the Akkadian ventive (with *-am* ending)[113]

(1) *From* yaqtulan(na). Some scholars advocate that the ending ָה of the long imperative is directly related to the modal form *yaqtulan(na)* found in

111. Kaufman, "An Emphatic Plea for Please," 195–98; Gottlieb, "The Hebrew Particle *nâ*"; T. O. Lambdin, "The Junctural Origin of the West Semitic Definite Article," in *Near Eastern Studies in Honor of William Foxwell Albright* (ed. Hans Goedicke; Baltimore: Johns Hopkins University Press, 1971) 326; GKC, §48i / p. 131.

112. A. F. Rainey, "The Ancient Hebrew Prefix Conjugation," *HS* 27 (1986) 8; Waltke and O'Connor, *Introduction to Biblical Hebrew Syntax,* 568; W. L. Moran, "Early Canaanite *yaqtula*," *Or* 29 (1960)19.

113. S. Fassberg, *Studies in Biblical Syntax* (Jerusalem: Magnes, 1994) 30 [Hebrew]; idem, "The Lengthened Imperative קָטְלָה in Biblical Hebrew," *HS* 40 (1999) 7–13; idem, "Imperative and Prohibitive: Pre-Modern," in *Encyclopedia of Hebrew Language and Linguistics* (Leiden: Brill, 2013) 2:243–44.

Ugaritic, EA Canaanite, and Arabic.[114] Kaufman, Lambdin, and Blau, who hold this view, add that the cohortative also reflects the features of this modal form. According to Moscati, the final הָ on the long imperative is possibly the same element found on the cohortative, but Moscati offers no suggestion about the origin and/or development of these two forms.[115] Evidence supporting *yaqtulan(na)* as the origin of the long imperative and the cohortative is based on the following three points.

In passages in which the long imperative and the cohortative are followed by the particle נָא, a *dagesh forte* appears in the *nun*. This doubling of the *nun* reflects the *-nn-* of the modal form *yaqtulan(na)*, before the ending *-(n)na* became a separate particle.

הַגִּידָה־נָּא שְׁמֶךָ

Please tell me your name (Gen 32:30)

versus:

בְּנִי שִׂים־נָא כָבוֹד לַיהוָה אֱלֹהֵי יִשְׂרָאֵל וְתֶן־לוֹ תוֹדָה וְהַגֶּד־נָא לִי מֶה עָשִׂיתָ אַל־תְּכַחֵד מִמֶּנִּי

My son, please give glory to the Lord God of Israel and give him thanks; *please* tell me what you have done; do not hide it from me (Josh 7:19)

An examination of the masculine-singular imperative with 3m/fs pronominal suffix reveals two forms: (a) the imperative with *-ehu*/*-eha* pronominal suffix, and (b) the imperative with *-ennu*/*-enna* pronominal suffix.[116] The following question naturally arises: can the two forms of the imperative (regular and long imperatives) be distinguished by their pronominal suffix? I believe that this sort of distinction can be made by looking at the context in which these imperatives are found. As a rule, a regular imperative is followed by another regular imperative, and a long imperative is followed by another long imperative.[117] An examination of sequences of imperatives (with and with-

114. Kaufman, "An Emphatic Plea for Please," 195–98; Gottlieb, "The Hebrew Particle *nâ*"; Lambdin, *Introduction to Biblical Hebrew*, 114; Blau, *Grammar of Biblical Hebrew*, 72.

115. S. Moscati et al., *An Introduction to the Comparative Grammar of the Semitic Languages: Phonology and Morphology* (ed. S. Moscati; Porta Linguarum n.s. 6; Wiesbaden: Harrassowitz, 1980) §16.36.

116. The Hebrew inscription from Arad includes an imperative with a *-n(n)u* pronominal suffix ונחלש 'Send it!' (Arad 4:2).

117. Kaufman identified this phenomenon in his article "An Emphatic Plea for Please." He states:

> This also explains why the *-n_* form of the pronominal suffixes, normally associated with the simple imperfect rather than the short preformative forms (jussive, imperfect consecutive, and imperative), can occur with the imperative. . . . The simple impera-

out pronominal suffix) should therefore show the distinction between the two forms:

וַיֹּאמֶר שְׁמוּאֵל אֶל־יִשַׁי שִׁלְחָה וְקָחֶנּוּ כִּי לֹא־נָסֹב עַד־בֹּאוֹ פֹה
Samuel said to Jesse: *Send someone to take him* for we will not sit down until he comes here (1 Sam 16:11)

אִם־אָמֹר אֹמַר לַנַּעַר הִנֵּה הַחִצִּים מִמְּךָ וָהֵנָּה קָחֶנּוּ וָבֹאָה
If I say to the boy: "Look, the arrows are by you; *pick them up*," then come (1 Sam 20:21)[118]

versus:

וַיֹּאמֶר מֶלֶךְ יִשְׂרָאֵל קַח אֶת־מִיכָיְהוּ וַהֲשִׁיבֵהוּ אֶל־אָמֹן
Then the king of Israel said: *Take* Micayah *and bring him* to Amon. (1 Kgs 22:26)

וְעַתָּה שָׂא הַשְׁלִכֵהוּ בַּחֶלְקָה כִּדְבַר יְהוָה
So now, *lift him up and throw him* on the plot of ground according to the word of the Lord (2 Kgs 9:26)

The first set of examples shows sequences of regular imperatives while the second set shows sequences of long imperatives. The third-person masculine-singular pronominal suffix *-ennu* occurs on the long imperative and reflects a *yaqtulan(na)* origin. Cohortatives, whose origin is also *yaqtulan(na)*, take the *-ennu* / *-enna* pronominal suffix.[119]

We know, from Ugaritic texts, that the ending *-nn* appeared not only on prefix conjugations but also on forms of the imperative (impv. *qtln*[*n* < *yqtln*[*n*]).[120] If the Hebrew cohortative with its final long *-a* corresponds to the modal form *yaqtulan(na)*, then the long imperative with its final long *-a* corresponds to the Ugaritic imperative with final *-n(n)*. This modal ending (*-nn*) originally

tive would have been חֲלַשְׁ וּהחֶקָ, whereas a phrase like הַחָלְשׁ וּהחֶקָ would, I think, be quite ungrammatical; וּנחֶקָ is simply the long imperative with a pronominal suffix.

118. Jonathan uses regular imperatives when the commands are directed solely toward the young boy and long imperatives as "code language" when the commands also affect David's behavior.

119. E.g., Gen 27:37, 45:28; Num 22:6; Deut 30:12, 13; 31:14; Judg 7:4; 14:13; 19:22.

120. According to Gottlieb and Hammershaimb, the regular imperative and the long imperative do not differ syntactically (Gottlieb, "The Hebrew Particle *nâ*," 51); E. Hammershaimb, *Das Verbum im Dialekt von Ras Schamra: Eine morphologische und syntaktische Untersuchung des Verbums in den alphabetischen Keilschrifttexten aus dem alten Ugarit* (Copenhagen: Hammershaimb, 1941) 112. I propose that, although specific nuances are difficult to depict in the literature, scribes would surely have used different verbal forms to express different modalities and would not have used different verbal forms as interchangeable morphemes.

appended to verb forms eventually became a separate morpheme, thus the Hebrew נָא.

qḥn . wtšqyn . yn (1 Aq 215)	*Do take* the wine and drink (it).
šrn (Krt A 110)	*Harrass!*[121]
wgr . nn . ʿrm (Krt A 110)	*Settle* by the town.

In his article on the Hebrew particle נָא, Gottlieb writes:

> In Ugaritic cuneiform writing the distinction between the words is indicated by a cuneiform character, the so-called word-divider, which in the transliteration is represented by a point. It is due to this linguistic instinct to conceive the energetic element *n* or *nn* as an independent word. Certainly, it is normal that the complete energetic mood is written as one word; but in a number of cases, the energetic element is separated from the rest of the verbal form by a word-divider: Thus the imperfect 1st person is found: *ašt.n.*, 67:V:5; *a*]*mṣḫ.nn.*, ʿnt pl. vi:V:9; imperfect 2nd femininum: *trḥṣ.nn.*, 127:10; imperfect 3rd masculinum: *yqbr.nn.*, 1 Aqht 147, cf. 68:31 [quoted above]; imperative: *št.nnh.*, 56:18, cf. Krt 110 [quoted above].[122]

(2) *From yaqtula.* The second view links the origin of the long imperative and the cohortative to the *yaqtula* volitive attested in EA Canaanite.[123] Lambdin disputes this view and raises the following question: "Unless the final vowel of *yaqtula* was long or anceps, how did it survive the general loss of short vowels in Pre-Hebrew?"[124] A close examination of the Ugaritic verbal system reveals that Hebrew possibly has three forms of imperative: one with no final vowel, one with a final short *-a* (< *yaqtula* with lost final *-a* in Hebrew), and one with a final long *-a*:

The regular imperative:

Ugaritic: *rd, tn, lk* Hebrew: רֵד, תֵּן, לֵךְ

The imperative with final short *-a*:

> *ša* . . . -"Lift up . . . !" ([Krt: 75 and Gordon, 51 VIII 5]; mostly undiscernable in Hebrew due to the loss of short vowel). In Ugaritic, the presence of the *-y* in imperatives of third *yod* verbs is no doubt a reflection of a final *-a* vowel (e.g., *ʿl*–"Go up!" *vs šty*–"Drink!" and *ṯny*–"Repeat!").

121. W. Moran, *A Syntactical Study of the Dialect of Byblos* (Ph.D. diss., Johns Hopkins University, 1950) 11.

122. Gottlieb, "The Hebrew Particle *nâ*," 51. In Arabic, the modal form loses its final *-n* when in pause, thereby producing a modal verbal ending with long *-a*.

123. Blau, "Studies in Hebrew Verb Formation," 138 n. 22. Blau does not seem to make a distinction between the verbal forms ending in *-a* (*yaqtula*) and those in *-â* (*qotĕlâ*). In his opinion, both forms have the same origin. See also Fassberg, *Studies in Biblical Syntax*, §41 [Hebrew]; A. F. Rainey, "The Ancient Hebrew Prefix Conjugation," *HS* 27 (1986) 8.

124. Lambdin, "The Junctural Origin," 320.

> The III-*he* imperatives of Hebrew mostly preserve their final *he* (e.g., קַוֵּה, קְנֵה, רְאֵה, עֲשֵׂה, שְׁתֵה), except for a few verbs that occur with and without the final *he* (e.g., גְּלֵה // גַּל; מְנֵה // מַן; צַוֵּה // צַו). The short form reflects a regular imperative while the form with final *he* possibly reflects an imperative with final short *-a* connected to the volitive *yaqtula*.

The imperative with *-n(n)*, evidenced in Hebrew by a final long *-a* (as is known from the Arabic *-nn* forms in pause):

Ugaritic: *wgr.nn, qḥn* Hebrew: לְכָה, קְחָה

(3) *From the Akkadian ventive.* The third view attempts to show that the long imperative and the cohortative are morphologically and syntactically related to the Akkadian ventive (*-am*). Fassberg advocates, with Shulman,[125] that the majority of the long imperatives are found in contexts in which the action focuses on the speaker, either "for him, to him, with him or towards him."[126] Fassberg writes:

> Due to the similarity between the ventive and the ending *-ā* on the long imperative in Hebrew, both in form and in function (which expresses movement, exclusively movement towards the speaker—like the first person pronoun in the dative), there is reason to ask if there is any connection between the Akkadian and the Hebrew morphemes. If there is a connection, it is possible to propose these two hypotheses: a. The vowel *-a* is the component which expresses the intent towards the speaker in both languages (therefore, the mimation is secondary in Akkadian . . .). If such is the case, it is possible to see in the ending *a(m)* in Akkadian and in the ending *-ā* in Hebrew . . . a common characteristic from proto-Semitic. . . . b. In the same way, it is possible to consider a different way and to propose that the use of *-am* in proto-Semitic was dative for the first person, while in Hebrew, the *-m* was dropped when the mimation disappeared.[127]

My research supports the first view, that the origin of the long imperative is directly related to that of the cohortative and originates from the modal prefix conjugation *yaqtulan(na)*. The Ugaritic evidence, the presence of pronominal suffixes with *-nn-*, and the development of the particle of entreaty נָא outweigh the evidence of the *yaqtula* origin with anceps vowel or the case of the ventive *-am*. Fassberg's and Shulman's view can be refuted by the fact that, in many cases, the long imperative is neither accompanied by a preposition with first-person pronominal suffix nor does it imply the idea of the action being done

125. Shulman, *Use of Modal Verb Forms*, 66.

126. Fassberg, *Studies in Biblical Syntax*, 41; Shulman, *Use of Modal Verb Forms*, 66. Both Fassberg and Shulman focus on the idea that the long imperative precedes one of the following particles: עַל־יָדִי, אוֹתִי, אֵלַי, עִמִּי, עָלַי, עִמָּדִי, אִתָּנוּ, אִתִּי, לָנוּ, לִי. In their view, even when the imperative is not followed by one of these particles with a suffix, the context often implies one.

127. Fassberg, *Studies in Biblical Syntax*, 34 n.100.

"for, to, with, or toward" the speaker. Its function is more closely related to a modal idea than to the idea of direction.

2.2.2.2 Theories on the Functions of the Long Imperative

According to scholars, long imperatives fulfill one or more of the following roles:[128]

1. an "emphatic" or "energic" form of the regular imperative[129]
2. a "polite" form of the regular imperative[130]
3. a "stylistic variation" of the regular imperative with no difference in meaning[131]
4. an indication that the action is to be "directed towards, or performed on behalf of the speaker"[132]

(1) *Emphatic/Energic.* The following scholars hold to the first view, that an "energic" form of the imperative exists in Biblical Hebrew: (a) GKC states that "the longer form [of the imperative] is frequently emphatic, e.g., קוּם *'rise up,'* קוּמָה *'up!'* תֵּן *'give,'* תְּנָה *'give up!'*"[133] (b) Joüon agrees with GKC's interpretation that the long imperative is "emphatic" in origin but adds that "in practice [it] does not often seem to add any particular nuance, though it often seems to carry an honorific one, being addressed to God (Ps 5.2), father (Gen 27.19), prophet (Num 22.6), and priest (1Sam 14.18)."[134] This interpretation, which links situations of "politeness" to the use of the long imperative, could also be included in the second group. Joüon also comments that, in some cases, the long form of the imperative may be used purely for reasons of euphony.

(2) *Politeness.* In addition to the idea of "honorific" language mentioned by Joüon, Kaufman and Lambert argue that the long imperative is marked for "politeness" and "respect" toward the addressee.[135] Kaufman states that the long imperative and the regular imperative with the particle of entreaty נָא are

128. C. E. Morrison, "Courtesy Expressions: Biblical Hebrew," in *Encyclopedia of Hebrew Language and Linguistics* (ed. Geoffrey Khan; Leiden: Brill, 2013) 2:911.

129. GKC, 130; Joüon, *A Grammar of Biblical Hebrew*, 143.

130. Kaufman, "An Emphatic Plea for Please," 195–98; M. Lambert, *Traité de grammaire hébraïque* (Paris: Presses universitaires de France, 1946) 255–57.

131. Waltke and O'Connor, *Introduction to Biblical Hebrew Syntax,* 571; M. Tsevat, *A Study of the Language of the Biblical Psalms* (JBL Monograph Series 9; Philadelphia: Society of Biblical Literature, 1955) 25.

132. Fassberg, *Studies in Biblical Syntax*, 13–33; Shulman, *Use of Modal Verb Forms*, 65–84.

133. GKC §48k. This statement is made without much support or examples to substantiate the proposed view.

134. Joüon, *A Grammar of Biblical Hebrew*, §48d.

135. Lambert, *Traité de grammaire hébraïque*, 255–57; Kaufman, "An Emphatic Plea for Please," 198.

"essentially equivalent." They both mean 'please'.[136] Kaufman's conclusion is based on the idea that the long imperative, the cohortative, and the particle נָא find their origin in the same modal form, *yaqtulan(na)*, a form used not to express an "energic" idea but, rather, to express requests, doubts, questions, "a softening rather than a strengthening!"[137]

(3) *Stylistic variation.* The third view identifies no difference between the regular imperative and the long imperative. Waltke and O'Connor barely treat the subject and conclude that "no differentiation is possible between the regular and long (הָ) forms of the imperative, since they occur in similar contexts."[138] In his study of the Psalms, Tsevat notes that, in proportion to the other books, the long imperative appears in the Psalms eight times more often than the regular imperative, and states that the two forms "can rightly be juxtaposed for comparison, since they have the same meaning.[139] Tsevat adds that "one would look in vain for a remark in the current grammars that this form, or others, is largely determined by literary species and their traditions. This cognition would have saved many an author from seeking special meanings behind this form where there are none."[140]

(4) *In the interest/direction of the speaker.* Fassberg and Shulman are the main proponents of the idea that, when the long imperative occurs, the action is expressed in the direction or interest of the speaker ("to, for, with, on behalf of, etc.").[141] Fassberg makes a distinction between passages in which:

- the action is directed toward the speaker;
- there is a general or specific relationship between the action and the speaker, "such as an action that benefits the speaker, or an action that will be performed with the speaker, or takes place near the speaker";[142]
- he action is directed against the enemies of the speaker, thereby bringing "relief and salvation for the speaker and his people Israel";[143]
- requests addressed to God are for the benefit of the speaker and of God's people.

Shulman and Fassberg note that a good percentage of the passages where this form occurs includes a long imperative accompanied by a preposition with a first-person suffix, implying that the speaker of the utterance desires that an

136. Ibid., 198.
137. Ibid., 197.
138. Waltke and O'Connor, *Introduction to Biblical Hebrew Syntax,* 571.
139. Tsevat, *A Study of the Language of the Biblical Psalms*, 80 n. 245.
140. Ibid., 246.
141. S. E. Fassberg, "The Lengthened Imperative *qōtlâ* in Biblical Hebrew," *HS* 40 (1999) 7–13, esp. p. 13; idem, "Imperative and Prohibitive," 66.
142. Idem, "The Lengthened Imperative *qōtlâ* in Biblical Hebrew," 10.
143. Ibid., 11.

Table 2.2. Long Imperative: Social Dynamics

	Long Impv. Greater > Lesser	*Long Impv. Lesser > Greater*	*Long Impv. Equals*	*Reg. Impv. ms (x = Long Impv.)*
Gen	15:9; 21:23; 27:4, 7, 21, 25, 26; 29:15, 19; 30:8; 39:7, 12; 47:31	27:19; 29:21; 30:26; 32:30; 42:37; 43:8; 45:9; 47:15	25:31, 33; 30:1; 37:16	(25) 97
Exod	32:10	—	—	(1) 97
Lev	—	—	—	(0) 31
Num	11:16; 10:29	10:35, 36; 22:6, 11, 17; 23:7; 27:4	—	(9) 65
Deut	—	26:15	—	(1) 61
Josh	—	10:6; 14:12; 15:19	—	(3) 27
Judg	11:13; 17:10	1:15; 4:18 (2×); 9:8, 29; 11:6; 14:13; 16:6, 10, 13, 26	—	(13) 42
Ruth	—	4:1, 4	—	(2) 2
1 Sam	9:23; 10:15; 14:18, 43; 16:11, 19; 20:21, 38; 22:23; 23:9, 27; 24:22; 30:7	2:15; 8:5, 6; 9:18; 14:41; 21:10; 30:15	17:44	(21) 79
2 Sam	3:14; 15:27	14:4	3:12	(4) 66
1 Kgs	21:2, 6; 22:9	13:7 (2×)	15:19	(6) 69
2 Kgs	4:6; 8:4; 10:15, 16	1:9, 11; 6:26	4:22, 14:9	(9) 76
Neh	—	1:11; 5:19; 6:13; 13:14, 22 (2×), 29, 31	—	(8) 10
Total	42	54	8	(102) 661

action be performed "for him, to him, with him or towards him."[144] If this is the case, what should we make of the regular imperatives (without final הָ) followed by a preposition or noun + first-person pronominal suffix?[145] Should we assume that the two constructions (regular impv. + preposition + 1st pron. suffix *and* long impv. + preposition + 1st pron. suffix) are stylistic variations, or do they actually represent different ideas? Table 2.2 shows the distribution of long imperatives and regular imperatives with first-person pronominal suffix on a noun or preposition in Genesis–2 Kings, Ruth, and Nehemiah.

2.2.2.3. Observations

(1) Fassberg's and Shulman's interpretation that the long imperative is the form used for commands "to, for, and toward the speaker" is challenged by the fact that the regular imperative occurs frequently with a first-person pronominal suffix on a preposition or a noun in contexts similar to those in where the long imperative appears (69 regular impvs. versus 102 long impvs.). When a command "to, for, and toward the speaker" is intended, both the regular imperative and the long imperative occur. Commands are generally given with the interest of the speaker in mind. When the speaker wishes to specify that the action is to be performed "in the interest *of the listener*," he uses an imperative with ethical dative (see §2.2.1.4).

(2) In prose, the long imperative is not restricted to contexts where a person with lower status (lesser) is addressing a person with higher status (greater). It appears frequently where a greater addresses a lesser, and between equals. Where a greater commands a lesser with a long imperative, he/she addresses the listener(s) with an element of respect or politeness. Expressions of politeness with the Long Imperative are not restricted to one type of social dynamic (lesser > greater) but are possible in all contexts and are used by kings, prophets, leaders of the community, officials, common men, and women.[146] In Proverbs, a father addresses his son on a number of occasions with a long

144. Shulman, *Use of Modal Verb Forms*, 66. The long imperative is often followed by these particles: עַל־יָדִי, אוֹתִי, אֵלַי, עִמִּי, עָלַי, עִמָּדִי, אִתָּנוּ, אִתִּי, לָנוּ, לִי. When the imperative is not followed by one of these particles with a suffix, the context often implies one.

145. E.g., Gen 13:9; 14:21; 16:2; 23:13; 26:16; 27:8, 9, 13, 43; 33:11; 34:4; Exod 3:10; 5:1; 4:23; 7:16, 26; 8:5, 16; 9:1, 13; 10:3, 17, 28; 13:2; 14:12; 17:9; 18:19; 20:19; 24:12; 32:1, 23; Num 23:1, 29; Deut 4:10; 5:31; 9:14; Josh 7:19; Judg 8:21 (2×); 9:14; 14:3; 18:19; 1 Sam 11:1, 3; 15:25 (2×), 30; 2 Sam 1:4, 9; 11:6; 19:34; 20:4; 1 Kgs 13:6, 15; 18:19; 19:4; 2 Kgs 9:12; 18:14.

146. Expressions of politeness are not restricted to situations in which subordinates address superiors. Superiors can also address subordinates with respect. For example, in English, a parent can command a child with a variety of modal nuances using the imperative form of the verb: "John, take out the trash NOW!!!" (Hebrew regular imperative) or "John, please take out the trash!" (Hebrew long imperative). Hebrew provides two forms of the imperative: regular imperative for all types of commands and long imperative marked for polite commands.

imperative (greater > lesser). The father respectfully commands his son to observe God's decrees, for his own good, and not for the good of the father.

(3) The long imperative does not appear in instructional/legal material (see table 2.2 on Exodus, Leviticus, and Deuteronomy). A polite form of command is not compatible with legal material. The regular imperative, *weqatal*, *yiqtol*, and infinitive absolute are normative for expressing commands in legal/instructional material.

(4) The long imperatives from greater to lesser appear more frequently at the beginning of a major corpus of material (e.g., Genesis, 1 Samuel). Kaufman explains this phenomenon with the following three points: (a) The more often a text has been copied, the greater the degree of both scribal corruption and, especially in the case of Jewish texts, scribal modification to which the text has been exposed. (b) The earlier portions of a heavily edited text have, in general, been copied more often than have later portions of the same text. Therefore, (c) the later portions of such a text should preserve a better textual tradition. . . . there is a tendency for scribes to "correct" a form the first few times it is encountered; after several such encounters, however, they may realize that the form is actually correct and stop modifying it. Eventually, after many generations of this sort of activity, these corrections will have made their way into the text itself. Thus, in general, the later the portion of the MS is, the more reliable it probably is.[147]

The distribution of long imperatives in Genesis and 1 Samuel demonstrates this effort by the scribes to "improve" passages where one would expect regular imperatives.[148] The number of scribes who copied these texts was no doubt greater than the number of scribes who copied the books of Numbers, Deuteronomy, Joshua, and Judges. The latter books give a more accurate representation of the use of the long imperative (from lesser to greater) than the books of Genesis and 1 Samuel.

2.2.2.4. Long Imperative with נָא

The long imperative with נָא occurs 25 times in the Hebrew Bible, with the majority of occurrences in prose texts. A noticeable number of this type of construction appears with *I-weak* verbs (20 out of 25) but, as mentioned above, since the long imperative is only identifiable in the masculine-singular form of the verb, it is likely that the nuance expressed by the long imperative occurs in all forms of the verb (ms, fs, mp, fp).[149]

---

147. S. A. Kaufman, "Of Beginnings, Ends, and Computers in Targumic Studies," in *To Touch the Text: Biblical and Related Studies in Honor of Joseph A. Fitzmyer, S.J.* (ed. Maurya P. Horgan and Paul J. Kobelski; New York: Crossroad, 1989) 53.

148. The distribution of cohortatives with *waw*-consecutive reflects this type of scribal improvement. Such cohortatives occur in: Gen 32:6; Judg 12:3; 1 Sam 2:28; Neh 2:6, 5:13, 13:8.

149. With נגד, נגשׁ, נתן, ישׁע, יהב, and הלך.

גְּשָׁה־נָּא וַאֲמֻשְׁךָ בְּנִי
Please come near so that I may touch you (Gen 27:21)

הַגִּידָה־נָּא שְׁמֶךָ
Please tell me your name (Gen 32:30)

הָבָה־נָּא אָבוֹא אֵלַיִךְ
Come on, let me sleep with you (Gen 38:16)

Additional occurrences appear with *III-guttural* verbs.[150]

וַתֹּאמֶר שִׁלְחָה נָא לִי אֶחָד מִן־הַנְּעָרִים
Then she said: *Please, send* me one of the young men (2 Kgs 4:22)

סַפְּרָה־נָּא לִי אֵת כָּל־הַגְּדֹלוֹת אֲשֶׁר־עָשָׂה אֱלִישָׁע
Please tell me all the great things that Elisha did (2 Kgs 8:4)

וְהַצְלִיחָה־נָּא לְעַבְדְּךָ הַיּוֹם
And please give success to your servant this day (Neh 1:11)

The emotional dispositions expressed in the passages where the long imperative appears with נָא are quite similar to those found in contexts where the regular imperative appears with נָא.[151] But, since the particle נָא expresses respect or politeness and the long imperative is marked for polite commands, we assume that the combination of these two elements includes a level of modality superior to that found in contexts where only one of the two features is present. The more numerous the modal elements, the higher the level of modality.[152] When the long imperative appears with נָא, we find the following nuances of modality:

1. *Urgency.* The matter must be attended to immediately:

וְעַתָּה לְכָה־נָּא אָרָה־לִּי אֶת־הָעָם הַזֶּה
Please come curse this people now for me (Num 22:6)

וַתִּקְרָא אֶל־אִישָׁהּ וַתֹּאמֶר שִׁלְחָה נָא לִי אֶחָד מִן־הַנְּעָרִים
So she cried out to her husband and said: *Send me now* one of the young men (2 Kgs 4:22)

150. With שלח, צלח, and ספר.

151. Kaufman, "An Emphatic Plea for Please," 198.

152. Ps 118:25 provides us with a clear example of the author's ultimate respect, politeness, and gratitude toward God, with its use of two נָא particles, two אָנָּא particles, and two long imperatives. This verse appears as the climax of a very emotionally charged outburst of thanksgiving to God: אָנָּא יְהוָה הוֹשִׁיעָה נָּא אָנָּא יְהוָה הַצְלִיחָה נָּא 'Please, O Lord, please save (me); please, O Lord, please grant (me) success!'

2. *Non-urgent request.* The situation requires action in the near future but not necessarily immediately:

תְּנָה־נָּא לָהֶם כִּכַּר־כֶּסֶף וּשְׁתֵּי חֲלִפוֹת בְּגָדִים

Give them a talent of silver and two changes of clothes (2 Kgs 5:22)

3. *Politeness.* The speaker shows respect for the listener(s):

וַיִּשְׁאַל יַעֲקֹב וַיֹּאמֶר הַגִּידָה־נָּא שְׁמֶךָ

Then Jacob asked (him) and said: *Please tell* me your name (Gen 32:30)

הַגִּידָה־נָּא לִי אֵי־זֶה בֵּית הָרֹאֶה

Please tell me where the seer's house is located (1 Sam 9:18)

4. *Manipulative petition.* The speaker is using deception in order to obtain his/her request:

הָבָה־נָּא אָבוֹא אֵלַיִךְ

Please let me sleep with you (Gen 38:16)

וַתֹּאמֶר דְּלִילָה אֶל־שִׁמְשׁוֹן הַגִּידָה־נָּא לִי בַּמֶּה כֹּחֲךָ גָדוֹל

Then Delilah said to Samson: *Please, tell* me where your strength comes from (Judg 16:6)

2.2.2.4.1. Social Dynamics

Table 2.3 shows the distribution of long imperatives with נָא, a distribution similar to that of the long imperative without נָא. The discourses that include this sort of construction take place on all social levels, with 9 occurrences from greater to lesser, 11 occurrences from lesser to greater, 4 interactions between equals, and 1 in which an individual addresses himself. At a glance, we notice that the occurrences from greater to lesser appear mostly in Genesis, 1 Samuel, and 2 Kings. This is also the case with the Long Imperative without נָא. I therefore conclude that Kaufman's idea of scribal "improvements" at the beginning of scrolls applies also to this syntagma (see discussion above in §2.2.2.2. Observations).

2.2.3. Negative Commands

In Biblical Hebrew, the positive and negative commands are grammatically asymmetrical.[153] Positive commands are generally expressed with im-

153. This phenomenon is common to Semitic languages. For example, the Ugaritic imperative does not appear with a negative particle. Rather, the negative particle precedes the jussive: *ʿal tqrb* 'Do not approach' (Gordon, *Ugaritic Textbook*, 51 VIII 15f); *ʿal yʾdbkm* 'Let him not make you' (ibid., 51 VIII 17); *ʿal tbkn* 'Do not weep!' (ibid., 125 25).

Table 2.3. Long Imperative with נָא

	Greater > Lesser	*Lesser > Greater*	*Equals*
Gen	27:21, 26; 32:30; 38:16	—	37:16
Num	—	22:6, 17, 23:27	—
Judg	—	16:6, 10, 19:11	—
1 Sam	10:15, 30:7	9:18	25:8
2 Kgs	5:22, 8:4	—	4:22
Neh	—	1:11	—

peratives while negative commands use one of the following grammatical constructions:[154]

1. The second- or third-person jussive preceded by the particle אַל. This construction, whether in the second or third person, expresses the same force of command as the positive imperative but in a negative-wish situation.

וַיֹּאמֶר אַל־תִּשְׁלַח יָדְךָ אֶל־הַנַּעַר וְאַל־תַּעַשׂ לוֹ מְאוּמָּה
Then he said: *Do not lay* your hand on the boy *(n)or do* anything to him (Gen 22:12—2nd person)

יַיִן וְשֵׁכָר אַל־תֵּשְׁתְּ אַתָּה וּבָנֶיךָ אִתָּךְ בְּבֹאֲכֶם אֶל־אֹהֶל מוֹעֵד וְלֹא תָמֻתוּ
Drink neither wine nor strong drink, you and your sons with you, when you come to the tent of meeting, lest you die (Lev 10:9—2nd person)

וַיֹּאמֶר גִּדְעוֹן אֶל־הָאֱלֹהִים אַל־יִחַר אַפְּךָ בִּי
Gideon said to God: *Do not let your anger burn* against me (Judg 6:39—3rd person)

אַל־יַחֲשָׁב־לִי אֲדֹנִי עָוֹן וְאַל־תִּזְכֹּר אֵת אֲשֶׁר הֶעֱוָה עַבְדְּךָ
May my lord not consider me guilty *(n)or remember* the wrong done by your servant (2 Sam 19:20—3rd person and 2nd person)

154. There is a consensus among scholars that the particles לֹא and אל are marked for specific functions when used in negative commands: as a rule, לֹא expresses an immediate or urgent negative command while אל appears in (strong) prohibitions, primarily in legislative texts. For a summary of views (by Seow, Davidson, Waltke and O'Connor, Watts, Joüon, Ewald, Bright, and Gerstenberger) on these two particles, see David K. Stabnow, *A Discourse Analysis Perspective on the Syntax of Clauses Negated by* אל *in the Primary History* (Ph.D. dissertation, Westminster Theological Seminary, 2000) 11–14. See also J. Bright, "Apodictic Prohibition: Some Observations," *JBL* 92 (1973) 185–204; Joosten, *The Verbal System of Biblical Hebrew*, 67–69.

2. The second-person imperfect preceded by לֹא, which is usually referred to as the"*prohibitive*.[155]

וְלֹא תִנְאָף לֹא תִרְצָח
Do not commit murder; do not commit adultery (Deut 5:17)

לֹא תָרִיעוּ וְלֹא־תַשְׁמִיעוּ אֶת־קוֹלְכֶם וְלֹא־יֵצֵא מִפִּיכֶם דָּבָר
Do not shout, do not let your voice be heard, do not let a word come out of your mouth (Josh 6:10)

3. The jussive preceded by לֹא, the least common of the negative command constructions. The majority of cases of לֹא + jussive (and of אַל + imperfect) are found in the Deuteronomistic History and may represent a scribal tradition different from that of the preexilic period.[156]

or mistakes!

אֵת כָּל־הַדָּבָר אֲשֶׁר אָנֹכִי מְצַוֶּה אֶתְכֶם אֹתוֹ תִשְׁמְרוּ לַעֲשׂוֹת לֹא־תֹסֵף עָלָיו וְלֹא תִגְרַע מִמֶּנּוּ
From all the words that I am commanding you, observe it; *do not add* to it (n)or take away from it (Deut 13:1)

וְלֹא־תוֹרֵד שֵׂיבָתוֹ בְּשָׁלֹם שְׁאֹל
And do not let his gray head go down to the grave in peace (1 Kgs 2:6)

Since the negative imperative is directly related to the jussive form of the verb, a discussion on the negative command will be covered below in the section on negative jussives (see §2.3.4).

2.2.4. Sequences of Verbs with the Imperative

2.2.4.1. Imperative Followed by *waw*-Imperative

In this type of construction, the relationship between the imperatives represents various syntactical functions.

1. *Sequentiality*. In the majority of cases where an imperative (nonadverbial) is followed by another imperative, the fulfillment of the second imperative must take place after the fulfillment of the first imperative, thereby expressing a *sequence* of actions. The events are irreversible.

syndetic

וְעַתָּה הִנֵּה אִשְׁתְּךָ קַח וָלֵךְ
So now, here is your wife; *take (her) and go!* (Gen 12:19)

---

155. The negative jussive usually refers to an action that should take place in the near future, while the prohibitive (imperfect with אל) usually refers to an action, the effects of which extend over a long period of time in the future.

156. E.g., Deut 7:16; 13:1, 9; 18:16; 25:12; 1 Sam 14:36; 2 Sam 18:14; 1 Kgs 2:6.

נְטֵה אֶת־מַטְּךָ וְהַךְ אֶת־עֲפַר הָאָרֶץ
Stretch out your staff *and strike* the dust of the ground (Exod 8:12)

עֲלֵה רֹאשׁ הַפִּסְגָּה וְשָׂא עֵינֶיךָ יָמָּה
Go up to Rosh Pisgah *and lift up* your eyes toward the sea (Deut 3:27)

2. *Conjunction.* The next most-common syntactic relationship between two imperatives is when the verbs express two reversible events that can appear in any order and produce the same outcome in the story. The *waw* functions as a simple conjunction.

וַיֹּאמֶר יְהוָה אֶל־מֹשֶׁה עֲבֹר לִפְנֵי הָעָם וְקַח אִתְּךָ מִזִּקְנֵי יִשְׂרָאֵל
Then the Lord said to Moses: *Cross* before the people, *taking* with you some of the elders of Israel (Exod 17:5)

שֻׁבוּ מִדַּרְכֵיכֶם הָרָעִים וְשִׁמְרוּ מִצְוֹתַי חֻקּוֹתַי כְּכָל־הַתּוֹרָה אֲשֶׁר צִוִּיתִי אֶת־אֲבֹתֵיכֶם
Repent of your evil ways *and observe* my commandments, my statutes, according to the whole law which I commanded your forefathers (2 Kgs 17:13)

3. *Synonymous/Parallel/Hendiadys.* Third, a number of pairs of imperatives include two verbs with similar meaning, in many cases separated by a different object, with the intent of producing only one result.

אֲנִי־אֵל שַׁדַּי הִתְהַלֵּךְ לְפָנַי וֶהְיֵה תָמִים
I am the Almighty; *walk* before me and *be* perfect (Gen 17:1)

הִתְאַבְּלִי־נָא וְלִבְשִׁי־נָא בִגְדֵי־אֵבֶל
Act as a mourner; *put on* clothes of mourning (2 Sam 14:2)

4. *Hendiadys.* Several verb pairs involve two imperatives with the same person, gender, and number, that are semantically related and aiming at producing only one result. These pairs are called idiomatic *hendiadys* and are commonly found in Biblical Hebrew.

פְּרוּ וּרְבוּ וּמִלְאוּ אֶת־הַמַּיִם בַּיַּמִּים
Be fruitful and multiply and fill the waters (Gen 1:22)

חִזְקוּ וְאִמְצוּ אַל־תִּירְאוּ וְאַל־תַּעַרְצוּ מִפְּנֵיהֶם
Be strong and courageous; do not be afraid (n)or tremble before them (Deut 31:6)

The imperative forms of the word pair יָדַע and רָאָה often appear together in a construction in which the direct object is governed by both verbs. Since these verbs usually indicate a sense of perception, the idea of the verbal pair or *hendiadys* usually takes the sense of "considering," "finding out," or "being aware" of something.[157]

וּדְעוּ וּרְאוּ בַּמָּה הָיְתָה הַחַטָּאת הַזֹּאת הַיּוֹם
Consider how great your sin is today (1 Sam 14:38)

לְכוּ־נָא הָכִינוּ עוֹד וּדְעוּ וּרְאוּ אֶת־מְקוֹמוֹ (1Sam 23:22 WTT)
Go prepare further and *consider* where the place is (1 Sam 23:22)

וּרְאוּ וּדְעוּ מִכֹּל הַמַּחֲבֹאִים אֲשֶׁר יִתְחַבֵּא שָׁם
Find out about all the hiding places where he is hiding (1 Sam 23:23)

וְעַתָּה דְּעִי וּרְאִי מַה־תַּעֲשִׂי
Now, *consider* what you should do (1 Sam 25:17)

דְּעוּ־נָא וּרְאוּ כִּי רָעָה זֶה מְבַקֵּשׁ
Please consider what evil this man is seeking (1 Kgs 20:7)

5. *Purpose/Result.* When a *waw*-imperative follows another imperative, it often introduces a purpose or result clause. In cases of this sort, the focus is placed on the subordinate clause. The events are logically sequential.

רְדוּ־שָׁמָּה וְשִׁבְרוּ־לָנוּ מִשָּׁם
Go down there *to buy* grain for us (Gen 42:2)

רְדוּ לִקְרַאת מִדְיָן וְלִכְדוּ לָהֶם אֶת־הַמַּיִם
Go down to the Midianites *in order to take over* their water (Judg 7:24)

In disjunctive syntax, an imperative is not syntactically related to the previous verb. It functions as an independent verb and can represent any of the nuances of the regular imperative (e.g., a strong command, a mitigated command, or an urgent request). The word order of the clause does not influence the meaning of the imperative.

תֶּן־לִי הַנֶּפֶשׁ וְהָרְכֻשׁ קַח־לָךְ
Give me the individual *but take* the goods for yourself (Gen 14:21)

157. Also וְיִתֵּן קֹלוֹת וּמָטָר וּדְעוּ וּרְאוּ כִּי־רָעַתְכֶם רַבָּה 'so that he may send thunder and rain; then you will see how great your evil is' (1 Sam 12:17); דַּע וּרְאֵה כִּי אֵין בְּיָדִי רָעָה 'Consider that there is no evil in my hand' (1 Sam 24:12); וְעַתָּה דְּעִי וּרְאִי מַה־תַּעֲשִׂי 'Now, consider what you should do' (1 Sam 25:17); עַתָּה דַּע וּרְאֵה מָה־אָשִׁיב שֹׁלְחִי דָּבָר 'Now, think about what answer I should give to the one who sent me' (2 Sam 24:13); לֵךְ הִתְחַזַּק וְדַע וּרְאֵה אֵת אֲשֶׁר־תַּעֲשֶׂה 'Go strengthen yourself and consider what you should do' (1 Kgs 20:22); אַךְ־דְּעוּ־נָא וּרְאוּ כִּי־מִתְאַנֶּה הוּא לִי 'Now, see how he wants to quarrel with me' (2 Kgs 5:7).

שִׁלְחוּ מִכֶּם אֶחָד וְיִקַּח אֶת־אֲחִיכֶם וְאַתֶּם הֵאָסְרוּ
Send one of your own and let him take your brother, *but as for you, stay* in prison (Gen 42:16)

6. *Other.* The transitive verbs לָקַח and שָׁלַח are often used without specified objects and imply the idea of "taking something/someone" and "sending someone."[158] This use of the verbs is not restricted to the imperative but also occurs in the cohortative.

וְעַתָּה הִנֵּה אִשְׁתְּךָ קַח וָלֵךְ
So now, here is your wife; *take (her) and go* (Gen 12:19)

וְעַתָּה שְׁלַח הָעֵז אֶת־מִקְנְךָ
So now, *send (someone and) have (him) shelter* the flock (Exod 9:19)

וְעַתָּה קְחוּ וַעֲשׂוּ עֲגָלָה חֲדָשָׁה אֶחָת
Now, *take (what you need) and make* a new cart (1 Sam 6:7)

וְעַתָּה שְׁלַח וְקַח אֹתוֹ אֵלַי
Now, *send (someone) and bring* him to me (1 Sam 20:31)

לְכוּ וּרְאוּ אֵיכֹה הוּא וְאֶשְׁלַח וְאֶקָּחֵהוּ
Go see how he is *so that I may send (someone)* and take him (2 Kgs 6:13)

2.2.4.2. Imperative Followed by Jussive

From the examples examined in BH prose, there are no instances in which the imperative in this sequence of verbs operates adverbially. The imperative and the jussive always express two independent actions, sometimes syntactically related and at other times independent from each other. In most cases, the clause that includes the jussive expresses *purpose* or *result*. This conforms to the rule of "modal congruence" presented by Moran for EA Canaanite:

> [I]f the verb of the first clause states a fact (perfect, indicative), then in the purpose clause the verb is in the indicative; if the verb of the first clause is an imperative, a jussive or *yaqtula* expressing wish, etc., then in the purpose clause the verb is a jussive—or *yaqtula*.[159]

This rule is common to several of the languages of the NWSemitic group. Among the languages examined for the application of this rule (Ugaritic, EA

158. Also שִׁלְחָה וְקָחֶנּוּ 'Send (someone) and take him' (1 Sam 16:11); וְעַתָּה שְׁלַח קְבֹץ אֵלַי אֶת־כָּל־יִשְׂרָאֵל 'Now, send (someone) to gather to me' (1 Kgs 1:19).

159. Moran, "Early Canaanite *yaqtula*," 9. Moran uses the term "indicative" in this context to refer to the *yaqtulu* indicative form in which the verb states a fact.

Canaanite, Phoenician, Epigraphic Hebrew, Biblical Hebrew, Moabite, Ammonite, Edomite, and Aramaic), the sequence of "Imperative followed by a Jussive (purpose/result clause)" is attested mostly in EA Canaanite and Biblical Hebrew. The limited corpus of texts in the minor languages prevents us from finding more evidence.

הַעְתִּירוּ אֶל־יְהוָה וְיָסֵר הַצְפַרְדְּעִים מִמֶּנִּי וּמֵעַמִּי

Pray to the Lord *that he may take away* the frogs from me and my people (Exod 8:4)

שְׁלַח־לְךָ אֲנָשִׁים וְיָתֻרוּ אֶת־אֶרֶץ כְּנַעַן

Send men *so that they may spy out* the land of Canaan (Num 13:2)

חַל־נָא אֶת־פְּנֵי יְהוָה אֱלֹהֶיךָ וְהִתְפַּלֵּל בַּעֲדִי וְתָשֹׁב יָדִי אֵלָי

Entreat the Lord *and pray for me so that my hand may be restored* (1 Kgs 13:6)

2.2.4.3. Imperative Followed by Cohortative

This sequence of verbs, common in Biblical Hebrew, can be separated into two groups: (1) the imperative operates adverbially; and (2) the imperative and the cohortative represent two separate actions.

In the first group, the imperative with adverbial functions is more often than not joined to the cohortative by a *waw,* except with the verb יָהַב. The imperative of יָהַב and its following cohortative are never joined by a *waw*:

הָבָה נִלְבְּנָה לְבֵנִים וְנִשְׂרְפָה לִשְׂרֵפָה

Let us make bricks and let us fire (them) (Gen 11:3)

הָבָה נֵרְדָה וְנָבְלָה שָׁם שְׂפָתָם

Let us go down and confuse their language (Gen 11:7)

The opposite is true of the verb קוּם. The imperative of קוּם and its following cohortative are always linked with a *waw.*

קוּמוּ וְנִבְרָחָה כִּי לֹא־תִהְיֶה־לָּנוּ פְלֵיטָה מִפְּנֵי אַבְשָׁלוֹם

Let us flee for we will not be able to escape from Absalom (2 Sam 15:14)

The verb הָלַךְ functions adverbially in this sequence with or without a *waw* on the cohortative. Out of 18 passages where such sequences occur with הָלַךְ, 14 are syndetic (with *waw*) and 4 are asyndetic (without *waw*). The difference in meaning between the two constructions is barely discernible. The following passages taken from 1 Samuel 9 show the variety of constructions used to express the same idea, with syndetic and asyndetic constructions. These passages taken from the same context show the difficulties in trying to determine a difference in meaning between syndetic and asyndetic constructions.

וְשָׁאוּל אָמַר לְנַעֲרוֹ אֲשֶׁר־עִמּוֹ לְכָה וְנָשׁוּבָה פֶּן־יֶחְדַּל אָבִי מִן־הָאֲתֹנוֹת
Saul said to the young man who was with him: *Let us go back* lest my father stop (being concerned) about the asses (1 Sam 9:5—syndetic with long imperative)

כֹּה־אָמַר הָאִישׁ בְּלֶכְתּוֹ לִדְרוֹשׁ אֱלֹהִים לְכוּ וְנֵלְכָה עַד־הָרֹאֶה
Thus said the man when he went to seek God: *Let us go* to the seer (1 Sam 9:9—syndetic with plural imperative)

וַיֹּאמֶר שָׁאוּל לְנַעֲרוֹ טוֹב דְּבָרְךָ לְכָה נֵלֵכָה וַיֵּלְכוּ אֶל־הָעִיר
Then Saul said to his young man: Your idea is great. *Let us go.* So they went into the city (1 Sam 9:10—asyndetic with long imperative)

As a rule, when an imperative with adverbial functions is followed by a cohortative, the imperative and cohortative do not agree in number. The imperative appears in the masculine-singular, feminine-singular, and plural forms while the cohortative is always plural. There are no occurrences where the adverbial imperative is followed by a singular cohortative.

הָבָה נֵרְדָה וְנָבְלָה שָׁם שְׂפָתָם
Let us go down and confuse their language (Gen 11:7—singular imperative + plural cohortative)

לְכָה וְנַעְבְּרָה אֶל־מַצַּב פְּלִשְׁתִּים
Let us go over to the outpost of the Philistines (1 Sam 14:1—singular imperative + plural cohortative)

When an imperative is followed by a cohortative, the imperative carries one of the following ideas:

1. *Motion.* when a change of location is required in order for the action of the cohortative to be fulfilled:

לְכָה וְנָשׁוּבָה פֶּן־יֶחְדַּל אָבִי מִן־הָאֲתֹנוֹת
Let us return lest my father ceases to be concerned about the donkeys (1 Sam 9:5)

וְעַתָּה לְכוּ וְנִפְּלָה אֶל־מַחֲנֵה אֲרָם
So now, *let us go* into the camp of the Arameans (2 Kgs 7:4)

2. *Suggestion.* Where no motion is required for the action of the cohortative to be fulfilled. The speaker is simply recommending a certain course of action, in the form of a suggestion:

וְעַתָּה לְכָה נִכְרְתָה בְרִית אֲנִי וָאָתָּה
Now, *let us cut* a covenant, you and I (Gen 31:44)

3. *Emphasis.* When the imperative and cohortative are from the same root.

וַיֹּאמֶר שְׁמוּאֵל אֶל־הָעָם לְכוּ וְנֵלְכָה הַגִּלְגָּל וּנְחַדֵּשׁ שָׁם הַמְּלוּכָה
Then Samuel said to the people: *Let us go* to Gilgal in order to renew the kindgom there (1 Sam 11:14)

חֲזַק וְנִתְחַזְּקָה בְּעַד־עַמֵּנוּ
Let us be strong for our people (1 Chr 19:13)

In the second group, independent actions are expressed by both the imperative and the cohortative. In passages of this sort, the cohortative is always preceded by a *waw*, unless found in a disjunctive clause.

1. *Purpose.* In the majority of cases, the clause introduced by the cohortative expresses *purpose*:

הוֹצִיאֵם אֵלֵינוּ וְנֵדְעָה אֹתָם
Bring them out to us *so that we may have intercourse* with them (Gen 19:5)

תְּנָה־לָּנוּ בָשָׂר וְנֹאכֵלָה
Give us food *so that we may eat* (Num 11:13)

לְכוּ סִפְרוּ אֶת־יִשְׂרָאֵל מִבְּאֵר שֶׁבַע וְעַד־דָּן וְהָבִיאוּ אֵלַי וְאֵדְעָה אֶת־מִסְפָּרָם
Go count the Israelites from Beersheva to Dan and bring me (a report) *so that I may know* how many of them there are (1 Chr 21:2)

2. *Circumstantial.* The cohortative can be found within disjunctive circumstantial clauses. In such cases, the verb does not appear at the head of the clause but is preceded by another element, as is typical of disjunctive syntax:

שְׁבוּ־לָכֶם פֹּה עִם־הַחֲמוֹר וַאֲנִי וְהַנַּעַר נֵלְכָה עַד־כֹּה וְנִשְׁתַּחֲוֶה וְנָשׁוּבָה אֲלֵיכֶם
Stay here with the ass *while the youth and I go* up there and worship; then we will return to you (Gen 22:5)

וַיֹּאמֶר בִּלְעָם לְבָלָק הִתְיַצֵּב עַל־עֹלָתֶךָ וְאֵלְכָה
Balaam said to Balak: *Stand* by your burnt offering *while I go* (Num 23:3)

2.2.4.4. Imperative Followed by *weqatal*

The majority of the *weqatal* verbs governed by an imperative appear in the second person and represent the syntactic functions listed below. Seven types of relationships have been observed from the passages examined for this study. They are as follows, the first category being the most common:

1. *Sequentiality.*[160] The majority of examples of "imperatives followed by *waw*-perfect" examined for this study require that the fulfillment of the action of the perfect follow the fulfillment of the action expressed by the imperative. This verbal sequence is marked for expressing consecutive actions in the imperative mood.[161] The events are irreversible.

וַיֹּאמֶר יְהוָה אֶל־מֹשֶׁה בֹּא אֶל־פַּרְעֹה וְאָמַרְתָּ אֵלָיו
The Lord said to Moses: *Go* to Pharaoh *and then say* to him (Exod 7:26)

קַח אֶת־פַּר־הַשּׁוֹר אֲשֶׁר לְאָבִיךָ וּפַר הַשֵּׁנִי שֶׁבַע שָׁנִים וְהָרַסְתָּ אֶת־מִזְבַּח הַבַּעַל
Take the bull that belongs to your father and a second bull of seven years old *and then pull* down the altar of Baal (Judg 6:25)

בְּנֵה־לְךָ בַיִת בִּירוּשָׁלִַם וְיָשַׁבְתָּ שָׁם
Build yourself a house in Jerusalem *and dwell* there (1 Kgs 2:36)

Among these examples, only two are found in a social relationship of "lesser to greater." The other examples represent discourse spoken by a "greater to a lesser".

2. *Hendiadys.* In a large number of cases, the imperative and the perfect use synonymous verbs in order to indicate a single action. The most common expression, דַּבֵּר וְאָמַרְתָּ 'Speak and say!' appears in the books of Leviticus and Numbers.[162] Other, similar expressions include: צַו וְאָמַרְתָּ 'Command and say!'; אֱמֹר וְאָמַרְתָּ 'Speak and say!'; שְׁמֹר וְשָׁמַעְתָּ

160. A. H. Bartelt, "On the Subtleties of Hebrew Verbs, Part II," *Concordia Journal* (2008) 301.

161. Endo contrasts the function of the imperative and the perfect when used in volitive constructions and concludes that "the imperatives basically function as non sequential forms. The suffix conjugation, i.e., (we)QATAL, on the other hand, is used as a sequential form." Endo, *The Verbal System of Classical Hebrew in the Joseph Story*, 230.

162. The second most-frequent expression is limited to the book of Ezekiel: הִנָּבֵא וְאָמַרְתָּ 'Prophesy and say!'

'Observe and take heed!'; הָבָה וְנָתַתָּה 'Give and give!'; מְשֹׁל וְאָמַרְתָּ 'Instruct with a parable and say!'; יִרְאוּ וַעֲבַדְתֶּם 'Fear and serve!' Wherever these expressions are found, the relationship between speaker and listener is that of "greater to lesser." Only in one case do we find the discourse originating with the lesser of the two individuals involved in the conversation.

3. *Purpose/Result.* The five passages in which this syntactical function is found include perfect consecutives in the third person, singular or plural.

נְטֵה אֶת־מַטְּךָ וְהַךְ אֶת־עֲפַר הָאָרֶץ וְהָיָה לְכִנִּם בְּכָל־אֶרֶץ מִצְרָיִם
Stretch out your rod *and strike* the dust of the ground *so that they may become gnats* throughout Egypt (Exod 8:12)

וְזֹאת עֲשׂוּ לָהֶם וְחָיוּ וְלֹא יָמֻתוּ
This *do* to them *so that they may live* and not die (Num 4:19)

קַח מֵאִתָּם וְהָיוּ לַעֲבֹד אֶת־עֲבֹדַת אֹהֶל מוֹעֵד
Accept (these) from them *so that they may serve* in the Tabernacle (Num 7:5)

4. *Adverbial imperative followed by waw-perfect in the imperative mood.* In a limited number of cases, the imperative functions adverbially before a *weqatal* in the imperative mood. These occurrences involve the two most common adverbial imperatives—the verbs הָלַךְ and קוּם.

לֵךְ וּבָאתָ־לְּךָ אֶרֶץ יְהוּדָה
Come to the land of Judah (1 Sam 22:5)

וַיֹּאמֶר יָרָבְעָם לְאִשְׁתּוֹ קוּמִי נָא וְהִשְׁתַּנִּית
Jeroboam said to his wife: Please *go disguise yourself* (1 Kgs 14:2)

5. *Temporal clause.* In a few cases, an imbedded temporal clause with perfect consecutive is inserted into the discourse, breaking the flow of commands. This *weqatal* is not governed by the imperative but forms a secondary story line in the discourse. The imperative mood introduced by the imperative is resumed by the appropriate verb after the temporal clause.

קוּם רְדֹף אַחֲרֵי הָאֲנָשִׁים וְהִשַּׂגְתָּם וְאָמַרְתָּ אֲלֵהֶם
Pursue after the men *and when you overtake them,* say to them (Gen 44:4)

חֲגֹר מָתְנֶיךָ וְקַח פַּךְ הַשֶּׁמֶן הַזֶּה בְּיָדֶךָ וְלֵךְ רָמֹת גִּלְעָד׃ וּבָאתָ שָׁמָּה וּרְאֵה־שָׁם יֵהוּא
בֶּן־יְהוֹשָׁפָט

Gird up your loins; *take* this flask of oil with you *and go* to Ramot Gilead; *when you get* there, look for Jehu, the son of Jehoshaphat (2 Kgs 9:1–2a)

2.2.4.4.1. Social Dynamics

The verbal construction under discussion (imperative *followed by* perfect consecutive) is peculiar for its pattern of relationship between speakers and listeners. In 98% of the cases we examined, when the imperative is followed by a perfect in the imperative mood, the relationship involved is that of "greater to lesser." And in 73% of these instances, God is the speaker of the utterance. Rare are the occasions when someone of lower social status uses a perfect consecutive in the imperative mood to address someone of higher social status.

2.2.4.5. Imperative Followed by *weyiqtol*

The major issues related to the modal use of the imperfect will be discussed in detail below. Here, I will address the modal use of the imperfect only where it is governed by an imperative. This sequence reflects *irrealis* modality where "the command is given with the intent of the future action happening . . . [and] can actually serve as a nuanced purpose clause."[163] In such passages, we find the following possibilities of sequences:

Imperative	*followed by*	*weyiqtol* (1st person)
Imperative	*followed by*	*yiqtol* (2nd person)[164]
Imperative	*followed by*	*weyiqtol* (3rd person)

First- and Third-Person Imperfect. The type of sequence in which an imperative precedes an imperfect in the first or third person is not common in Biblical Hebrew. However, these sorts of occurrences have not gone without notice by scholars who, over the years, have attempted either to emend the text or to explain such "inconsistencies" in the language. In several passages, the imperfect *seems* to deviate from normal behavior, especially when it is accompanied by a *waw* and appears at the head of the clause. In most of these cases, the imperfect indicates purpose and seems to function exactly as a volitive would in the same context. These imperfects need not be emended or explained away but have their place in the language. I believe they represent a *yaqtula* volitive form common in EA Canaanite texts and not an indicative *yaqtulu*.[165]

163. Bartelt, "On the Subtleties of Hebrew Verbs, Part II," 302.

164. In such cases, the imperfect does not appear at the head of the clause but is preceded by an adverb, an object, or a subject. When the syntax requires that the verb appear first in the clause, the *weqatal* or another imperative continues the command of the first imperative.

165. See more-detailed discussion on the modal use of the Imperfect in the section on "Additional Verbs with Modal Functions" (in §2.5.1).

Since the final short vowel of the indicative *yaqtulu* and the volitive *yaqtula* was lost, the two verb forms have merged into one and given us the *yiqtol* imperfect. The majority of *waw*-imperfect verbs identify in function with the *yaqtula*.

When passages with the *waw*-imperfect are examined by themselves, they appear to be problematic and seem to represent scribal errors, but when these examples are added to the list of passages where the imperfect functions as a volitive (e.g., imperative in the 2nd person, sometimes accompanied by the negative particle אַל, in the jussive and cohortative mood, as a negative imperative), there is no need to resort to emendations. The imperfect has its place in the modal system of classical Hebrew. If these imperfects represent the *yaqtula* volitive, it is not surprising that in most cases where an imperative is followed by a *waw*-imperfect, we find a purpose clause.

לֵךְ הָפֵרָה אֶת־בְּרִיתְךָ אֶת־בַּעְשָׁא מֶלֶךְ־יִשְׂרָאֵל וְיַעֲלֶה מֵעָלָי

Go break your alliance with Baasha, the king of Israel, *so that he may go away* from me (1 Kgs 15:19)

וַיִּתְפַּלֵּל אֱלִישָׁע וַיֹּאמַר יְהוָה פְּקַח־נָא אֶת־עֵינָיו וְיִרְאֶה

Then Elisha prayed and said: *Please open* his eyes *that he may see* (2 Kgs 6:17)

This construction is common to Canaanite languages, especially with purpose clauses.

Second-Person Imperfect. When following an imperative, the second-person imperfect often expresses a command. In these cases, the syntax of the sentence demands that one or more elements precede the imperfect. When the syntax requires the verb to be at the head of the clause, the *weqatal* is used. Therefore, in such verbal sequences, the nuances expressed by the *weqatal* equal those of the *yiqtol*. Our examples of second-person imperfect expressing commands can be grouped into three categories:

all these have to do with some word preceding the verb in the second clause

- Where the imperfect follows an adverb of time, place or manner
- Where the imperfect is found in a circumstantial clause, indicates a contrast, or emphasizes the direct or indirect object
- Where the clause with the imperfect provides additional information on the manner in which the first command is to be performed (especially where the same verb is appears in both clauses).

1. *After an adverb.* The imperfect is preceded by an adverb of time, place, or manner and is governed by the imperative.

בַּשְּׁלוּ אֶת־הַבָּשָׂר פֶּתַח אֹהֶל מוֹעֵד וְשָׁם תֹּאכְלוּ אֹתוֹ

Cook the meat at the entrance of the tent of meeting *and eat it there* (Lev 8:31)

וַיָּשֶׂם יְהוָה דָּבָר בְּפִי בִלְעָם וַיֹּאמֶר שׁוּב אֶל־בָּלָק וְכֹה תְדַבֵּר
The Lord put a message in the mouth of Balaam, so he said: *Return* to Balak *and say thus* (Num 23:5)

סְעָד לִבְּךָ פַּת־לֶחֶם וְאַחַר תֵּלֵכוּ
Strengthen yourself with a bit of food *and after that, go* (Judg 19:5)

2. *Circumstantial, marking object or subject, contrast.* In cases of disjunctive syntax, the imperfect is preceded by another element (e.g., subject, object).

וַיֹּאמֶר אֶל־עֲבָדָיו עִבְרוּ לְפָנַי וְרֶוַח תָּשִׂימוּ בֵּין עֵדֶר וּבֵין עֵדֶר
Then he said to his servants: *Cross over* before me, *keeping* some space between the herds (Gen 32:17)

וְקַח מֵאִתָּם מַטֶּה מַטֶּה לְבֵית אָב מֵאֵת כָּל־נְשִׂיאֵהֶם לְבֵית אֲבֹתָם שְׁנֵים עָשָׂר מַטּוֹת
אִישׁ אֶת־שְׁמוֹ תִּכְתֹּב עַל־מַטֵּהוּ
And take a staff from each family, of all the leaders according to their father's household, *and write* the name of each man upon his staff (Num 17:17)

קוּם לֵךְ אִתָּם וְאַךְ אֶת־הַדָּבָר אֲשֶׁר־אֲדַבֵּר אֵלֶיךָ אֹתוֹ תַעֲשֶׂה
Go with them, *but do* what I say for you to do (Num 22:20)

קְרַב אַתָּה וּשֲׁמָע אֵת כָּל־אֲשֶׁר יֹאמַר יְהוָה אֱלֹהֵינוּ וְאַתְּ תְּדַבֵּר אֵלֵינוּ אֵת כָּל־אֲשֶׁר
יְדַבֵּר יְהוָה אֱלֹהֵינוּ אֵלֶיךָ
Get close and listen to everything the Lord our God is saying, *then tell* us everything the Lord our God said to you (Deut 5:27)

3. *Explanatory.* In some passages, the commands are expressed by the same verb—in the imperative in the first clause, and in the imperfect in the second clause. The imperfect carries the imperative mood of the first verb and usually provides explanations for the command given by the imperative.

עֲשֵׂה לְךָ תֵּבַת עֲצֵי־גֹפֶר קִנִּים תַּעֲשֶׂה אֶת־הַתֵּבָה וְכָפַרְתָּ אֹתָהּ מִבַּיִת וּמִחוּץ בַּכֹּפֶר
Make an ark of gofer-wood; *make* the ark with rooms and cover it with pitch inside and out (Gen 6:14)

פְּקֹד אֶת־בְּנֵי לֵוִי לְבֵית אֲבֹתָם לְמִשְׁפְּחֹתָם כָּל־זָכָר מִבֶּן־חֹדֶשׁ וָמַעְלָה תִּפְקְדֵם
Number the Levites according to their father's house, by family; *number* each male from age one month up (Num 3:15)

עֲשֵׂה לְךָ שְׁתֵּי חֲצוֹצְרֹת כֶּסֶף מִקְשָׁה תַּעֲשֶׂה אֹתָם
Make two silver trumpets; *make* them from hammered material (Num 10:2)

שְׁלַח־לְךָ אֲנָשִׁים וְיָתֻרוּ אֶת־אֶרֶץ כְּנַעַן אֲשֶׁר־אֲנִי נֹתֵן לִבְנֵי יִשְׂרָאֵל אִישׁ אֶחָד אִישׁ אֶחָד לְמַטֵּה אֲבֹתָיו תִּשְׁלָחוּ כֹּל נָשִׂיא בָהֶם
Send men to inspect the land of Canaan which I am giving to the Israelites; *send* a man from each ancestral tribe, a leader from among them (Num 13:2)

2.2.5. Speaker/Listener Relationship

The three types of imperatives (regular imperative, long imperative, imperative with נָא) appear in the following social contexts:

1. From greater to lesser
2. From lesser to greater
3. With individuals of equal status

The following points are significant:

(1) An individual of higher social status is more likely to address one of lower social status with the regular imperative than with another type of imperative. When a speaker addresses someone of lower status with the particle נָא, he seems to identify with the listener on a more intimate level, using a "softening" construction marked for politeness.

(2) An individual of lower social status is more likely to address someone of higher status with the imperative with נָא or with the long imperative. The notion of politeness or submission before someone of higher social status is emphasized by the particle נָא.[166]

(3) When the regular imperative is used by an individual of lower social status, the context is often that of prayer to God. In these cases, the imperative represents a mitigated form of command or a request, rather than an order.

(4) The nuances expressed by the regular imperative are more closely related to those of the imperative with נָא than to those of the long imperative.

2.2.5.1. Verb Sequences in Which the Imperative Governs the Mood

The following points are significant:

(1) Commands governed by an imperative are common when a greater is addressing someone of lower social status.

(2) When the *weqatal* expresses a command and is governed by an imperative, 98% of the cases are found in the category of greater to lesser. Seventy-three percent of these passages are found in prescriptive discourse, with God

166. See Kaufman, "An Emphatic Plea for Please," 198.

as the speaker of the utterance. In these cases, the commands given do not represent one action but represent habitual/repeated actions in the future.

(3) When the infinitive absolute is governed by an imperative and expresses a command, the social dynamics are that of greater to lesser. This sort of construction is rare in narrative prose.[167]

2.2.6. Summary of the Imperative

(1) My study shows that the Hebrew language includes a variety of verbal forms and nuances to express commands. Longacre identifies four different types of commands and associates them with specific verbal forms:[168]

- *Unmitigated command* expressed by the imperative
- *Partially mitigated command* expressed by the *weqatal* preceded by an imperative
- *Completely mitigated command* expressed by the *weqatal* without the presence of an imperative
- *Deferential command* expressed by the jussive

(2) From the standpoint of discourse analysis, the imperative provides the main line of the story in hortatory discourse, described by Longacre as "discourse in which one person tries to influence the conduct of another" or "tries to impose his or her will on another person."[169] In instructional and judicial discourse, the imperative initiates a series of commands continued by the *weqatal* for foreground information and the *yiqtol* for background information.[170]

(3) Marked for simple commands, the regular imperative can represent nuances such as: *strong commands, mitigated commands, pleas of desperation, urgent and nonurgent requests, and wishes.*

(4) When a command is marked for *politeness* or *respect*, the author uses the imperative with נָא or the long imperative. These two forms are close in

167. Josh 4:3, 2 Kgs 11:15. The majority of occurrences appear in prophetic material, outside of our corpus.

168. Longacre, *Joseph*, 113, 123–25.

169. Idem, "Discourse Perspective on the Hebrew Verb: Affirmation and Restatement," in *Linguistics and Biblical Hebrew* (ed. W. R. Bodine; Winona Lake, IN: Eisenbrauns, 1992) 119, 186. The terms *mainline* and *off-line* or *secondary line* are also designated "foreground information" and "background information." See D. A. Dawson, *Text-Linguistics and Biblical Hebrew* (JSOTSup 17; Sheffield: Sheffield Academic Press, 1994) 102. Dawson describes "foreground" material as "that which moves the story/exhortation/instructions/etc. toward its essential goal," and "background" material is "that which does not significantly advance the story" (p. 102).

170. Dawson states that "'background' material can be categorized in terms of 'distance from the main-line' or 'degree of backgrounding'; the more unlike the main-line clause-type and off-line clause-type can be shown to be (in terms of its tense-aspect-mood values, for example), the further off-line it can be said to be" (ibid., 102).

meaning and function in similar contexts. Since both forms find their origin in the Canaanite modal form *yaqtulanna*, it is understandable that they overlap in meaning and function. Although the imperative with נָא and the long imperative are marked for specific types of modality, they appear in contexts similar to those of the regular imperative: *pleas of desperation, urgency, non-urgent requests, politeness,* and *strong petitions.*

(5) The long imperative and the imperative with ethical dative emphasize different participants. The long imperative focuses on *the interests of the speaker*, while the imperative with ethical dative *focuses on the interests of the listener.*

(6) When preceding an imperative or a cohortative, certain verbs in the imperative play an adverbial role. In these constructions, the imperative expresses one of the following ideas: *motion* (e.g., בּוֹא, הָלַךְ, קוּם), *repetition* (e.g., שׁוּב), or *causation* (e.g., שָׁלַח). The imperative may or may not be joined to the following verb by a conjunctive *waw*. In many cases, a distinction in meaning between the two constructions is hardly discernible.

(7) *Interjections* are sometimes represented by the imperative (e.g., רְאֵה, הִשָּׁמֶר, הָבָה, הוֹאִיל). These imperatives seek to draw the attention of the listener to the information that follows.

2.2.6.1. Sequences with Imperatives

(1) When strings of imperatives occur, the syntactic relationships between the verbs is one of the following:

- *Conjunctive.* The fulfillment of the commands can occur in any order and produce the same outcome.
- *Hendiadys/synonymous ideas.* Two semantically related verbs appear in the context, and refer to only one event.
- *Sequentiality.* The fulfillment of the first command must occur before the fulfillment of the second command. The events are irreversible.
- *Purpose.* The event of the main clause points to the subordinate purpose clause in order to give meaning to its stated event.

(2) When the imperative is found in a *disjunctive* clause (the imperative is preceded by another element in the clause), it can represent any of the nuances of the imperative listed above (*strong commands, mitigated commands, pleas of desperation, urgent* and *nonurgent requests*, and *wishes*). The word order of the clause does not affect the meaning of the imperative.

(3) In most cases in which imperatives are followed by jussives and cohortatives, the second clause is a *purpose* or *result* clause. This phenomenon is common in EA Canaanite syntax.

(4) Unlike the cohortative, the jussive is never preceded by an adverbial imperative. When an adverbial imperative precedes the cohortative, the two

verbs may or may not be connected by a *waw*. The semantic distinction between the two syntagmas (imperative followed by *waw*-cohortative; imperative followed by cohortative) is often difficult to detect, especially when the imperative and the cohortative are both verbs of motion. Therefore, I conclude that the two syntagmas simply reveal stylistic variation.

(5) The imperative often governs the imperative mood of a following *weqatal* or imperfect in procedural discourse.[171] When a sequence of commands is expressed, the *weqatal* appears at the head of the clause, but when disjunctive syntax is required, the imperfect appears within the clause, preceded by another element.

(6) When an imperative governs the imperative mood of a *weqatal*, imperfect, or infinitive absolute, the social dynamics between the speaker and the listener are in the majority of cases that of "greater" to "lesser."

2.2.6.2. Conditional Sentences with Imperatives

Imperatives are usually found in main clauses, but in a few cases, the imperative introduces the apodosis of a conditional clause. In such cases, the imperative is asyndetic, without *waw*. This phenomenon is also common with the other volitives. In most cases when jussives and cohortatives introduce the apodosis of a conditional, a temporal, or an interrogative clause, they appear without a *waw* at the head of the clause (examples for the jussive and cohortatives are given in their respective sections below).

וְעַתָּה אִם־יֶשְׁכֶם עֹשִׂים חֶסֶד וֶאֱמֶת אֶת־אֲדֹנִי הַגִּידוּ לִי וְאִם־לֹא הַגִּידוּ לִי
Now, if you are going to deal mercifully and truthfully with my lord,
then tell me, but if not, *then tell* me (Gen 24:49)

וְאִם רַע בְּעֵינֵיכֶם לַעֲבֹד אֶת־יְהוָה בַּחֲרוּ לָכֶם הַיּוֹם אֶת־מִי תַעֲבֹדוּן
If it is evil in your eyes to serve the Lord, *then choose* this day whom
you will serve (Josh 24:15)

אִם־לְשָׁלוֹם יָצָאוּ תִּפְשׂוּם חַיִּים וְאִם לְמִלְחָמָה יָצָאוּ חַיִּים תִּפְשׂוּם
If they have come out in peace, *then take* them alive, and if they have
come out for war, *take* them while you are alive (1 Kgs 20:18)

2.3. The Jussive

In order to determine the syntactical functions of the jussive, I will note its usage both in contexts where it functions independently from other volitives

171. R. Longacre, "Building for the Worship of God: Exodus 25:1–30:10," in *Discourse Analysis of Biblical Literature: What It Is and What It Offers* (ed. W. R. Bodine; Atlanta: Scholars Press, 1995) 23.

and in contexts where it is syntactically related to other volitives. The following list shows the constructions and verb sequences considered for the study:

Jussive		
Jussive	*with* נָא	
Jussive	*followed by*	(*waw*-) Cohortative
Jussive	*followed by*	(*waw*-) Imperative
Jussive	*followed by*	(*waw*-) Jussive
Jussive	*followed by*	(*waw*-) Imperfect
Negative Jussives / Imperatives		

In this section, I will examine the relationships between speaker and listener in order to determine patterns of speech identified with the jussive. Such relationships can be grouped as follows:

1. from greater to lesser
2. from lesser to greater
3. between individuals of equal social status

Finally, the significance of word order will be addressed, followed by a discussion on the types of clauses in which the jussive is found, briefly commenting on Moran's rule of "modal congruence" in relationship to the jussives of BH and EA Canaanite.

2.3.1. Morphology

The Hebrew jussive appears in the first, second, and third persons. In the Qal stem, only verbs with final ה/י and medial ו/י show a morphological difference between the singular jussive and imperfect forms (יְהִי/יִהְיֶה and יָקֹם/יָקוּם). In the Hiphil stem, the jussive appears with a reduced theme vowel (יַפְקֵד) when compared with the imperfect (יַפְקִיד).

First person. First-person jussives are the least common attested forms of the jussive and occur mostly in poetry.[172]

וַיֹּאמֶר שָׁאוּל נֵרְדָה אַחֲרֵי פְלִשְׁתִּים לַיְלָה וְנָבֹזָּה בָהֶם עַד־אוֹר הַבֹּקֶר וְלֹא־נַשְׁאֵר בָּהֶם אִישׁ
Saul said: Let us go down after the Philistines tonight and plunder them until the morning, but *let us not allow* one man among them to remain (1 Sam 14:36)

In the following examples, a prefix conjugation in the first person introduces a purpose clause. The verb is one of the following three forms: (1) an indicative imperfect (*yaqtulu*); (2) a jussive (*yaqtul*); or (3) a volitive (*yaqtula*). Since the syntax of each sentence requires that the verb of the purpose clause

172. Only 13 morphologically identifiable apocopated first-person forms appear in the Hebrew Bible—Deut 18:16; 1 Sam 14:36; Isa 41:23, 28; Ezek 5:16; Hos 9:15; 11:4; Job 23:9, 11; Zeph 1:2, 3 [2×]); Neh 1:4.

be a volitive (conforming to the rule of "modal congruence"), the indicative imperfect (*yaqtulu*) is therefore excluded from our possibility of choices. Since the functions of the Hebrew jussive and the volitive *yiqtol* (*yaqtula*) are quite similar, both are possible choices.

קִבְצוּ אֶת־כָּל־יִשְׂרָאֵל הַמִּצְפָּתָה וְאֶתְפַּלֵּל בַּעַדְכֶם אֶל־יְהוָה
Gather all the Israelites at Mitzpah *so that I may pray* to the Lord for you (1 Sam 7:5)

וַיֹּאמֶר הֲדַד אֶל־פַּרְעֹה שַׁלְּחֵנִי וְאֵלֵךְ אֶל־אַרְצִי
Hadad said to Pharaoh: *Send me away that I may go* to my own land (1 Kgs 11:21)

In the following examples, the first-person verbs express volition. In each case, the verb is preceded by an imperative with adverbial functions, a construction common with volitives. Morphologically, the first-person verb is either an imperfect (*yaqtulu*), a volitive *yiqtol* (*yaqtula*), or a jussive (*yiqtol*). Based on the syntax, the verb can only be a volitive *yiqtol* (*yaqtula*) or a jussive (*yiqtol*).

וַיֹּאמֶר יְהוֹנָתָן אֶל־דָּוִד לְכָה וְנֵצֵא הַשָּׂדֶה
Then Jonathan said to David: *Let us go out* to the field (1 Sam 20:11)[173]

חֲזַק וְנִתְחַזַּק בְּעַד־עַמֵּנוּ וּבְעַד עָרֵי אֱלֹהֵינוּ וַיהוָה יַעֲשֶׂה הַטּוֹב בְּעֵינָיו
Let us strengthen ourselves for the sake of our people and the cities of our God, and may the Lord do what is good in his eyes (2 Sam 10:12—a cohortative appears in the parallel passage in 1 Chr 19:13, חֲזַק וְנִתְחַזְּקָה)

Second person. Second-person jussives appear more often with the negative particle אַל as negative commands than in the affirmative. A Hebrew negative command is not expressed by the imperative form of the verb but, rather, with the second-person jussive (see discussion in §2.3.4).

וְלָאֲתֹנוֹת הָאֹבְדוֹת לְךָ הַיּוֹם שְׁלֹשֶׁת הַיָּמִים אַל־תָּשֶׂם אֶת־לִבְּךָ לָהֶם
As for your asses lost three days ago, *do not worry* about them (1 Sam 9:20)

Third person. The most frequently attested form of the jussive is in the third person.[174] It is common both with and without the negative particle אַל.

173. The verb יָצָא appears in the cohortative in Gen 19:8, Judg 19:24, and 2 Chr 1:10. The author of Samuel chose the *yaqtula* volitive form rather than the cohortative. This phenomenon is noticeable elsewhere in the book of Samuel.

174. There are at least 690 morphologically identifiable third-person apocopated forms in the Hebrew Bible.

וַיֹּאמֶר אֱלֹהִים יְהִי אוֹר וַיְהִי־אוֹר
Then God said: *Let there be* light, and light was (Gen 1:3)

וַיֹּאמֶר אַבְרָם אֶל־לוֹט אַל־נָא תְהִי מְרִיבָה בֵּינִי וּבֵינֶיךָ
Then Abraham said to Lot: *Please let there not be* a feud between us (Gen 13:8)

2.3.2. Theories about the Origin of the Jussive

Scholars have proposed three origins of the jussive:

(1) *From the imperfect* (yaqtulu). The most commonly accepted view about the origin of the jussive is with regard to the imperfect (*yaqtulu*), the basic form of which was (1) shortened to express volition in the second and third persons, and (2) lengthened to express volition in the first person (cohortative).[175] This view is flawed because the internal lengthening and shortening of verbal forms is normally related to the system of stems and not to modality. Semitic languages express modality through paradigmatic forms (e.g., *yaqtulanna, yaqtula*) and through the addition of particles to existing verbal forms (e.g., *liprus, yiqtol* + נָא).

(2) *One* yaqtul *form.* Huehnergard suggests that "the early Semitic zero form *yaqtul* was a single morpheme, perfective in meaning, that occurred both in statements and in injunctions."[176] He supports his view by pointing to the multifunctions of the imperfect that occur both in statements and in injunctions. According to Huehnergard, there is no need for an additional independent morpheme, since the language provides verbal forms that are used for more than one purpose.[177] Huehnergard's statement is problematic in that an injunctive verb form cannot be considered "perfective in meaning." Injunctions are not related to aspect but to modality. Joosten points to the loss of final short vowel in the effacing of the opposition between the *yaqtulu* (nonjussive)

175. S. R. Driver, *A Treatise on the Use of the Tenses in Hebrew* (3rd ed.; Oxford: Clarendon, 1892) 50–53; Blau, *Grammar of Biblical Hebrew*, 63; Shulman, *Use of Modal Verb Forms*, 1; idem, "Jussive," in *Encyclopedia of Hebrew Language and Linguistics* (ed. Geoffrey Khan; Leiden: Brill, 2013) 2:437–40. Joüon describes the jussive as a third-person (sometimes second-person and rarely first-person) volitive form of verb that appears with "modifications of the future indicative *yiqtol*" in certain types of weak verbs (§114 a). GKC describes the jussive as a "shortened form" of the imperfect (§48b) and speaks of its general characteristic as being "rapidity of pronunciation, combined with a tendency to retract the tone from the final syllable, in order by that means to express the urgency of the command in the very first syllable" (§48f). In addition, GKC mentions that, in other cases, the jussive simply displays a shorter vowel with no change in accent, and finally, mentions that some jussives are morphologically identical to the imperfect.

176. J. Huehnergard, "The Early Hebrew Prefix-Conjugations," *HS* 29 (1988) 20–23; H. Fleisch, "Sur le système verbal du sémitique commun," *MUSJ* 27 (1947–48) 39–60.

177. Huehnergard, "The Early Hebrew Prefix-Conjugations," 22.

and the *yaqtul* (jussive and preterite).[178] In my opinion, since the nonmodal *yiqtol* (*yaqtulu*) appears in statements, while the modal *yiqtol* (*yaqtula*) appears in injunctions, I conclude that the Hebrew imperfect represents two prefix conjugations: the *yaqtulu* indicative and the *yaqtula* volitive.

(3) *Two* yaqtul *forms.* Since the Hebrew jussive (*yaqtul*) and the preterite (*yaqtul*) express different types of ideas, it is unlikely that they would have the same etymology. Such is the view of G. R. Driver, who believes that "semantically it is impossible to see any connection between their usages. It is impossible to conceive any transition of sense whereby *ikšud* meaning 'he captured' can have come to mean also 'let him capture,' or vice versa."[179] According to McFall, the *iqat(t)al* was the origin of the preterite *yáqtul*, while the jussive *yaqtúl* would have appeared later, developing from the imperative *qutúl*.[180] Rainey agrees with McFall's view that the imperative was the origin of the jussive.[181]

2.3.3. Functions of the Jussive[182]

1. *Petitions in prayer.* Jussives are often used in *blessings* and *prayers*, when the one uttering the prayer wishes for God to intervene in his/her life and in the life of another:

יִצֶף יְהוָה בֵּינִי וּבֵינֶךָ

May the Lord keep watch between me and you (Gen 31:49)

יָקֵם יְהוָה אֶת־דְּבָרוֹ

May the Lord fulfill his word (1 Sam 1:23)

יְחִי אֲדֹנִי הַמֶּלֶךְ דָּוִד לְעֹלָם

May my lord, King David, *live* forever (1 Kgs 1:31)

2. *Commands.* The jussive can also express *commands*: (1) direct commands when the jussive is in the second person, and (2) indirect commands when the jussive is in the third person. According to Longacre, third-person jussives express "deferential" commands in hortatory discourse, and represent the mildest form of command, after

178. Joosten, *Verbal System of Biblical Hebrew*, 333.

179. L. McFall, *The Enigma of the Hebrew Verbal System* (Sheffield: Almond, 1982) 131. See G. R. Driver, *Problems of the Hebrew Verbal System* (Edinburgh: T. & T. Clark, 1936), 33.

180. See McFall, *Enigma of the Hebrew Verbal System*, 129–31.

181. Rainey, "Ancient Hebrew Prefix Conjugation," 5.

182. Joosten lists the functions of the jussive as commands, requests, recommendations, wishes, blessings, and curses (*The Verbal System of Biblical Hebrew*, 121, 336–40).

the imperative (unmitigated) and the *weqatal* (partially and completely mitigated).

וַיֹּאמֶר מֹשֶׁה אֲלֵהֶם אִישׁ אַל־יוֹתֵר מִמֶּנּוּ עַד־בֹּקֶר
Then Moses said to them: *Let no one of them remain* until morning (Exod 16:19)

שִׁבְעַת יָמִים תּוֹחֵל עַד־בּוֹאִי אֵלֶיךָ
Wait seven days until I come to you (1 Sam 10:8)

3. *Desire, wish.* In some passages, the jussive indicates a *desire* or *wish* that may or may not be fulfilled by the hearer:

וַיֹּאמֶר אֱלֹהִים תַּדְשֵׁא הָאָרֶץ דֶּשֶׁא
Then God said: *Let the earth bring forth* vegetation (Gen 1:11)

וַיֹּאמֶר שִׁמְשׁוֹן תָּמוֹת נַפְשִׁי עִם־פְּלִשְׁתִּים
Then Samson said: *Let me die* with the Philistines (Judg 16:30)

4. *Suggestion.* The jussive often carries the idea of *suggestion* when the speaker recommends a course of action to his/her audience. The majority of our examples include conversations with a king:

וְעַתָּה יֵרֶא פַרְעֹה אִישׁ נָבוֹן וְחָכָם
Now, *may the king look* for an understanding and wise man (Gen 41:33)

וְיַפְקֵד הַמֶּלֶךְ פְּקִידִים בְּכָל־מְדִינוֹת מַלְכוּתוֹ וְיִקְבְּצוּ אֶת־כָּל־נַעֲרָה־בְתוּלָה טוֹבַת מַרְאֶה אֶל־שׁוּשַׁן
And *may the king appoint* officers in all the provinces of his kingdom so that they may gather every good-looking young woman in the palace of Shushan (Esth 2:3)

2.3.4. Jussives with נָא

As with the imperative, the jussive is often accompanied by the particle נָא. This syntagm is rare in the Pentateuch and occurs mostly in historical books. According to Shulman, when the verbal forms are identical, the particle נָא distinguishes a jussive from an imperfect.[183] When a jussive appears without נָא, the actor is a third person (unidentified or nonidentified), but when the jussive appears with נָא, the actor is the addressee.[184] Similarly to the imperative and the cohortative, this particle is used with the jussive in a variety of emotional contexts such as:

183. Shulman, "The Particle נָא in Biblical Hebrew Prose," 60.
184. Ibid., 61.

1. *Plea of desperation.* The situation is one of life and death:

תְּחִי־נָא נַפְשִׁי

Please let me live! (1 Kgs 20:32)

2. *Urgency.* The request must be fulfilled immediately, without delay: *Please let our petition come* before you and pray for us to the Lord (Jer 42:2)

תִּפָּל־נָא תְחִנָּתֵנוּ לְפָנֶיךָ וְהִתְפַּלֵּל בַּעֲדֵנוּ אֶל־יְהוָה

3. *Nonurgent request.* The petition is not one of urgency yet will require attention in the near future:

תְּהִי־נָא לְךָ תַּחְתֶּיהָ

Now, let her [*younger sister*] *be* yours instead of her [older sister] (Judg 15:2)

4. *Politeness.* The speaker expresses respect for the listener:

יָבֹא־נָא אֵלַי וְיֵדַע כִּי יֵשׁ נָבִיא בְּיִשְׂרָאֵל

Please let him come to me so that he may know that there is a prophet in Israel (2 Kgs 5:8)

5. *Manipulative petition.* The speaker is using deception in order to obtain his/her request:

תָּבֹא נָא תָמָר אֲחוֹתִי וְתַבְרֵנִי לֶחֶם

Please let Tamar my sister come and feed me some bread (2 Sam 13:5)

6. *Strong petition.* Additional emphasis is placed on the request:

יְהוָה אֱלֹהָי תָּשָׁב נָא נֶפֶשׁ־הַיֶּלֶד הַזֶּה עַל־קִרְבּוֹ

O Lord my God, *please let the life of this child return* to him (1 Kgs 17:21)

2.3.4.1. Social Dynamics

The jussive with נָא is used at every level of society, from king to common man, and more often than not, from one of lower status to one of higher status.

2.3.5. Negative Jussive

The negative jussive and the negative imperfect appear with different particles of negation. These not only indicate the mood involved in the passage but also serve to distinguish between the imperfect and the jussive when they are morphologically identical.[185] As mentioned above, the imperative form never appears with a negative particle. Negative commands and prohibitions appear

185. Phoenician also has a particle of negation for the indicative (בל) and a particle of negation for modal forms (אל): e.g., אל יפתח אל יבקש ואל ישא 'May he not open and may

in one of two forms: (1) with the negative particle אַל before a jussive (second or third person), or (2) with the negative particle לֹא followed by the imperfect (second person).[186] In most cases, the jussive is accompanied by the particle אַל while the imperfect is preceded by לֹא.[187] Hendel distinguishes the two syntagmas in terms of aspect. He states that

> the construction *ʾal + Juss.* is used for perfective prohibitions, while *loʾ + Impf.* is used for imperfective prohibitions. The latter construction is used for situations seen as unbounded by the speaker, as in perpetual commands or legal prohibitions (consistently in apodictic law), while the former is used to prohibit specific, punctual events.[188]

According to Hendel, the beginning and end of an event is depicted in the construction אַל + jussive while the construction לֹא + imperfect provides no end point for the event.[189] Waltke and O'Connor attribute the use of אַל + jussive to urgent situations and the use of לֹא + imperfect to the imperfective aspect in legislative material.[190] GKC addresses the issue not on the basis of aspect but on the basis of expectation. According to the authors,

> the imperfect with לֹא represents a more emphatic form of prohibition than the jussive with אַל, and corresponds to our *thou shalt not do it!* with the strongest expectation of obedience, while אַל with the jussive is rather a simple warning, *do not that!*[191]

In his research on negative commands, David Stabnow surveys the major views presented before 2000 and concludes that John Bright's explanation best represents the major functions of the two constructions. In Bright's view,

---

he not seek and may he not lift' (Eshmunazar, lines 4–5); e.g., בל תבאן וחצר אדרך בל תדרכן 'You shall not enter and the courtyard I tread, you shall not tread' (Arslan Tash i, lines 6–8).

186. This is also the case in other NWSemitic languages. For example, in Ugaritic, the negative command is expressed by a negative particle + prefix conjugation: e.g., *al . yšt* 'May he not put . . .' (2.38:27); *ʾal tqrb* 'Do not approach' (51 VIII 15f); *ʾal yʿdbkm* 'Let him not make you' (51 VIII 17).

187. There are a few exceptions to the rule, such as 1 Sam 12:19, 25:25, 2 Sam 13:25, and 1 Chr 21:13, where the particle of negation אַל accompanies the imperfect rather than the jussive. There are also a few examples in which the negative particle לֹא precedes a jussive, such as Gen 4:12, 24:8; and 1 Kgs 2:6. This inconsistent phenomenon has been treated by GKC as a possible "attempt to moderate . . . by means of the jussive (voluntative) form what was at first intended to be a strict command" or a possible misunderstanding of defective writing of the imperfect form of the verb (§109d). Since most of the examples are found in Samuel/Kings, I propose that this peculiarity is attributed to a specific scribal tradition rather than to errors in the text. This idea will be discussed in greater detail below in the section on the Imperfect (§2.5.1.2).

188. Hendel, "In the Margins of the Hebrew Verbal System," 170.

189. Ibid., 171.

190. Waltke and O'Connor, *Introduction to Biblical Hebrew Syntax,* 567.

191. GKC, 317.

> It is generally agreed that the *lōʾ* prohibitive has a much stronger force than the *ʾal* prohibitive. One might express the difference as follows: Whereas the *ʾal* prohibitive expresses a specific command for a specific occasion, the *lōʾ* prohibitive expresses a categorical prohibition of binding validity both for the present and the future (or the future so far as it is envisioned).[192]

Bright and Stabnow point out that the two constructions are distinguished in function by the social contexts in which they appear. While the negative command with אַל occurs from "greater to lesser," from "lesser to greater," and among "equals," the negative command with לֹא is found primarily when someone of "higher" social status addresses someone of "lower" status, often with God or his messenger as the speaker.[193]

The negative jussive appears in the following contexts:

1. *Negative command*

לֹא תִשָּׂא שֵׁמַע שָׁוְא אַל־תָּשֶׁת יָדְךָ עִם־רָשָׁע
Do not offer a false report; *do not join* with the wicked (Exod 23:1—the negative imperative appears parallel to the prohibitive when both seem to carry the same force)

וְאִישׁ לֹא־יַעֲלֶה עִמָּךְ וְגַם־אִישׁ אַל־יֵרָא בְּכָל־הָהָר
Let no man go up with you *nor let any man be seen* on the whole mountain (Exod 34:3—this negative jussive also appears parallel to a negative imperfect, with similar negative force)

וְאַל־יָבוֹא בֵית־יְהוָה כִּי אִם־הַכֹּהֲנִים
Let no one enter *the house of the Lord except the priests*" (2 Chr 23:6)

2. *Desire or wish*

אִם־נָא מָצָאתִי חֵן בְּעֵינֶיךָ אַל־נָא תַעֲבֹר מֵעַל עַבְדֶּךָ
If I have found favor in your eyes, *please do not pass by* your servant (Gen 18:3—as is common with the volitives in the apodosis of conditional clauses, the verb is not preceded by a *waw*)

---

192. Bright, "Apodictic Prohibition," 187. The survey appears in Stabnow, *Discourse Analysis Perspective*, 11–12. C. L. Seow, *Grammar for Biblical Hebrew* (Nashville: Abingdon, 1987) 144, 173: אַל for negative commands and לֹא for prohibitions; A. B. Davidson, *Davidson's Introductory Hebrew Grammar* (3rd ed.; Edingurgh: T. & T. Clark, 1989) 76: אַל for negative commands, לֹא for very strong prohibitions; Waltke and O'Connor, *Introduction to Biblical Hebrew Syntax*, 567: אַל for urgent situations, לֹא for nonperfective legislative material; J. D. W. Watts, *Survey of Syntax in the Hebrew Old Testament* (Grand Rapids, MI: Eerdmans, 1964) 23: אַל contingent in nature; Joüon, *A Grammar of Biblical Hebrew*, 371–72: לֹא for more solemn situations; V. DeCaen, "Ewald and Driver on BH 'Aspect': Anteriority and the Orientalist Framework," *ZAH* 9 (1996) 140–41: אַל for subjectivity and לֹא for objectivity; GKC, 261–62: לֹא for objective, unconditional negations.

193. Stabnow, *Discourse Analysis Perspective*, 13–14.

יְהוָה אֱלֹהִים אַל־תָּשֵׁב פְּנֵי מְשִׁיחֶיךָ
O Lord God, *do not turn* from your anointed one (2 Chr 6:42)

וַיֹּאמֶר אֶל־הַמֶּלֶךְ אַל־יַחֲשָׁב־לִי אֲדֹנִי עָוֹן וְאַל־תִּזְכֹּר אֵת אֲשֶׁר הֶעֱוָה עַבְדְּךָ
Then he said to the king: *May my Lord not impute* iniquity on me *and may he not remember* the evil of your servant (2 Sam 19:20)

3. *Suggestion.* This suggestion may or may not be adhered to by the listener:[194]

וְלָאֲתֹנוֹת הָאֹבְדוֹת לְךָ הַיּוֹם שְׁלֹשֶׁת הַיָּמִים אַל־תָּשֶׂם אֶת־לִבְּךָ לָהֶם
Do not worry about your lost asses of three days (1 Sam 9:20)

וְעַתָּה אַל־יָשֵׂם אֲדֹנִי הַמֶּלֶךְ אֶל־לִבּוֹ דָּבָר
Now, *may my lord the king not take* the thing to heart (2 Sam 13:33)

אַל־יַשִּׁיא לָכֶם חִזְקִיָּהוּ כִּי־לֹא יוּכַל לְהַצִּיל אֶתְכֶם מִיָּדוֹ׃ וְאַל־יַבְטַח אֶתְכֶם חִזְקִיָּהוּ אֶל־יְהוָה
Do not let Hezekiah deceive you since he is not able to deliver you from my hand, *and do not let him make you trust* in the Lord (2 Kgs 18:29–30)

4. *Purpose.* Sequences of negative jussives also produce purpose clauses:

אַל־תָּצַר אֶת־מוֹאָב וְאַל־תִּתְגָּר בָּם מִלְחָמָה
Do not harass the Moabites *so that you engage not* with them in battle (Deut 2:9)

2.3.5.1. Adverbial Use of the Negative Jussive

The negative jussive of the verb יָסַף often serves an adverbial function. In some instances, the jussive of יָסַף appears with the particle לֹא rather than with the negative particle לֹא.

כִּי תַעֲבֹד אֶת־הָאֲדָמָה לֹא־תֹסֵף תֵּת־כֹּחָהּ לָךְ
When you work the land, *may it not give* you of its produce *any more* (Gen 4:12)

לֵךְ מֵעָלָי הִשָּׁמֶר לְךָ אֶל־תֹּסֶף רְאוֹת פָּנַי

194. Although *wishes* and *suggestions* are closely related in meaning, I separate them because wishes are uttered in the interest of the speaker, while suggestions are made for the sake of the listener.

Go away from me; make sure *you do not see my face again* (Exod 10:28—the vocalization of the negative particle differs from the regular form)

אַל־תּוֹסֶף דַּבֵּר אֵלַי עוֹד בַּדָּבָר הַזֶּה
Do not speak to me about this matter *again* (Deut 3:26)

לֹא אֹסֵף לִשְׁמֹעַ אֶת־קוֹל יְהוָה אֱלֹהָי
Let me not hear again the voice of the Lord my God (Deut 18:16)

2.3.5.2. Negative Jussive with נָא

The negative jussive occasionally appears with the particle נָא. In such cases, the speaker politely requests that the addressee not perform a certain action. In most cases, someone of lower social status is addressing one of higher status.[195] Most of the passages where someone of higher social status addresses one of lower social status with this syntagm (contrary to the norm) appear in Samuel.[196] The book of Samuel is peculiar in that it uses a number of syntactic structures that reflect a scribal tradition other than that generally found in preexilic narratives.[197] In some cases, the negative particle נָא (which is normally associated with volitives) precedes a non-volitive, and the negative particle אַל (which is normally associated with nonvolitives) precedes a volitive.

וַיַּעַן הַמֶּלֶךְ וַיֹּאמֶר אֶל־הָאִשָּׁה אַל־נָא תְכַחֲדִי מִמֶּנִּי דָּבָר אֲשֶׁר אָנֹכִי שֹׁאֵל אֹתָךְ
Then the king answered and said to the woman: *Please do not hide* from me anything I ask of you (2 Sam 14:18)

2.3.5.3. Social Dynamics

As a rule, negative commands with jussives appear much more frequently when the speaker addresses someone of lower social status. Where someone

195. Gen 18:3, 30, 32; Num 10:31; 12:11, 12; 22:16; Judg 6:18; Jonah 1:14.

196. E.g., 1 Sam 3:17; 2 Sam 13:25, 14:18. The book of Samuel also includes an occurrence of נָא-אַל followed by an imperfect, 1 Sam 25:25.

197. Examples of unusual syntax include: (1) *Imperative* followed by a *waw-Imperfect*: 1 Sam 7:5, 12:3, 20:11; 2 Sam 10:12; (2) *Jussive* followed by a *waw-Imperfect*: 1 Sam 2:10, 7:8; (3) *Cohortative* followed by a *waw-Imperfect*: 1 Sam 11:14, 2 Sam 19:27; (4) אַל + *Imperfect*: 1 Sam 12:19, 2 Sam 13:25, 1 Chr 21:13 (// 2 Sam 24:14); (5) לֹא + *Jussive*: 1 Sam 14:36, 2 Sam 18:14; (6) in 1 Sam 20:13, an imperfect (III-*he* verb) parallels a jussive; (7) in 2 Sam 14:17, we find the only imperfect (III-*he* verb) appearing with the particle of politeness, נָא; (8) there is no purpose clause with לְמַעַן + imperfect in Samuel; the construction *waw*-imperfect (purpose clause) after a volitive (main clause) appears almost strictly only in Samuel; (9) after the particle כֹּה, the imperfect expresses a wish, desire, and request 12 times in the book of Samuel/Kings. This use of כֹּה with the imperfect is not common in Hebrew.

expresses a negative wish or desire (and not a command) with a jussive, the speaker addresses someone of higher social status.[198]

2.3.6. Sequences of Verbs with the Jussive

2.3.6.1. Jussive Followed by Jussive

In this type of construction, the relationships between the jussives represent various syntactical functions:

1. *Adverbial function of the first jussive.* The first jussive describes the action of the second jussive. The following examples appear with the verbs קוּם and הָלַךְ as the first verb of the sequence. These two verbs often function as adverbial imperatives,[199] as narrative preterites,[200] as cohortatives,[201] and here, as jussives. The verb הָלַךְ also fulfills this adverbial function in the infinitive absolute.

מִי־הָאִישׁ אֲשֶׁר בָּנָה בַיִת־חָדָשׁ וְלֹא חֲנָכוֹ יֵלֵךְ וְיָשֹׁב לְבֵיתוֹ
Whoever has built a new house and has not dedicated it, *let him return* to his house lest he die in battle (Deut 20:5—also vv. 6, 7, 8)

הָבוּ לָכֶם שְׁלֹשָׁה אֲנָשִׁים לַשָּׁבֶט וְאֶשְׁלָחֵם וְיָקֻמוּ וְיִתְהַלְּכוּ בָאָרֶץ וְיִכְתְּבוּ אוֹתָהּ לְפִי נַחֲלָתָם
Provide three men per tribe so that I may send them out *to walk about* the land and record it according to their inheritance (Josh 18:4)

2. *Purpose.* Purpose clauses generated by sequences of volitives are common to several of the Semitic languages of the northwest corpus.[202] Moran demonstrated it from the EA Canaanite texts of Byblos and developed his rule of "modal congruence" based on this syntactic structure.[203]

וְהָיָה יְהוָה לְדַיָּן וְשָׁפַט בֵּינִי וּבֵינֶךָ וְיֵרֶא וְיָרֵב אֶת־רִיבִי וְיִשְׁפְּטֵנִי מִיָּדֶךָ
May the Lord be judge and rule between you and me, and *may he notice and plead* my cause, *so that he may vindicate* me from your hand (1 Sam 24:16)

198. The first-person jussive is rare in Biblical Hebrew, and whenever it appears in a negative expression, it is always preceded by the particle לֹא. This construction only appears with the following verbs: יָסַף (3×), סוּף (3×), שָׁאַר (1×), רָאָה (2×), נָטָה (2×), חָזָה (1×) and הָיָה (1×).

199. E.g., Gen 13:17, Deut 9:12.

200. E.g., Gen 22:19, 31:21; Judg 13:11.

201. E.g., Gen 35:3, 43:4.

202. Muraoka departs from this widely accepted view and advocates that the sequence "jussive *followed by* jussive" does not produce purpose clauses ("The Alleged Final Function of the Biblical Hebrew Syntagm '*WAW* + a Volitive Verb Form,'" in *Narrative Syntax and the Hebrew Bible: Papers of the Tilburg Conference 1996* [ed. Ellen van Wolde; Leiden: Brill, 1997] 229–41).

203. Moran, "Early Canaanite *yaqtula*," 9.

וְאִם־לְרַמּוֹתַנִי לְצָרַי בְּלֹא חָמָס בְּכַפַּי יֵרֶא אֱלֹהֵי אֲבוֹתֵינוּ וְיוֹכַח
and if you (have come) to betray me to my adversaries, even though I am innocent, (then) *may the God of our fathers notice so that He may pronounce judgement* (1 Chr 12:18)

3. *Synonymous/parallel/hendiadys.* Clauses that refer to the same event:

יְשַׁלֵּם יְהוָה פָּעֳלֵךְ וּתְהִי מַשְׂכֻּרְתֵּךְ שְׁלֵמָה מֵעִם יְהוָה אֱלֹהֵי יִשְׂרָאֵל
May the Lord repay your deeds *and may your reward from the Lord God of Israel be* complete (Ruth 2:12)

וְשָׁאוּל אָמַר אַל־תְּהִי יָדִי בּוֹ וּתְהִי־בוֹ יַד־פְּלִשְׁתִּים
For Saul had said: *Do not let my hand be* against him, *but rather, let the hand of the Philistines be* against him (1 Sam 18:17)

4. *Sequential.* The action of the first jussive must occur before the action of the second jussive. The events are irreversible:

וַיֹּאמֶר אֲרַוְנָה אֶל־דָּוִד יִקַּח וְיַעַל אֲדֹנִי הַמֶּלֶךְ הַטּוֹב בְּעֵינָיו רְאֵה הַבָּקָר לָעֹלָה
Then Araunah said to David: *May my lord the king take and offer up* what seems good in his eyes (2 Sam 24:22)

2.3.6.2. Jussive Followed by Cohortative

In the few passages where this sequence occurs, the functions of the cohortative indicate the following:

1. *Purpose.* This verb sequence conforms to Moran's rule of "modal congruence."[204]

וְיָבֹאוּ אַחֲרֵיהֶם וְאִכָּבְדָה בְּפַרְעֹה וּבְכָל־חֵילוֹ בְּרִכְבּוֹ וּבְפָרָשָׁיו
"So let them come after them *so that I may be glorified* through Pharaoh and through all his mighty men, through his charioteers and through his horsemen" (Exod 14:17)

2. *Protasis of a conditional sentence.* In these cases, the protasis (with cohortative) appears after the apodosis (with jussive).

וַיֹּאמֶר אַל־נָא יִחַר לַאדֹנָי וַאֲדַבֵּרָה אוּלַי יִמָּצְאוּן שָׁם שְׁלֹשִׁים
Then he said: Please, may my Lord not be angry *if I say:* Perhaps thirty can be found there (Gen 18:30)

וַיֹּאמֶר גִּדְעוֹן אֶל־הָאֱלֹהִים אַל־יִחַר אַפְּךָ בִּי וַאֲדַבְּרָה אַךְ הַפָּעַם אֲנַסֶּה נָּא־רַק־הַפַּעַם בַּגִּזָּה
Then Gideon said to God: Let your anger not burn against me *if I say*: Let me try only one more time with a fleece (Judg 6:39)

204. Ibid. Moran uses the term "indicative" in this context to refer to the *yaqtulu* indicative form in which the verb expresses a statement of fact.

3. *Circumstantial.* In such cases, syntax requires that the verb of the circumstantial clause be preceded by another element.

יַעֲבָר־נָא אֲדֹנִי לִפְנֵי עַבְדּוֹ וַאֲנִי אֶתְנָהֲלָה לְאִטִּי

Let my lord please cross over before his servant *since I travel* slowly (Gen 33:14)

2.3.6.3. Jussive Followed by Imperative

Following a jussive, an imperative expresses purpose or result. The events of the two clauses are therefore logically sequential and conform to the rule of "modal congruence":[205]

יֻקַּח־נָא מְעַט־מַיִם וְרַחֲצוּ רַגְלֵיכֶם וְהִשָּׁעֲנוּ תַּחַת הָעֵץ

Let a little water be brought *so that you may wash* your feet *and rest* under the tree (Gen 18:4)

יִתֵּן יְהוָה לָכֶם וּמְצֶאןָ מְנוּחָה אִשָּׁה בֵּית אִישָׁהּ

May the Lord grant you *to find* rest in each one in the household of her husband (Ruth 1:9)

2.3.6.4. Jussives Followed by *weyiqtol*

The sequence of a jussive followed by *weyiqtol* is rare in Biblical Hebrew. When the imperfect (*yiqtol*) functions as a volitive in this sort of verb sequence, it undoubtedly represents a volitive *yiqtol* (< *yaqtula*) rather than an indicative imperfect (< *yaqtulu*; see discussion in §2.5.1). The syntactic relationships between the jussive and the imperfect are as follows:

1. *Synonymous or parallel ideas.* The two clauses refer to the same event:

אַל־יַשִּׁיא לָכֶם חִזְקִיָּהוּ כִּי־לֹא יוּכַל לְהַצִּיל אֶתְכֶם מִיָּדוֹ׃ וְאַל־יַבְטַח אֶתְכֶם חִזְקִיָּהוּ אֶל־יְהוָה

Do not let Hezekiah deceive you because he will not be able to deliver you out of his hand, *neither let him make you trust* in the Lord (2 Kgs 18:29–30—note the imperfect with the negative particle אַל rather than with לֹא; this peculiarity is common to Samuel and Kings)

2. *Disjunction.* The volitive imperfect (*yaqtula*) is preceded by other elements in the clause, which typically happens in disjunctive syntax:

יְהִי־נָא חֹרֶב אֶל־הַגִּזָּה לְבַדָּהּ וְעַל־כָּל־הָאָרֶץ יִהְיֶה־טָּל

Let there please be dryness on the fleece only, *but* upon the ground *let there be* dew (Judg 6:39—disjunctive syntax)

205. Additional examples appear in Gen 19:8, 34; 20:7; 45:18; Exod 3:10, 18:22; Judg 8:24, 19:24; 1 Sam 25:24, 28:22; 2 Sam 2:7, 19:38, 21:3; 1 Kgs 1:12; Ruth 4:11.

2.3.7. Speaker/Listener Relationship

The following points are significant:

(1) The jussive by itself is well distributed between the different social groups.

(2) In the majority of cases where the jussive is followed by the particle נָא, someone of "lower" social status is addressing someone of "higher" status. This strengthens the view that the main use of the particle נָא is for *respect* and *politeness.*

2.3.8. Summary of the Jussive

(1) My study shows that the jussive exhibits much flexibility in the system of modality of Biblical Hebrew. In independent clauses, the jussive expresses one of the following nuances: *desire* or *wish, command, suggestion.*

(2) In *disjunctive* clauses, where the jussive is preceded by another element in the clause, the jussive expresses one of the following nuances: *desire* or *wish, command, suggestion.* The word order of the clause does not affect the nuance of the jussive.

(3) In the context of discourse analysis, the jussive (also the imperative and the cohortative) provides the main line for hortatory discourse.[206]

(4) The jussive with נָא is used mostly when someone of "lower" status addresses one of "higher" status. This construction appears in the following contexts: *pleas of desperation, urgent requests, nonurgent requests, polite petitions, manipulative petitions,* and *strong petitions.*

(5) Two Hebrew verbs commonly used to indicate *motion* are הָלַךְ and קוּם. Although these more often play an *adverbial* role in the imperative than in any other form, they appear occasionally as adverbs in the jussive. The jussive of יָסַף, both in the affirmative and in the negative, is sometimes used *adverbially* to qualify the following conjugated verb with the idea of *repetition.*

(6) In the second person, the negative jussive functions as a negative imperative. The choice between the prohibitive with לֹא and the negative imperative with אַל depends on two elements:

- whether the negative command represents a one-time prohibition related to a specific situation (אַל with jussive) or a prohibition related to future lifestyle (לֹא with imperfect).
- whether the prohibition comes from a "greater" person to a "lesser" person (mostly with לֹא with imperfect) or represents a negative command unrelated to the social dynamics between speaker and listener (אַל with jussive).

206. Longacre, "Discourse Perspective on the Hebrew Verb," 186.

2.3.8.1. Conditional Sentences with Jussives

When jussives introduce the apodosis of a conditional sentence, they are never accompanied by a *waw*.[207] These jussives appear at the head of the clause, immediately following the protasis. This asyndetic feature is also common with the cohortative in conditional sentences.

אִם־אֱלֹהִים הוּא יָרֶב לוֹ כִּי נָתַץ אֶת־מִזְבְּחוֹ
If he is a god, *let him defend* himself, when someone has torn down his altar (Judg 6:31)

וְאִם־אִישׁ אֱלֹהִים אָנִי תֵּרֶד אֵשׁ מִן־הַשָּׁמַיִם וְתֹאכַל אֹתְךָ
And if I am a man of God, *let fire come down* from heaven so that it may consume you (2 Kgs 1:10)

אִם־מָצָאתִי חֵן בְּעֵינֵי הַמֶּלֶךְ וְאִם־עַל־הַמֶּלֶךְ טוֹב לָתֵת אֶת־שְׁאֵלָתִי וְלַעֲשׂוֹת אֶת־
בַּקָּשָׁתִי יָבוֹא הַמֶּלֶךְ וְהָמָן אֶל־הַמִּשְׁתֶּה
And if it seems good to the king to grant my petition and to do my request, *let the king and Haman come* to the feast (Esth 5:8)

2.3.8.2. Sequences with Jussives

(1) When strings of jussives occur, the syntactic relationships between the verbs is one of the following:

- *Adverbial function of the first jussive.* The first jussive qualifies the action of the second jussive.
- *Purpose.* The jussive of the second clause introduces a purpose clause.
- *Synonymous/Parallel.* The two jussives refer to the same event, repeated for the sake of emphasis.
- *Sequentiality.* The actions represented by the jussives must occur in the order in which they are stated.

(2) When a jussive is followed by a cohortative or an imperative, the following syntactic relationship occurs:

- *Purpose.* The clause with the cohortative or imperative expresses purpose.

(3) In some cases, a cohortative introduces the protasis of a conditional sentence and is placed after the apodosis with a jussive.

207. See also 2 Sam 13:26, 2 Kgs 1:12, and 1 Chr 12:18.

(4) When an imperfect with volitive functions (< *yaqtula*) follows a jussive, the two clauses can express *synonymous* ideas. When the imperfect is preceded by other elements in the clause, it functions *disjunctively*.

2.4. The Cohortative

My analysis of the cohortative includes a short section on morphology, followed by a discussion on the various theories regarding the origin of the cohortative. My observations on the functions of the cohortative are derived from two contexts: (1) from sentences in which the cohortative functions independently from other verbs, (2) from sentences in which the cohortative is syntactically related to other verbs in the sentence.

The following constructions and verb sequences were taken into consideration for my study:

Cohortatives		
Cohortatives	*with* נָא	
Cohortative (Adverbial)	*followed by*	Cohortative
Cohortative	*followed by*	Cohortative
Cohortative	*followed by*	Jussive
Cohortative	*followed by*	Imperative
Cohortative	*followed by*	Imperfect
Negative Cohortatives		

In order to determine the existence of social patterns of speech involving cohortatives, I grouped the utterances into the following three categories:

1. from greater to lesser
2. from lesser to greater
3. between individuals of equal social status

2.4.1. Morphology

The Biblical Hebrew volitive of the first person, whether singular or plural, is the cohortative. This prefix conjugation form usually appears with a paragogic ָה appended to the verb. This sufformative does not occur with III-*yod* verbs.[208] When a pronominal suffix is added to the cohortative, the paragogic ָה is lost, making the imperfect and the cohortative morphologically identical.[209]

208. Revell notes that the III-*ʾalep* verbs do not take the ָה affix on first-person modals, but the Hebrew text reveals otherwise: אָבוֹאָה (Gen 29:21, Judg 15:1, 2 Kgs 19:23, Ps 43:4), אֵצְאָה (2 Chr 1:10, Gen 19:8, Judg 19:24; Revell, "The System of the Verb in Standard Biblical Prose," 17). Unfortunately, Joosten follows Revell and states that "third-weak verbs do not distinguish between cohortative and YIQTOL in the first person" (Joosten, *Verbal System of Biblical Hebrew*, 320).

209. Shulman identifies these morphologically indistinguishable cohortatives as "neutral" forms (Shulman, *Use of Modal Verb Forms*, 1).

We find a few rare occurrences of second- and third-person verbs in the prefix conjugation with a paragogic ָה.[210]

2.4.2. Theories on the Origin of the Cohortative

Scholars have proposed two possible origins for the Hebrew cohortative:

1. *Yaqtulan(na)*
2. *Yaqtula*

(1) *From yaqtulan(na).*[211] In my discussion of the "long imperative," I mentioned that some scholars link the origin of the cohortative and the long imperative to the modal form *yaqtulan(na)*. A comparison of the Hebrew cohortative, Ugaritic *yaqtulan(na)*, and Arabic *yaqtulan(na)* reveals a definite connection between these morphemes, both in morphology and syntax.[212] Evidence to support this view is as follows:

When the Hebrew cohortative (and the long imperative) appears with the particle of entreaty נָא, the *nun* includes a *dagesh forte*, an indication that the verb and the particle were originally one morpheme (*yaqtulanna*). Lambdin states that, "by virtue of the existence of junctural doubling, [the cohortative] is reinterpretable as **yaqtula* + *nā*."[213] The separation of the modal particle נָא from the verbal form first appears in Ugaritic, where a word divider separates the verb from the modal ending.[214] In Hebrew, the particle נָא appears as a separate morpheme that can be added to a verb or to another element.[215] When the particle נָא follows a jussive, it never includes a *dagesh forte*.

Although the cohortative occurs mainly in the first person, there is clear evidence of second- and third-person cohortatives with final ָה in the Hebrew

---

210. תָּבוֹאתָה (Deut 33:16); יָחִישָׁה, and תָּבוֹאָה (Isa 5:19); תָּעֻפָה (Job 11:17); יְדַשְּׁנֶה (Ps 20:4).

211. Kaufman, "An Emphatic Plea for Please," 198; Lambdin, "The Junctural Origin," 315–33; Gottlieb, "The Hebrew Particle *nâ*," 130.

212. The EA Canaanite texts provide only one clear example of a modal *yaqtulan(na)* in negative purpose clauses (EA 77.37). Semitic forms with *-nn* endings are often referred to as "energic," but there is no evidence to support this designation. Modal forms with *-nn* ending occur in passages where the speaker expresses modal subjectivity, in many cases, providing a softening rather than an energizing. Regarding the Ugaritic forms with ending *-nn*, Williams states that "there is no discernible difference in meaning between the energic and the forms lacking final /n/" (R. J. Williams, "Energic Verbal Forms in Hebrew," in *Studies on the Ancient Palestinian World* [ed. J. W. Wevers and D. B. Redford; Toronto: University of Toronto Press, 1972] 79). Gordon agrees with Williams and attributes the use of the long form to "stylistic variation" rather than to special meaning (Gordon, *Ugaritic Textbook*, 73 n. 1). Although differences in meaning are often barely distinguishable to today's reader, I advocate that two forms cannot represent the same nuance; they express two levels of modality.

213. Lambdin, "The Junctural Origin," 326.

214. Gottlieb, "The Hebrew Particle *nâ*," 51.

215. E.g., הִנֵּה־נָא, אִם־נָא, אַיֵּה־נָא.

text.[216] The *yaqtulan(na)* of Ugaritic and Arabic appears in the first, second, and third persons and expresses nuances similar to those expressed by the Hebrew cohortative in independent and subordinate clauses.

Ugaritic—1st person

rd . lmlk . amlk . ldrktk . ***a***<u>***t***</u>***bnn***

Descend from the kingship that I may rule, from your dominion *that I may sit* thereon (Gordon, 127.37)

Ugaritic—1st person

iqran *. ilm . nʿmm*

Let me indeed invoke the good gods (Gordon, 52:23)

Ugaritic—3rd person

bḥrb . ***tbqʿnn*** *.* ***bḫṯr . tdrynn*** *. bišt .* ***tšrpnn*** *. brḥm .* ***ṯṭḥnn*** *. bšd .* ***tdrʿnn***

With a sword *she cleaves him,* with a fan *she winnows him,* with fire *she burns him,* with a millstone *she grinds him,* in the field *she sows him* (Gordon, 49 II 31)

Arabic—1st person

lanaʾxuδan *hadaa alγulaʾma* ***falanadhabanna*** *bihi illay malikinaʾ*

Let us take this boy *and bring* him to our king (Ibn-Hish^{a}m, 167)

Arabic—2nd person

lataūdunna *fiy millabinaʾ*

You will return to our religion (Qurʾan, surat ʾibrāhīm, verse 13.14)

Arabic—3rd person

*la****yabaθannahu*** *allahu fa****layuqaṭṭaanna*** *ayadiya*

Let Allah *send him and let him cut* the hands . . . (Ṣaḥīḥ al-Bukhārī, vol. 6, ḥadīth 495)

216. תָּבוֹאתָה (Deut 33:16); יָחִישָׁה and תָּבוֹאָה (Isa 5:19); תָּעֻפָה (Job 11:17); יְדַשְּׁנֶה (Ps 20:4).

In pause, the Arabic *yaqtulan* loses its final *nun* and ends with a long *-a*. This final long vowel is reflected in the ending of the Hebrew cohortative.

(2) *From yaqtula.*[217] In his article "Early Canaanite *yaqtula,*" Moran examines the prefix conjugations that display an *-a* ending (*yaqtula*) in the EA Canaanite texts from Byblos, a form that is foreign to Akkadian dialects in general.[218] Moran compares the functions of this modal form with the functions of the Hebrew cohortative and concludes that the *yaqtula* of EA Canaanite is at the origin of the Hebrew cohortative, based on the similarity of usages between the two morphemes.[219] Moran shows that, in *independent clauses*, the *yaqtula* indicates a wish, a request, or a command and fulfills syntactic functions similar to those fulfilled by the Biblical Hebrew cohortative. In *dependent clauses*, the EA Canaanite *yaqtula* often expresses purpose or result, as does the Hebrew cohortative, especially when following another volitive such as an imperative, a jussive, or another cohortative. In conditional sentences, the Canaanite *yaqtula* and the Hebrew cohortative function similarly, in both the protasis and the apodosis.

Blau also advocates that the Hebrew cohortative is directly related to *yaqtula* and adds that, based on the similarities of functions between the *yaqtula* and the Hebrew cohortative, "the possibility of deriving the Hebrew cohortative from the energic [*yaqtulanna*] is out of the question."[220] Korchin supports Blau's view and points to first-person (cohortative) examples in the Joseph narrative (e.g., Gen 37:17, 42:34, 43:8, 45:28, 46:30–31, 50:5), dismissing the possibility that these examples may represent a Semitic *yaqtulan(na)* modal form.[221]

---

217. Moran, "Early Canaanite *yaqtula*," 1–19; idem, "The Hebrew Language in Its Northwest Semitic Background," in *The Bible and the Ancient Near East* (ed. G. E. Wright; Winona Lake, IN: Eisenbrauns, 1979) 64; Joüon, *A Grammar of Biblical Hebrew*, 373–74; Blau, "Studies in Hebrew Verb Formation," 133–58; Rainey, "Ancient Hebrew Prefix Conjugation," 8; idem, "Further Remarks on the Hebrew Verbal System," *HS* 29 (1988) 36; Huehnergard, "The Early Hebrew Prefix-Conjugations," 22–23; Waltke and O'Connor, *Introduction to Biblical Hebrew Syntax,* 564, 568.

218. Moran, "Early Canaanite *yaqtula.*" 1–19.

219. Ibid., 19.

220. Blau, "Studies in Hebrew Verb Formation," 135, 140; R. Hasselbach, "The Verbal Endings *-u* and *-a*: A Note on Their Functional Derivation," in *Language and Nature: Papers Presented to John Huehnergard on the Occasion of His 60th Birthday* (ed. R. Hasselbach and Naʿama Pat-El; Studies in Ancient Oriental Civilization 67; Chicago: University of Chicago Press) 130.

221. Korchin, *Markedness in Canaanite and Hebrew Verbs*, 308–16; idem, "Grammaticalization and the Biblical Hebrew Pseudo-Cohortative," in *Language and Nature: Papers Presented to John Huehnergard on the Occasion of His 60th Birthday* (ed. R. Hasselbach and Naʿama Pat-El; Studies in Ancient Oriental Civilization 67; Chicago: University of Chicago Press. 2012) 278–79.

Rainey states that, in Hebrew, "the volitive (**yaqtula*) survives chiefly as the first person injunctive"[222] and that cohortatives with *nun* in the accusative suffix probably do not reflect an injunctive energic with *-an(na)* ending but are simply cases of "later attraction." These verb forms with final long *-a* would have attracted to themselves "heavier forms of the accusative suffixes."[223]

Huehnergard takes issue with Rainey's theory of "later attraction," stating that "it is not certain that, synchronically, *-énnu* was really 'heavier' than *-éhu*."[224] Huehnergard attributes the presence of the *nun* in the object suffix *-ennu* on cohortatives to the ancient modal form *yaqtulanna* yet states that the cohortative is a reflex of the Canaanite volitive *yaqtula* and not of the modal form *yaqtulanna.*[225] According to Huehnergard, when the cohortative with third-person masculine-singular pronominal suffix appears as *ʾeqtlénnu*, it reflects the modal *yaqtulanna*, but when it appears with *waw*-consecutive and third-person masculine-singular pronominal suffix as *wa-ʾeqtléhu*, it reflects the *yaqtula.*[226]

2.4.2.1. Observations

As mentioned above, we see a closer connection between the morphology and syntax of the Hebrew cohortative and that of the modal *yaqtulan(na)* than we see between the cohortative and the Canaanite *yaqtula*. In my discussion on the Hebrew *yiqtol*, I will demonstrate that the Hebrew imperfect *yiqtol* embodies two prefix conjugations: (1) the indicative *yaqtulu*, and (2) the volitive *yaqtula*. Due to the loss of a final short vowel, both forms have become morphologically identical. In contexts in which an indicative is expected, the imperfect represents the *yaqtulu*, and in contexts in which a volitive is expected, the imperfect represents the volitive *yaqtula*. The Canaanite volitive *yaqtula* is therefore present in Hebrew in the *yiqtol* imperfect and not in the cohortative.

2.4.3. Functions of the Cohortative

The Hebrew cohortative functions as a "direct" volitive in independent clauses and as an "indirect" volitive in dependent clauses.[227] According to Joosten, the cohortative expresses "the intention to act when the speaker is able (Exod 3:3), but a request for help or permission when he is not (Num 20:7)"[228]

---

222. Rainey, "Ancient Hebrew Prefix Conjugation," 13; Waltke and O'Connor, *Introduction to Biblical Hebrew Syntax*, 568.

223. Rainey, "Ancient Hebrew Prefix Conjugation," 12.

224. Huehnergard, "The Early Hebrew Prefix-Conjugations," 22.

225. Ibid., 23.

226. Elizabeth Robar, "Nunation," in *Encyclopedia of Hebrew Language and Linguistics* (ed. Geoffrey Khan; Leiden: Brill, 2013) 2:909.

227. Hasselbach, 2012: 128.

228. Joosten, *Verbal System of Biblical Hebrew*, 121.

and that the cohortative "indicates in principle that the speaker wants to engage in the process expressed by the verb."[229] In independent clauses, it expresses the following nuances:

1. *Wish* and *Desire*. In independent clauses, the cohortative often expresses the *wishes* of the speaker. This idea may be indicated by "I (we) want to/would like to," "let me (us)/allow me (us) to" or, as Kaufman suggests, "I (we) think it may be a good idea to."[230]

וַיֹּאמְרוּ אֵלָיו בְּנֵי־יִשְׂרָאֵל בַּמְסִלָּה נַעֲלֶה וְאִם־מֵימֶיךָ נִשְׁתֶּה אֲנִי וּמִקְנַי וְנָתַתִּי מִכְרָם
The Israelites said to him: *We would like to go up* on your highways. Now if we drink your water, I and my animals, we will pay for it (Num 20:19)

כִּי־יַרְחִיב יְהוָה אֱלֹהֶיךָ אֶת־גְּבוּלְךָ כַּאֲשֶׁר דִּבֶּר־לָךְ וְאָמַרְתָּ אֹכְלָה בָשָׂר
When the Lord your God enlarges your border, just as he spoke to you, and you say: *I want to eat* meat (Deut 12:20)

אָשִׂימָה עָלַי מֶלֶךְ כְּכָל־הַגּוֹיִם אֲשֶׁר סְבִיבֹתָי
I would like to set a king over me like all the nations which are around me (Deut 17:14)

2. *Declaration*. In some instances, the desire of the speaker is expressed in a *declarative/determinative* sense. This nuance is common when the cohortative occurs in the apodosis of conditional clauses. In most cases where the *apodosis* of a conditional clause is introduced by a cohortative, the construction is asyndetic, without *waw* and immediately follows the protasis.[231]

אִם־יֶשְׁךָ מְשַׁלֵּחַ אֶת־אָחִינוּ אִתָּנוּ נֵרְדָה וְנִשְׁבְּרָה לְךָ אֹכֶל
If you send our brother with us, *then we will go down* in order to obtain grain for you to eat (Gen 43:4)

וְעַתָּה אִם־רַע בְּעֵינֶיךָ אָשׁוּבָה לִּי
Now if it does not please you, *I will go back* (Num 22:34)

In only a few cases does the cohortative introduce the apodosis with a *waw*.

אִם־הַשְּׂמֹאל וְאֵימִנָה וְאִם־הַיָּמִין וְאַשְׂמְאִילָה
If you go to the left, *then I will go to the right;* and if you go to the right, *then I will go to the left* (Gen 13:9)

229. Ibid., 321.
230. Kaufman, "An Emphatic Plea for Please," 198.
231. See also Gen 18:21; 30:31; 1 Sam 20:29; 2 Chr 20:9.

וְאִם־מְעָט וְאֹסִפָה לְּךָ כָּהֵנָּה וְכָהֵנָּה

And if it is too little, *then I will give* to you such and such things (2 Sam 12:8)

3. *Suggestion.* The cohortative is also found in contexts where the speaker(s) *suggests* a certain course of action.

שָׁמַעְתִּי אֹמְרִים נֵלְכָה דֹּתָיְנָה

I have heard them say: *Let us go* to Dothan (Gen 37:17)

נֵלְכָה וְנַעַבְדָה אֱלֹהִים אֲחֵרִים אֲשֶׁר לֹא־יְדַעְתֶּם

Let us follow after other gods which you have not known *and let us serve* them (Deut 13:14)

4. *Deliberative.* In a few cases, the cohortative expresses *deliberation*, when the individual speaking is debating within himself/herself whether or not to act and pursue a certain course of action.[232] In some of these passages, the cohortative is followed by the particle נָא; the use of this volitive with such a particle seems to indicate that the construction cannot represent the idea of politeness, since one would not address him/herself with such an emphasis.

אֵרְדָה־נָּא וְאֶרְאֶה הַכְּצַעֲקָתָהּ הַבָּאָה אֵלַי עָשׂוּ כָּלָה וְאִם־לֹא אֵדָעָה

Let me go down now and see if they have done everything according to the outcry that has come to me; if not, then I will know (Gen 18:21)

כִּי־אָמַר אֲכַפְּרָה פָנָיו בַּמִּנְחָה הַהֹלֶכֶת לְפָנָי וְאַחֲרֵי־כֵן אֶרְאֶה פָנָיו

For he thought: *I will (try to)* appease him with the present which goes before me; then I will see his reaction (Gen 32:21)

5. *Request for permission.* The cohortative is also used in contexts where one asks for *permission*.

וַיִּפְקֹד שִׁמְשׁוֹן אֶת־אִשְׁתּוֹ בִּגְדִי עִזִּים וַיֹּאמֶר אָבֹאָה אֶל־אִשְׁתִּי הֶחָדְרָה

Samson went to visit his wife bringing a kid; he said: *Let me go into* the bedroom with my wife (Judg 15:1)

וְעַתָּה אִם־מָצָאתִי חֵן בְּעֵינֶיךָ אִמָּלְטָה נָּא וְאֶרְאֶה אֶת־אֶחָי

So now, if I have found favor in your eyes, *let me go and see* my brothers (1 Sam 20:29)

232. Shulman, "The Particle נָא in Biblical Hebrew Prose," 77–78. Christiansen goes a step further and states that "the grammatical function of *na'* extends beyond that of the polite/honorific to that of an exhortation, or propositive, particle. The particle functions to signal that the speaker is *proposing* a course of action with which the addressee may or may not agree or choose to accommodate" (Christiansen, "Linguistic Analysis of the Biblical Hebrew Particle *na'*," 385, 391).

2.4.4. Cohortative with נָא

The particle נָא often accompanies the cohortative. Passages where this construction occurs express nuances similar to those expressed by a cohortative without נָא. As explained above, the particle נָא adds a certain degree of modality not easily represented in the translation.

1. *Polite request for permission.* The speaker expresses respect for the listener:

אֵלְכָה נָּא וְאָשׁוּבָה אֶל־אַחַי אֲשֶׁר־בְּמִצְרַיִם
Please let me go so that I may return to my brothers who are in Egypt (Exod 4:18)

נַעְבְּרָה־נָּא בְאַרְצֶךָ
Please, let us cross over through your land (Num 20:17)

אָרוּצָה נָּא וַאֲבַשְּׂרָה אֶת־הַמֶּלֶךְ כִּי־שְׁפָטוֹ יְהוָה מִיַּד אֹיְבָיו
Please let me run off, so that I may announce to the king that the Lord has vindicated him from the hand of his enemies (2 Sam 18:19)

2. *Plea of desperation.* The situation includes matters of life and death:

וַיֹּאמַר אַל־נָא אַחַי תָּרֵעוּ׃ הִנֵּה־נָא לִי שְׁתֵּי בָנוֹת אֲשֶׁר לֹא־יָדְעוּ אִישׁ אוֹצִיאָה־נָּא אֶתְהֶן אֲלֵיכֶם וַעֲשׂוּ לָהֶן כַּטּוֹב בְּעֵינֵיכֶם
Then they said: Please do no evil to my brothers. Look, I have two daughters who have never known a man. *Please, let me bring them out* to you and do to them according to what pleases you (Gen 19:7–8)

וַיֹּאמֶר דָּוִד אֶל־גָּד צַר־לִי מְאֹד נִפְּלָה־נָּא בְיַד־יְהוָה כִּי־רַבִּים רַחֲמָיו וּבְיַד־אָדָם אַל־אֶפֹּלָה
David said to Gad: I am extremely distressed. *Please let us fall* into the hands of the Lord for his mercies are great, but *do not let me fall* into the hand of man (2 Sam 24:14, WTT)

3. *Strong statement* or *declaration.* A proposition is made either by one of higher social status addressing one of lower status or vice versa:

וַיָּקָם הַמֶּלֶךְ לַיְלָה וַיֹּאמֶר אֶל־עֲבָדָיו אַגִּידָה־נָּא לָכֶם אֵת אֲשֶׁר־עָשׂוּ לָנוּ
The king arose at night and said to his servants: *Let me tell* you what the Arameans have done to us (2 Kgs 7:12)

4. *Polite suggestion.* The speaker *suggests* a change in the established course of action:

וְגַם־אֲנִי אַחַי וּנְעָרַי נֹשִׁים בָּהֶם כֶּסֶף וְדָגָן נַעַזְבָה־נָּא אֶת־הַמַּשָּׁא הַזֶּה

Even I, my brothers and my young men are exacting silver and grain from them; *please, let us abandon* this exacting of money (Neh 5:10)

5. *Deliberative.* The speaker is thinking about an action he/she wishes to perform himself/herself:

וַתֹּאמֶר שִׁפְחָתְךָ אֲדַבְּרָה־נָּא אֶל־הַמֶּלֶךְ אוּלַי יַעֲשֶׂה הַמֶּלֶךְ אֶת־דְּבַר אֲמָתוֹ
Your handmaiden said: *Let me (I should) speak* to the king; perhaps the king will grant the request of his handmaid (2 Sam 14:15)

וַיֹּאמֶר דָּוִיד שְׁלֹמֹה בְנִי נַעַר וָרָךְ וְהַבַּיִת לִבְנוֹת לַיהוָה לְהַגְדִּיל לְמַעְלָה לְשֵׁם
וּלְתִפְאֶרֶת לְכָל־הָאֲרָצוֹת אָכִינָה נָּא לוֹ
David said (thought): Solomon, my son, is young and tender, and the house to be built for the Lord must be magnificent to win fame and honor for all the lands; *let me (it would be a good idea for me to) prepare* it for him (1 Chr 22:5)

This last category shows an interesting feature of the cohortative with נָא whereby someone addresses himself/herself using this type of construction. These passages obviously exclude the idea of politeness but seem to carry the idea of deliberation: the speaker is thinking about performing a certain action. Kaufman's translation 'I think it would be a good idea for . . .' is fitting in such contexts.[233] Shulman interprets these sorts of passages as follows:

> In soliloquy passages the narrator presents the speaker in self-reflection. The speaker formulates his thoughts in his own words, expressing his desire to act. . . . [T]he speaker is portrayed as debating with himself whether or not to act. נָא is used when the speaker is still contemplating his course of action, possibly trying to persuade himself to act.[234]

The cohortative with נָא is never preceded by an adverbial imperative (e.g., הָבָה, קוּמָה, לְכָה). The cohortative is never followed by the particle נָא in passages where it functions as an indirect volitive. In the majority of cases where a plural cohortative appears with נָא, the speaker is not expected to participate in the fulfillment of the event. The particle נָא with the cohortative, imperative, or jussive never appears in the first 11 chapters of Genesis or in the legal portions of Leviticus and Deuteronomy but appears often in historical narratives. The absence of נָא in the first 11 chapters of Genesis is one of the elements that distinguishes the two independent parts of the book. The two sections have different themes and purposes: (1) primeval history in a Mesopotamian context (chaps. 1–11); and (2) patriarchal history in a western Levant context, mostly

233. Kaufman, "An Emphatic Plea for Please," 198.
234. Shulman, "The Particle נָא in Biblical Hebrew Prose," 77–78.

through narrative (chaps. 12–50). The legal material of Leviticus and Deuteronomy contains God's instructions for day-to-day living and leaves little room for "politeness," "requests," "encouragement," and other such types of modality.

2.4.4.1. Social Dynamics

In the majority of cases when the cohortative is followed by the particle נָא, someone of lower social status is addressing someone of higher social status.

2.4.5. Negative Cohortative

The negative cohortative is rare in Biblical Hebrew and is usually formed with the particle אַל. Although it is unusual, we find one occurrence of לֹא with the cohortative in 1 Sam 14:36. As will be discussed below in §2.5, "Additional Verbs with Modal Functions: The Imperfect," there is a possibility that a particular scribal tradition is reflected in Samuel. In many cases in Samuel, the negative particles are used with a form of the prefix conjugation other than what is normally expected. In addition, the imperfect often plays the role of an injunctive. Contexts where negative cohortatives appear involve the following nuances:

1. *Negative desire* or *wish*[235]

אִם־מָצָאתִי חֵן בְּעֵינֶיךָ וְאַל־אֶרְאֶה בְּרָעָתִי
If I have found favor in your eyes, *do not let me look* upon my misery (Num 11:15)

נִפְּלָה־נָּא בְיַד־יְהוָה כִּי־רַבִּים רַחֲמָיו וּבְיַד־אָדָם אַל־אֶפֹּלָה
Let me please fall into the hands of the Lord because great is his compassion, but *do not let me fall* into the hands of man (2 Sam 24:14)

2. *Negative declaration* or *strong statement*

וַיֹּאמֶר יוֹאָב לֹא־כֵן אֹחִילָה לְפָנֶיךָ
Joab said: *I will not wait* for you this way (2 Sam 18:14—note the unusual use of the negative particle אל with a cohortative)

2.4.6. Sequences of Verbs with the Cohortative

2.4.6.1. Cohortative (Adverbial) Followed by Cohortative

Two of the most common verbs of motion— הָלַךְ and קוּם—function adverbially, not only in sequences of imperatives and sequences of jussives, but

235. Both examples presented here are morphologically identical with first-person imperfects, but the presence of the negative particle אַל indicates that the verb is a volitive rather than an indicative.

also in sequences with cohortatives. These are the only two verbs that fulfill adverbial functions as cohortatives. These two verbs are found in the singular and plural forms and always agree in number with the second cohortative of the sequence. This is not always the case in passages where the imperatives of הָלַךְ and קוּם function adverbially before an imperative or before a cohortative. In cases of this sort, the imperative does not always agree in number with the second verb of the sequence. Whenever the cohortative of the verb הָלַךְ functions adverbially, it appears in syndetic constructions with *waw* or in asyndetic constructions without a connecting *waw*.

1. Cohortative *followed by* Cohortative
2. Cohortative *followed by* *waw*-Cohortative

As mentioned in §2.2.1.2, "Imperative as Adverb," in an economic language such as Hebrew, two constructions should express two different ideas; however, as we have discussed above, the difference in nuance is not always evident. The following examples show that the two constructions can carry similar meaning:

אֵלְכָה נָּא וְאָשׁוּבָה אֶל־אַחַי אֲשֶׁר־בְּמִצְרַיִם
Please *let me return* to my brothers who are in Egypt (Exod 4:18—syndetic)

נֵלְכָה וְנַעַבְדָה אֱלֹהִים אֲחֵרִים אֲשֶׁר לֹא יָדַעְתָּ
Let us go serve other gods that you did not know (Deut 13:7—syndetic)

versus:

עַל־כֵּן הֵם צֹעֲקִים לֵאמֹר נֵלְכָה נִזְבְּחָה לֵאלֹהֵינוּ
Therefore they cry out: *Let us go sacrifice* to our God (Exod 5:8—asyndetic)

עַל־כֵּן אַתֶּם אֹמְרִים נֵלְכָה נִזְבְּחָה לַיהוָה
Therefore you say: *Let us go sacrifice* to the Lord (Exod 5:17—asyndetic)

In the case of the verb קוּם, the first cohortative is always connected to the second cohortative by a *waw*.

וְנָקוּמָה וְנַעֲלֶה בֵּית־אֵל וְאֶעֱשֶׂה־שָּׁם מִזְבֵּחַ
Let us go up to Bethel so that I may build an altar there (Gen 35:3)

וַיֹּאמֶר אַבְנֵר אֶל־דָּוִד אָקוּמָה וְאֵלֵכָה וְאֶקְבְּצָה אֶל־אֲדֹנִי הַמֶּלֶךְ אֶת־כָּל־יִשְׂרָאֵל
Abner said to David: *Let me go* and gather to my lord the king, all the Israelites (2 Sam 3:21)

2.4.6.2. Cohortative Followed by Cohortative

Two cohortatives may be syntactically related in a number of ways.

1. *Sequentiality.* A sequence of cohortatives can express *sequentiality*, meaning that the action of the first cohortative takes place before the action of the second cohortative.

הָבָה נִלְבְּנָה לְבֵנִים וְנִשְׂרְפָה לִשְׂרֵפָה
Let us make bricks and then burn them thoroughly (Gen 11:3)

אֶשְּׁקָה־נָּא לְאָבִי וּלְאִמִּי וְאֵלְכָה אַחֲרֶיךָ
Let me please go kiss my father and my mother, *then I will follow* you (1 Kgs 19:20)

2. *Purpose/result.* This type of sentence follows the rule of "modal congruence":

לְכָה נַשְׁקֶה אֶת־אָבִינוּ יַיִן וְנִשְׁכְּבָה עִמּוֹ וּנְחַיֶּה מֵאָבִינוּ זָרַע
Let us give our father some wine *and lie* with him *so that we may preserve* his posterity (Gen 19:32)

וְעַתָּה נֵלְכָה־נָּא דֶּרֶךְ שְׁלֹשֶׁת יָמִים בַּמִּדְבָּר וְנִזְבְּחָה לַיהוָה אֱלֹהֵינוּ
Let us now go on a three days hike into the desert *in order to offer* sacrifice to the Lord (Exod 3:18)

אֶבְחֲרָה נָּא שְׁנֵים־עָשָׂר אֶלֶף אִישׁ וְאָקוּמָה וְאֶרְדְּפָה אַחֲרֵי־דָוִד הַלָּיְלָה
Let me please choose twelve thousand men *so that I may pursue* David tonight (2 Sam 17:1)

3. *Disjunction*: In disjunctive syntax, the verb is normally preceded by one or more elements, but in the following passage, the cohortative appears at the head of the clause in a *circumstantial* clause.

וַיֹּאמֶר נִסְעָה וְנֵלֵכָה וְאֵלְכָה לְנֶגְדֶּךָ
So he said: *Let us go* on our journey, with me *going* before you (Gen 33:12)

2.4.6.3. Cohortative Followed by Jussive

As expected in this type of sequence, the jussive introduces a *purpose* clause and follows the rule of "modal congruence."

אַךְ נֵאוֹתָה לָהֶם וְיֵשְׁבוּ אִתָּנוּ
Now, *let us agree* with them *so that they may live* with us (Gen 34:23)

אִמָּלְטָה נָּא שָׁמָּה הֲלֹא מִצְעָר הִוא וּתְחִי נַפְשִׁי
Let me please flee there (is it not a small one) *so that my life be spared* (Gen 19:20—this could also be interpreted as a result clause)

נִשְׁלְחָה אֲנָשִׁים לְפָנֵינוּ וְיַחְפְּרוּ־לָנוּ אֶת־הָאָרֶץ
Let us send men before us *to spy out* the land *and bring us back* a report (Deut 1:22)

נִקְחָה אֵלֵינוּ מִשִּׁלֹה אֶת־אֲרוֹן בְּרִית יְהוָה וְיָבֹא בְקִרְבֵּנוּ וְיֹשִׁעֵנוּ מִכַּף אֹיְבֵינוּ
Let us take the ark of the covenant of the Lord from Shiloh *so that it may be* in our midst *and save* us from the hand of the our enemies (1 Sam 4:3)

וַיֹּאמֶר שָׁאוּל אֶתְּנֶנָּה לּוֹ וּתְהִי־לוֹ לְמוֹקֵשׁ
Saul thought: *Let me give* her to him *that she may become* a snare to him (1 Sam 18:21)

2.4.6.4. Cohortative Followed by Imperative

As expected, this sequence of volitives produces purpose or result clauses:[236]

וְאֶעֶשְׂךָ לְגוֹי גָּדוֹל וַאֲבָרֶכְךָ וַאֲגַדְּלָה שְׁמֶךָ וֶהְיֵה בְּרָכָה
And I wish to make you into a great nation and to bless you, and to make your name great s*o that you may be* a blessing (Gen 12:2)

הִנֵּה־נָא לִי שְׁתֵּי בָנוֹת אֲשֶׁר לֹא־יָדְעוּ אִישׁ אוֹצִיאָה־נָּא אֶתְהֶן אֲלֵיכֶם וַעֲשׂוּ לָהֶן כַּטּוֹב בְּעֵינֵיכֶם רַק לָאֲנָשִׁים הָאֵל אַל־תַּעֲשׂוּ דָבָר
Look! I have two daughters who have never been with a man. Let me bring them out to you *that you may do* to them according to what seems good to you; but do not do a thing to the men of God (Gen 19:8)

וְעַתָּה לְכָה וְאֶשְׁלָחֲךָ אֶל־פַּרְעֹה וְהוֹצֵא אֶת־עַמִּי בְנֵי־יִשְׂרָאֵל מִמִּצְרָיִם
Now, let me send you to Pharaoh *that you may bring out* my people, the Israelites, from Egypt (Exod 3:10)

וַיֹּאמֶר אֲלֵהֶם גִּדְעוֹן אֶשְׁאֲלָה מִכֶּם שְׁאֵלָה וּתְנוּ־לִי אִישׁ נֶזֶם שְׁלָלוֹ
Then Gideon said to them: Let me ask a request, *that you give* to me, each one of you, the earring of his spoil (Judg 8:24)

236. For a discussion on the sequence of volitives in purpose/result clauses in Genesis 12, see Patrick Miller, "Syntax and Theology in Genesis XII 3a," *VT* 34 (1984) 473; Joel S. Baden, "The Morpho-Syntax of Genesis 12:1–3: Translation and Interpretation," *CBQ* 72 (2010) 223–37.

2.4.7. Speaker/Listener Relationship

As with the jussive, the distribution of the cohortative is well balanced between the three groups, except when the cohortative and the jussive appear with the particle נָא. As expected, the cohortative with נָא appears more often when someone of lower social status is addressing a person of higher status, and in most cases (60% of the time), it carries the idea of *politeness*.

2.4.8. Summary Regarding the Cohortatives

(1) According to my study, the cohortative is directly related (morphologically and syntactically) to the modal form *yaqtulan(na)*. The final *-(n)na* became a separate particle, leaving the Hebrew volitive with a long final *-a*, as is found on the Arabic *yaqtulan* in pause.

(2) The cohortative expresses a variety of nuances: *desires* or *wishes, declarations* (especially in the apodosis of conditional sentences), *suggestions, deliberations*, and *requests for permission*.

(3) The cohortative with נָא expresses nuances similar to those expressed by the cohortative without נָא, with an additional modal element indicating "politeness." Where the speaker addresses himself with the particle נָא, the idea is not that of politeness but of "self-encouragement." In such cases, the speaker considers performing a certain action, and through the process of deliberation, he/she proceeds with the act.

(4) In the context of discourse analysis, the cohortative (with the imperative and jussive) provides the main line for hortatory discourse.[237]

(5) When the cohortative forms of הָלַךְ and קוּם appear immediately before another cohortative, they function as adverbs of manner, indicating *motion*. The cohortative of הָלַךְ appears with and without a connecting *waw*, while the cohortative of קוּם is never connected to the following cohortative by a *waw*. The distinction between the two constructions (with connecting *waw*, without connecting *waw*) is hard to discern.

2.4.8.1. Sequences with Cohortatives

(1) Where strings of cohortatives occur, the syntactic relationship is one of the following:

- *Sequentiality.* The actions stated by the cohortatives must occur in the order in which they are stated.
- *Purpose/Result.* One of the cohortatives other than the first one in the string introduces a purpose clause.

(2) When a cohortative is syntactically related to a following jussive or imperative, the jussive and the imperative introduce a *purpose* clause.

237. Longacre, "Discourse Perspective on the Hebrew Verb," 186.

2.4.8.2. Cohortatives in Conditional Sentences

(1) In most cases when a cohortative introduces the apodosis of a conditional sentence, the cohortative appears at the head of the clause without a preceding *waw*. This is also the case with the imperative and jussive in the apodosis of conditional sentences.

(2) When the protasis and apodosis are connected by a *waw*, the two clauses express contrasting information (e.g., Gen 13:9–"right" versus "left"; 2 Sam 12:8–"little" versus "much").

(3) In conditional sentences, the cohortative expresses a *declarative* statement.

2.5. Additional Verbs with Modal Functions

In the following sections, we will examine the *yiqtol*, *weyiqtol*, *qatal*, *weqatal*, and infinitive absolute, and we will determine their level of interaction in the system of modality in Classical Hebrew. As stated by Joosten, "[I]n practically all types of utterances normally associated with the volitives—wishes, commands, requests—YIQTOL (and WEQATAL) may be found as well."[238] As noted by scholars, the volitives are linked to immediate requests, while the *qatal, weqatal, yiqtol, weyiqtol*, and infinitive absolute with modal functions point to an indefinite future event.[239]

2.5.1. *Yiqtol, weyiqtol*

Scholars have long noted that the *yiqtol* and *weyiqtol* regularly assume the functions of volitives. In his *Treatise on the Use of the Tenses in Hebrew*, S. R. Driver lumps the *yiqtol* with simple *waw* together with the jussive and cohortative and points to the preceding verbs in the discourse (volitives) to determine that the *weyiqtol* belongs to the category of volitives.[240] Blau states unequivocally that "a *yqtl* form connected by *we* to a preceding imperative/jussive, becomes assimilated to the jussive mood (by a sort of *consecutio modorum*), thus shifting into the cohortative in the first person, and into the jussive otherwise (insofar as it can be distinguished morphologically from ordinary *yqtl*)."[241]

238. Joosten, *Verbal System of Biblical Hebrew*, 316; Galia Hatav, "The Deictic Nature of the Directives in Biblical Hebrew," *Studies in Language* 30 (2006) 733–75; idem, *The Semantics of Aspect and Modality: Evidence from English and Biblical Hebrew* (Studies in Language Companion Series 34; Amsterdam: John Benjamins); Andrason, "The Panchronic *Yiqtol*: Functionally Consistent and Cognitively Plausible"; idem, "An Optative Indicative? A Real Factual Past? Toward A Cognitive-Typological Approach to the Precative Qatal," *JHS* 13 (2013).

239. Hatav, "The Deictic Nature of the Directives in Biblical Hebrew," 735; Shulman, *The Use of Modal Verb Forms in Biblical Hebrew Prose*; idem, "Imperative and Second Person Indicative Forms in Biblical Hebrew Prose," *HS* 42 (2001) 271–87.

240. S. R. Driver, *Treatise on the Use of the Tenses in Hebrew*, 64.

241. Blau, *Grammar of Biblical Hebrew*, 87.

Lambdin speaks of one form—the *yiqtol* imperfect—that "may be used in an indirect imperative sense in all persons" in sequence with volitives.[242] In other words, in his view, only a verbal sequence with a *weyiqtol* in a purpose or result clause distinguishes the volitive *yiqtol* from the indicative *yiqtol* (imperfect). For Waltke and O'Connor, the *weyiqtol* after a volitive expresses the consequence of a previous action rather than a purpose or result.[243]

In his analysis of the *weyiqtol*, J. S. Baden states that, since the *weyiqtol* is "so uncommon that it does not fit into the standard verbal system, it must be associated with a specific meaning or usage."[244] He concludes that this specific meaning can only be linked to purpose and result in verbal sequences when a volitive is followed by *weyiqtol*. Joosten takes issue with Baden's conclusions and proposes that the *weyiqtol* belongs to the category of volitives and is intended to express consequence and subordination. According to Joosten, "[T]he nature and degree of subordination are determined by contextual factors. The meaning of the first verb plays a role, as does the meaning of the second verb."[245] Joosten points out that the *weyiqtol* seems to lose its peculiar function "in Late Biblical Hebrew [LBH] and Qumran Hebrew, and disappears completely in Mishnaic Hebrew."[246] Joosten adds that "cases where a YIQTOL form occurs instead of an expected volitive, or vice versa, are probably attributable to the fact that the Hebrew verbal system is undergoing a transition: the distinction between volitive forms and YIQTOL is slowly eroding."[247] Unfortunately, Baden and Joosten limited their research to the biblical and post-biblical Hebrew corpora and, consequently, any external evidence that could have pointed to the origin of the *weyiqtol* volitive (e.g., EA *yaqtula*) was left untouched. Had Baden and Joosten (and others) ventured outside the Biblical Hebrew text, they could have discovered a Semitic volitive equivalent to the *weyiqtol* in the EA Canaanite *yaqtula*.

Hatav proposes that the *weyiqtol* is linked to the jussive or cohortative and not to the indicative *yiqtol* (< *yaqtulu*).[248] She supports her argument by pointing to the facts that (1) the *weyiqtol* appears strictly in direct speech, and (2) most of these *weyiqtol* in direct speech are morphologically identical to the jussive and cohortative.[249] According to Andrason, the *yiqtol* can express intention and desire from the standpoint of the speaker and "provides all ranges of the optative-injunctive values: when the action is directed to the 2nd persons

242. Lambdin, *Introduction to Biblical Hebrew*, 118.
243. Waltke and O'Connor, *Introduction*, 562–63.
244. J. S. Baden, "The *weyiqtol* and the Volitive Sequence," *VT* 58 (2008) 152.
245. J. Joosten, "Short Note: A Note on *weyiqtol* and Volitive Sequences," *VT* 59 (2009) 497.
246. Ibid., 498.
247. Idem, *Verbal System of Biblical Hebrew*, 314.
248. Hatav, "The Deictic Nature of the Directives in Biblical Hebrew," 771.
249. Ibid.

(both singular and plural), the gram functions as an imperative or a prohibitive, while in the case of the first and third persons, the construction corresponds respectively to the jussive and the cohortative."[250] It functions as a "prototypical modally tinted future"[251] and often reflects the modal-optative functions of the cohortative, imperative, and jussive.

Based on his comprehensive study of the panchronic *yiqtol*, Andrason identifies the following functions of the *yiqtol* and proposes the paradigm that follows for the development of the verb form from Proto-Semitic (PS) **yaqattal* to Central Semitic (CS) *yaqtulu* and finally to Biblical Hebrew (BH) *yiqtol*:[252]

Functions:

1. Principal and dependent clauses (also subordinated)
    - root possibility
    - epistemic possibility
    - permission
    - obligation
    - deliberation
    - volitional-optative: intention-desire; injunctive; prohibitive
    - modal future (modal prospectivity)
2. Dependent clauses (including subordinated [see above])
    - finality (purpose): positive and negative
3. Conditional phrases
    - real (nuances of uncertainty)
    - (infrequently) unreal or counterfactual

See the Panchronic Model of the Biblical Hebrew *yiqtol* (fig. 2.1). In Andrason's view, the uses of the *yiqtol* range from "the explicit modality to the modally colored future; and from the independent modality to the syntactically based mood,"[253] regardless of the presence or absence of explicit modal lexemes, and contextual syntactic relationships with other verbs.[254] According to Andrason's comprehensive taxonomy, the *yiqtol*'s

> universal functional path traverses various semantic and pragmatic domains. . . . It embraces a large set of different values: ones correspond to more original stages of the development . . . while others reflect more advanced segments of

250. Andrason, "The Panchronic *Yiqtol*: Functionally Consistent and Cognitively Plausible," 10.

251. Ibid., 12.

252. Ibid., 16. The "panchronic" perspective is defined by Andrason as a method used to explain synchronic observations in diachronic terms (p. 19).

253. Ibid., 35.

254. Ibid., 36.

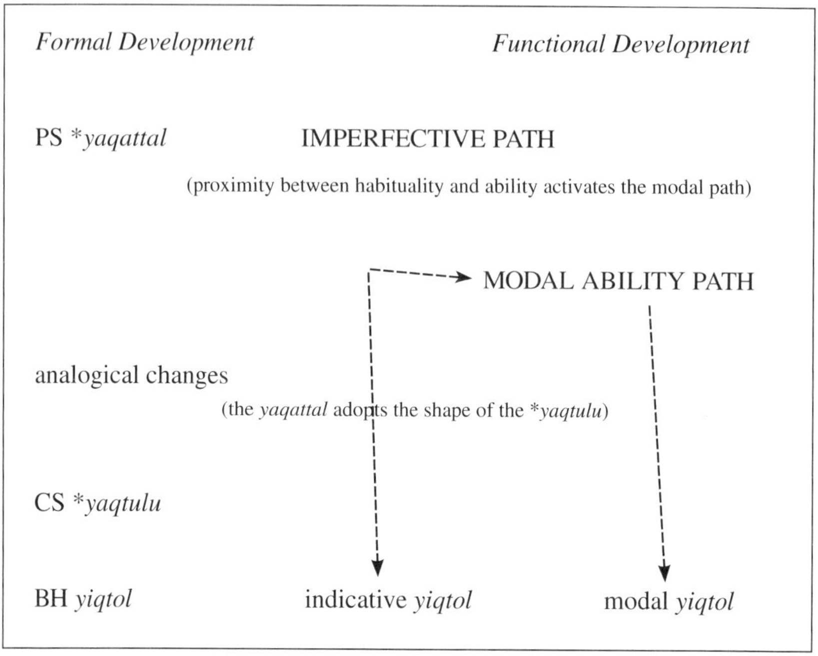

Fig. 2.1. *Panchronic Model of the Biblical Hebrew* yiqtol.

a given path. . . . In that way, taxis, aspectual, temporal, modal (agent/speaker/hearer, root/epistemic and independent/syntactical types), and pragmatic-textual functions are constantly interwoven.[255]

2.5.1.1. Morphological Issues

As mentioned above, in Hebrew, the imperfect (*yiqtol*) and the jussive (*yiqtol*) cannot always be distinguished morphologically.[256] In order to identify a volitive *yiqtol*, one must consider its place in the sentence and its function, and consider the presence or absence of other volitives in the discourse. The

255. Ibid., 56.

256. Regarding the identification of verbal forms, Joosten notes that "what might appear to be a routine operation [of identification] in fact constitutes a major hurdle in the study of the Hebrew verb. Hebrew forms that look the same are in reality to be distinguished" (Joosten, *Verbal System of Biblical Hebrew*, 11). This observation applies to the identification of the forms hidden in the *yiqtol* (e.g., *yaqtulu*, *yaqtula*, *yaqtul*) due to the loss of final short vowels in Hebrew. Andrason shows a direct relationship between the morphosyntax of the Proto-Semitic **yaqattal*, the Central Semitic *yaqtulu*, and the Hebrew *yiqtol* ("The Panchronic *Yiqtol*," 38–46).

verbs that display a morphological distinction between the jussive *yiqtol* and the imperfect *yiqtol* are:[257]

1. Verbs with final ה/י (III-*he*; e.g., יִהְיֶה *versus* יְהִי)
2. Verbs with medial ו/י (*biconsonantal*; e.g., יָקוּם *versus* יָקֹם)
3. Strong and weak verbs in the Hiphil stem, when the theme vowel is long in the imperfect and short in the jussive form (e.g., יַקְדִּים *versus* יַקְדֵּם)

The morphological difference between the imperfect and the jussive of these verb types is evident in the first-, second-, and third-singular forms.[258] In the plural, the imperfect and the jussive are indistinguishable, except in pause. For reasons discussed below, I propose that the Hebrew *yiqtol* embodies two prefix conjugations: (1) the *yaqtulu* – indicative; and (2) the *yaqtula* – volitive. Due to the loss of final short vowels, both forms merged into what appears in Hebrew as *yiqtol*.[259] It is therefore understandable that the Hebrew *yiqtol* appears in contexts where an indicative normally occurs **and also** in contexts where a volitive is expected.[260] Since the jussive and the cohortative are not always distinguishable from the imperfect through morphological features, their identification depends on their function in context.[261] In this book, I focus on the verbal forms that are identifiable as imperfects, with and without *waw*.

2.5.1.2. Functions of *yiqtol*, *weyiqtol*

Most traditional grammars indicate that the Hebrew imperfect (> *yaqtulu*) has the basic functions of expressing present-future and iterative past,[262] but

---

257. As stated by Baden, "[I]t is imperative that only forms which are morphologically distinguishable as imperfects be used for this study" (Baden, "The *weyiqtol* and the Volitive Sequence," 151). Although this approach limits the corpus, it establishes parameters to identify morphological differences between the imperfect *yiqtol* and the volitive *yiqtol*.

258. *First*-person examples: אֹסֵף (Deut 18:16, Exod 5:16), נַשְׁאֵר (1 Sam 14:36). *Second*-person examples: תַּשְׁמֵט (Deut 15:3), תּוֹחֵל (2 Sam 10:8), אַל־תַּעַשׂ (Gen 22:12), אַל־תָּחֹס (Gen 45:20), אַל־תָּשֶׁת (Exod 23:1, Lev 10:9, Num 12:11), אַל־תּוֹסֶף (Deut 3:26). *Third*-person examples: יְהִי (Gen 1:3, 6, 14; Exod 7:9; 9:22), יַפְתְּ (Gen 9:27), וְיַעַל (Exod 10:12), יֹסֵף (Lev 27:31, Num 5:7), וְיָשֵׂם (Num 6:26).

259. This idea was suggested in passing by Wright, who mentions that, in Classical Hebrew, when the imperfect appears after particles such as כִּי, לְמַעַן, אֲשֶׁר, יַעַן, פֶּן, the *yiqtol* may represent a subjunctive *yaqtula* rather than an indicative *yaqtulu*, but due to the loss of final short vowels, the two forms can no longer be distinguished (W. Wright, *A Grammar of the Arabic Language* [3rd ed.; Cambridge: Cambridge University Press, 1991] 2:34).

260. From here on, we will distinguish the indicative *yiqtol* (< *yaqtulu*) from the volitive *yiqtol* (< *yaqtula*).

261. For example, the cohortative/jussive with pronominal suffix, strong verbs in the jussive.

262. Joüon, *A Grammar of Biblical Hebrew*, 366–73; GKC, 313–19; Waltke and O'Connor, *Introduction to Biblical Hebrew Syntax*, 502–14; Rainey, "Ancient Hebrew Prefix Conjugation," 6; Revell, "System of the Verb in Standard Biblical Prose," 3, 9.

the imperfect has long been recognized for its flexibility of functions in the system of modality of Biblical Hebrew. Gropp's study of the finite verb in Classical Hebrew identifies the imperfect as "the least marked form in the system" with "the widest range of contextual meanings . . . [which] cannot be generally characterized by any one or two of its contextual meanings."[263] GKC recognizes that the imperfect belongs to the Hebrew system of modality, noting that it sometimes takes the place of a cohortative, an imperative, or a jussive.[264] Joüon points out the flexibility of the *yiqtol* and mentions that it expresses modal nuances such as *can, may, must,* and *want* "rather poorly."[265] Joüon hardly acknowledges the volitive functions of the imperfect. Joosten notes that, in the majority of cases, the *yiqtol* imperfect has a future-modal function, and "according to the context, the usage may shade into various kinds of modality: futurity, necessity, potentiality, likelihood, desirability, and others."[266]

The Hebrew text provides many passages where the imperfect expresses volitive nuances similar to those expressed by the jussive and cohortative. Attempts have been made to emend passages such as these in order to replace the imperfects by the appropriate volitive form (jussive or cohortative) and to identify the type of scribal error present in the passage.[267]

In "On the Cohortative and Jussive after an Imperative or Interjection in Biblical Hebrew," Orlinsky examines passages where an imperative is followed by a *waw*-imperfect (*weyiqtol*) and concludes that, in each case, the imperfect is a cohortative or a jussive and not an imperfect. In his opinion, the *waw*-imperfect occurs due to one of the following errors and should be emended to the appropriate volitive: (1) haplography; (2) passages of uncertain character; (3) misunderstood orthography; (4) pseudo-haplography; and (5) manuscript variants.[268] Orlinsky fails to recognize that Hebrew has a volitive form (*yaqtula*) that is morphologically identical to the imperfect (*yaqtulu*). Had Orlinsky included this volitive morpheme in his paradigm of the prefix conjugations, he would have seen that all the "unusual" *waw*-imperfects function like typical *waw-yaqtula* volitives.

In "The Imperfect with Simple *Waw* in Hebrew," F. Kelly lists all the passages where *waw*-imperfect appears.[269] He concludes that the *waw*-imperfect falls into one of the following categories: (1) coordinate usage, where the *waw* simply represents a conjunction; (2) sequential "then," where the order

263. Gropp, "The Function of the Finite Verb in Classical Biblical Hebrew," 56.

264. GKC, 317.

265. Joüon, *A Grammar of Biblical Hebrew*, 370.

266. Joosten, *Verbal System of Biblical Hebrew*, 266.

267. Gropp, "The Function of the Finite Verb in Classical Biblical Hebrew," 48 n. 9; H. M. Orlinsky, "On the Cohortative and Jussive after an Imperative or Interjection in Biblical Hebrew," *JQR* 31 (1940–41) 371–82; 32 (1941–42) 191–205 and 273–77.

268. Orlinsky, "On the Cohortative and Jussive," 375.

269. F. Kelly, "The Imperfect with Simple *Waw* in Hebrew," *JBL* 39 (1920) 1–23. According to Kelly, there are 1,287 of these passages.

of events follows the order in which the verbs are listed; (3) purpose/result, where the *waw*-imperfect is governed by a preceding verb and produces a purpose/result clause; and (4) synonymous/parallel, where the *waw*-imperfect elaborates on a previous idea (especially in poetry). Unfortunately, Kelly's list includes a great number of morphologically identifiable jussives and cohortatives; therefore, his conclusions do not accurately represent the behavior of the *waw*-imperfect only but represent the behavior of several Hebrew *waw*-prefix conjugations (imperfect, jussive, and cohortative). Consequently, in order to identify the true functions of the *waw*-imperfect, I will treat it separately from other prefix conjugations, unless the *waw*-jussive/cohortative is needed for comparison.

(1) Yiqtol *with volitive functions.* The volitive *yiqtol* (without *waw*) appears in main clauses and in disjunctive clauses (with typical "*waw* + non-verb initial" word order). In such passages, the imperfect follows or precedes (and governs) the volitive of the preceding or following clause:

> וַיֹּאמְרוּ נִקְרָא לַנַּעֲרָ וְנִשְׁאֲלָה אֶת־פִּיהָ
> So they said: *Let us call in* (imperfect) the young woman so that we may ask (cohortative) for her opinion (Gen 24:57)

> וַיֹּאמֶר שָׁאוּל אֶל־דָּוִד לֵךְ וַיהוָה יִהְיֶה עִמָּךְ
> Saul said to David: Go (imperative) and *may the Lord be* (imperfect) with you (1 Sam 17:37)

> חֲזַק וְנִתְחַזַּק בְּעַד־עַמֵּנוּ וּבְעַד עָרֵי אֱלֹהֵינוּ וַיהוָה יַעֲשֶׂה הַטּוֹב בְּעֵינָיו
> *Let us strengthen ourselves* (imperative/imperfect) on account of our people and for the cities of our God, and *may the Lord do* (imperfect) according to what seems good in his eyes (2 Sam 10:12)

The second-person *yiqtol* often expresses a command (affirmative and negative with לֹא). In these cases, the imperative mood is established by a preceding imperative or by a preceding infinitive absolute. The nature of the commands given with a second-person imperfect differs from that given by an imperative. The imperative is the unmarked form used to express various types of commands that require immediate attention. It is used in social dynamics of "greater to lesser," "lesser to greater," and between equals. The imperfect, on the other hand, is marked for commands that affect the long-term behavior of the listener(s). It is found mostly in social contexts of "greater to lesser," typically appears in legal material, and often addresses the whole community rather than a single individual. Commands expressed by the imperfect are atemporal, while the commands given by the imperative are time related.[270]

270. Shulman, "Imperative and Second Person Indicative Forms in Biblical Hebrew Prose," 271–87.

וְהִתְחַתְּנוּ אֹתָנוּ בְּנֹתֵיכֶם תִּתְּנוּ־לָנוּ וְאֶת־בְּנֹתֵינוּ תִּקְחוּ לָכֶם
Marry among us; *giv*e us your daughters and *take* our daughters for yourselves (Gen 34:9)

זָכוֹר אֶת־יוֹם הַשַּׁבָּת לְקַדְּשׁוֹ׃ שֵׁשֶׁת יָמִים תַּעֲבֹד וְעָשִׂיתָ כָּל־מְלַאכְתֶּךָ
Remember the Sabbath by keeping it holy; six days, *wor*k and do your business (Exod 20:8–9—following an infinitive absolute)

בְּכָל־הַדֶּרֶךְ אֲשֶׁר צִוָּה יְהוָה אֱלֹהֵיכֶם אֶתְכֶם תֵּלֵכוּ לְמַעַן תִּחְיוּן וְטוֹב לָכֶם
"Walk *in all the way which the Lord your God has commanded you, so that you may live and that it may be well with you*" (Deut 5:33—preceded by an imperative)

Consequently, prohibitions, including those found in the Ten Commandments and in legal material, are expressed with the negative particle לֹא + the imperfect, because they relate to habitual events and not to one-time events. One-time negative commands are expressed by the particle אַל + second-person jussives.

13 לֹא תִּרְצָח׃ 14 לֹא תִּנְאָף׃ 15 לֹא תִּגְנֹב׃ 16 לֹא־תַעֲנֶה בְרֵעֲךָ עֵד שָׁקֶר
Do not commit murder; do not commit adultery; do not steal; do not bear false witness against your neighbor (Exod 20:13–16)

כְּמַעֲשֵׂה אֶרֶץ־מִצְרַיִם אֲשֶׁר יְשַׁבְתֶּם־בָּהּ לֹא תַעֲשׂוּ וּכְמַעֲשֵׂה אֶרֶץ־כְּנַעַן אֲשֶׁר אֲנִי מֵבִיא אֶתְכֶם שָׁמָּה לֹא תַעֲשׂוּ וּבְחֻקֹּתֵיהֶם לֹא תֵלֵכוּ
Do not do according to the deeds of the land of Egypt in which you dwelt, and *do not do* according to the deeds of the land of Canaan where I am bringing you, *neither observe* their statutes (Lev 18:3—preceded by an imperative)

(2) Weyiqtol *with volitive functions. Weyiqtol* functions as a direct or indirect volitive in the following contexts:

(2.1) The *weyiqtol* follows an imperative with adverbial functions (e.g., הָבָה, לְכָה, חֲזַק, בֹּאוּ): e.g., Gen 38:16, 1 Sam 20:11, 2 Sam 10:12, Jer 35:11.

(2.2) After an imperative, the *weyiqtol* introduces a purpose clause: e.g., Judg 16:26; 1 Sam 7:5; 1 Kgs 11:21, 15:19; 2 Kgs 6:17; 1 Chr 16:3.

(2.3) After a cohortative, the *weyiqtol* introduces a purpose clause: e.g., Judg 19:11, 1 Sam 11:14, 2 Sam 19:27 (2×), and 1 Kgs 20:31.

Purpose clauses involving volitives are normally represented by the following verbal sequences:[271]

Imperative	*followed by*	*waw*-jussive
Imperative	*followed by*	*waw*-cohortative

271. Purpose clauses are also introduced by other constructions: for example, the infinitive construct with לְמַעַן; לְ + imperfect.

Jussive	*followed by*	*waw*-jussive
Jussive	*followed by*	*waw*-cohortative
Cohortative	*followed by*	*waw*-cohortative
Cohortative	*followed by*	*waw*-jussive
Imperative	*followed by*	*waw-yiqtol* (*yaqtula*)
Cohortative	*followed by*	*waw-yiqtol* (*yaqtula*)

As mentioned above, if the Hebrew verbal system includes a volitive *yaqtula* (represented by the imperfect), there is no need to emend passages where the *weyiqtol* functions as a typical volitive in main clauses and in purpose clauses, nor is there a need to list potential "scribal errors" in order to explain its presence in contexts where volitives normally appear. In order to understand the functions of the Hebrew *weyiqtol* better, we must look beyond the Hebrew verbal system to compare *weyiqtol* with its counterparts in other Semitic languages. As I will demonstrate below, the functions of the volitive *weyiqtol* reflect some of the main functions of the Canaanite volitive *yaqtula* and the Arabic subjunctive.

2.5.1.3. Comparison of EA Canaanite (*ù*)*yaqtula* and Hebrew (*we*)*yiqtol*

In "Early Canaanite *yaqtula*,"[272] Moran compares the volitive *yaqtula* of Byblos texts with the Hebrew cohortative and concludes, based on the similar functions of both forms in independent and purpose clauses, that the cohortative derives from the *yaqtula* modal verb. I deviate from Moran's conclusion for the following reasons: (1) morphologically, as discussed above, the *qameṣ he* ending of the cohortative finds its origin in the *-anna* ending of the *yaqtulanna* modal verb in EA Canaanite and Ugaritic, not in the *yaqtula*; (2) morphologically, the loss of final short vowels in Hebrew points to the *yaqtula* as the background form for the modal (*we*)*yiqtol*; (3) syntactically, a comparison between Hebrew (*we*)*yiqtol* and EA Canaanite *yaqtula* reveals that, in independent and purpose clauses, the two verb forms fulfill the same functions. Since the Hebrew cohortative and the (*we*)*yiqtol* cannot find their origin in the same Semitic modal form, I propose that the Hebrew counterpart of the EA Canaanite *yaqtula* is the *weyiqtol* (*yaqtula* > *yiqtol*), and the Hebrew counterpart of the EA Canaanite *yaqtulanna* is the cohortative.[273]

A systematic comparison shows that a parallel between the Canaanite volitive *yaqtula* and the Hebrew volitive *yiqtol* is evident in the following contexts:

1. In independent clauses
2. In purpose clauses
3. In negative clauses

272. Moran, "Early Canaanite *yaqtula*," 1–19.

273. For further discussion on a *yaqtula* origin for the cohortative, see §2.4.1.

(1) *In independent clauses.* When comparing EA Canaanite *yaqtula* and Hebrew *yiqtol* in main clauses, we find that both verb forms can function as direct volitives, expressing wishes, requests, or commands.[274]

2.5.1.3.1. EA Canaanite[275]

The EA Canaanite *yaqtula*[276] functioning as a direct volitive is placed at the head of the clause (with or without *ù-*) or appears after an adverb (e.g., *šanitam, kinana*), after the subject, after an object, or after a particle (e.g., *ul*).[277] Independent clauses introduced by *ù-yaqtula* can be rendered 'so, and also, moreover, furthermore, now'.[278]

> **ù a-da-bu-ba** *ka-ki ip-ši*[*-š*]*u-nu ù yi-di LUGAL-ru i-nu-ma ARAD ki-ti a-na-ku a-na ša-šu*
> *Now let me tell* about all their deeds so that the king may know that I am a loyal servant of his (119.23)

> *šu-te-ra a-wa-tam a-na ia-ši ù i-pu-ša a-na-ku ki-ta it-ti mÌR-A-ši-ir-ta ki-ma mIa-pa-dIM ù mZi-im-ri-*[*d*]*a*
> Send back word to me *or I will make* an alliance with Abdi-Aširta, like Iapa-Hadda and Zimrida (EA 83.23)

2.5.1.3.2. Classical Hebrew

As a rule, Hebrew *yiqtol* does not appear at the head of a clause but appears after an adverb (e.g., כֹּה, לְעוֹלָם), after the subject, after an object, or after a particle (e.g., אַל, לֹא). In the following passages, the *yiqtol* functions as a typical volitive in independent clauses, in that it expresses wishes and petitions. This is also the case with the Canaanite volitive *yaqtula.*[279]

> יְהִי־נָא חֹרֶב אֶל־הַגִּזָּה לְבַדָּהּ וְעַל־כָּל־הָאָרֶץ יִהְיֶה־טָּל
> Please let there be dryness on the fleece, but *let there be* dew on the land (Judg 6:39)

> וַתֹּאמֶר אֶל־אָבִיהָ יֵעָשֶׂה לִּי הַדָּבָר הַזֶּה

---

274. In Ugaritic, the *yaqtula* also functions as a direct volitive in main clauses: for example, iqra . ilm . n[ʿmm] 'Let me invoke the good gods' (Gordon, *Ugaritic Textbook*, 52:1).

275. For *ù-yaqtula*: e.g., 74.54, 85.17, 19, 117.66, 78, 118.16, 119.23, 124.46; *AO* 7093.40–41, 60–61). For *yaqtula*: e.g., 71.28–31, 79.33, 83.16–20, 43–44, 117.76–80, 129.77–80.

276. Since the EA Canaanite *yaqtula* can represent a jussive + ventive ending, I will only provide examples with verbs that are not commonly attested with the ventive in Akkadian and that I believe are true *yaqtula* volitives. Issues related to the ventive as the origin of the *yaqtula* are treated in the EA Canaanite chapter (chap. 3).

277. At the head of the clause, see EA 74.60, 79.29, 85.76, 117.77, 118.33. After a subject, object, or adverb, see EA 79.33, 85.37, 117.72.

278. See J. Huehnergard, *A Grammar of Akkadian* (HSS 45; 3rd ed.; Atlanta: Scholars Press, 2011) 50.

279. See also 1 Sam 1:23, 10:5, 17:37; 2 Sam 2:6.

Then she said to her father: *Let this thing be done* to me (Judg 11:37)[280]

אַל־נָא תְכַחֵד מִמֶּנִּי כֹּה יַעֲשֶׂה־לְּךָ אֱלֹהִים וְכֹה יוֹסִיף אִם־תְּכַחֵד מִמֶּנִּי דָּבָר
Do not hide from me; *May God do* thus to you and more, if you hide anything from me (1 Sam 3:17—for similar blessings with הכ + *yiqtol*, see also 1 Sam 14:44; 20:13; 2 Sam 3:9, 35; 19:14; 1 Kgs 2:23; Ruth 1:17)

אַל־נָא יָשִׂים אֲדֹנִי אֶת־לִבּוֹ אֶל־אִישׁ הַבְּלִיַּעַל הַזֶּה עַל־נָבָל
May my lord please not set his heart against this wicked man, against Nabal (1 Sam 25:25)

וָאֹמַר לַמֶּלֶךְ הַמֶּלֶךְ לְעוֹלָם יִחְיֶה
Then I said to the king: *May the king live* forever (Neh 2:3)

(2) *In purpose clauses*

2.5.1.3.3. EA Canaanite

In his 1950 dissertation on the EA texts from Byblos, Moran introduced the rule of "modal congruence." The rule is described as follows:

> [I]f the verb of the first clause states a fact (perfect, indicative), then in the purpose clause the verb is in the indicative; if the verb of the first clause is an imperative, a jussive or *yaqtula* expressing wish, etc., then in the purpose clause the verb is a jussive— or *yaqtula* . . . [and] . . . an indicative never expresses purpose except when virtually dependent on another indicative, so that if the governing verb is a volitive, purpose in a following clause can only be expressed by another volitive, never by an indicative.[281]

The following examples show verb sequences that conform to Moran's rule of "modal congruence":

uš-ši-ra [*3*] *LÚ* **ù ib-lu-ṭá ù i-na-ṣí-ra** *URU a-na LUGAL-ri*
Send the three men *so that I may live and guard* the city for the king (123.23–28—imperative *followed by* first-person volitives)

ša-ni-tam yu-wa-ši-ra LUGAL-ru ANŠE.KUR.RA a-na ARAD-šu **ù a-na-ṣa-ra** *URU.KI LUGAL*
Moreover, may the king send horses to his servant *so that I may protect* the royal city (117.71–74—third-person volitive *followed by* first-person volitive)

uš-ši-ru-na-ni 50 ta-pal ANŠE.KUR.RA ù 2 ME ERÍN^{MEŠ} *GÌR*^{MEŠ} **ù i-zi-za** *i-na URU Ši-ga-ta i-na pa-ni-šu*

280. For examples of III-*he* jussives in the Niphal stem, see Exod 34:3; Lev 9:6; Esth 5:7, 7:2, 9:12.

281. Moran, "Early Canaanite *yaqtula*," 9, 81.

Send me 50 teams of horses and 200 infantry men *in order that I may resist* him in Sigata (71.23–26—imperative *followed by* first-person volitive)

2.5.1.3.4. Classical Hebrew

My assumption of the presence of a *yaqtula* volitive in Hebrew led me to test Moran's rule of "modal congruence" in Hebrew purpose clauses with (*we*) *yiqtol*. As I surveyed the text, I noticed that, following a volitive (imperative, jussive, cohortative) in the main clause, the purpose clause is not only introduced by a volitive (*waw* + imperative, jussive, cohortative) but also by a *weyiqtol*. When the (*we*)*yiqtol* appears in sequences of volitives and expresses volition or purpose, I identify it as a volitive *yiqtol* (< *yaqtula*) and not an indicative *yiqtol* (< *yaqtulu*).

לְכָה־נָּא וְנָסוּרָה אֶל־עִיר־הַיְבוּסִי הַזֹּאת וְנָלִין בָּהּ
Let us turn into this city of the Jebusites *in order to lodge* in it (Judg 19:11—cohortative *followed by weyiqtol*—imperfect)

לֵךְ הָפֵרָה אֶת־בְּרִיתְךָ אֶת־בַּעְשָׁא מֶלֶךְ־יִשְׂרָאֵל וְיַעֲלֶה מֵעָלָי
Go break your alliance with Baasha, king of Israel, *so that he may withdraw* from me (1 Kgs 15:19 // 2 Chr 16:3—imperative followed by *weyiqtol*)

וַיִּתְפַּלֵּל אֱלִישָׁע וַיֹּאמַר יְהוָה פְּקַח־נָא אֶת־עֵינָיו וְיִרְאֶה
(Elisha prayed and said:) Lord, please open his eyes *so that he may see* (2 Kgs 6:17—imperative *followed by weyiqtol*)

This evidence is found throughout the Hebrew Bible and is especially consistent in Samuel. Therefore, I believe that the Hebrew verbal system includes a prefix conjugation morphologically identical to the imperfect but syntactically identifiable as a volitive.

(3) *In negative clauses with* lā/ul—לֹא/אַל. As in most languages, EA Canaanite and Hebrew have several particles of negation, some associated with volitives and others with nonvolitives. My examination of negative clauses shows a correspondence between the EA Canaanite particle *ul* and Hebrew אַל, and between EA Canaanite *lā* and Hebrew לֹא. The presence of EA Canaanite *lā* with volitives sheds light on passages where Hebrew לֹא occurs with volitives and demonstrates that the negative particle normally associated with nonvolitives (לֹא) also finds its place with volitives in West Semitic languages.

2.5.1.3.5. EA Canaanite with *ul*

The EA Canaanite negative particle *ul* appears more frequently with volitives than with nonvolitives. This phenomenon is due to West Semitic influence since, in Akkadian, injunctives are negated with *lā*.[282]

282. Rainey, *Canaanite in the Amarna Tablets*, 3:226.

LÚ.pa-qá-ri-ka **ul ya-qá-ar-ri-ib** it-ti-šu-nu
May your customs inspector *not come near* them! (39.18–20)

ú-ul yu-pa-ḫi-ra ka-li LÚ^{MEŠ} GAZ^{MEŠ} ù yi-ìl-qa URU Ši-ga-t[a] ù URU Am-pí
Let him not gather together all the Apiru that he may take Figata and Ampi (71.28–31)

ú-ul yi-iš-ma ^{m}ARAD-a-ši-i[r-ta] ù ma-an-nu ìl-ti-qa-n[i] e[š]-tu qa-ti-šu
Let not Abdi-Aširta hear (about it) or who could rescue me from him? (82.23–24)

[i]a-di-na LÚ^{MEŠ} a-na na-ṣa-ar [UR]u-šu **ú-ul yu-pa-ḫi-ra** ka-li [LU]^{MEŠ} GAZ^{MEŠ} ù DI.AB.t[u]
Let him give men to guard his city, *lest he muster* all the Apiru and they seize [the city] (85.77–79)

[ú]-ul yi-iš-me LUGAL kar$_5$-ṣi ÌR ki-ti-šu
May the king not listen to the slander of his royal servant! (119.26–27)

2.5.1.3.6. EA Canaanite with *lā*

The EA Canaanite particle *lā* occurs predominantly in main clauses, with volitives and with nonvolitives. My interest focuses on passages where the negative particle occurs in passages with volitives.

ù la-a <y>a-qúl-mì LUGAL EN-ia iš-tu URU Ṣu-mu-ur^{KI}
So *may the king, my lord, not keep silent* concerning Ṣu-mur! (68.14–16; 139.5–6, 10; compare 68.30–32 with *ul*)

ù **la-a i-qa-al I**.Šàr-ru EN-ia
And *may the king not keep silent!* (185.67–68)

la-a yi- iš-mé LUGAL be-li a-wa-te^{MEŠ} ša-nu-ti
May the king, my lord, not listen to the words of other men (362.48–49 // 126.62–63)

2.5.1.3.7. Classical Hebrew with אַל

In Hebrew, the most common negative particle with volitives is אַל. There are a number of cases, however, where אַל occurs with the *yiqtol* rather than with a volitive (cohortative, imperative, jussive). Since, in all of these cases, the *yiqtol* is accompanied by a volitive or by a modal particle (e.g., אַל, נָא) and functions as a volitive, I conclude that, in these passages, the verb is a volitive *yiqtol* (< *yaqtula*) and not an indicative *yiqtol* (< *yaqtulu*).

The first three examples include the negative particle אַל followed by first-person imperfects, in independent and purpose clauses, in contexts where other volitives or modal particles appear. Since in Hebrew, the first-person cohortative always appears with the negative particle אַל and never with לֹא, it comes as no surprise that the first-person volitive *yiqtol* (< *yaqtula*) appears with the negative particle אַל and not with לֹא in volitive sequences.[283] This feature confirms that the following first-person "imperfects" are indeed volitives (< *yaqtula*) and not indicatives (< *yaqtulu*).[284]

> וַיֹּאמְרוּ כָל־הָעָם אֶל־שְׁמוּאֵל הִתְפַּלֵּל בְּעַד־עֲבָדֶיךָ אֶל־יְהוָה אֱלֹהֶיךָ וְאַל־נָמוּת
> Then all the people said to Samuel: Pray to the Lord your God for your servants *so that we may not die* (1 Sam 12:19—imperative followed by אַל + *yiqtol*)

> וַיֹּאמֶר הַמֶּלֶךְ אֶל־אַבְשָׁלוֹם אַל־בְּנִי אַל־נָא נֵלֵךְ כֻּלָּנוּ וְלֹא נִכְבַּד עָלֶיךָ
> The king said to Absalom: No, my son. *Let us not all go,* so that we be not burdensome to you (2 Sam 13:25—אַל + *yiqtol* following the modal particle אַל)

> אַל־תָּסוּר מִמֶּנּוּ יָמִין וּשְׂמֹאול
> *Do not turn* from it to the right or to the left (Josh 1:7—imperative *followed by* אַל + *yiqtol*)

> אַל־נָא יָשִׂים אֲדֹנִי אֶת־לִבּוֹ אֶל־אִישׁ הַבְּלִיַּעַל הַזֶּה עַל־נָבָל
> *May my lord not take to heart,* this wretched man, Nabal (1 Sam 25:25—אַל + *yiqtol*)

2.5.1.3.8. Classical Hebrew with לֹא

Although the negative particle לֹא appears mostly with indicative verbs, there are a number of passages where it appears before a volitive. In these cases, I believe that the syntagma reflects a Canaanite construction (*lā* + volitive) and is not a scribal/textual error. This construction parallels the negative syntagma with l^a found in EA Canaanite texts.

> רַק אֶת־בְּנִי לֹא תָשֵׁב שָׁמָּה
> But *do not bring* my son back there (Gen 24:8 + second-person jussive)

The Hebrew text includes a sufficient number of examples of אַל with *yiqtol* and לֹא with volitives to show that the syntagmas are not anomalies of the text but, rather, features of the language associated with certain scribes. These features occur in Samuel more frequently than in any other book and may reflect a tradition known to the scribes who participated in the composition of the book.

2.5.1.3.9. Conclusion

The examples presented above show clear similarities in the functions of the EA Canaanite *yaqtula* and the Hebrew volitive *yiqtol* (< *yaqtula*), in in-

283. Additional examples appear in 2 Sam 24:14; Jer 17:18, 18:18; Ps 25:2; 31:2, 18; 69:15; 71:1; 73:17.

284. The verbs of the second and third examples could also be interpreted as first-person jussives.

dependent clauses, in purpose clauses, and in negative clauses. The following paradigm shows the distribution and functions of the *yiqtol, yaqtula, weyiqtol* and *ù-yaqtula* in Hebrew and EA Canaanite:

	EA	**Hebrew**
Main clause	*yaqtula* / *ù-yaqtula*	*yiqtol* / *weyiqtol*
Purpose clause	*ù-yaqtula*	*weyiqtol*
Negative volitive	*ul* / *lā yaqtula*	אַל/לֹא *yiqtol*

The EA Canaanite *yaqtula* is often preceded by the conjunction *ù* in independent clauses and in purpose clauses. The particles of negation *ul* and *lā* both occur before volitives (jussive and *yaqtula*). In Hebrew, when the *yiqtol* with volitive nuances appears in independent clauses, it is preceded by a *waw* only after an imperative with adverbial functions. In purpose clauses, it is always preceded by a *waw* (equivalent to *ù-yaqtula*). In most cases, the volitive *yiqtol* is negated with the particle אַל, as is the case with the other volitives. A remnant of לֹא with volitives reflects the EA Canaanite negative construction with *lā*.

From this comparison, I conclude that the Hebrew *weyiqtol*, when functioning as a volitive in independent clauses, purpose clauses, and negative sentences reflects a Canaanite volitive *yaqtula*. The Canaanite indicative *yaqtulu* represented by the Hebrew imperfect, is limited to contexts where an indicative is expected (e.g., indicating statements of fact or modal *would, should, could, may,* or *might*).

2.5.1.4. Comparison of Arabic Subjunctive *yaqtula* with Hebrew *yiqtol*[285]

The EA Canaanite volitive *yaqtula* and the Arabic subjunctive are morphologically identical. Both introduce purpose clauses (positive and negative), especially when preceded by a volitive in the main clause. Since I concluded above that the EA Canaanite *yaqtula* in purpose clauses finds its counterpart in the Hebrew *yiqtol*, I posit that the Arabic subjunctive is also related morphologically and syntactically to the Hebrew volitive *yiqtol*. The Arabic subjunctive *yaqtula* is restricted to subordinate clauses, after selected particles, while the Hebrew *yiqtol* (< *yaqtula*) with volitive meaning appears in both independent and subordinate clauses. In Arabic, when the purpose clause follows an imperative in the main clause, the purpose clause is introduced by a particle

285. According to Fleisch, the earliest form of the Arabic subjunctive was *yaqtulu* (H. Fleisch, "*Yaqtula* cananéen et subjonctif arabe," in *Studia Orientalia in Memoriam Caroli Brockelmann* [ed. M. Fleishhammer; Wissenschaftliche Zeitschrift der M. Luther Universität 17/2–3; Wittemberg: Martin-Luther Universität, 1968] 65–76). Fleisch notes: "À notre avis, *yaqtula* (subjonctif de l'arabe) est une création récente dans le sémitique de l'Ouest. Il y eut un temps où les Arabes, ou des Arabes, employaient indistinctement *yaqtulu* pour les fonctions d'indicatif ou de subjonctif. Des Arabes ont continué cet usage. Le système à *yaqtula* (subjonctif) s'est propagé dans la langue arabe au point de paraître le seul normal" (H. Fleisch, *L'Arabe classique: Esquisse d'une structure linguistique* [Beirut: Dar El-Machreq, 1968] 200).

of subordination followed by a subjunctive or by the particle *fa* followed by a subjunctive.[286] These syntagmas can be compared to the following constructions in Hebrew: לְמַעַן, פֶּן + *weyiqtol* (< *yaqtula*). My observations are based on the functions of the syntagmas "particle + subjunctive" in purpose clauses, even when the Arabic particles are not direct cognates of Hebrew.

In this section, I will compare the Arabic subjunctive *yaqtula* with the Hebrew *yiqtol* in positive and negative purpose clauses. My aim is to show that the Hebrew verbal system includes a volitive/subjunctive *yaqtula*, the morphological features of which are identical to those of the indicative *yiqtol* and the functions of which correspond to the Arabic subjunctive, especially in purpose clauses.

(1) *In purpose clauses*

2.5.1.4.1. Arabic

After an imperative, the Arabic *yaqtula* with *li, liʾan, kay, likay, ḥattā* produces a purpose clause.

Aktub illay biʿuδraka ***liʾaʿrifahu***
Write your excuse to me *so that I may know* it (Jâḥ. 85)[287]

Tub ***liyaγfira*** *laka* ***Allahu***
Repent, *that* God *may forgive* thee[288]

Taʿallamuʾ ***likay tuʿallamu***
Learn *that you may teach*[289]

2.5.1.4.2. Arabic

After an imperative, the *yaqtula* with *fa* introduces a purpose clause.

ʾiγfir liy yaʾrabu ***faʾadxula*** *ʿalĵannaha*
Pardon me, O my Lord, *so that I may enter* paradise[290]

Rabbi ʾanṣuryi ***faʾla ʿaxδala***
O my Lord, help me, *so that I be not forsaken*[291]

2.5.1.4.3. Classical Hebrew

After a volitive, לְמַעַן + *yiqtol* or *weyiqtol* introduce a purpose clause. In my opinion, this *yiqtol* represents the *yaqtula* volitive/subjunctive.

אִמְרִי־נָא אֲחֹתִי אָתְּ לְמַעַן יִיטַב־לִי בַעֲבוּרֵךְ וְחָיְתָה נַפְשִׁי בִּגְלָלֵךְ

286. The presence of prepositions + subjunctive in purpose clauses is common to many languages: e.g., Latin, *ut* + subjunctive; French, *pour que* and *afin que* + subjunctive; in Italian, *in modo che, affinché* and *cosicché* + subjunctive.

287. R. Blachère and M. Gaudefroy-Demombynes, *Grammaire de l'arabe classique: Morphologie et syntaxe* (3rd ed.; Revue et remaniée; Paris: Maisonneuve, 1952) 441.

288. Wright, *Grammar of the Arabic Language*, 2:28.

289. Ibid.

290. Ibid., 2:31.

291. Ibid.

Please say that you are my sister, *in order that it may be well* with me on account of you (Gen 12:13)

וַיֹּאמֶר הַגִּשָׁה לִּי וְאֹכְלָה מִצֵּיד בְּנִי לְמַעַן תְּבָרֶכְךָ נַפְשִׁי

Then he said: Come to me so that I may eat from the game, my son, *so that I may bless you* (Gen 27:25)

שְׁלַח יָדְךָ וֶאֱחֹז בִּזְנָבוֹ וַיִּשְׁלַח יָדוֹ וַיַּחֲזֶק בּוֹ וַיְהִי לְמַטֶּה בְּכַפּוֹ׃ לְמַעַן יַאֲמִינוּ כִּי־נִרְאָה אֵלֶיךָ יְהוָה אֱלֹהֵי אֲבֹתָם

Stretch out your hand and grab it by the tail . . . *so that they may believe* that the Lord has appeared to you (Exod 4:4–5)

וְעַתָּה יִשְׂרָאֵל שְׁמַע אֶל־הַחֻקִּים וְאֶל־הַמִּשְׁפָּטִים אֲשֶׁר אָנֹכִי מְלַמֵּד אֶתְכֶם לַעֲשׂוֹת לְמַעַן תִּחְיוּ וּבָאתֶם וִירִשְׁתֶּם אֶת־הָאָרֶץ

So now, O Israel, listen to the statutes and the judgments that I am teaching you to observe, *so that you may live,* and come and inherit the land (Deut 4:1—cf. 4:40)

אַל־תָּסוּר מִמֶּנּוּ יָמִין וּשְׂמֹאול לְמַעַן תַּשְׂכִּיל בְּכֹל אֲשֶׁר תֵּלֵךְ

Do not turn from it to the right or to the left *so that you may understand* the way in which you should walk (Josh 1:7)

שִׁמְרוּ וְדִרְשׁוּ כָּל־מִצְוֺת יְהוָה אֱלֹהֵיכֶם לְמַעַן תִּירְשׁוּ אֶת־הָאָרֶץ הַטּוֹבָה

Keep and pursue all the commands of the Lord your God *so that you may inherit* the good land (1 Chr 28:8)

In the book of Samuel, there are no occurrences of לְמַעַן with *yiqtol* in purpose clauses. This construction is not used by the scribes of Samuel, while the *we-yiqtol* (< *yaqtula*) in a purpose clause, following a volitive in the main clause is quite common. Since the scribes of Samuel included the volitive *yiqtol* (< *yaqtula*) in their paradigm of volitives, they did not need to use the construction לְמַעַן + *yiqtol* to indicate purpose.[292]

2.5.1.4.4. Classical Hebrew

Following a volitive, the *weyiqtol* introduces a purpose clause.

הַנִּיחָה אוֹתִי וַהֲמִשֵׁנִי אֶת־הָעַמֻּדִים אֲשֶׁר הַבַּיִת נָכוֹן עֲלֵיהֶם וְאֶשָּׁעֵן עֲלֵיהֶם

Let go of me and let me feel the pillars upon which the temple stands *so that I may lean* against them (Judg 16:26)

אִם־תִּגְאַל גְּאָל וְאִם־לֹא יִגְאַל הַגִּידָה לִּי וְאֵדְעָה כִּי אֵין זוּלָתְךָ לִגְאוֹל

If you redeem, redeem; but if he will not redeem, tell me *so that I may know,* for there is no other redeemer (Ruth 4:4)

292. The book of Samuel is unique in its use of volitives, *weyiqtol*, and negative particles.

נָשִׂימָה נָּא שַׂקִּים בְּמָתְנֵינוּ וַחֲבָלִים בְּרֹאשֵׁנוּ וְנֵצֵא אֶל־מֶלֶךְ יִשְׂרָאֵל אוּלַי יְחַיֶּה אֶת־נַפְשֶׁךָ

Let us put on sackcloth on our loins and turbans on our heads *to go out* to the king of Israel; perhaps he will let you live (1 Kgs 20:31)

(2) *In negative purpose clauses.* The same phenomenon occurs in negative purpose clauses, where the clause is introduced by a "particle + subjunctive" in Arabic, and פֶּן + *yiqtol* in Hebrew, even though the particles are not direct cognates.

2.5.1.4.5. Arabic

After *kaylā, likaylā, liʾallā, ʾillā*, the Arabic *yaqtula* expresses negative purpose.

zawwaxnnaʾ kahaʾ ***likaylā yakūna*** *ʿalay ʿalmūminiyna ḥaranĵa*
We gave her to you for a wife so *that there be no trouble* among the believers (Cor. XXXIII 37)[293]

2.5.1.4.6. Classical Hebrew

After the particle פֶּן, the Hebrew *yiqtol* appears in a negative purpose clause. This construction often follows a clause with an imperative.

דַּבֵּר־אַתָּה עִמָּנוּ וְנִשְׁמָעָה וְאַל־יְדַבֵּר עִמָּנוּ אֱלֹהִים פֶּן־נָמוּת

Speak with us and we will listen, but do not let God speak with us *lest we die!* (Exod 20:19)

הִשָּׁמֶר לְךָ פֶּן־יִהְיֶה דָבָר עִם־לְבָבְךָ בְלִיַּעַל

"*Be careful* lest an evil thought be *in your heart*" (Deut 15:9)

וְעַתָּה אֱסֹף אֶת־יֶתֶר הָעָם וַחֲנֵה עַל־הָעִיר וְלָכְדָהּ פֶּן־אֶלְכֹּד אֲנִי אֶת־הָעִיר וְנִקְרָא שְׁמִי עָלֶיהָ

Now, gather the rest of the people and encamp against the city and capture it, *lest I capture* the city and call it by my name (2 Sam 12:28)

(3) *After verbs of emotion* (e.g., fear, wish, know).[294] In Arabic, the clause which follows a verb of emotion is introduced by a particle + subjunctive. One could posit that כִּי clauses with *yiqtol*, after a verb of emotion, are its Hebrew counterpart.

---

293. Blachère and Gaudefroy-Demombynes, *Grammaire de l'arabe classique*, 441.

294. Unfortunately, EA Canaanite yields only one example of *yaqtula* after a "verb of fearing" (EA 131:27–28; see Rainey, *CAT*, 2:260; Moran, *Syntactical Study of the Dialect of Byblos*, 90.

Table 2.4. Biblical Hebrew *yiqtol/yaqtula*

EA yaqtula	*Hebrew* yiqtol	*Arabic* yaqtula
Independent clauses: wishes, commands, petitions	Independent clauses: wishes, commands, petitions	—
Purpose clauses after a volitive	Purpose clauses after a volitive, or with לְמַעַן	Purpose clauses after *fa*, or after particles *li, liʾan, kay, liʾkay, ḥattā*
—	Negative purpose clauses with פֶּן	Negative purpose clauses after particles *kaylā, likaylā, liʾallā*
Subordinate clauses after verbs of emotion (EA 131.27–28)	Subordinate clauses after verbs of emotion, knowing, wishing, after particle כִּי	Subordinate clauses after verbs of emotion, knowing, wishing, after particles *ʾan* and *ʾanna*
Negative volition with *ul*	Negative volition with אַל	—
Negative volition with *lā*	Negative volition with לֹא	—

2.5.1.4.7. Arabic

The Arabic *yaqtula* appears in subordinate clauses with *ʾan* or *ʾanna* after verbs of emotion, knowing, and wishing.

*ʾ**ariyduʾan** tanūba ʿanniy*
I would like you to replace me (1 Q. III 80)[295]

***γašiytuʾan** taʾkulahumu ʿalaḍḍabuḥu*
I was afraid *that the hyena would eat them* (Buḫ. III 113)[296]

ʾinniy ʾaγaʾfu ***ʾallaʾtatrukaniy***
I am afraid *he will not leave me.*[297]

2.5.1.4.8. Classical Hebrew

The Hebrew *yiqtol* appears in כִּי clauses after verbs of emotion, knowing, and wishing.

וַיֹּאמַר אֲדֹנָי יֱהוִה בַּמָּה אֵדַע כִּי אִירָשֶׁנָּה
Then he said: My Lord, how will I know *that I will inherit it?* (Gen 15:8)

295. Blachère and Gaudefroy-Demombynes, *Grammaire de l'arabe classique*, 436.
296. Ibid., 437.
297. Wright, *Grammar of the Arabic Language*, 2:25.

הֲיָדוֹעַ נֵדַע כִּי יֹאמַר הוֹרִידוּ אֶת־אֲחִיכֶם

Could we know *that he would say:* Bring your brother down? (Gen 43:7)

וְיָדַעְתִּי כִּי־תוֹשִׁיעַ בְּיָדִי אֶת־יִשְׂרָאֵל כַּאֲשֶׁר דִּבַּרְתָּ

Then I will know *that you will deliver* by my hand the Israelites, just as you said (Judg 6:37)

2.5.1.4.9. Conclusion

The comparison between the Arabic subjunctive *yaqtula* and the Hebrew *yiqtol* in purpose clauses and after verbs of emotion shows an undeniable relationship between the two verbal forms. Though the Hebrew volitive *yaqtula* cannot be recognized morphologically, its use in these types of clauses places it closer to the EA Canaanite and Arabic *yaqtula* than to the indicative *yaqtulu*.

2.5.1.5. Is There a *yaqtula* Volitive/Subjunctive in Hebrew?

A comparison of the EA Canaanite volitive *yaqtula*, the Arabic subjunctive *yaqtula*, and the Hebrew *yiqtol* reveals the presence of a volitive/subjunctive in Hebrew expressed with the *yiqtol*. Due to the loss of short vowels, this volitive/subjunctive became morphologically identical to the imperfect. I suspect that it appears in more contexts than those mentioned above (e.g., independent clauses, purpose clauses), but the examples presented here are sufficient to establish its presence in Classical Hebrew. Table 2.4 shows the similarity of the *yaqtula*'s functions in EA Canaanite, Arabic, and Hebrew and demonstrates that, in Hebrew, the volitive/subjunctive functions of the Semitic *yaqtula* are fulfilled by the volitive *yiqtol* (< *yaqtula*).

2.5.1.5.1. Conclusion

The evidence presented above reveals that the *yiqtol* plays a major role in the system of modality of Classical Hebrew, often functioning as a typical volitive in independent and dependent clauses or as a subjunctive in subordinate clauses. Its volitive functions occur in the first, second, and third persons, singular and plural. I propose that, when the *yiqtol* occurs in passages where a volitive (cohortative, imperative, jussive) is expected, it reflects a volitive/subjunctive *yaqtula* and is not related to the indicative *yaqtulu*.

1. In the first person, the Hebrew *yiqtol* (< *yaqtula*) expresses volition in independent clauses and subordinate clauses, as does the cohortative.
2. In the second person, the Hebrew *yiqtol* frequently functions as an imperative, expressing commands.
3. In the third person, the Hebrew *yiqtol* (< *yaqtula*) plays the role of a jussive, indicating a wish, petition, or command.

2.5.1.6. Common Use of Volitive *yiqtol* in Samuel

In the course of my research, I noticed that a great number of the volitive/subjunctive (*we*)*yiqtol*, which function as direct and indirect volitives and in subordinate clauses after particles, are found in Samuel. The following list shows its regular appearance in contexts where other volitives and particles of volition are found.

- Imperatives *followed by yiqtol* include: 1 Sam 7:5, 12:3, 17:37, 20:11; 2 Sam 10:12
- Jussives *followed by yiqtol* include: 1 Sam 2:10, 7:8
- Cohortatives *followed by yiqtol* include: 1 Sam 11:14; 2 Sam 19:27
- אַל + *yiqtol* include: 1 Sam 12:19, 2 Sam 13:25, 1 Chr 21:13 (2 Sam 24:14)
- לֹא + *Jussive* include: 1 Sam 14:36, 2 Sam 18:14
- In 1 Sam 20:13, a *yiqtol* (III-*he* verb) parallels a jussive
- In 2 Sam 14:17, we find the only *yiqtol* (probably *yaqtula*) appearing with the particle of politeness נָא
- There is no purpose clause with לְמַעַן + *yiqtol* in Samuel; the *weyiqtol* (purpose clause) construction after a volitive (main clause) is common in Samuel

Is the presence of the volitive *yiqtol* in Samuel a coincidence, or should we suspect a scribal tradition in which the volitive functions of the *yiqtol* (< *yaqtula*) were well known? Could the scribes of Samuel have been familiar with the Hebrew volitive *yaqtula* while the scribes of other books expressed volition strictly through the jussive, imperative, and cohortative? Since a concentration of "volitive followed by *yiqtol*" is found in Samuel, I advocate for a literary style peculiar to a specific scribal tradition rather than suggesting emendations for all the passages traditionally interpreted as textual errors. The scribes of Samuel, who were certainly familiar with the Canaanite volitive *yaqtula*, give us a glimpse into their understanding of the modal system of Hebrew.

2.5.2. *(We)qatal*

The *qatal* is typically included in the indicative (*realis*) paradigm due to its high percentage of occurrences identified by grammarians as perfective past tense morphemes.[298] Less frequently, the *qatal* functions as a precative with modal nuances to express wishes or orders (deontic modality).[299] This

298. Matthew P. Anstey, "The Biblical Hebrew *qatal* Verb: A Functional Discourse Grammar Analysis," *Linguistics* 47 (2009) 825–44.

299. This optative usage of the perfect is also found in Arabic in wishes, prayers, and curses (Wright, *Grammar of the Arabic Language*, 2:2). According to Andrason, 98% of all uses of the *qatal* are indicative, while 1.5% represent various shades of modal meanings. Based on this inequality of distribution, grammarians have treated the *qatal* primarily as a nonmodal (*realis*; Andrason, "An Optative Indicative? A Real Factual Past?" 1–2). Van der Merwe, Naudé, and Kroeze note that the "precative perfective" is rare and appears primarily in Psalms (~20 occurrences; Christo H. J. van der Merwe, Jackie A. Naudé, and Jan H. Kroeze, *A Biblical Hebrew Reference Grammar* [Biblical Languages: Hebrew 3; Sheffield: Sheffield Academic Press, 1999] 146). Andrason reviews the two scholarly trends related to

function of the *qatal* is familiar to the larger world of Semitic languages (e.g., Akkadian *parkāsu*, Arabic *qatala*) in both positive and negative syntagma.[300] Andrason notes that in the process of "modalization of an original indicative . . . a change may be detected whereby the temporal and aspectual load of the underlying gram is modified for modal purposes."[301] In other words, by the first millennium B.C.E., the earlier indicative *qatal* (and its Semitic equivalents) had evolved from factual modality (*realis*) toward real modality (*irrealis*; diachronic evolution).

Distinguished from the indicative *qatal*, the *weqatal* finds a place as a modal (*irrealis*) in the verbal system of Biblical Hebrew.[302] Max Rogland notes that the *weqatal* "indicates various kinds of imperfective situations, in contrast to the *qatal* form, which marks a non-imperfective past tense."[303] In Joosten's view, the *weqatal* expresses primarily iterativity in the past.[304] This observation is echoed by Rogland, who adds that this function of *weqatal* decreases significantly in exilic and postexilic literature.[305] Notarius points to the "modal theory of possible worlds" as a place for the modal functions of the *weqatal*.[306]

The *weqatal* represents two syntagmas that can be distinguished by their accent and by their use in context:[307]

---

the interpretation of the precative *qatal*: (1) recognition of this use of the *qatal* by Ewald, Davidson, Joüon and Muraoka, G. R. Driver, Ginsberg, Moran, Buttenwieser, Dahood, Hughes, Rundgren, and Waltke and O'Connor; and (2) rejection of a precative *qatal* by S. R. Driver, Gesenius, Kautzsch and Cowley, Bergsträsser, and Cook (Andrason, "An Optative Indicative? A Real Factual Past?" 3–4). Hatav notes that, "when its antecedent is a modal clause, or if it has a modal particle, such as the world 'if', it [*qatal*] is interpreted as modal" (Hatav, "The Deictic Nature of the Directives in Biblical Hebrew," 764 n. 2).

300. Andrason, "An Optative Indicative? A Real Factual Past?" 15.

301. Ibid., 21.

302. Unfortunately, Robert Kawashima resorts to the outdated and confusing designation "converted perfect" in his study of the *weqatal* (Robert S. Kawashima, "'Orphaned' Converted Tense Forms in Classical Biblical Hebrew Prose," *JSS* 55 [Spring 2010] 30–35).

303. Max Rogland, "Abram's Persistent Faith: Hebrew Verb Semantics in Genesis 15:6," *WTJ* 70 (2008) 239.

304. Jan Joosten, "Biblical Hebrew *w^eqatal* and Syriac *hwā qātel*: Expressing Repetition in the Past," *ZAH* 5 (1992) 2–8.

305. Rogland, "Abram's Persistent Faith," 239–40.

306. Tania Notarius, "Prospective *weqatal* in Biblical Hebrew: Dubious Cases or Unindentified Category?" *JNSL* 34 (2008) 39.

307. As a rule, in the first- and second-person singular, the accent on the *weqatal* with "conjunctive" *waw* appears on the second syllable, while the accent of the *weqatal* with "consecutive" *waw* appears on the last syllable. There are many exceptions that I do not treat in this book. See discussion in S. R. Driver, *Treatise on the Use of the Tenses in Hebrew*, 138–39; GKC, §112; Joüon, *A Grammar of Biblical Hebrew*, 115 and 119; Waltke and O'Connor, *Introduction*, 519ff.; Endo, *The Verbal System of Classical Hebrew in the Joseph Story*, 68ff.

- Perfect with conjunctive *waw*[308] (= Arabic *wa*)
- Perfect with consecutive *waw*[309] (= Arabic *fa*)

(1) Weqatal-*perfect with conjunctive* waw. In this category, the *weqatal* functions in an independent clause, expresses an idea in the past tense, and is linked to a previous past-perfective *qatal* by a simple conjunction.[310] In such cases, the verbs of both independent clauses belong to the indicative (*realis*) modal system. This structure is rare in preexilic biblical literature and increases in frequency in exilic and postexilic literature. This category of *qatal* is normally linked to the indicative system.

וְעַתָּה הִנֵּה הַמֶּלֶךְ מִתְהַלֵּךְ לִפְנֵיכֶם וַאֲנִי זָקַנְתִּי וָשַׂבְתִּי וּבָנַי הִנָּם אִתְּכֶם

Look, it is the king who will lead you now; I am old *and gray,* but my sons are here before you (1 Sam 12:2)

וּבְנֵי יִשְׂרָאֵל הָתְפָּקְדוּ וְכָלְכְּלוּ וַיֵּלְכוּ לִקְרָאתָם

After the Israelites had assembled *and had been provisioned,* they went against them (1 Kgs 20:27)

(2) Weqatal-*perfect with consecutive* waw. As noted by Cook, the Perfect Consecutive (*weqatal*) "is more closely aligned syntactically and semantically with these modal forms [jussive, cohortative, and imperative], than with the non-modal or indicative forms."[311] While the *qatal* reflects primarily the indicative mood, the *weqatal* consistently reflects modal nuances.[312] The *weqatal* appears at the head of the clause, and unlike the *qatal* indicative verb, it reflects *irrealis* (nonindicative) modality or the mood of "contingency."[313] Bartelt calls the *weqatal* a "'wild card' that adapts to whatever verbal aspect begins and thus controls the sequence in which the waw *consecutive* follows. The force of the following verb can often be translated with the adverb *then* to indicate this

308. Joüon, *A Grammar of Biblical Hebrew*, §115—*waw* "conjunctive," or §120—*waw* of "juxtaposition"; S. R. Driver, *Treatise on the Use of the Tenses in Hebrew*, 137—"weak" *waw*; Waltke and O'Connor, *Introduction*, 519—*waw* "copulative."

309. Joüon, *A Grammar of Biblical Hebrew*, §115—*waw* "energetic"; S. R. Driver, *Treatise on the Use of the Tenses in Hebrew*, 137—"strong" and "conversive" *waw*; Waltke and O'Connor, *Introduction*, 519—*waw* "relative"; E. Lipińsky, *Semitic Languages: Outline of a Comparative Grammar* (Orientalia Lovaniensia Analecta 80; Louvain: Peeters, [1997] 518); Hatav, "The Deictic Nature of the Directives in Biblical Hebrew," 747.

310. R. Longacre, "*Weqatal* Forms in Biblical Hebrew Prose: A Discourse-Modular Approach," in *Biblical Hebrew and Discourse Linguistics* (ed. R. D. Bergen; Dallas: Summer Institute of Linguistics, 1994) 68–69.

311. Cook, "The *Vav*-Prefixed Verb Forms," 6.

312. Ibid., 7.

313. Ibid., 10; Andrew H. Bartelt, "The Hebrew Infinitive," *Concordia Journal* (Winter 2010) 36.

action as sequential."[314] According to Longacre, the *weqatal* forms the "*backbone structures* in predictive, procedural, and instructional discourses."[315] Instructional discourse is logically connected to hortatory discourse, where the imperative, jussive, and cohortative prevail and where the *weqatal* expresses primarily the result or outcome of the command(s).[316]

2.5.2.1. *Weqatal* Governed by a Preceding Verb

The *weqatal* appears in a number of verbal sequences, where its mood is dictated by a preceding verb. When related to verbs that express wishes, requests, and commands, the *weqatal* appears in the following verb sequences:

Imperative	*followed by*	*weqatal* (command)
Infitive absolute (command)	*followed by*	*weqatal* (command)
Cohortative	*followed by*	*weqatal* (purpose)
Jussive	*followed by*	*weqatal* (purpose)
לְמַעַן and פֶּן + *yiqtol*	*followed by*	*weqatal* (purpose)

The examples and verb sequences presented below show that, in Classical Hebrew, the traditional functions of the suffix conjugation evolved under the influence of modal verbs. As a result of this influence, the *weqatal* developed a secondary volitive nature, and began appearing in contexts where volition is expressed, without the presence of other volitives.

2.5.2.2. Imperative Followed by *weqatal*[317]

The contribution of the *weqatal* to the modal system of Biblical Hebrew is more closely related to the idea of command than to any other idea expressed by the volitives. Gentry compares the functions of the imperatives with those of the *weqatal* (impv. mood) and concludes that "imperatives and jussives (that is, short prefix forms) mark modals which are immediate and urgent whereas indicatives like *weqatal* and long prefix forms mark commands which refer to the distant future and are non-immediate."[318] Shulman reached the same conclusions and adds that, when a command is expressed by a *weqatal*, it "typically occurs in contexts where a superior speaker presents instructions, laws and commandments."[319]

314. Idem, "On the Subtleties of Hebrew Verbs," *Concordia Journal* (January–April 2008a) 62; idem, "On the Subtleties of Hebrew Verbs, Part II," 301.

315. Longacre, "*Weqatal* Forms in Biblical Hebrew Prose," 51.

316. Ibid., 54–55; Alviero Niccacci, "Consecutive Waw," in *Encyclopedia of Hebrew Language and Linguistics* (ed. Goeffrey Khan; Leiden: Brill, 2013) 1:569–70.

317. So as not to repeat the material discussed above, I will treat here the two main features represented by the construction "imperative *followed by weqatal*." They are: "greater-to-lesser" social dynamics and "sequentiality of events."

318. Gentry, "The System of the Finite Verb in Classical Biblical Hebrew," 23.

319. Shulman, "Imperative and Second Person Indicative Forms in Biblical Hebrew Prose," 271.

וַיֹּאמֶר הַמֶּלֶךְ שְׁבוּ בִירֵחוֹ עַד־יְצַמַּח זְקַנְכֶם וְשַׁבְתֶּם

Then the king said: *Stay* in Jericho until your beard grows, *and reside* there (2 Sam 10:5)

וַיֹּאמֶר לוֹ בְּנֵה־לְךָ בַיִת בִּירוּשָׁלִַם וְיָשַׁבְתָּ שָׁם וְלֹא־תֵצֵא מִשָּׁם אָנֶה וָאָנָה

Then he said to him: *Build* yourself a house in Jerusalem *and dwell* there; do not go out from there (1 Kgs 2:36)

According to Longacre, when the *weqatal* functions in the imperative mood, it expresses a *mitigated* form of command rather than a strong command.[320] The evidence does not support this view but shows instead that the *weqatal*, when governed by an imperative, carries the same nuance as the imperative that introduced the verbal sequence (see examples above). Since, in the majority of cases in which the *weqatal* expresses a command, the social dynamics are from "greater to lesser," it is unlikely that the *weqatal* will be marked for *mitigated* commands. On the contrary, it is more likely that the *weqatal* represents an *unmitigated* type of command. While acknowledging that the *weqatal* and the imperative are both rendered in English by simple commands, Revell highlights the difference between them, stating that "[o]ne imperative is followed by another where the command is urgent, or is addressed to someone who is inferior in status, or is despised. Where an imperative is followed by a perfect with *waw* consecutive, the situation is not urgent, and the command is given to someone who is esteemed."[321]

I agree with Revell's first point regarding the social status of the parties involved, but I disagree with his second point related to the urgency of the command. An examination of passages where the *weqatal* expresses a command reveals two main issues. These are unrelated to the type of command expressed by the *weqatal* (e.g., mitigated versus unmitigated, immediate versus non-immediate) but, instead, they identify (1) *social dynamics* and (2) *sequentiality of events.*

2.5.2.2.1. Social Dynamics

1. In the majority of cases where the *weqatal* follow an imperative and expresses a command, one of "higher" social status (speaker) addresses one of "lower" status (listener) (98%).
2. In a great number of these passages (73%), the speaker is God.
3. The idea that God would use a mitigated form of command to address humans is unlikely. On the contrary, his commands require serious attention and demand a change in behavior.

320. Longacre, *Joseph*, 123, 127–32.

321. Revell, "System of the Verb in Standard Biblical Prose," 24.

4. The particle of entreaty נָא never accompanies a *weqatal* when it is governed by an imperative.[322]

2.5.2.2.2. Sequentiality

In the majority of cases, the commands must be fulfilled in the order in which they are stated (imperative first, *followed by* the action of the *weqatal*).

וַיֹּאמֶר אֵלָיו יְהוָה לֶךְ־רֵד וְעָלִיתָ אַתָּה וְאַהֲרֹן עִמָּךְ

The Lord said to him: *Go down, then come up,* you and Aaron with you (Exod 19:24)

וַיֹּאמֶר לוֹ יְהוָה קַח אֶת־פַּר־הַשּׁוֹר אֲשֶׁר לְאָבִיךָ וּפַר הַשֵּׁנִי שֶׁבַע שָׁנִים וְהָרַסְתָּ אֶת־מִזְבַּח הַבַּעַל

The Lord said to him: *Take* your father's bull . . . *then pull down* the altar of Baal (Judg 6:25)

וַיֹּאמֶר יְהוָה אֶל־דָּוִד לֵךְ וְהִכִּיתָ בַפְּלִשְׁתִּים וְהוֹשַׁעְתָּ אֶת־קְעִילָה

The Lord said to David: *Go and smite* the Philistines, *then save* Keilah (1 Sam 23:2)

2.5.2.3. Infinitive Absolute (Command) Followed by *weqatal*

When the infinitive absolute functions as an imperative, the following *weqatal* normally expresses a second command with similar nuance.[323] Since the infinitive absolute is marked for commands involving continuous or habitual action in the future, it is not surprising that the *weqatal* in such a verb sequence also expresses continuous or habitual action in the future. As mentioned above, the *weqatal* in the imperative mood is primarily linked to *social context* and to *sequentiality*; and secondarily, it adopts its nuance from the verb that governs it (for further discussion, see §2.5.3 on the Infinitive Absolute).

פָּתוֹת אֹתָהּ פִּתִּים וְיָצַקְתָּ עָלֶיהָ שָׁמֶן מִנְחָה הִוא

Break a piece of it, *then pour* oil over it; it is a grain offering (Lev 2:6)

צָרוֹר אֶת־הַמִּדְיָנִים וְהִכִּיתֶם אוֹתָם

Harrass the Midianites, *then smite* them (Num 25:17)

322. We find one example of *weqatal* with the modal particle of entreaty, נָא (Gen 40:14). The command expressed by the *weqatal* in this text is not preceded by an imperative but by a perfect (2nd person) in the imperative mood.

323. This sequence of verbs is discussed in greater detail below, in §2.5.3, on the Infinitive Absolute.

2.5.2.4. Cohortative/Jussive Followed by *weqatal*[324]

The cohortative/jussive followed by *weqatal* is not common in Classical Hebrew, but when it appears, the *weqatal* introduces a purpose clause. Purpose clauses are commonly formed by sequences of volitives, and since under the influence of volitives the *weqatal* developed an independent modal nature, it is fitting that a verbal sequence of "volitive *followed by weqatal*" also produces purpose clauses. As mentioned above, the *weqatal* is marked for events that carry long-term effects rather than for one-time events. The purpose clauses of the following examples denote long-term implications, rather than one-time results:

וַיֹּאמֶר אֱלֹהִים יְהִי מְאֹרֹת בִּרְקִיעַ הַשָּׁמַיִם לְהַבְדִּיל בֵּין הַיּוֹם וּבֵין הַלָּיְלָה וְהָיוּ
לְאֹתֹת וּלְמוֹעֲדִים וּלְיָמִים וְשָׁנִים

God said: Let there be lights in the firmament of the heavens to divide between the day and the night, *so that they may become* signs for seasons, days and years (Gen 1:14)

וְאֵל שַׁדַּי יְבָרֵךְ אֹתְךָ וְיַפְרְךָ וְיַרְבֶּךָ וְהָיִיתָ לִקְהַל עַמִּים

And may the Almighty bless you, make you fruitful, and multiply you, *so that you may become* an assembly of people (Gen 28:3)

וְעַתָּה לְכָה נִכְרְתָה בְרִית אֲנִי וָאָתָּה וְהָיָה לְעֵד בֵּינִי וּבֵינֶךָ

Now let us cut a covenant, me and you, *so that it may be* a testimony between me and you (Gen 31:44)

וַיֹּאמֶר לְנַעֲרוֹ לְךָ וְנִקְרְבָה בְּאַחַד הַמְּקֹמוֹת וְלַנּוּ בַגִּבְעָה אוֹ בָרָמָה

Then he said to his servant: Let us approach one of these places *in order to lodge* either in Gibeah or in Ramah (Judg 19:13)

וַתֹּאמֶר אֲלַקֳטָה־נָּא וְאָסַפְתִּי בָעֳמָרִים אַחֲרֵי הַקּוֹצְרִים

Then she said: Let me please glean *so that I may gather* sheaves after the reapers (Ruth 2:7)

2.5.2.5. *Weqatal* in Purpose Clauses after לְמַעַן/פֶּן + *yiqtol*[325]

Following לְמַעַן/פֶּן + *yiqtol*, the *weqatal* carries the same idea as that expressed by the preceding *yiqtol*, or introduces a result clause.

(1) With לְמַעַן

אִמְרִי־נָא אֲחֹתִי אָתְּ לְמַעַן יִיטַב־לִי בַעֲבוּרֵךְ וְחָיְתָה נַפְשִׁי בִּגְלָלֵךְ

Please say you are my sister *so that it may be well* with me on account of you, *and so that I may remain alive* because of you (Gen 12:13)

---

324. See also Gen 28:3, 1 Kgs 1:2, 1 Chr 22:11.

325. See also Exod 10:2; Num 15:40; Deut 6:18, 13:18; 1 Chr 28:8.

וְעַתָּה יִשְׂרָאֵל שְׁמַע אֶל־הַחֻקִּים וְאֶל־הַמִּשְׁפָּטִים אֲשֶׁר אָנֹכִי מְלַמֵּד אֶתְכֶם לַעֲשׂוֹת לְמַעַן תִּחְיוּ וּבָאתֶם וִירִשְׁתֶּם אֶת־הָאָרֶץ
Now Israel, listen to the statutes and to the judgments which I am teaching you to do *so that you may live, and enter and inherit* the land (Deut 4:1)

וְלֹא־תִדְרְשׁוּ שְׁלֹמָם וְטוֹבָתָם עַד־עוֹלָם לְמַעַן תֶּחֶזְקוּ וַאֲכַלְתֶּם אֶת־טוּב הָאָרֶץ וְהוֹרַשְׁתֶּם לִבְנֵיכֶם עַד־עוֹלָם
Do not seek their peace and their good ever, *in order that you may be strong and eat* the good of the land and leave it as an inheritance for your sons forever (Ezra 9:12)

(2) With פֶּן

הִשָּׁמְרוּ לָכֶם פֶּן יִפְתֶּה לְבַבְכֶם וְסַרְתֶּם וַעֲבַדְתֶּם אֱלֹהִים אֲחֵרִים וְהִשְׁתַּחֲוִיתֶם לָהֶם
Beware *lest he entice* your heart *and you turn and serve* other gods *and bow down* to them (Deut 11:16—the *weqatal* appears in result clauses)

וְרַק־אַתֶּם שִׁמְרוּ מִן־הַחֵרֶם פֶּן־תַּחֲרִימוּ וּלְקַחְתֶּם מִן־הַחֵרֶם וְשַׂמְתֶּם אֶת־מַחֲנֵה יִשְׂרָאֵל לְחֵרֶם וַעֲכַרְתֶּם אוֹתוֹ
As for you, keep away from the accursed thing, *lest you bring about the curse, and take* from the accursed thing, *bring* the curse upon the camp of the Israelites, *and destroy* it (Josh 6:18—result clauses)

לְכָה וְנָשׁוּבָה פֶּן־יֶחְדַּל אָבִי מִן־הָאֲתֹנוֹת וְדָאַג לָנוּ
Let us return *lest my father stop being concerned* with the asses and *worry* about us (1 Sam 9:5)

וַיֹּאמֶר שָׁאוּל לְנֹשֵׂא כֵלָיו שְׁלֹף חַרְבְּךָ וְדָקְרֵנִי בָהּ פֶּן־יָבוֹאוּ הָעֲרֵלִים הָאֵלֶּה וּדְקָרֻנִי וְהִתְעַלְּלוּ־בִי
Then Saul said to the one who was carrying his belongings: Draw out your sword and pierce me with it, *lest these uncircumcised come and slay me and make a mockery* of me (1 Sam 31:4)

מַהֲרוּ לָלֶכֶת פֶּן־יְמַהֵר וְהִשִּׂגֻנוּ וְהִדִּיחַ עָלֵינוּ אֶת־הָרָעָה וְהִכָּה הָעִיר לְפִי־חָרֶב
Go quickly, *lest he quickly overtake us, inflict* this evil upon us, *and destroy* the city by the sword (2 Sam 15:14)

2.5.2.6. *Weqatal* with Modal Functions, Syntactically Independent from Other Verbs

The *weqatal* appears in a number of passages in which it introduces a wish or command of a general or habitual nature without being governed by a preceding volitive.[326] As mentioned above, under the influence of volitives, the *weqatal* adopted an independent volitive nature of its own. Consequently, it appears in contexts where a volitive normally occurs and expresses volition with nuances similar to those expressed by the jussive and cohortative. Such is the case with blessings and curses, where jussives commonly occur.[327]

As I compared passages with jussives and with *weqatal* in blessings and prayers, I noticed no semantic distinction between the two verbs and therefore concluded that the *weqatal* became, over time, an alternative form for expressing wishes and petitions in blessings, prayers, and curses.

וְהָיָה יְהוָה לְדַיָּן וְשָׁפַט בֵּינִי וּבֵינֶךָ
May the Lord be judge; *may he judge* between me and you (1 Sam 24:16)[328]

versus:

יִשְׁפֹּט יְהוָה בֵּינִי וּבֵינֶךָ וּנְקָמַנִי יְהוָה מִמֶּךָּ
May the Lord judge between me and you and may the Lord avenge me (from you) (1 Sam 24:13)

וַתֵּרֶא כִּי הָרָתָה וָאֵקַל בְּעֵינֶיהָ יִשְׁפֹּט יְהוָה בֵּינִי וּבֵינֶיךָ
When she saw that she was pregnant, I was belittled in her eyes: *May the Lord judge* between me and you (Gen 16:5)

וַיֹּאמֶר יִשְׂרָאֵל אֶל־יוֹסֵף הִנֵּה אָנֹכִי מֵת וְהָיָה אֱלֹהִים עִמָּכֶם וְהֵשִׁיב אֶתְכֶם אֶל־אֶרֶץ אֲבֹתֵיכֶם
Then Israel said to Joseph: I am about to die; *may the Lord be* with you and may He bring you to the land of your forefathers (Gen 48:21)

versus:

וַיֹּאמֶר שָׁאוּל אֶל־דָּוִד לֵךְ וַיהוָה יִהְיֶה עִמָּךְ
Then Saul said to David: Go and *may the Lord be* with you (1 Sam 17:37)

326. This modal nuance introduced by *weqatal* is often continued by jussives.

327. The *weqatal* appears at the head of the clause, while the imperfect plays this role within a clause (e.g., 1 Sam 17:37). This use of the perfect in oaths, blessings, and curses also appears in Phoenician and in Arabic after *fa*; e.g., Karatepe A III 2/3: וברך בעל כרנתריש 'May Baal *Krntryš* bless'; Karatepe A III 7–8: וכן הקרת . . . ז ועם ז יכן 'May this city be . . . and may this people be . . .'.

328. Verse 15 in *BHL* (Hebrew), KJV, NRSV, NIV, NJPS, etc.

וְאָמַר הַכֹּהֵן לָאִשָּׁה יִתֵּן יְהוָה אוֹתָךְ לְאָלָה וְלִשְׁבֻעָה בְּתוֹךְ עַמֵּךְ בְּתֵת יְהוָה אֶת־
יְרֵכֵךְ נֹפֶלֶת וְאֶת־בִּטְנֵךְ צָבָה

Then the priest shall say: *May the Lord make* you an execration and an oath in the midst of your people, when the Lord causes your uterus to fall and your womb discharge (Num 5:21)

versus:

וַיִּכְרֹת יְהוֹנָתָן עִם־בֵּית דָּוִד וּבִקֵּשׁ יְהוָה מִיַּד אֹיְבֵי דָוִד

Then Jonathan cut a covenant with the house of David: *May the Lord seek out* the enemies of David (1 Sam 20:16)

The following passage shows a series of *weqatal*s expressing commands, without the presence of an imperative.

וַיִּקְרְבוּ יְמֵי־דָוִד לָמוּת וַיְצַו אֶת־שְׁלֹמֹה בְנוֹ לֵאמֹר: אָנֹכִי הֹלֵךְ בְּדֶרֶךְ כָּל־הָאָרֶץ
וְחָזַקְתָּ וְהָיִיתָ לְאִישׁ: וְשָׁמַרְתָּ אֶת־מִשְׁמֶרֶת יְהוָה אֱלֹהֶיךָ לָלֶכֶת בִּדְרָכָיו

The days of David's death approaches, so He commanded Solomon, his son, saying: I am about to go the way of all the earth, so *be strong, be a man, and keep* the observances of the Lord your God, by walking in his ways (1 Kgs 2:1–3)

2.5.3. Infinitive Absolute

It is widely acknowledged that, in Hebrew, the infinitive absolute can express a command.[329] My study of passages with infinitives of this sort will show that commands expressed by them differ on several levels from commands expressed by the imperative. In order to determine these differences, I will examine the following features: (1) the syntactic relationships of the infinitives with other verbs in the context; (2) the types of discourse in which these infinitives appear; and (3) the social dynamics occurring within the pericope.

329. GKC, 346; Joüon, *A Grammar of Biblical Hebrew*, §123u; Lambdin, *Introduction to Biblical Hebrew*, 157; Davidson, *Hebrew Syntax*, 122; Waltke and O'Connor, *Introduction*, 593; J. M. Solá-Solé, *L'infinitif sémitique: Contribution à l'étude des formes et des fonctions des noms d'action et des infinitifs sémitiques* (Bibliothèque de l'École Pratique des Hautes Études; Paris: Honoré Champion, 1961), 98; Craig E. Morrison, "Infinitive: Biblical Hebrew," in *Encyclopedia of Hebrew Language and Linguistics* (ed. Geoffrey Khan; Leiden: Brill, 2013) 3:693–94. This use of the infinitive absolute is found in other Semitic languages: e.g., Ugaritic: *dk.aḥdh wyṣq baph* 'mix (it) together and pour (it) into his presence!' (55:9, 56:20). Phoenician: עבר 'pass away!' (Arsl. Tash 1:20); הלך 'go away!' (Arsl. Tash 1:21). Since no vocalization is present in Phoenician, these verbs have been interpreted by some as imperatives and by others as infinitives absolute. Hebrew inscriptions: Compare נתן 'give!' (Arad 1:2, 2:1, etc.) with תן 'give!' (Arad 3:2, 4\\:1, etc.).

2.5.3.1. Syntactic Relationship of the Infinitive Absolute with Other Verbs

The infinitive absolute can express a command in one of the following contexts: (1) when it is independent from other verbs; (2) before or after an imperative; and (3) before or after a *weqatal* or *yiqtol*.

(1) *Independent from other verbs.* Infinitives absolute expressing commands are usually accompanied the *weqatal* and *yiqtol* in the imperative mood, but in a few cases, the infinitive absolute is neither governed by another verb nor does it govern the mood of another verb. I therefore conclude that the infinitive absolute has, as a secondary function, an imperative nature of its own.

> נָשֹׂא אֶת־רֹאשׁ בְּנֵי קְהָת מִתּוֹךְ בְּנֵי לֵוִי לְמִשְׁפְּחֹתָם לְבֵית אֲבֹתָם
> *Take* a census of the Kohathites from among the Levites, by family, per their ancestors' household (Num 4:2; see also v. 22)

> זָכוֹר אֶת־הַדָּבָר אֲשֶׁר צִוָּה אֶתְכֶם מֹשֶׁה עֶבֶד־יְהוָה לֵאמֹר יְהוָה אֱלֹהֵיכֶם מֵנִיחַ לָכֶם וְנָתַן לָכֶם אֶת־הָאָרֶץ הַזֹּאת
> *Remember* what Moses, the servant of the Lord, command you, saying: The Lord your God is giving you rest, and will give to you this land (Josh 1:13)

> עָשֹׂה הַנַּחַל הַזֶּה גֵּבִים גֵּבִים
> *Make* this valley full of ditches (2 Kgs 3:16)[330]

---

330. Several modern versions translate the infinitive as a finite verb with a first-common singular, nonstated subject, making God the agent of the infinitive. For example, עָשֹׂה הַנַּחַל הַזֶּה גֵּבִים גֵּבִים (2 Kgs 3:16, NRSV) 'I will make this wadi full of pools'. Other translations interpret the passage with the "wadi" as the subject of the infinitive absolute. For example, 'This wadi shall be full of pools' (JPS). But the most common interpretation is that of the infinitive in the imperative mood. For example, 'Make this valley full of ditches' (KJV); 'Make this valley full of trenches' (ASV); 'Make this valley full of ditches' (NIV). One finds a similar interpretation with the infinitives absolute in 1 Kgs 22:30. In some modern translations, the infinitives are translated as imperatives, while in other translations, the infinitives are interpreted as finite verbs with a first-common singular, nonstated agent: וַיֹּאמֶר מֶלֶךְ יִשְׂרָאֵל אֶל־יְהוֹשָׁפָט הִתְחַפֵּשׂ וָבֹא בַמִּלְחָמָה וְאַתָּה לְבַשׁ בְּגָדֶיךָ וַיִּתְחַפֵּשׂ מֶלֶךְ יִשְׂרָאֵל וַיָּבוֹא בַּמִּלְחָמָה 'The king of Israel said to Jehoshaphat, *"I will enter the battle in disguise,* but you wear your royal robes." So the king of Israel disguised himself and went into battle' (NIV); 'And the king of Israel said unto Jehoshaphat, *"I will disguise myself, and enter* into the battle; but put thou on thy robes." And the king of Israel disguised himself, and went into the battle' (KJV); 'The king of Israel said to Jehoshaphat, *"I will disguise myself and go* into battle, but you wear your robes." So the king of Israel disguised himself and went into battle' (NRSV); 'The king of Israel said to Jehoshaphat, *"Disguise yourself and go* into the battle; but you, wear your robes." So the king of Israel went into the battle disguised' (JPS). The context of the discourse lacks the information needed to clarify the textual issue and contributes to the ambiguity encountered by translators.

(2) *Infinitive absolute followed by* weqatal or yiqtol

Adverbial function of הָלוֹךְ *before a* weqatal. As previously mentioned (see §2.2.1.2), when the verb הָלַךְ appears immediately before another verb, it often carries an adverbial function. This function of the verb הָלַךְ is common when it is in its imperative, jussive, imperfect, narrative preterite, and cohortative forms. In passages where it precedes a *weqatal*, the infinitive הָלוֹךְ governs the imperative mood of the following *weqatal* and indicates motion.[331]

וְעַתָּה הָלֹךְ הָלַכְתָּ כִּי־נִכְסֹף נִכְסַפְתָּה לְבֵית אָבִיךָ
Now, *go*, for you longed for your father's house (Gen 31:30)

הָלוֹךְ וְדִבַּרְתָּ אֶל־דָּוִד
Go and speak to David (2 Sam 24:12)

וַיִּשְׁלַח אֵלָיו אֱלִישָׁע מַלְאָךְ לֵאמֹר הָלוֹךְ וְרָחַצְתָּ שֶׁבַע־פְּעָמִים בַּיַּרְדֵּן
Then Elijah sent a messenger to him saying: *Go and wash* seven times in the Jordan (2 Kgs 5:10)

Infinitive absolute with weqatal *or* yiqtol. Generally speaking, the choice between a *weqatal* and a *yiqtol* depends on the word order required by the clauses and not on the value of the imperative. The *weqatal* appears in clauses expressing sequentiality while, in disjunctive clauses, the *yiqtol* is preceded by a *waw* + a nonverbal element.

וַיֹּאמֶר מֹשֶׁה אֶל־הָעָם זָכוֹר אֶת־הַיּוֹם הַזֶּה אֲשֶׁר יְצָאתֶם מִמִּצְרַיִם מִבֵּית עֲבָדִים כִּי בְּחֹזֶק יָד הוֹצִיא יְהוָה אֶתְכֶם מִזֶּה וְלֹא יֵאָכֵל חָמֵץ׃ ⁴ הַיּוֹם אַתֶּם יֹצְאִים בְּחֹדֶשׁ הָאָבִיב׃ ⁵ וְהָיָה כִי־יְבִיאֲךָ יְהוָה אֶל־אֶרֶץ הַכְּנַעֲנִי וְהַחִתִּי וְהָאֱמֹרִי וְהַחִוִּי וְהַיְבוּסִי אֲשֶׁר נִשְׁבַּע לַאֲבֹתֶיךָ לָתֶת לָךְ אֶרֶץ זָבַת חָלָב וּדְבָשׁ וְעָבַדְתָּ אֶת־הָעֲבֹדָה הַזֹּאת בַּחֹדֶשׁ הַזֶּה
Moses said to the people: *Remember* this day when you came out of Egypt, from the house of bondage, for with a mighty hand, the Lord has brought you out from here; do not let anyone eat leaven. . . (v. 4). . . . When the Lord bring you to the land of the Canaanites, the Hittites, the Amorites, the Hivites, and the Jebusites, as he swore to your fathers to give to you, a land of milk and honey, *observe* this practice during this month" (Exod 13:3–5—infinitive absolute followed by *weqatal*)

וָאֲצַוֶּה אֶת־שֹׁפְטֵיכֶם בָּעֵת הַהִוא לֵאמֹר שָׁמֹעַ בֵּין־אֲחֵיכֶם וּשְׁפַטְתֶּם צֶדֶק בֵּין־אִישׁ וּבֵין־אָחִיו וּבֵין גֵּרוֹ

331. This verbal construction with הָלַךְ appears as a common feature in prophetic books (which is outside our corpus) and is especially found clustered in the book of Jeremiah: 2:2, 3:12, 13:1, 17:19, 19:1, 28:13, 34:2, 35:13, 39:16; and in Isa 38:5.

So I commanded your judges at that time saying: *Listen* to your brothers, *and judge them* righteously, between a man, his brother, and his stranger (Deut 1:16–17—infinitive absolute followed by *weqatal*)

שָׁמוֹר אֶת־חֹדֶשׁ הָאָבִיב וְעָשִׂיתָ פֶּסַח לַיהוָה אֱלֹהֶיךָ כִּי בְּחֹדֶשׁ הָאָבִיב הוֹצִיאֲךָ
יְהוָה אֱלֹהֶיךָ מִמִּצְרַיִם לָיְלָה

Observe the month of Abib; *do* the passover of the Lord your God (then), for it was in the month of Abib that the Lord your God brought you out of Egypt by night (Deut 16:1–3—infinitive absolute followed by *weqatal*)

לָקֹחַ אֵת סֵפֶר הַתּוֹרָה הַזֶּה וְשַׂמְתֶּם אֹתוֹ מִצַּד אֲרוֹן בְּרִית־יְהוָה אֱלֹהֵיכֶם וְהָיָה־שָׁם
בְּךָ לְעֵד

Take this book of the Torah *and place* it next to the ark of the covenant of the Lord your God, and it will be there as a testimony for you (Deut 31:26—infinitive absolute followed by *weqatal*)

זָכוֹר אֶת־הַדָּבָר אֲשֶׁר צִוָּה אֶתְכֶם מֹשֶׁה עֶבֶד־יְהוָה לֵאמֹר יְהוָה אֱלֹהֵיכֶם מֵנִיחַ לָכֶם
וְנָתַן לָכֶם אֶת־הָאָרֶץ הַזֹּאת׃ נְשֵׁיכֶם טַפְּכֶם וּמִקְנֵיכֶם יֵשְׁבוּ בָּאָרֶץ אֲשֶׁר נָתַן לָכֶם
מֹשֶׁה בְּעֵבֶר הַיַּרְדֵּן וְאַתֶּם תַּעַבְרוּ חֲמֻשִׁים לִפְנֵי אֲחֵיכֶם כֹּל גִּבּוֹרֵי הַחַיִל וַעֲזַרְתֶּם
אוֹתָם

Remember what Moses, the servant of the Lord, commanded you saying: The Lord your God is giving you rest and will give you this land; have your women, children, and cattle dwell in the land which Moses assigned to you on the other side of the Jordan; all of you strong men, cross over by fifties before your brothers, and help them (Josh 1:13–14—infinitive absolute followed by *yiqtol*)

(3) *Infinitive absolute with imperatives.* Rare are the occurrences where the infinitive absolute expresses a *command* and is followed by an imperative. The first example is Isaiah's utterance to King Hezekiah (cf. Isa 37:30). The second passage is from the Late Biblical Hebrew corpus:

אָכוֹל הַשָּׁנָה סָפִיחַ וּבַשָּׁנָה הַשֵּׁנִית סָחִישׁ וּבַשָּׁנָה הַשְּׁלִישִׁית זִרְעוּ וְקִצְרוּ וְנִטְעוּ
כְרָמִים וְאִכְלוּ פִּרְיָם

Eat what grows of itself the first year and in the second year, (eat) what springs from it, but during the third year, *sow, harvest* and *plant* vineyards, then *eat* of its fruit (2 Kgs 19:29)

וְנָתוֹן הַלְּבוּשׁ וְהַסּוּס עַל־יַד־אִישׁ מִשָּׂרֵי הַמֶּלֶךְ הַפַּרְתְּמִים וְהִלְבִּישׁוּ אֶת־הָאִישׁ
אֲשֶׁר הַמֶּלֶךְ חָפֵץ בִּיקָרוֹ וְהִרְכִּיבֻהוּ עַל־הַסּוּס בִּרְחוֹב הָעִיר וְקָרְאוּ לְפָנָיו

Let them bring the royal clothes . . . and the horse . . . and *give* the clothes and the horse to one of the most noble officials of the king then dress the man . . . and *make him ride* the horse in the city square and *shout* before him (Esth 6:9)

Imperatives followed by infinitives absolute are rare and are restricted to prophetic material, except for the following example:

וְעַד הֵם עֹמְדִים יָגִיפוּ הַדְּלָתוֹת וֶאֱחֹזוּ וְהַעֲמֵיד מִשְׁמְרוֹת יֹשְׁבֵי יְרוּשָׁלַם
And while they are standing there, let them close the doors, then *bar* them and *appoint* guards from among the inhabitants of Jerusalem (Neh 7:3)

2.5.3.2. Proposed Functions for the Use of the Infinitive Absolute as a Volitive

In their attempt to determine the value of the command expressed by the infinitive absolute, scholars have suggested four possible interpretations:

(1) The infinitive expresses a command that is *softer* than a command expressed by a regular imperative. In his article on the infinitive absolute, entitled "Infinitive Absolute as Imperative and the Interpretation of Exodus 20:8," John Watts advocates that the infinitive absolute, when syntactically related to the preceding or following verb, is never "as strong as the accompanying finite construction."[332] Its imperative nuance is governed by the mood of other verbs in the passage. Watts remarks that, since the infinitive absolute does not function as an imperative outside this type of context, it cannot have an imperative nature of its own and therefore cannot be considered equivalent to or stronger than the imperative itself.[333] Unfortunately, Watts fails to note that, when the infinitive expresses a command, it is rarely accompanied by an imperative. In most cases, the *weqatal* and *yiqtol* carry the imperative mood previously established by the infinitive absolute.

(2) The infinitive absolute expresses a command *comparable* to that of the imperative. Joüon holds this position, stating that the infinitive absolute functions as an "equivalent of the imperative," producing the same effects as an imperative.[334] In his study of the infinitive in Semitic languages, Solá-Solé concludes that the Biblical Hebrew infinitive absolute functions as an imperative equal in function to a regular imperative, except in legal material, where the infinitive tends more toward a future injunctive than a regular imperative. In these cases, the infinitive is found amid a number of imperfects with injunctive functions.[335] In his doctoral dissertation, B. Goddard advocates that, since

332. J. D. W. Watts, "Infinitive Absolute as Imperative and the Interpretation of Exodus 20:8," *ZAW* (1962) 143.

333. Ibid., 143.

334. Joüon, *A Grammar of Biblical Hebrew*, §123u.

335. Solá-Solé, *L'infinitif sémitique*, 92–93.

Table 2.5. Punctiliar and Nonpunctiliar Commands

	Imperative (Punctiliar)	*Infinitive Absolute (Nonpunctiliar)*
שְׁמַע	Gen 4:23, 21:12, 23:8, 27:43, Exod 18:19, Num 12:6, 16:8, Deut 5:27, Josh 3:9, 1 Sam 22:7	Deut 1:16
לְקַח	Gen 12:19, 22:2, 24:51, Exod 7:19, 9:8, Lev 8:2, Num 17:1, 20:8, Josh 4:2, Judg 6:20, 1 Sam 6:7	Deut 31:26
מוֹל	Josh 5:2	Gen 17:10 Exod 12:48
אֱכֹל	Gen 27:19, Exod 16:25, Lev 10:12, 1 Sam 9:24, 28:22, 1 Kgs 13:15, 18:41, 19:5, Neh 8:10	2 Kgs 19:29

the Septuagint translates most of these infinitives absolute with imperatives, in such contexts, the two verbal forms should be considered equivalents.[336]

(3) The infinitive expresses a *strong* or *emphatic* command. Davidson states that the infinitive absolute is used as a command when "the verbal action . . . is to be forcibly presented . . . ; but [appears] also in any case where the action in itself, apart from its conditions, is to be vividly expressed."[337] GKC agrees with Davidson's view and adds that such infinitives absolute are used primarily for "emphatic promises."[338] Hospers rejects the idea that the imperative and infinitive absolute function as equivalents and states that, when the infinitive expresses a command, a certain nuance of emphasis is present. Hospers suggests that the term *focus* may be more accurate than the term *emphasis*, since the term *emphasis* is often used indiscriminately to refer to the use of a wide variety of morphemes and syntagmas.[339] *Focus* is found on the semantic level and, therefore, represents well a verbal form that is morphologically

336. B. L. Goddard, *The Origin of the Hebrew Infinitive Absolute in the Light of the Infinitive Uses in Related Languages and Its Use in the Old Testament* (Ph.D. diss., Harvard Divinity School, 1943) 59.

337. Davidson, *Hebrew Syntax*, 121.

338. GKC, §113ee.

339. J. H. Hospers, "Some Remarks about the So-called Imperative Use of the Infinitive Absolute (*Infinitivus pro Imperativo*) in Classical Hebrew," in *Studies in Hebrew and Aramaic Syntax* (ed. K. Jongeling, H. L. Murre van den Berg, and L. van Rompay; Leiden: Brill, 1991) 102. Hosper's choice of designation is based on van der Merwe's study on the word *emphasis*. According to van der Merwe, interpretations of *emphasis* are too subjective, and criteria for applying it to certain words or constructions have not been well defined. Therefore, it has been used indiscriminately and vaguely, rather than with defined purpose. *Focus*, on the other hand, has been well defined and functions on the semantic level. It can be of phonological, grammatical, semantic, or lexical nature and is contrasted with background information. See C. H. J. van der Merwe, "The Vague Term 'Emphasis,'" *JSem* 1/1 (1989) 118–32.

Table 2.7. Hebrew Prefix Conjugations: Revised Paradigm

Traditional Paradigm	*New Paradigm*
Prefix Conjugation Volitives	**Prefix Conjugation Volitives**
yiqtol jussive	*yiqtol* jussive
ʾqtelah cohortative	*ʾqtelah* cohortative
—	*yiqtol* (*yaqtula*) volitive/subjunctive
Prefix Conjugation Nonvolitives	**Prefix Conjugation Nonvolitives**
yiqtol preterite	*yiqtol* preterite
yiqtol (*yaqtulu*) imperfect	*yiqtol* (*yaqtulu*) imperfect

unmarked for modality and occurs in contexts where authoritative commands are expressed.

(4) The "strength" of the infinitive absolute expressing a command is secondary to its durative–adverbial nature.[340] Solá-Solé notes that a comparison of the mood expressed by the imperative and the infinitive absolute should not be the main focus, since both forms are inherently different. The imperative centers on the mood of the utterance, while the inherent meaning of the infinitive absolute is aspectual, focusing on the durative value of the form.[341] Shulman also notes that the issue is not related to the "strength" or "weakness" of the command, but to the time frame in which the command must be fulfilled. She states,

> The time reference for the performance of the action is not indicated, since the action is not limited to a certain time and not contingent on future events. In contrast to the imperative, the application of the command presented by an infinitive absolute is general, and not just immediate, it presents an action which must be done continuously, whereas imperatives present one-time commands.[342]

2.5.3.3. My Observations

(1) As a rule, the Hebrew imperative expresses a punctiliar command, while the infinitive absolute expresses an injunction that denotes *habitual and durative action in the future* or *an action that has long-term effects* on its hearer(s). Since the infinitive is by nature an atemporal verbal form, it comes as no surprise that a nonpunctiliar command is expressed by an infinitive absolute rather than by an imperative. Table 2.5 provides examples in which the same

340. Adverbs are a-temporal, and are used to describe situations. Since one of the main functions of infinitives is that of adverb, where it expresses a command, the command is atemporal, and presents a wish of long-term effects.

341. Solá-Solé, *L'infinitif sémitique*, 93.

342. Shulman, *Use of Modal Verb Forms*, 132.

verb expresses a punctiliar command in the imperative and expresses a command with long-term effects in the infinitive absolute.

(2) With verbs the inherent meaning of which is durative, the imperative and infinitive are used in similar ways (e.g., שָׁמֹר, זָכֹר).[343]

(3) Expectations differ regarding *the fulfillment of the commands* expressed by the infinitive absolute and the imperative. The command expressed by the imperative requires immediate attention, while the command expressed by the infinitive absolute is of a *more-general nature, carrying long-term effects* and *implying the long term involvement of the hearers.*

(4) Common *in instructional and judicial discourse*, the infinitive absolute is considered more as a "rule" to be observed than as a "command" that requires one-time fulfillment.[344]

(5) The infinitive absolute expresses a command *only when someone "greater" is addressing someone "lesser."* In these cases, the speaker is either God or a leader of the community. The commands are either divine instructions given to humans,[345] laws presented to the community by the leader,[346] or simple commands given by someone "greater" to someone "lesser."[347] This use of the infinitive absolute is similar to that of the *weqatal* in the imperative mood. In 98% of the prose passages where the *weqatal* expresses a command, someone of "higher" social status is addressing someone of "lower" status. In 75% of these cases, God is giving the command.

(6) The infinitive absolute is normally found when the speaker is *addressing the whole community* or *a selected group of leaders* within the community.[348] Infinitives absolute that express a command to an individual are less common

343. שָׁמֹר—imperative (Deut 12:28, Josh 6:18, 2 Sam 18:12), infinitive (Deut 5:12, 16:1, 27:1); זָכֹר—imperative (Exod 32:13; Deut 9:27–29; Judg 16:21; 2 Kgs 9:25, 20:3), infinitive (Exod 13:3, 20:8; Deut 24:9, 25:17; Josh 1:13).

344. For example, Exod 20:8, 12; Deut 5:12, 16. Based on its morphological features, the verb כַּבֵּד could be either an imperative or an infinitive absolute. BDB identifies the verb in Exodus 20 as an imperative but makes no mention of the Deuteronomy 5 passage when speaking of morphology (BDB, 457). Muraoka identifies both verbs (Exodus 20 and Deuteronomy 5) as infinitives absolute (see Joüon, *A Grammar of Biblical Hebrew*, §123v, n. 1). Muraoka's identification is more likely since there are no other imperatives in the contexts, and both passages include another infinitive absolute in the imperative mood. The commands of the Decalogue are expressed by the imperfect, the *weqatal*, and the infinitive absolute and not by imperatives. Muraoka's interpretation is also consistent with the idea that the infinitive absolute expresses a command of a more-general nature, often related to lifestyle, while the imperative represents a command that requires more-immediate attention.

345. E.g., Gen 17:10; Exod 12:48; 13:3; 20:8, 12; Lev 2:6; 6:7; Num 4:2, 22; 6:5; 25:17; Deut 5:12, 16; 2 Kgs 3:16; 19:29.

346. E.g., Deut 16:1, 24:9, 25:17.

347. E.g., Deut 1:16, 31:26; Josh 1:13, 4:3; 2 Kgs 5:10, 11:15; Neh 7:3; Esth 6:9.

348. E.g., Gen 17:10; Exod 12:48; 13:3; 20:8; Lev 2:6; 6:7; Num 4:2, 22; 25:17; Deut 1:16; 5:12, 16; 15:2; 16:1; 24:9; 25:17; 27:1; 31:26; Josh 1:13; 4:3; 2 Kgs 3:16; 19:29; Esth 6:9; Neh 7:3.

than imperatives and appear in specific contexts: (a) in prophetic material;[349] and (b) where הָלוֹךְ functions adverbially before a *weqatal*.[350]

(7) The infinitive absolute *never appears with the particle of politeness* נָא. This feature is understandable since the contexts in which the infinitive expresses a command are not conducive to ideas of "politeness." The commands expressed are *authoritative* and *serious* and *entail long-term behavior.*

(8) When the infinitive absolute introduces a string of commands, the subsequent commands are normally expressed by the *weqatal* and the *yiqtol*. The *weqatal* is typical of commands that are given by a superior to an inferior, as is the infinitive absolute. The imperfective *yiqtol* represents commands that do not require immediate fulfillment, as does the infinitive absolute. It is therefore understandable that a string of commands introduced by an infinitive absolute is continued by the *weqatal* and the *yiqtol* and not by an imperative. The infinitive absolute of הָלַךְ often appears immediately followed by a *weqatal*. In such cases, הָלוֹךְ introduces the imperative mood, governs the mood of the *weqatal*, and can be interpreted as an adverb of motion. This function of the verb הָלַךְ appears in the narrative preterite, imperative, cohortative, and so on.

(9) The verb נָשָׂא carries a similar nuance in the imperative and in the infinitive absolute. In Num 1:2 and 26:2, Moses is instructed by the Lord to take a census of all the Israelites (using imperatives).

> שְׂאוּ אֶת־רֹאשׁ כָּל־עֲדַת בְּנֵי־יִשְׂרָאֵל לְמִשְׁפְּחֹתָם לְבֵית אֲבֹתָם
> *Take* a census of the whole congregation of Israel . . . from twenty years old and up, everyone who goes out into the army in Israel (Num 1:2)

> שְׂאוּ אֶת־רֹאשׁ כָּל־עֲדַת בְּנֵי־יִשְׂרָאֵל מִבֶּן עֶשְׂרִים שָׁנָה וָמַעְלָה לְבֵית אֲבֹתָם
> *Take* a census of the whole congregation of Israel, from twenty years old and up, from the household of their ancestors, everyone who goes out into the army in Israel (Num 26:2)

In Num 4:2 and 22, Moses is instructed by the Lord to take a census of the Kohathites and Gershonites (infinitives absolute).

> נָשֹׂא אֶת־רֹאשׁ בְּנֵי קְהָת מִתּוֹךְ בְּנֵי לֵוִי לְמִשְׁפְּחֹתָם לְבֵית אֲבֹתָם
> *Take* a census of the Kohathites, from among the Levites, by family, by the house of their ancestors (Num 4:2)

> נָשֹׂא אֶת־רֹאשׁ בְּנֵי גֵרְשׁוֹן גַּם־הֵם לְבֵית אֲבֹתָם לְמִשְׁפְּחֹתָם
> *Take* a census of the Gershonites also, according to the house of their ancestors, by family (Num 4:22)

The variations can be explained in one of two ways:

349. E.g., Jer 7:9, 35:2; Ezek 21:31, 24:5; Zech 6:10 (this is outside our corpus).
350. E.g., 2 Sam 24:12, 2 Kgs 5:10.

- The infinitive absolute and the imperative of נָשָׂא are used interchangeably in the whole book, by the same scribe, to express commands; or
- we are faced with redaction or transmission issues involving more than one scribal hand. It is possible that the redactor of 4:22 (regarding the Gershonites) repeats the infinitive absolute he previously used in v. 2 (regarding the Kohathites), while the redactor of 26:2 copies the expressions used in 1:2 almost verbatim (both passages referring to the Israelites).

(10) Table 2.6 represents the major differences between commands expressed by imperatives and commands expressed by infinitives absolute.

2.5.4. Summary of Additional Verbs with Modal Functions

2.5.4.1. *Yiqtol/weyiqtol*

(1) My study shows that the Hebrew *yiqtol* embodies a number of prefix conjugations: the indicative *yaqtulu*, the jussive *yiqtol*, and the volitive *yaqtula*.[351] On certain types of verbs, the morphological features of the jussive differ from those of the indicative *yaqtulu* and the volitive *yaqtula*, but due to the loss of final short vowels, the *yaqtulu* and the *yaqtula* became morphologically indistinguishable in Hebrew.

(2) In independent sentences, the volitive *yiqtol* (*yaqtula*) functions as a typical Canaanite *yaqtula*, expressing wishes, requests, and commands.

(3) After an imperative or a cohortative, the *weyiqtol* introduces a purpose clause in the same manner as the Canaanite *yaqtula*. If such a *weyiqtol* represents a Canaanite volitive *yaqtula*, it comes as no surprise that these verb sequences in Hebrew follow Moran's rule of "modal congruence."[352]

(4) A comparison of the EA Canaanite (*ù-*) *yaqtula* and the Hebrew *weyiqtol* reveals that the Hebrew counterpart of the EA Canaanite volitive *yaqtula* is the volitive *yiqtol*. This phenomenon is evident in three contexts: (a) in independent clauses; (b) in purpose clauses; and (c) in negative sentences.

(5) A comparison of the Arabic subjunctive *yaqtula* and the Hebrew *yiqtol* reveals that the Hebrew *yiqtol* often functions as a subjunctive in subordinate clauses. Such a *yiqtol* is therefore the counterpart of the Arabic subjunctive *yaqtula*. This phenomenon is evident in the following contexts: (a) in purpose clauses (affirmative and negative) and (b) after verbs of emotion (e.g., fearing, wishing, knowing).

(6) In Arabic, the *yaqtula* is normally preceded by a particle of subordination (e.g., *li, liʾan, kay, liʾkay*). The Hebrew subjunctive *yiqtol* is also preceded

351. From here on, the *yaqtula* will be referred to as the "volitive *yiqtol*."

352. Rule of "modal congruence": if the verb of the first clause states a fact (perfect, indicative), then in the purpose clause the verb is in the indicative; if the verb of the first clause is an imperative, a jussive, or *yaqtula* expressing a wish, etc., then in the purpose clause the verb is a jussive—or *yaqtula* (Moran, "Early Canaanite *yaqtula*," 9).

Table 2.6. Imperative and Infinitive Absolute as Commands

	Imperative	*Infinitive Absolute*
Social contexts	All social contexts	Restricted to "greater to lesser"
Audience	Individuals and communities	Communities and specific groups of leaders within the community
Types of discourse	Typical of narratives	Typical of legal, instructional
Fulfillment of command	Immediate attention required	Habitual, long-term lifestyle effect
Type of command	From soft to strong command	Authoritative command

by particles (e.g., לְמַעַן, כִּי). The similarity of the syntagmas, both in construction and in function, reveals that the Hebrew *yiqtol* reflects the Arabic subjunctive *yaqtula*.

(7) The redactors of the book of Samuel seem to have been familiar with the Hebrew volitive *yaqtula*, because they regularly used the *yiqtol* in contexts where volitives are normally expected.

2.5.4.2. *Weqatal*

(1) The mood of the *weqatal* is often dictated by a preceding volitive. This phenomenon occurs more frequently with an imperative than with any other verb form. In these cases, the *weqatal* also expresses a command.

(2) After an imperative, a *weqatal* represents a "sequential" command. The fulfillment of the imperative must precede that of the *weqatal*.

(3) The *weqatal* is typical of commands whereby someone of "higher" social status addresses someone of "lower" social status. In the majority of cases, God is the speaker of the utterance. This phenomenon shows that the *weqatal* cannot be marked for "mitigated" commands but, on the contrary, represents an authoritative command.

(4) After a jussive or cohortative, the *weqatal* introduces a purpose clause. Under the influence of volitives, the *weqatal* adopted some of the functions of the volitives.

(5) The *weqatal* functions as a subjunctive when the preceding clause includes לְמַעַן or פֶּן + *yiqtol* (< *yaqtula*). The subjunctive mood is carried by the *weqatal*.

(6) When the *weqatal* introduces a wish or command without being governed by a volitive, the wish or command is of a general nature and does not require immediate fulfillment. Under the influence of volitives, the *weqatal*, over time, adopted a volitive nature of its own.

2.5.4.3. Infinitive Absolute

(1) The infinitive absolute can express commands without being governed by an imperative. When used in this manner, the infinitive shows an independent secondary imperative nature.

(2) The command expressed by the infinitive absolute does not require immediate fulfillment but suggests the continuous and habitual implication of the hearer. This feature of the infinitive absolute also applies to commands expressed by a *weqatal* or *yiqtol*.

(3) The most common types of discourse in which the infinitive absolute expresses a command are instructional and judicial. Therefore, the absence of the particle נָא with such infinitives is normal because the command is meant to be authoritative and official.

(4) When the infinitive absolute expresses a command, the social dynamics are clearly "greater" to "lesser." And in most cases, the speaker is addressing a community or a group of leaders within the community.

2.6. Conclusion

My study of the Biblical Hebrew verbal system shows that the imperative, the jussive, and the cohortative are flexible, fulfilling a number of syntactical functions and expressing various nuances related to volition. These depend on the context in which the verbs are found, the word order in the clause, the type of discourse in which they occur, and the intent of the speaker. In addition, the three traditional volitives (imperative, jussive, and cohortative) are supplemented by verbal forms that participate in the system of modality (*yiqtol*, *weqatal*, and infinitive absolute).

2.6.1. "Commands" in Biblical Hebrew

The Hebrew language uses several morphemes to express commands:

(1) קְטוֹל. The *unmarked command* appears in the regular imperative form, and its fulfillment is connected to a specific time frame in that it requires immediate attention. Frequent between individuals of all social classes, the imperative represents the greatest variety of nuances, from "mitigated" to "strong" commands. A *polite* variation of commands expressed by the regular imperative appears in the long form (קָטְלָה) and/or with the particle of entreaty נָא.

(2) קָטוֹל. The command expressed by the infinitive absolute is *atemporal*. Its focus is on the *durative* or *long-term effects* of the command in the life of the listener(s) and on the *authoritativeness* of the injunction.[353] Common in legal and instructional material, the infinitive absolute never appears with the

353. The command is considered authoritative based on the following phenomena: (1) the social dynamics are from "greater" to "lesser"; and (2) the speaker is either God or a ruler of the community.

particle of entreaty נָא since laws given to a community are not conducive for expressing politeness.

(3) יִקְטוֹל/וְקָטַל. The *yiqtol* and the *weqatal* both function as commands. The word order required by the clause determines the choice of the form. The *weqatal* appears at the head of a clause while the *yiqtol* is preceded by another (other) element(s). In the majority of cases, the command expressed by the *weqatal* and *yiqtol* is given by one whose social status is "higher" than that of the listener.[354] When the *weqatal* and the *yiqtol* express commands, they do not appear with the particle of entreaty נָא.[355]

(4) The idea expressed by the jussive is closer to that of a request than to that of an command. It is therefore not surprising that, in hortatory discourse, deferential or indirect requests, the jussive is often accompanied by the particle of entreaty נָא.

(5) Negative commands are expressed by אַל + jussive and by לֹא + imperfect. A scribal tradition peculiar to Deuteronomistic literature (especially Samuel) shows a certain flexibility in the use of the negative particles: (a) in a number of cases, the particle אַל appears with the imperfect where the jussive is expected; and (2) the particle לֹא appears with the jussive where the imperfect is expected.

2.6.2. Volitives with נָא

When indicating politeness, the particle נָא appears more frequently with the jussive and cohortative than with the imperative. When it appears with the imperative, the command is softened and nonurgent, unless it appears in utterances expressing "pleas of desperation."

When the particle נָא follows a jussive or a cohortative, it expresses politeness twice as often as with the imperative.[356] The idea of politeness is directly related to social contexts in which an indirect command is expressed and, more specifically, when a "lesser" person is addressing a "greater."

2.6.3. Volitives with Adverbial Functions

The first verb of a sequence does not always indicate an action but may function as an adverb to describe the manner in which the following verb is to be performed. At least eight Hebrew verbs regularly function as adverbs, in volitive or nonvolitive forms. The most common are הָלַךְ and קוּם. These carry the idea of "motion," while other verbs such as שׁוּב include nuances such as "repetition" and "causation."[357] The verb הָלַךְ remains the most flexible, ap-

354. The infinitive absolute is also identified with this phenomenon.

355. This is also the case with the infinitive absolute.

356. When the speaker addresses himself/herself using a cohortative + נָא, the idea is not *politeness* but *deliberation* or *self-encouragement*.

357. See §2.2.1.2.

pearing in the imperative, jussive, cohortative, narrative preterite, imperfect, perfect consecutive, and infinitive absolute forms.

2.6.4. Additional Verbs with Modal Functions

Within the Hebrew verbal system, the *weqatal*, the *yiqtol*, and the *infinitive absolute* may function as modals, both in situations where they are governed by volitives, and also in contexts where no volitives are present. The *weqatal* and the *infinitive absolute* express commands in similar social contexts. In 98% of the cases where the *weqatal* is governed by an imperative and functions in the imperative mood, the speaker/listener relationship is that of "greater to lesser." In 73% of these cases, God is the speaker of the utterance. This is also the case whenever the *infinitive absolute* expresses a command. In every case, the relationship between the speaker and listener is that of "greater to lesser," and in 74% of these cases, God is the speaker.

The *yiqtol* is the most flexible of the so-called "nonvolitive" modal verbs. It functions in the first, second, and third persons in contexts where the cohortative, imperative, and jussive are also found. However, to label the *yiqtol* as an indicative is misleading and restrictive. In fact, based on my findings, it is clear that the Hebrew *yiqtol* verbal form represents two prefix conjugations: (1) the indicative *yaqtulu* and (2) the volitive/subjunctive *yaqtula*. Since this is the case, the paradigm of the Hebrew prefix conjugations is as follows:

Volitives		**Nonvolitives**	
yiqtol-∅	jussive	*yiqtol-∅*	preterite
yiqtol-(a)	volitive / subjunctive	*yiqtol-(u)*	imperfect
ʾqtelah	cohortative		

It appears, therefore, that the Hebrew system of modality is more complex than previously assumed. My study demonstrates that the verbal system includes an additional form that has not previously been identified as a volitive. Table 2.7 shows the traditional paradigm of the prefix conjugations in Hebrew and the view presented here.

2.6.5. Syntax of Volitives in Verbal Sequences

When volitives appear in verbal sequences, the following syntactic functions can be identified:

1. *Sequentiality*, when the actions appear in the order in which they are stated.
2. *Conjunctivity*, when no specific order is required.
3. *Parallel/synonymous ideas* (including *hendiadys*), when the two verbs are conveying the same idea.
4. *Purpose/result*, when the volitive expressing purpose or result is governed by the verb of a previous clause. *Disjunctive-circumstantial*,

when the volitive is governed by a previous verb, is preceded by another (other) element(s) in the clause, and describes the circumstances surrounding the event.

5. *Disjunctive-adversative*, when the volitive is governed by a previous verb, is preceded by another (other) element(s) in the clause, and indicates contrast with the idea expressed by the main clause.

The most flexible verbal sequence is an "imperative *followed by* an imperative." It represents all of the syntactical functions mentioned above (§2.2.4.1) The "imperative *followed by weqatal*" (§2.2.4.4) and the "imperative *followed by* volitive *yiqtol*" (§2.2.4.5) fulfill similar functions (a., b., c., d.). The choice between the *weqatal* and the volitive *yiqtol* depends on word order, rather than on the basic functions of the independent forms.[358] When the infinitive absolute introduces a string of commands, it is normally followed by a series of *weqatal* or *yiqtol* and not by imperatives. Sequences introduced by imperatives emphasize the *immediacy* of the requests, while sequences introduced by the infinitive absolute highlight the *authorativeness* and *long-term effects* of the command. In the majority of cases, when a volitive is followed by a *waw* + volitive, the second clause expresses *purpose* or *result*. The fact that a purpose clause after a volitive can be introduced by a *weyiqtol* confirms the presence of a volitive *yiqtol* (*yaqtula*) in Hebrew.

358. For discussion on the volitive *yiqtol*, see §2.5.1.

Chapter 3
El Amarna Canaanite

3.1. Introduction

Around 1887, an Egyptian peasant who lived in the area of Akhenaten's ancient capital of Akhetaten (modern Tell Amarna) found a number of cuneiform clay tablets inscribed with correspondence between Egyptian and Canaanite rulers of the fourteenth century B.C.E.[1] Additional tablets that included myths, epics, syllabaries, lexical texts, a god list, and other texts of various genres were also uncovered in the same area. Except for a very small number of texts written in Assyrian, Hurrian, and Hittite, the correspondence represents different dialects of the Babylonian language (e.g., northern, southern, and peripheral traditions) in which a number of West Semitic elements have been inserted.[2]

The El-Amarna (EA) texts, especially the vassal correspondence between the Egyptian administration and its territories in Syria–Palestine, provide important information for our understanding of the phonology, morphology, and syntax of early Canaanite and Ugaritic.[3] The most significant contribution

1. Texts, transliterations, and translations used in this chapter are from the following publications: J. A. Knudtzon, *Die El-Amarna Tafeln* (2 vols; Leipzig: Hinrich, 1915); Otto Schroeder, *Die Tontaffeln von El-Amarna* (Leipzig: Hinrich, 1915); W. L. Moran, *A Syntactical Study of the Dialect of Byblos* (Ph.D. diss., Johns Hopkins University Press, 1950); A. F. Rainey, *El Amarna Tablets 359–379; Supplement to T. A. Knudtzon, Die El Amarna Tafeln* (AOAT 8; Kevelaer: Butzon & Bercker / Neukirchen-Vluyn: Neukirchener Verlag, 1970); idem, *Canaanite in the Amarna Tablets: A Linguistic Analysis of the Mixed Dialect Used by the Scribes from Canaan*, vol 2: *Morphosyntactic Analysis of the Verbal System* (Leiden: Brill, 1996); R. F. Youngblood, *The Amarna Correspondence of Rib-Haddi, Prince of Byblos (EA 68–96)* (Ph.D. diss., Dropsie College, 1961); S. Izre'el, "The Gezer Letters of the El-Amarna Archive: Linguistic Analysis," *IOS* 8 (1978) 13–90.

2. W. L. Moran, ed. and trans., *The Amarna Letters* (Baltimore: Johns Hopkins Univ. Press, 1992) xx–xxii; S. Izre'el, *The Amarna Scholarly Tablets* (Groningen: Styx, 1997) 10–11; idem, "The Amarna Letters from Canaan," in *Civilizations of the Ancient Near East* (ed. Jack M. Sasson; New York: Scribners, 1995) 2411–19; Z. Cochavi-Rainey, "Amarna Canaanite and Hebrew," in *Encyclopedia of Hebrew Language and Linguistics* (ed. Geoffrey Khan; Leiden: Brill, 2013) 1:96–98.

3. S. Izre'el, "Canaano-Akkadian: Linguistics and Sociolinguistics," in *Language and Nature: Papers Presented to John Huehnergard on the Occasion of His 60th Birthday* (ed. R. Hasselbach and Naʿama Pat-El; Studies in Ancient Oriental Civilization 67; Chicago: University of Chicago Press. 2012) 171–218.

of the EA texts to the study of West Semitic languages is the verbal system. Since the language of the EA letters is vocalized, it sheds light on unvocalized morphemes of other NWSemitic languages. In addition to using the Akkadian language, the scribes of the EA texts included hybrid forms built on both Akkadian and Canaanite features and applied Canaanite syntax to their compositions (i.e., West Semitic word order). As a result, the language expressed a new code "only vaguely intelligible (if at all) to the West Semite because of the lexicon, and to the Babylonian because of the grammar."[4] This new language, colored by its Canaanite vocabulary, syntax, morphology, and phonology displayed "a Canaanite substratum in the mind of the scribe."[5] Albright states:

> In short, the language of the Amarna Letters was a scholastic and diplomatic jargon, the use of which had become acceptable for written communication between Canaanites and foreigners, as well as among Canaanites who did not wish to use either of the native consonantal alphabets which we know to have been current at the time.[6]

Shlomo Izre'el addresses the possibility that the "Amarna language" may have been spoken "by a certain upper social class of officials or the like, as was the case, for instance, with the Latin spoken by French officials and scholars side by side with French."[7] Nevertheless, he concludes that the variety of spelling and formulaic conventions, the presence of Akkadianisms, and the inconsistency of hybrid forms seem to indicate, at this point at least, that the chancellery language of the letters was not spoken, except in scribal schools.[8]

The particular linguistic features encountered in these texts attracted scholars' attention so that the first half of the twentieth century provided us with numerous publications.[9] However, it was Professor W. L. Moran, in his 1950, groundbreaking doctoral dissertation entitled *A Syntactical Study of the Dialect*

---

4. Moran, *Amarna Letters*, xxii.

5. W. F. Albright, "The Amarna Letters from Palestine," in *The Cambridge Ancient History*, vol. 2/2: *History of the Middle East and the Aegean Region, 1380–1000 B.C.* (ed. I. E. S. Edwards et al.; Cambridge: Cambridge Univ. Press, 1975) 98–116.

6. Ibid., 4.

7. Izre'el, "The Gezer Letters of the El-Amarna Archive," 83.

8. Ibid.

9. W. F. Albright, (numerous articles on EA texts from 1924–75); C. Bezold and E. W. Budge, eds., *The Tell el-Amarna Tablets in the British Museum* (London: British Museum, 1892); Franz M. Böhl, *Die Sprache der Amarnabriefe: Mit besonderer Berücksichtigung der Kanaanismen* (Leipziger semitistische Studien 5/2; Leipzig: Hinrich, 1909); P. E. Dhorme, "La langue de Canaan," *RB* n.s. 10 (1913) 369–93; n.s. 11 (1914) 37–59, 334–72; E. Ebeling, "Das Verbum der El-Amarna Briefe," *BASS* 8 (1910) 39–79; Knudtzon, *El-Amarna Tafeln*; Moran, *Syntactical Study of the Dialect of Byblos*; Schroeder, *Tontaffeln von El-Amarna*; J.-G. Heintz, *Index Documentaire d'El-Amarna—I.D.E.A.*, vol. 2: *Bibliographie des textes babyloniens d'El-Amarna [1888 à 1993] et Concordance des sigles EA* (Wiesbaden: Harrassowitz, 1995) 3–33.

of Byblos as Reflected in the Amarna Tablets and in his abundant articles, who initiated serious study of the EA material.[10] His work became instrumental in the explosion of research on the subject during the last 50 years.[11] The most comprehensive descriptive work on the EA Canaanite language as a whole was produced in 1996 by Anson Rainey who rightly aknowledges that Moran's research and study "on the verbal system of the Byblos texts became the magic key to unlocking the secrets of the interlanguage reflected in the EA texts from Canaan."[12]

As we will see below, scholars have proposed various paradigms for the verbal system of EA Canaanite. Finding the *authentic* verbal system used by the people of the region is hampered by the fact that the language of the letters includes a blend of typical Akkadian verbal forms, hybrid forms, scribal errors, Canaanite morphemes, and West Semitic syntax. The scribes who participated in the writing of these texts reveal that they had a poor command of the Akkadian language. Consequently, they resorted to Canaanite linguistic elements with which they were familiar, thereby providing a glimpse into the linguistic system of the region.

At times, scribes of specific locales (e.g., Gezer, Jerusalem, Byblos) used more than one verbal form in order to express a single nuance (e.g., wishes expressed by the jussive, the precative, or the volitive *yaqtula*); thus, an accurate representation of the verbal system is obscured by the presence of seemingly interchageable forms.[13] Based on his study of the Gezer letters, Izre'el notes that the functions of the jussive *yaqtul* and the volitive *yaqtula* "are essentially the same"[14] in the Gezer corpus as they are at Byblos, as elucidated by Moran.[15]

The EA texts most relevant to our study are the letters written from or to Canaan, between the Egyptian pharaoh and his vassals (e.g., Byblos and Ṣumur: EA 68–135; Jerusalem: EA 286–90; Gezer: EA 267–71, 292–94, 297–300, 378; Lachish: EA 328–29, 332; Ashkelon: EA 320–26; and various Canaanite rulers: EA 362–67). Texts from Babylonia (EA 1–14), Mittani (EA 19–23, 26–30), and Alašiya (EA 33–40) will be considered when they shed light on morphological and syntactical features found in Canaanite letters and contribute to our study.

10. W. L. Moran, "An Unexplained Passage in an Amarna Letter from Byblos," *JNES* 8 (1949) 124–25; idem, "The Use of the Canaanite Infinitive Absolute as a Finite Verb in the Amarna Letters from Byblos," *JCS* 4 (1950) 169–72; idem, "New Evidence on Canaanite *taqtuï(na)*," 33–35; "Does Amarna Bear on Karatepe?— An Answer," *JCS* 6 (1952) 76–80; idem, "Amarna *shumma* in Main Clauses," *JCS* 7 (1953) 78–80; idem, "Early Canaanite *yaqtula*," *Or* 29 (1960) 1–19.

11. Heintz, *Bibliographie des textes babyloniens d'El-Amarna*, 34–113.

12. Rainey, *Canaanite in the Amarna Tablets*, 1:xx.

13. Izre'el, "The Gezer Letters of the El-Amarna Archive," 51.

14. Ibid., 82; Izre'el quotes from Moran, *Syntactical Study of the Dialect of Byblos*, 105.

15. Ibid., 105.

3.2. Proposed Paradigms for the Canaanite Verbal System

Several scholars (e.g., Moran, Rainey, Izre'el, and Korchin) have proposed that a West Semitic verbal paradigm can be depicted through the writings of the EA scribes, even though the letters include hybrid forms, Akkadianisms, West Semitic morphemes, and scribal errors. On the other hand, others see the language of the EA letters as a linguistic code that is not representative of the language of the region but that was created to serve as a bridge between rulers of various regions where different languages were spoken.[16] For this reason, a representation of the *actual verbal system* used by the people of Canaan is not easily defined. The following paradigms proposed by Moran, Rainey, and Izre'el need to remain flexible and open to further interpretation as additional data appear in the West Semitic corpus.

Moran. From his study of the Byblos texts, Moran concludes that the West Semitic and Akkadian verbal forms familiar to EA Canaanite scribes belong to the following three groups:

1. *Indicative*	imperfect (*yaqtulu*—possible modal functions)
	perfect (*qatala*—possible modal functions)
	preterite (*yaqtul*)[17]
2. *Modal*	imperative (*qutul, qitil, qital*)
	jussive (*yaqtul*)
	precative (*liprus*)[18]
	volitive (*yaqtula*)
2. *Modal*	energic[19]
	imperfect—energic (*yaqtuluna*)
	imperative—energic (*qutula*)
	volitive—energic (*yaqtulan(na)*)

16. Tarsee Li, *The Expression of Sequence and Non Sequence* (Ph.D. diss., Hebrew Union College–Jewish Institute of Religion, 1999) 24.

17. Moran notes that

> the use of *yaqtul* referring to the past (pres. perf. or historical perf.) is relatively rare. . . . It is very significant that the instances of the perfect (175) with the same meaning greatly outnumber those of *yaqtul*. Almost every example of the past *yaqtul* can be paralleled by perfects either in parallel passages or in similar contexts. All of which indicates that in Byblian the perfect was *normally* used to express a present or historical perfect, though it is impossible to say that *yaqtul* could not, at least in certain circumstances, have a similar use. (Moran, *Syntactical Study of the Dialect of Byblos*, 51)

18. Canaanite scribes often used the Akkadian precative *liprus* as a semantic equivalent to the West Semitic jussive. Rainey points out that the precative often begins a string of injunctives (Rainey, *Canaanite in the Amarna Tablets*, 2:217). Korchin uses the term *precative* for the *yqtl-Ø* modal form (Korchin, 2008: 80).

19. The term *energic* is used here to follow the traditional designation of modal forms with *-a* or *-an(na)*.

Rainey. With regard to the Canaanite prefix conjugations, Rainey proposes a "bi-partite modal system, with a tri-partite subdivision in each mode."[20] His suggested paradigm is as follows:

Indicative		**Injunctive**	
Preterite	*yaqtul*	Jussive	*yaqtul*
Imperfect	*yaqtulu*	Volitive	*yaqtula*
Energic	*yaqtulun(n)a*	Energic	*yaqtulan(n)a*

Korchin disputes Rainey's proposed paradigm, stating that the model "is constructed upon a mixture of functional and formal criteria that appear to be at least somewhat influenced by a desire for symmetry."[21] Korchin contends that the data in his study do not consistently reveal the presence of two distinct morphosyntactic *yqtl-Ø* patterns "but rather one uniform paradigmatic morphological structure that is capable of functioning in various syntactic environments, both indicative and injunctive."[22]

Izre'el. S. Izre'el's morphosyntactic analysis of the Gezer letters reveals a verbal paradigm that includes the following forms:[23]

perfect (*qatala*)	imperfect (*yaqtulu*)
preterite (*yaqtul*)	jussive (*yaqtul*)
precative (*liqtul*)	volitive (*yaqtula*)
imperative (*qutul*, *qitil*, *qital*)	long impv (*id-na-m*[*i*])[24]

Tropper. Refuting Rainey's proposed binary *yqtl-Ø* paradigm, Tropper proposes one *yqtl-Ø* form with multiple modal functions and *yqtl-u/a-(n)na* as secondary forms (nonparadigmatic) on the formal and functional levels.[25] In his view, the *yqtl-a* reveals the presence of an Akkadian ventive marker *-(a)m* or volitive ending *-a* on the *yqtl-Ø* paradigmatic form.[26] His proposed model for the Canaanite prefix conjugation is as follows:

Indikativ	
Kurzform	**Langform**
yaqtul-Ø (Präteritum)	*yaqtulu* (Imperfekt)
Volitiv	
yaqtul-Ø (Jussiv)	*'lnaqtulā* (Kohortativ)

20. Rainey, "Further Remarks on the Hebrew Verbal System," *HS* 29 (1988) 35–42; Cochavi-Rainey, "Amarna Canaanite and Hebrew."

21. Korchin, *Markedness in Canaanite and Hebrew Verbs*, 325.

22. Ibid.

23. Izre'el, "The Gezer Letters of the El-Amarna Archive," 13–90.

24. EA 270.18.

25. J. Tropper, "Kanaanäisches in dem Amarnabriefen" (Review of *Canaanite in the Amarna Tablets*, by Anson Rainey), *AfO* 44–45 (1997–98) 136.

26. J. Tropper, "Das altkanaanäische und ugaritische Verbalsystem," in *Ugarit: Ein ostmeditarranes Kulturzentrum im Alten Orient* (ed. M. Dietrich and O. Loretz; Abhandlungen zur Literatur Alt-Syrien-Palästinas 7; Münster: Ugarit-Verlag, 1995) 165.

Korchin. In his study on the markedness of the prefix conjugations of Canaano-Akkadian and Biblical Hebrew, Korchin concludes that two structural paradigms are represented in the EA corpus of Gubla, Gazru, and Gimtu: the *functional structure* and the *formal structure*. In the *formal structure* paradigm, the *yqtl-u* (A) versus *yqtl-a* (B) and the *yqtl-u-(n)a* (A′) versus *yqtl-a-(n)a* (B′) are viewed as equipollent binary oppositions "with respect with the primary associational matrix underlying the system (*y-qtl-*)."[27]

yqtl-∅[28]
(unmarked)

yqtl-u[29] (singly marked) | *yqtl-a* (singly marked)

yqtl-u-(n)na (doubly marked) | *yqtl-a-(n)na* (doubly marked)

In the *functional structure* paradigm, the unmarked *yqtl-∅* form is less restricted in function than the marked *yqtl-u* and *yqtl-a*. The *yqtl-u* (realis—marked nonanterior) functions in temporal opposition to *yqtl-∅* (unmarked ant/nonanterior) while the *yqtl-a* (irrealis—marked nonindicative) functions in modal opposition to the *yqtl-∅* (unmarked ind/nonindicative).[30] The prefix conjugations with *-(n)na* endings are not considered intrinsic to the Canaanite verbal system. Rather, they are interpreted by Korchin as prefix conjugations with an enclitic particle "appended to temporally marked *yqtl-u-* and to modally marked *yqtl-a-*."[31]

yqtl-∅

(Ant/non-Ant) (unmarked) | **(Ind/non-Ind)** (unmarked)

yqtl-u **(non-Ant)** (singly marked) | *yqtl-a* **(non-Ind)** (singly marked)

yqtl-u-(n)na **(non-Ant + Cont)** (doubly marked) | *yqtl-a-(n)na* **(non-Ind + Cont)** (doubly marked)

27. Korchin, *Markedness in Canaanite and Hebrew Verbs*, 324.

28. Korchin treats the *yqtl-0* of precative and declarative clauses together, dismissing the possiblity of two *yqtl-∅* forms in which the accents distinguish the precative *yqtl-∅* from the declarative *yqtl-∅* form. Tropper and Hetzron advocate for two functionally distinct *yqtl-∅* identified by their accents (Tropper, "Das altkanaanäische und ugaritische Verbalsystem," 159–70; Robert Hetzron, "The Evidence of Perfect **y'aqtul* and Jussive **yaqt'ul* in Proto-Semitic," *JSS* 14 [1969] 1–21).

29. Declarative.

30. Korchin, *Markedness in Canaanite and Hebrew Verbs*, 324.

31. Ibid., 325.

The *yqtl-Ø* serves as the "primary associational matrix" in precative, declarative, causal, temporal, referential, and epistolary performative clauses. The *yqtl-u* is found in declarative, conditional, referential, prohibitibite, purpose, circumstantial, and asseverative clauses. The *yqtl-a* appears in precative, volitive result, interrogative, and conditional clauses.[32]

3.3. The Imperative

3.3.1. Regular Imperatives

The regular imperative is the unmarked form of command and, in Canaanite letters, appears at the head of the clause.[33] This word order is a West Semitic feature and is in contrast to the typical Akkadian word order, where the imperative, like all other verbs, appears at the end of the clause.[34] The EA Canaanite imperative frequently appears in independent clauses and occasionally in the apodosis of conditional sentences (e.g., EA 112.33, 114.25). The regular imperative is used by individuals of higher social status (e.g., kings, officials) toward individuals of lower social status (e.g., vassals), and vice versa.[35] Its nuances are similar to those of the Biblical Hebrew imperative in that it expresses injunctions that range from regular commands in epistolary formulas to strong commands within the body of the letter.

(1) *In epistolary formulas.* The regular imperative often appears in the introductory formula of letters. The following formula with *qabû*, *a-na PN **qí-bí-ma*** '*Say* to PN', appears in the introduction of letters from Babylonia (e.g., EA 1.2, 2.2, 6.2, 7.2, 8.2, 9.2, 12.2), Mittani (e.g., EA 19.3, 20.2, 21.4, 23.3, 28.3), Alašiya (e.g., EA 35.1, 37.2, 38.1, 39.2, 40.2), and Canaan (e.g., EA 82.2, 84.2, 85.1, 87.2, 90.2, 95.1, 96.2, 102.2, 104.2, et passim). Scribes from Canaan, though familiar with the alternate form, *qibami* (with modal ending), never include the imperative with an *-a* ending in the introductions of letters.[36]

---

32. Korchin, *Markedness in Canaanite and Hebrew Verbs*, 323, nn. 1–3.

33. Regular imperative—in contrast to the imperative with *-na* and the imperative with modal ending *-a*, which are marked for specific use. This feature will be discussed in greater detail below. Word order—here a "function word" (e.g., *šanitam, ù*)—appears before the imperative; it "serves to indicate the relation of a sentence to a previous sentence or to modify the whole sentence, hence the name function. These words occur before the V-S-O-C complex" (A. Gianto Kentjanaputra, *A Study of Word Order Variations in the Byblos Amarna Letters* [Ph.D. diss., Harvard University, 1987] 11).

34. J. Huehnergard, *A Grammar of Akkadian* (HSS 45; 3rd ed.; Atlanta: Scholars Press, 2011) 144.

35. Since the correspondence is of a political nature, the possible social contexts are quite restricted and only include kings, officials, and rulers. The letters cannot be said to represent the spoken dialects of the communities where the letters were composed, since their content strictly represents communication between officials of the administrative segment of the population.

36. Some of the letters from Canaan include both *qibima* and *qibami* in the body of the letter, with no obvious difference in meaning (e.g., EA 73.28, 43). In other cases, (e.g., EA

Their scribal training no doubt included the appropriate Akkadian use of formulaic syntagmas, both in the introduction of letters and, as we will see below, within the body of the correspondence.

(2) *The imperative in rhetorical statements.* A number of phrases involving imperatives are repeated within the body of letters by scribes who had obviously received training in political-correspondence rhetoric.

With ***lamādu***. In several cases, scribes use the imperative of *lamādu* in a formula whereby the reader is told to "be informed (about)" a specific event or message (e.g., 34.4–5 [Alašiya], 79.8, 90.5, 101.37–38, 113.10, 284.6, 292.52 [Canaan]). The verb *lamādu* occurs more frequently as a jussive or precative in a phrase that serves a similar purpose: "May the king, my lord, be informed (that)" (see discussion below in §3.3)

> **li-ma-ad** i-nu-ma iš-tu ka-ša-ad ^{m}A-ma-an-Ap-pa a-na mu-ḫi-ia ka-li LÚ^{MEŠ} GAZ^{MEŠ} na-a[d]-nu pa-ni-šu-nu
> *Be informed* that, since Amanappa reached me, all the ʿApiru have turned (against me) (EA 79.8)

> **li-ma-ad** [i-nu-ma] KALAG.GA nu-kúr-tum UGU-[ia]
> *Be informed* [that] the war against me is severe (EA 90.5)

With ***naṣāru***. The imperative of *naṣāru* also appears in similar rhetorical statements, in letters written by scribes in Egypt (EA 99.7–8, 367.4, 12 [2×], 370.5).[37] Where correspondence from Canaan includes the command with *naṣāru*, the scribe quotes from letters written in Egypt (EA 112.9, 117.84, 125.9, 10). In a number of these cases, the imperative is followed by the modal particle *lū* + the stative form of *naṣāru*, e.g., lū na-ṣa-ra-ta / lū na-ṣir-ta (EA 99.8, 112.9, 117.84, 367.4, 370.5). The combinations of both syntagmas is probably for emphasis:

> a-nu-ma ṭup-pa an-na-a uš-te-bi-la-ku qá-bé-e a-na ka-a-ša ù uṣ-ṣur lu-ú **na-ṣa-ra-ta**
> This tablet I have sent to you to say to you: *"Guard! Be on your guard"* (EA 367.4 and 12 [2×])

> a-na mi-ni yi-iš-ta-pa-ru [š]arru^{ru} beli^{li} a-na ia-ši ú-ṣur-mi lu-ú **na-ṣir-ta**
> Why does the king, my lord, write to me: *"Guard! Be on your guard"*? (EA 117.84)

With ***malāku***. A third verb, the imperative of which appears frequently in rhetorical statements is *malāku*. In these cases, the Canaanite scribe addresses the king, requesting that he "give thought to" his servant or his city

---

85.1, 48), the scribe uses the Akkadian formula with *qibima* in the introduction (line 1), and the West Semitic modal form with final *-a* in the body of the letter (line 48).

37. Rainey, *Canaanite in the Amarna Tablets*, 3:199.

(EA 114.54, 116.17, 124.10, 132.8). This function of the verb *malāku* is not restricted to the imperative but also plays a similar role in the jussive/precative (for examples, see below, §3.3).

> **mi-lik** a-na arad ki-ti-k[a]
> *Give thought* to your loyal servant (EA 114.54)

> ša-ni-tú **mi-li-ik** [alu]gub-la àl ki-ti-ka
> Moreover, *give thought* to Gubla, your loyal city (EA 132.8)

With ***wuššuru***. The imperative of *wuššuru* appears frequently in the EA correspondence from Canaan, with and without the ventive ending (*uššir/uššira/mušera*): "*Send* me 50 pairs of horses and 200 infantry" (e.g., EA 70.10, 71.23–24); "*Send* a large force of archers" (e.g., EA 76.38–39, 85.38, 90.58, 94.15, 103.27, 107.29); "*Send* me a garrison to guard the city" (e.g., EA 79.15–16, 85.45, 96.28, 103.37, 130.46); "*Send* men to take the city" (e.g., EA 90.15–16, 108.66); "*Send* the commissioner" (e.g., EA 118.14, 33); "*Send* ships to get me" (EA 129.50, 132.53). Three suggestions have been made regarding the ending *-a* that appears on the imperative *uššira* and *muššera*:

(2.1) Since "*-ā* is the Akkadian correspondent to Canaanite *-ū* as the plural masculine imperative morpheme," it is possible that *uššira* indicates the presence of a plural of majesty.[38]

(2.2) The imperative *uššira* includes the ventive ending, and since in most cases it can logically be translated 'Send me', the additional expression *a-na ia-ši*, which is found with other verbs, is not needed.[39] In EA 82.15 and EA 87.9, Canaanite scribes quote from a letter originally written by an Egyptian scribe. In both quotations, the imperative *uššira* is followed by *it-ti-ia*. This additional element, not found elsewhere with *uššira* in Canaanite letters, may indicate that Egyptian scribes were less familiar with the use of the Akkadian ventive and, as a result, included this feature.

(2.3) When the imperative *uššira* is accompanied by the first-person-singular pronominal suffix *-ni* (e.g., *uš-ši-ra-ni*, EA 70.17, 76.24; *mu-še-ra-an-ni*, 287.51), the form *uššira* either includes a modal ending *-a* or has become the accepted form of the imperative for the verb *wuššuru*.[40]

An examination of the contexts in which *uššira* occurs supports the second view, that the verb appears with the ventive ending. As we will see below, where imperatives occur with the modal ending *-a*, they are normally preceded

38. Although Youngblood suggests this possibility, he states that such a conclusion is highly unlikely. He favors the second view, that the imperative *uššira* includes the ventive ending (Youngblood, *Amarna Correspondence of Rib-Haddi*, 94).

39. Ibid., 95; Rainey, *Canaanite in the Amarna Tablets*, 2:205.

40. Although Rainey strongly advocates that most imperatives with an *-a* ending include the ventive, he acknowledges the possibility that the *-a* ending on *uššira* could be a volitive affix (Rainey, *Canaanite in the Amarna Tablets*, 2:268–69).

by a particle of emphasis or by an interjection (e.g., *ša-ni-tam*, *ši-me ia-ši*). This is never the case with *uššira*.

(3) *Commands/requests.* The imperative, unmarked for commands, appears in contexts where both urgent and nonurgent commands are given. Polite requests and indirect commands are normally expressed with the jussive.

In Rib-Hadda's letter (EA 69) to an Egyptian official, the tone of the message is clearly one of desperation and critical need. The polite introductory formula is followed immediately by a vivid description of the threatening situation at hand. The text includes a number of strong comments in which the pressing needs are reinforced by the repetition of the adverb *ša-ni-tam* (lines 12, 15, 18, 24, 30). In this context, the commands are expressed by regular imperatives (*ša-a*[*l*], *ku-ru-u*[*b-mi*] 'Interrogate! Urge!') and require immediate attention, lest the situation deteriorate and Rib-Hadda perish at the hand of his enemies.[41]

(4) *In conditional sentences.* The imperative occurs in the apodosis of conditional sentences, with and without connecting *ù*. The contexts range from polite situations to circumstances involving matters of life and death.

> ù šum-[ma] da-mi-[ik] i-na pa-ni-ka ù š[u]-ku-un i-na ^{amêlu}rabiṣi ši-mi-rum i-n[a] pa-ni ^{amêlūtu} ḫa-za-nu-ti š[arri]
> So if it pleases you, *then appoint* as its commissioner someone respected by the king's mayors (EA 107.22–24)

> šum-[ma] libbi^{bi} šarri^{ri} a-na ba-la-aṭ ardi-šu ù ali^{li}-šu **uš-ši-ra** [m]a-ṣa-ar-ta ù ti-na-ṣa-ru ala-ka ù arda-ka
> If the king wants his servant and his city to survive, (then) *send* a garrison to guard your city and your servant (EA 112.31–33)

3.3.1.1. Imperatives as Interjections

With ***amāru***. In addition to expressing a regular command, the imperative of *amāru* functions as an interjection.[42] In these cases, it appears at the head of the sentence and draws attention to the information that immediately follows.

41. According to Moran, "urge with lo[ud cries] the king," based on EA 87.25 (Moran, "An Unexplained Passage in an Amarna Letter from Byblos," 124–25). Youngblood translates the passage: "pay hom[age] to the king." According to Moran, the word *karābu* is paralleled in *Enuma Elish* IV 28, with the same meaning.

42. Rainey and Cochavi-Rainey treat this verb as a "presentation particle" (Rainey, *Canaanite in the Amarna Tablets*, 2:274 and Z. Cochavi-Rainey, "Canaanite Influence in the Akkadian Texts Written by Egyptian Scribes in the 14th and 13th Centuries B.C.E.," *UF* 21 [1989] 41). Mark Mangano notes that it is one of the Canaanite verbs "used to mark a logical arrangement of thought" in EA texts (M. J. Mangano, *Rhetorical Content in the Amarna Correspondence* [Ph.D. diss., Hebrew Union College–Jewish Institute of Religion, 1990] 149).

a-mur URU Gu-ub-la la ki-(ma) URU.KI.ḪI.A [x x] URU Gu-ub-la URU ki-it-ti LUGAL B[E-ia] iš-tu da-ri-ti
Look! Gubla is not like (other) cities. Gubla is the loyal city of the king, my lord, from ancient times (EA 88.42–45)

a-mur a-na-ku NU.KÚR.TUM UGU-ia 5 MU.MEŠ
Look! As for me, there has been war against me for 5 years (possibly: '*Look at me.* There has been . . . !') (EA 106.16–17)

a-mur a-na-ku ia-nu ḫa-za-na i-na ar-ki-ti-ia ìš-tu URU Ṣu-mu-ra
Look! In my case, there is not a mayor from „umur that supports me (possibly: '*Look at me!* There is not . . .') (EA 117.9–11)

This use of *amāru* is not known in Classical Babylonian but appears in EA texts from Canaan, Egypt, Alašiya, and Hattusas.[43] This function of the *amāru* imperative finds its parallel in the Classical Hebrew verb רָאָה and in the Egyptian verb *ptr.*[44] Cochavi-Rainey writes:

> So it looks as though we have a three-way calque, Egyptian *ptr*, Akkadian *amur* and a West Semitic imperative like Hebrew *rᵉʾēʰ* (Dt. 1:8, 12; 4:5; 11:26; 30:15). Whether the usage originated among the Canaanites or among the Egyptians, or whether it may have been a purely independent development in the two languages, is impossible to determine. The indisputable fact is that both Egyptian and Canaanite scribes used the imperative *amur* in the Akkadian letters and documents.[45]

Cochavi-Rainey provides no answer for the origin of this idiom. Rainey, on the other hand, seems to favor a West Semitic provenance, since "by far the largest number of examples come from the Amarna letters written in Canaan. Therefore, one may at least suggest tentatively that the idiom is originally West Semitic, specifically Canaanite."[46] The distribution of occurrences seems to support this view, but one can also propose that, since verbs related to the physical senses are natural candidates for this sort of function, in Semitic and non-Semitic languages, there is no need to identify a source for this usage of *amāru*. For example, the English verbs *to look* and *to listen* often function as

43. For examples, see EA 1.28; 34.7; 60.6; 71.7; 84.38; 106.18; 107.8; 117.34; 118.39–40; 139.7, 39; 162.30, 67; 174.8; 175.7; 179.28; 187.9; 189.rev. 9; 209.7, 8; 211.7, 15; 227.5; 239.18; 254.10; 257.78; 264.5, 14–15; 287.25, 29, 32; 288.5, 9; 289.18; 362.62; 363.7; 365.15. Rainey, *CAT* 2:274–75. See also idem, "The Imperative 'See' as an Introductory Particle: An Egyptian–West Semitic Calque," in *Go to the Land I Will Show You: Studies in Honor of Dwight W. Young* (ed. J. Coleson and V. Matthews; Winona Lake, IN: Eisenbrauns, 1996) 309–16.

44. For examples with רָאָה, see above, §2.2.1.1; for examples in Egyptian, see Cochavi-Rainey, "Canaanite Influence in the Akkadian Texts Written by Egyptian Scribes," 42–44.

45. Ibid., 44.

46. Rainey, "The Imperative 'See' as an Introductory Particle," 316.

interjections. This is also the case with the French verbs *regarder* 'to look' and *écouter* 'to listen':

> **Regarde! / Écoute!** Je te l'ai dis hier!
> *Look!/Listen!* I told you so yesterday.

The issue is neither verbal form nor Semitic versus non-Semitic origin; it is semantics.

With ***šemû***. The imperative of *šemû* plays a similar role in a number of Canaanite letters. It is used to emphasize the urgency of the situation and is meant to draw attention to the message that immediately follows:

> **ši-me** ia-ši
> *Listen* to me! (EA 79.20, 83.14, 85.47, 93.9, 95.21–22, 102.29, 122.53 [2×])

In a number of cases, the verb *šime* is followed by one or more imperatives, thereby emphasizing the urgency of the situation and the importance of paying attention to the speaker's words (e.g., 85.47, 93.9, 102.29).

3.2.1.2. Imperatives as Adverbs

When it appears immediately before another imperative, the imperative of *alāku* functions adverbially.[47] Although rare in EA correspondence, this function of the verb *to go* is common to several of the Semitic languages (see §2.2.1.2 for the adverbial functions of הָלַךְ in Biblical Hebrew).

> **a-lik-mi** i-zi-iz a-na ^{alu}ṣu-mu-ur a-di ka-ši-di-ia
> *Go* stay in Ṣumur until I arrive (EA 102.15)

3.3.1.3. Imperatives with *-na* Ending

The NWSemitic particle of modality *-na* is well known in Ugaritic, EA Canaanite, and Hebrew. In EA texts, it is most commonly found on the indicative *yaqtulu* (e.g., *yaqtulu*[*n*]*na*);[48] it rarely appears with the volitive *yaqtula* (e.g., *yaqtula*[*n*]*na*)[49] and appears appears only a few times with the imperative (see examples below).

As discussed in the chapter on Biblical Hebrew (§2.2.1.3), the ending *-(n)na* became a separate particle in Ugaritic (separated from the verb by a word divider) and in Hebrew (as נָא). Due to the nature of the written language, in which no word division occurs, it is impossible to know whether the ending

47. Rainey describes this function of *al^{a}ku* as one of "exhortation" (idem, *Canaanite in the Amarna Tablets*, 2:276).

48. For examples with *īpušuna*, see 74.63, 90.22, 91.26, etc.; *inaṣ(ṣ)aruna*, see 112.10, 125.12; *tiliʾuna*, see 82.6; and *tištapruna*, see 117.8.

49. *ul timaḫḫaṣanī* (77.37).

-(n)na in EA Canaanite appears independently from the verb, or whether it is always attached to the verb.

Ebeling first discussed the presence of EA verbal forms with *-(n)na* endings in his 1910 publication "Das Verbum der El-Amarna Briefe."[50] He recognized that the ending normally occurred on the prefix conjugations, with a few cases with the imperative.[51] Moran, Rainey, and Zewi mention that the modal ending *-na* appears on only two imperatives in letters from Canaan (*uš-ši-ru-na-ni*, EA 71.23, and *le-qú-na*, EA 117.63).[52]

The imperative of *uššuru* is quite common in EA letters but not with the modal affix *-na*.[53] The imperative normally appears as *uššir* (regular form), *ušširu* (plural of majesty), or *uššira* (with ventive or modal ending). In EA 71.23, the scribe uses the plural of majesty in addressing the king, plus the modal affix *-na*.[54] He includes this affix not only on the imperative but also on two singular indicatives, verbal forms upon which the ending *-na* often appears (see discussion on *yaqtulu(n)na* in §3.5.3.1): *ù yu-wa-ši-ru-na* (l.13), *ù ti-ìl-qú-na* (l.15), *uš-ši-ru-na-ni* (l.23).

> **ù uš-ši-ru-na-ni NINNU ta-pal** ANŠE.KUR.RA
> *So send* 50 teams of horses (EA 71.23)

The affix *-na* appears on a number of verbs in EA 117: *le-qú-na* (line 63), *ti-eš-tap-ru-na* (line 8), *tu-ba-lu-na* (line 18), *tu-ṣa-na* (line 55), *ti-íl-qu-na* (line 64), *yu-ú-ul-qu-na* (line 68). The modal ending was obviously very familiar to the scribe who composed the letter.

> šum-ma lìb-bi LUGAL ba-li uš-ša-[ar] ERÍN^{MEŠ} pí-ṭá-ti ia-aš-pu-ur a-na ^{I}Ia-an-ḫa-mì ù a-na ^{I}Pí-ḫu-ra al-ku-mi qa-du LÚ^{MEŠ} ḫa-za-ni-ku-nu **le-qú-na** ^{KUR}a-mur-ri
> If the king wishes not to send the archer host, let him write to Yanʿʿamu and to Piʾʾura: Go on! Together with your mayors, *take* the land of Amurru (EA 117.63)

---

50. Ebeling, "Das Verbum der El-Amarna Briefe," 39–79.

51. For further discussion on *yaqtula(n)na*, see §3.4.1; on *yaqtulu(n)na*, see §3.5.3.1.

52. Moran, *Syntactical Study of the Dialect of Byblos*, 11; Rainey, *Canaanite in the Amarna Tablets*, 2:271; T. Zewi, *A Syntactical Study of Verbal Forms Affixed by -(n)n Endings in Classical Arabic, Biblical Hebrew, El-Amarna Akkadian and Ugaritic* (AOAT 260; Münster: Ugarit-Verlag, 1999) 170. An EA letter from Amurru gives us another case of an imperative with *-na*: EA 62.30, *še-ez-zi-bá-an-na-ši-mi*. Compare with EA 318.8, 14, *še-zi-ba-an-ni*.

53. For examples with *uššir*, see EA 82.28, 120.36, 121.42; *uššira*, see EA 75.43; 76.24, 38; 82.15; 83.37; 84.41, 44; 85.45, 80; 86.49, 90.15, 58, 60; 94.10.

54. Youngblood, *Amarna Correspondence of Rib-Haddi*, 94; Rainey, *Canaanite in the Amarna Tablets*, 2:272.

3.3.2. Imperatives with Final *-a*

EA texts include a great number of imperatives with the ending *-a* (e.g., *mu-še-ra*, EA 287.52, 289.45; *te-ra-ni*, EA 114.25; *bu-a$_4$-mi*, EA 96.24; *še-zi-ba-an-ni*, EA 318.8, 14; *šu-te-ra*, EA 83.23; *uš-ši-ra*, EA 70.17, et passim; *qí-ba-mi*, EA 73.33, 83.39, 85.48, 86.31, 93.10). The forms have been treated as either Akkadian ventives or as West Semitic modal injunctives equivalent to the long imperative of Hebrew.[55] In the early days of EA scholarship, P. E. Dhorme distinguished two forms of the imperative: the regular imperative and the imperative with final *-a* as "energic" forms equivalent to the Hebrew long imperative.[56]

ù qí-bi a-na LUGAL **ku-uš-da** ki-ma ar-ḫi-ìš
and say to the king: *Come* quickly! (EA 82.52)

bu-ʾa$_4$-mi ANŠE$^{\text{MEŠ LUGAL}}$
Search for the donkeys of the king (EA 96.24)

Shlomo Izre'el noted that the imperative of *nadanu* with final *-a* in EA 270.18 is a good Babylonian form with ventive ending but that one can also "see in this form an adaptation of the Canaanite long imperative," since its Hebrew cognate נָתַן regularly occurs as a long imperative תְּנָה.[57]

ù **id-na-ni** 20 ta-pal sisē a-na ia-ši
Give me 20 pairs of horses (EA 270.18; see also EA 103.42, 333.12)

In his publications, Rainey emphasizes that most EA verbal forms with the *-a* ending (e.g., *yaqtula* and imperatives) represent ventive forms rather than injunctive forms.[58] In his examination of the corpus, he observes that "many verbs with *-a* suffix are those which naturally took the ventive in Akkadian."[59] In cases where the ventive would have been unlikely in Akkadian, he attributes the presence of the *-a* ending to *modus attraction*, whereby a verb in injunctive contexts would attract the volitive *-a* ending to itself.[60] In his estimation, the only occurrence of a true Canaanite long imperative appears in the following passage:

i$_{15}$-nu-ma / iq-bi LUGAL be-li-ia \\ **ku-na** / a-na pa-ni ERIN.MEŠ GAL ù iq-bi / IR-du a-na be-li-šu

55. See discussions in Rainey, *CAT* 2, chap. 11; Izre'el, "The Gezer Letters," 64, 82.

56. Dhorme, "La langue de Canaan, part 1," 373. Dhorme mentions that long imperatives can be identified in Assyrian where the endings *-am* and *-amma* appear on imperatives: e.g., *i-ziz-za-am-ma* 'arise!'; *en-di-im-ma* 'stand up!'; and in Arabic where endings *-an* and *-anna* appear on imperatives.

57. Izre'el, "The Gezer Letters of the El-Amarna Archive," 64.

58. Rainey, *Canaanite in the Amarna Tablets*, 2:202–11, 265–73.

59. Ibid., 255.

60. Ibid., 205, 257.

> When the king, my lord, said: "*Be ready* for (the coming of) the great army," the servant answered (EA 147:35–38)

Rainey states that, in this case, the final *-a* ending could be a plural form or a ventive but, more likely, an injunctive ending related to the ending found on the long imperative of Biblical Hebrew. Rainey adds that the imperative *uššira* may also, in some cases, include the injunctive final vowel rather than the ventive suffix.[61] In Akkadian, the ventive ending *-a(m)* can be added to any finite verb, including the imperative. This ending is "essentially a directional element that denotes motion or activity in the direction of, or to a point near, the speaker (or a person being addressed, when the speaker places herself in the location of the person addressed)"[62] and occurs mainly with verbs of motion. EA texts from Babylonia (e.g., EA 9.12–18 and 35) and texts in peripheral Akkadian (e.g., EA 35.25–26) are consistent in their use of the imperative with ventive ending.

The picture is not as clear in the Canaanite texts. Verb forms ending with *-a* can be identified as either ventives or as modal injunctives. Verbs of motion, which are prone to appear with the ventive, can also denote modal nuances. For example, the imperative of *uššuru*, which commonly takes the ventive in Akkadian, often appears as *uššira* in Canaanite letters. Since in West Semitic languages, a final *-a* is a marker often appended to finite verbs to indicate politeness, it is possible to interpret *uššira* as a ventive or as a modal form.[63] The nature of the letters, in which the addressee is either the king or one of his officials, adds to the possibility that a verbal form with final *-a* indicates politeness or respect.[64]

In his review of *CAT*, Huehnergard challenges Rainey's view that imperatives with final *-a* are all ventives (except for *ku-na*) by arguing that the presence of ventive forms in the singular should be complemented by the presence of ventive forms in the plural. Huehnergard writes:

> It is worth noting here . . . that if such forms are indeed ventive, we should expect at least a few examples of plural verbs with the ventive allomorph *-ni* (*iprusūni*), which the scribes would presumably have learned at the same time as the singular; yet such forms are lacking, the plural counterpart to singular *yaqtula* being, in fact, the expected *tiqtulū*, which is also the plural of the apocopate *yaqtul*, just as in Ugaritic and Arabic. In other words, we find injunctive singulars written both *yaqtul* and *yaqtula*, and injuntive plurals written *tiqtulū*; this is just what we expect if both *yaqtul* and *yaqtula* represent NWS modal forms, and contrary to what is expected if *yaqtula* forms are ventive, viz., plural written *tiqtulūni*. The

61. Ibid., 268–69.

62. Huehnergard, *Grammar of Akkadian*, 133–34.

63. For further discussion, see §2.2.2.2 on the Hebrew long imperative.

64. As discussed in chap. 2, scribes frequently used long imperatives to mark politeness in contexts where someone lesser in status was addressing someone greater.

same considerations apply to the forms of the imperative with final *-a*, which Rainey (II 265–73) also considers to be ventive (although admitting that the purely Canaanite form *ku-na* probably contains the NWS modal *-a*; p. 266): plural imperatives regularly end in *-ū*, while the ventive *-ūni* is quite rare. (It might be added that it is not clear, to me at least, *why* Rainey is so keen to rid Amarna Canaanite of a form that is both perfectly understandable and, indeed, expected.)[65]

The nature of the EA letters is such that singular forms are much more common than plural forms, since, in most cases, the speaker addresses only one individual (e.g., king, vizier). Evidence from Canaanite letters reveals that the ventive occurs both in the singular (with *-a*) and in the plural (with *-nim*) on the imperative (e.g., pu-ḫu-ru-nim-mi EA 73.31) and on the indicative prefix conjugation (ù la i-nam-mu-šu-nim, EA 87.23; i-qa-bu-nim, EA 127.10; i-ri-bu-nim, EA 127.19). Canaanite scribes were therefore familiar with the ventive plural ending and used it appropriately. However, they did not append the ventive ending *-nim* on jussives, precatives, and *yaqtula* plural forms, even with verbs that commonly take the ventive in Akkadian.

In Canaanite letters, some verbs commonly found with the ventive in Akkadian occur with a final *-a* in the singular and with *-ū* in the plural rather than with the expected ending *-nim*. Although one may be tempted to conclude that the Canaanite plural ventive ending is *-ū*, the limited number of examples do not provide sufficient data to reach a definite conclusion on this matter. Nevertheless, based on the attested forms, two interpretations are possible:

(1) *The ending -ū is a ventive morpheme.* Since there is no morphological distinction between the singular ventive and the singular modal form with *-a* ending, it is possible that there is no morphological difference between the plural ventive and the plural modal injunctive *-ū*. Consequently, it is at times difficult to determine which idea the scribe intended to convey, especially in cases where both the ventive and the modal form are a possibility. In order to identify one form over another, one must consider the syntax of the whole sentence.

For example, the verb *leqû*, which commonly takes the ventive in Akkadian, appears in Canaanite letters in the singular with final *-a* in the first person (e.g., EA 362.23), in the second person (e.g., EA 95.37, 162.18), and in the third person (e.g., EA 71.30, 81.32, 84.34). In the plural, it appears with the *-ū* ending (e.g., EA 84.34, 137.82) but not with the *-nim* plural ending. The following passage includes the singular *ìl-ti-qa*, which can be identified as a ventive or as a Canaanite injunctive. If *ìl-ti-qa* is a ventive, then we could assume that *ti-ìl-qú* is also a ventive. But, since both verbs are dependent on a previous modal form (*lu-wa-ši-ra*) and express purpose, we conclude that both *ìl-ti-qa* and *ti-ìl-qú* are injunctives. Moreover, the social dynamics of the letter

65. J. Huehnergard, "Review of 'A Grammar of Amarna Canaanite,'" *BASOR* 310 (1998) 71.

(from a lesser party to a greater party) are conducive to the use of forms that express politeness.

> ù lu-wa-ši-ra be-li-ia LÚ^{MEŠ} **ú ti-ìl-qú** mi-im-mi^{MEŠ} ^{d}DA.MU-ia a-na ma-ḫar BE-ia **ù ú-ul ìl-ti-qa** mi-im-ma^{MEŠ} [š]a DINGIR^{MEŠ}-ka
> So may my lord send men *so that they may take* the property of my Tammuz to my lord and that the property of you gods *may not be taken* (EA 84.34)

(2) *The -ū ending and the "plural of majesty."* The ending *-ū* indicates a "plural of majesty" in passages where the subject of the verb is in the singular. For example, the singular imperative of *wuššuru* appears frequently as *uššira* both in Akkadian and in EA letters but never appears with *-nim* in the plural in Canaanite correspondence. The only plural form attested is *wuššurū* (EA 71.23 and 90.45). As suggested by Youngblood, both occurrences should be interpreted as a "plural of majesty" since, in both cases, the speaker is addressing a sole individual, and the addressee is of higher social status.[66]

> **ù uš-ši-ru-na-ni NINNU ta-pal ANŠE.KUR.RA ù MIN me** ERÍN^{MEŠ} GÌR^{MEŠ} ù i-zi-za i-na ^{URU}Ši-ga-ta i-na pa-ni-šu
> *So send me* fifty teams of horses and two hundred foot soldiers so that I might withstand him in ſiigata (EA 71.23, addressing Ḫaya, the vizier)

> ša-ni-tam yi-ì[š]-mé [LUGAL a-w]a-t[e] Ì[R]-šu ù uš-ši-ru [LIMMU me LÚ]^{MEŠ} ù EŠ t[a-p]al [A]NŠ[E].KU[R].R[A] ù [a-n]a-ṣ[a-r]a URU [a-n]a ka-[t]am
> Moreover, may [the king] listen to the [wo]rd of his [ser]vant. So *send* four hundred [troo]ps and thirty teams of [hor]ses so that I may [gu]ard the city for [y]ou (EA 90.45, addressing the king)

The verb ***qabû***. The Canaanite scribes did not restrict their use of the ending *-a* to verbs of motion (e.g., EA 147.36, *ku-na*; EA 93.10, *qí-ba-mi*; EA 74.56, *a-na-ṣa-ra*; EA 123.26, *ib-lu-ṭa*). Among these, the verb *qabû* displays peculiar features. The imperative *qí-bí* occurs within the body of letters as the unmarked form of the imperative (e.g., EA 73.43, 82.51, 86.28, 230.1). The form *qí-bí* appears with the enclitic *-ma* only in the Akkadian epistolary formula of introduction (e.g., EA 1.2, 9.2, 19.3, 28.3, 38.1, 82.2, 84.2, 85.1, 87.2, 363.2, 365.2, 366.2).[67] A third form, *qí-ba-mi* (impv. + *-a* + enclitic *-mi*) occur within the body of the letters (e.g., EA 73.33, 83.39, 85.48, 86.31, 93.10).

66. Youngblood, *Amarna Correspondence of Rib-Haddi*, 94, 346–47. The "plural of majesty" also appears with the jussive *ti-di-nu* in the introduction of several Canaanite letters: e.g., EA 71.5, 86.4. See ibid., 84; Moran, "New Evidence on Canaanite *taqtul(na)*," 35 n. 14; Rainey, *Canaanite in the Amarna Tablets*, 2:246.

67. Ibid., 2:273; Izre'el, "The Gezer Letters of the El-Amarna Archive," 39.

With ***qí-bi***. The regular imperative *qí-bi* is the unmarked form used for commands. Without the enclitic *-ma*, it appears within the body of letters:

> ti-i-de pa-ar-ṣa-ia i-nu-ma i-ba-ša-ta i-na [^{U}]^{RU}[Ṣ]u-mu-ra i-nu-ma [Ì]R [k] i-it-ti-ka a-na-ku **ù qí-bi** a-na LUGAL
> You know my conduct when you were in Ṣumur, that I am your loyal servant. *So say* to the king (EA 73.43)

> ú-ul ta-ša-aš / na-aq-ṣa-pu / **ù qí-bi** a-na LUGAL
> Have they not been distressed / angry /? *So say* to the king (EA 82.51)

> [a-mi-ni la táq-b]i a-na ia-ši [. . . **ù**] **qí-bi** a-na LUGAL
> Why do you not speak to me? . . . [*So*] *say* to the king[68] (EA 86.28; with *qí-ba* in line 31)

> a-na LUGAL BE-ia **qí-bi**
> *Speak* to the king, my lord (EA 230:1)

With ***qí-bí-ma***. The regular imperative of *qabû* is accompanied by the enclitic *-ma* only in the typical Akkadian epistolary formula, both in Canaanite and non-Canaanite letters.[69]

> a-na ni-ip-ḫu-ur-ri-ia LUGAL ^{KUR}m[i-iṣ-ri-i] **qí-bí-m[a]**
> *Say* to Niphuria, the king of Egypt (EA 19.3, non-Canaanite)

> a-na LUGAL^{ri} ^{KUR}mi-iṣ-ri ŠEŠ-ia **qí-bí-ma**
> *Say* to the king of Egypt, my brother (EA 38.1, non-Canaanite)

> [a-na] LUGAL BE-ia ^{d}UTU KUR$^{\text{KI.DIDLI.ḪI.A}}$ [q]í-bí-ma
> *Say* to the king, my lord, the sun-god of the two lands (EA 84.2, Canaanite)

> e.g., [a-na ^{m}]A-ma-an-ap-pí B[E-ia] **qí-bí-ma**
> *Say* to Aman-Appa, [my l]ord (EA 87.2, Canaanite)

With ***qí-ba-mi***. The imperative *qí-ba* is always accompanied by the enclitic *-mi*. In Akkadian, the enclitic *-mi* functions as a marker of direct speech and is appended to a word at the beginning of the quotation. In the EA Canaanite correspondence, it occurs both within and outside reported speech.[70] The enclitic *-mi* of these texts not only marks direct speech but also functions as a

68. Youngblood reconstructs [*ši-me ia-ši*] before *ù qíbi*, while Moran omits the reconstrution. Since I have shown that *ši-me ia-ši* is normally followed by *qí-ba-mi* rather than by *qí-bi*, I agree with Moran that the reconstruction of Youngblood is unlikely.

69. For examples, see EA 1.2, 9.2, 19.3, 28.3, 38.1, 82.2, 84.2, 85.1, 87.2, 90.2, 95.1, 96.2, 102.2, 104.2, 118.2, 120.2, 126.1, 130.2, 132.2, 141.3, 286.1, 287.65, 290.2, 292.2, 363.2, 365.2, 366.2, 367.2.

70. Huehnergard, *Grammar of Akkadian*, 136; idem, *The Akkadian of Ugarit* (HSS 34; Atlanta: Scholars Press, 1989) 209; G. Buccellati, *A Structural Grammar of Babylonian*

"focus marker" for emphasis and as a marker of the logical predicate (some of the functions fulfilled in Akkadian by the enclitic *-ma*).[71]

It is possible that some Canaanite scribes considered the letters to be direct speech, since a great number of them begin with instruction to "speak" to the ruler, thereby giving justification for the use of the direct-speech marker *-mi* throughout the letters.[72] It is also likely that NWSemitic languages had a marker of emphasis indicated by *-m(*v*)* since Ugaritic also includes an enclitic *-m*. When it is appended to an injunctive, the Canaanite enclitic *-mi* adds to the level of markedness and indicates a certain aspect of modality not expressed by the injunctives alone.

Since *qí-ba* always appears with the enclitic *-mi*, never occurs in reported speech, is always preceded by a syntagma that indicates emphasis (except in EA 73.33),[73] and includes the ending *-a*, I deduce that, in each case, the scribe intended to express strong modality (the urgency of the situation at hand).[74]

ša-ni-tam qí-ba-mi a-na ^{m}Ia-<an>-ḫa-mi
Moreover, say to (EA 83.39)

ša-ni-tam qí-ba-mi a-na [LUGAL]
Moreover, say to (EA 86.31)

ši-me ia-a-ši qí-ba-mi a-na LUGAL^{ri}
Listen to me, say to (EA 93.10)

ša-ni-tam ši-me ia-a-ši qí-ba-mi a-na ^{m}Ia-an-ḫa-mi
Moreover, listen to me, say to (EA 85.48)

(Wiesbaden: Harrassowitz, 1996) 366; S. Izre'el, *Amurru Akkadian: A Linguistic Study*, vol. 1 (HSS 40; Atlanta: Scholars Press, 1991) 329.

71. Moran, *Syntactical Study of the Dialect of Byblos*, 9–10; S. Izre'el, *Canaano-Akkadian* (Languages of the World / Materials 82; Munich: Lincom Europa, 1998) 41–42. In EA texts, the enclitic *-ma* occurs mostly in typical Akkadian introductory formulas (e.g., *qi-bí-ma*, EA 82.2, 84.2, 85.1, 87.2, 90.2, 95.1, 96.2, 102.2, 104.2, 118.2, 120.2, 126.1, 130.2, 132.2, 141.3, 286.1, 287.65, 290.2, 292.2, 363.2, 365.2, 366.2, 367.2; *ÌR-ka-ma*, EA 85.2; 87.3; 103.3; 118.3; 130.3; 132.3; 286.2, 62; 287.66; 288.2; 290.3). For a full discussion of the enclitic *-mi* in EA correspondence, see Rainey, *Canaanite in the Amarna Tablets*, 3:234.

72. Ibid., 3:237.

73. Although all the examples that follow present an intransitive *qí-ba-mi*, the verb in EA 73.33 is transitive. It is possible that the modal nuance introduced by *ša-ni-tam* and *ši-me ia-ši* in EA 83.39, 85.48, 86.31, and 93.10 is found in the accusative *a-wa-tam* in EA 73.33.

74. Other imperatives with final *-a* and enclitic *-mi* are *uš-ši-ra-mi* (with ventive ending, always in direct speech, e.g., EA 82.15, 28; 87.9; 90.15; 94.10; 132.13), and *bu-a-mi* (not in direct speech, EA 96.24). The imperative *uš-ši-ra* + *-mi* only occurs outside direct speech in EA 96.28 in a context where the ventive is unlikely. Rib-Hadda's father instructs his son to send men to guard the city. It is therefore possible that the final *-a* on *uš-ši-ra* is a modal ending rather than an indicator of the ventive.

In conclusion, the imperative of *qabû* is used to express unmarked commands (*qí-bí*), in typical Akkadian introductory epistolary formulas with *-ma* (*qí-bí-ma*) and with the ending *-a* and the enclitic *-mi* to accentuate a modal nuance (*qí-ba-mi*).

3.3.3. Negative Imperatives

The imperative never appears with a negative particle. A negative command is expressed by insertion of the particle *ul* or *la* before an imperfect (*yaqtulu*), a jussive, or a precative. Therefore, our discussion on negative commands and on the use of *ul* and *la* will appear with the discussion on negative jussives (see §3.4.1).

3.4. The Jussive

In EA texts, wishes and indirect commands are expressed by the West Semitic *yqtl-∅* jussive (in the first, second, and third persons), by its Akkadian counterpart, the precative *liqtul* (*lū +iprus*), and by the West Semitic *yaqtula* injunctive.[75] As demonstrated below, the jussive and precative express injunctions both in formulaic and nonformulaic statements. A review of the data reveals that one of the ways scribes from Canaan and Egypt learned their Akkadian was by mastering lists of rhetorical statements appropriate for political correspondence.[76]

(1) *In epistolary formulas.* As mentioned in our discussion of the imperative, a number of formulas appearing in the introduction of Canaanite letters contain jussives.[77] Although the precative and *yaqtula* are often used interchangeably with the jussive in the body of the letters, they never appear in the introduction of Canaanite letters. When a wish is expressed, Canaanite introduction epistolary formulas only include jussives. Non-Canaanite EA correspondence normally includes the nonverbal sentence *a-na . . .* (*da-an-ni-iš*) *lu-ú šul-mu* (e.g., EA 1, 2, 3, 6, 7, 8, 9, 10, 12, 15, 16, 17, 19, 20, 21, 23, 27, 28, 29, 33, 35, 37, 38, 39, 40, 41, 42). The most common Canaanite EA epistolary formula with jussives contains the verb *nadānu*:

> ^{d}NIN ša ^{URU}Gub-la **ti-din / ti-di-in$_4$ / ti-id-di-in$_4$** KALAG.GA i-na pa-ni LUGAL^{ri} EN-ia
> (**ti-din**, EA 75.4, 92.5; **ti-di-in$_4$**, EA 76.4, 79.4, 105.3, 107.3, 108.3, 109.3, 114.3, 116.4, 117.3, 118.7, 119.4, 121.4, 122.5, 123.5, 125.6, 130.5, 132.4; **ti-id-di-in$_4$**, EA 68.5)
> *May* the lady of Gubla *grant* power to the king, my lord.

---

75. In some instances, the third-person masculine-singular or plural jussive may appear with a preformative *t-* rather than the usual West Semitic *y-* affixed to the root of the verb (*taqtul*[*ū*] / *yaqtul*[*ū*]). See Moran, "New Evidence on Canaanite *taqtul(na)*," 33–35.

76. M. J. Mangano, *Rhetorical Content in the Amarna Correspondence from the Levant* (Ph.D. diss., Hebrew Union College–Jewish Institute of Religion, 1990) 125.

77. For examples on the imperative used in such formulas, see §3.3.1 (1).

(2) *In rhetorical statements.* The correspondence of the EA letters includes a number of formulaic expressions for wishes and indirect commands with jussives and precatives.[78] These phrases repeated two or three times in the body of letters reveal a writing technique that served to strengthen the scribe's learning (e.g., EA 103.5, 23, 33; and 107.12, 25, 35, "May the king heed the words of his servant"; EA 116.6, 10; 144.10, 17, 22; 161.41, 46; 273.8, 18, 25; 287.11, 49, 57, "May the king know that"; EA 136.35, 43; 149.8, 53, "May the king, my lord, give thought to."

Although the *yaqtula* functions as an injunctive and is used, in some contexts, interchangeably with the jussive, it never appears in the formulaic expressions listed here. The *yaqtula* is restricted to West Semitic usage and does not participate in Akkadian frozen expressions learned by the scribes. Some of the verbs found in formulaic expressions with jussives are also commonly found in formulas with imperatives.[79]

With ***lamādu:***

Imperative. "Be informed that . . ." (EA 34.4–5; 79.8; 90.5; 101.37–38; 113.10; 284.6; 292.52; see §3.2.1)

Jussive/Precative: "May the king be informed that" (EA 64.8; 75.35; 142.19; 143.36; 237.8; 238.23; 264.23; 281.31; 282.8, 16; 283.18; 292.26; 294.14, 25; 295.4; 298.20; 335.8, 13; 366.11, 17), **yi-il-ma-ad** LUGAL be-li-ia // **li-il-ma-ad** LUGAL be-li-ia . . .

With ***qâlu:***

Imperative. "Do not be negligent" (EA 74.13, 90.57, 139.5, negative particle *ul* or *la* + 2nd-person jussive)

Jussive. "May the king not neglect" (EA 68.16–17, 32; 132.43–44; 137.25, 59, 77, 94; 138.109; 149.40, with negative particles *ul* or *la* + 3rd-person jussive), la-a / ú-ul **ia-ku-ul / ia-qúl-me** LUGAL EN-ia

With ***malāku:***

Imperative. "Give thought" (EA 114.54; 116.17; 124.10; 132.8)

Jussive/Precative. "May the king, my lord, give thought" (EA 105.6; 114.20; 136.35, 43; 149.8, 53; 155.14; 263.17; 288.23; 299.16; 364.27), ù LUGAL EN-ia **yi-im-lu-uk / ya-am-li-ik / yi-am-li-ik / li-im-li-ik-mi / li-im-lu-uk-mi** a-na ÌR-šu

With ***wuššuru:***

78. Mangano, *Rhetorical Content in the Amarna Correspondence*, 127.

79. For comments on the word order, deixis, mood, *Zeibezug*, tense and aspect of the *yqtl-Ø* in precative and purpose functions in EA Canaanite, see Korchin, *Markedness in Canaanite and Hebrew Verbs*, 80–100, 119–33.

Imperative. "*Send* (archers, a garrison, men, etc.)" (EA 70.17; 75.43; 76.24, 38; 82.15; 83.37; 84.41; 85.45, 80; 87.9; 90.15, 58; 94.10; 96.28; 114.45; 118.14, 34; 121.42; 123.34; 126.43, 48; 129.50; 130.46; 132.13, 53)

Jussive/Precative. "(Moreover) may the king, my lord, send" (EA 84.28; 95.31; 104.14; 117.72; 149.18; 160.33; 162.58; 182.8; 216.15; 255.21; 263.24; 269.11, 15; 270.24; 271.17; 279.14; 281.12, 27; 282.12; 283.25; 284.16; 285.29; 286.46; 288.59; 289.43; 300.15; 366.31) (ša-ni-tam) **lu-wa-ší-ra-am / yu-wa-ši-ra / yu-ši-ra** LUGAL EN-ia

Additional formulaic statements with jussives and precatives that appear within the body of letters are:

li-ìš-mé / yi-iš-mé / yi-iš-mi LUGAL^{ru} a-wa-te ÌR-šu
May the king *heed* the words of his servant
(EA 74.53–54; 75.20; 79.13; 85.16; 89.55; 100.30; 103.5, 23, 33; 107.12, 25, 35; 108.65; 116.44; 122.44; 136.6; 137.38; 164.27; 169.6; 234.10; 263.5)

ù li-it-ri-iṣ / li-it-ru-uṣ / yi-it-ru-uṣ i-na pa-ni LUGAL^{ri} EN-ia
May it seem good to the king to
(EA 64.12; 74.60; 92.46–47; 103.40; 106.35; 250.25; 286.44; 366.28)

yi-de / li-di-mi / lu-ú i-de LUGAL EN-ia
May the king, my lord, *know*
(EA 68.8; 70.24–25; 75.6; 100.8; 104.6; 114.8; 116.6, 10; 139.29; 144.10, 17, 22; 152.54; 154.29; 155.20, 40, 57; 157.6; 161.41, 46; 174.18; 175.14; 177.10; 180.8; 182.6; 220.20; 226.6; 230.20; 244.8; 246.1; 248.9, 21; 250.4, 9; 257.8; 267.15; 268.8; 270.9, 22; 271.9; 273.8, 16, 25; 279.9; 280.36; 286.25; 287.11, 49, 57; 289.35; 304.24; 305.23; 306.28; 307.12; 330.9, 17; 333.4; 364.24; 365.8, 31)

(3) *Interchange of jussive, precative and* yaqtula. In many cases, Canaanite scribes use the jussive, the *yaqtula* volitive, and the precative in the same letter to express similar types of injunction. Rainey noticed that, when this phenomenon occurs, the precative is "first in a chain of injunctive clauses, the subsequent verb forms being either WS jussives or volitives."[80] According to Moran, the jussive and *yaqtula* are "essentially the same with the accidental difference of emphasis, the latter [*yaqtula*] probably the more emphatic form. . . . In other words, the Byblian scribes used interchangeably *yaqtul* and

80. Rainey, *Canaanite in the Amarna Tablets*, 2:217; idem, "The Use of the Precative by Canaanite Scribes in the Amarna Letters," in *Mesopotamica – Ugaritica – Biblica* (ed. M. Dietrich and O. Loretz; AOAT 232. Kevelaer: Butzon & Bercker / Neukirchen-Vluyn: Neukirchener Verlag, 1993) 331–41

yaqtula, though undoubtedly with some slight difference of meaning which escapes us."[81] Korchin's analysis of the Canaanite *yqtl-Ø* prefix conjugation presents data and conclusions not previously discussed in EA scholarship regarding "markedness" and the Canaanite verbal system. He notes that

> *yqtl-Ø* constitutes the unmarked form in opposition to the other prefixed verb forms of EA CanAkk. Morphologically, *yqtl-Ø* exhibits the absence of any paradigmatic (nonplural) suffix morphemes, thereby being structurally opposed to those prefixed verb forms—*yqtl-u, yqtl-a, yqtl-u-(n)na, yqtl-a-(n)na*—that do entail such morphemes. At a strictly formal level, therefore, the paradigm that does not exhibit overt specificity is unmarked, while the paradigms that do exhibit overt specificity are marked.[82]

Where we have verbs of motion with final *-a*, the possibilities include: (1) a jussive with ventive ending; (2) an injunctive (*yaqtula*); or (3) a combination of both forms, through which the scribe indicates both direction and modality.

Our first example includes two verbs with final *-a*. The first one (*ia-di-na*) is a verb of motion that typically occurs with the ventive in Akkadian and in Canaanite letters. It can therefore be interpreted as a jussive with ventive ending (more likely) or as a volitive *yaqtula* (less likely). The second verb (*a-na-ṣa-ra*) does not typically occur with the ventive and should be interpreted as a first-person volitive. The first sentence includes two independent clauses while the second sentence includes a main clause and a purpose clause (conforming to the rule of "modal congruence").

> **ìš-mé** LUGAL^{ru} a-wa-te ÌR-šu **ù ia-di-na** ba-la-ṭá ÌR-šu **ù yu-ba-li-iṭ** ÌR-šu ù **a-na-ṣa-r[a** URU k]i-it-ti-šu
> *May* the king listen to the word of his servant *and give* his servant life. *May he preserve the life* of his servant *so that he may protec*[*t*] his [l]oyal [city] (EA 74.53–56)

The following example includes two verbs with final *-a*. The first one (*lu-wa-ši-ra*) is a verb of motion that appears frequently with the ventive both in Akkadian and in Canaanite letters. Its precative form provides the modal aspect while the final *-a* indicates the ventive. The second verb (*ú-ul ìl-ti-qa*), although common with the ventive, introduces a negative purpose clause in which a volitive is expected. The form *ìl-ti-qa* can therefore represent a jussive with ventive ending (more likely) or a volitive *yaqtula* (less likely).

> **ù lu-wa-ši-ra** be-li-ia LÚ.^{MEŠ} ú **ti-ìl-qú** mi-im-mi^{MEŠ} ^{d}DA.MU-ia a-na ma-ḫar BE-ia ù ú-ul **ìl-ti-qa** mi-im-ma^{MEŠ} [š]a DINGIR^{MEŠ}-ka

81. Moran, *Syntactical Study of the Dialect of Byblos*, 105.
82. Korchin, *Markedness in Canaanite and Hebrew Verbs*, 146–47.

> *Let my lord send* me men, *that they may take* the property of my Tammuz to my lord *and that the* property [belon]ging to your gods *may not be taken* (EA 84.31–35)

In our next example, the precative marker on *li-di-na* indicates volition, while the final *-a* indicates the ventive—as is common with the verb *na-dā-nu*. The following two verbs of the sequence are first-person jussives in purpose clauses.

> **ù li-di-na** LUGAL EN-ia ERÍN^{MEŠ} pí-ṭá-ta ù **ni-pu-uš** URU.DIDLI.ḪÁ LUGAL EN-ia ù **ni-ša-ab** a-na URU.DIDLI.ḪÁ LUGAL EN-ia DINGIR-ia ^{d}UTU-ia
> So *may* the king, my lord, *provide* troops *so that we may rebuild* the cities of the king, my lord, *and so that we may settle* in the cities of the king, my lord, my son (EA 363.17–23)

The scribes who wrote EA letters outside Canaan never used the jussive and the volitive *yaqtula* to express volition (e.g., letters from Babylonia, Mittani, Alašiya) but expressed wishes with the precatives at the end of clauses, as is expected in Akkadian. In Canaanite texts, on the other hand, the precative and the jussive appear at the head of the clause, as expected in West Semitic syntax, and is often accompanied by other West Semitic injunctives:

Non-Canaanite with precative (typical Akkadian word order):

> -ḫu-ú-a ḫurâṣa ba-na-a ma-ʾa-da **li-še-bi-la-am-ma** a-na du-ul-li-ia **lu-uš-ku-un**
> *May* my brother *send me* much fine gold *so that I may use* it on my work (EA 7.64–65—Babylonia)

> ištar a-na ša-me-e aḫi-ia ù ia-ši **li-iṣ-ṣur-an-na-ši I me li-im šanāti ù ḫe-du-ta ra-bi-ta bêltum** *annîtum* a-na ki-la-a-al-li-ni **li-id-din-an-na-ši-ma**
> *May* Šauška, the mistress of heaven, *protect us*, my brother and me, 100,000 years, and *may* our mistress *grant* both of us great joy (EA 23.27–29—Mittani)

Canaanite with precative and/or jussive (typical West Semitic word order):

> ša-ni-tam **lu-wa-ší-ra-am** LUGAL [BE-i]a ^{LÚ}MAŠKIM-šu ša da-an qa-d[u ERÍN^{MEŠ}] ù **li-iṣ-ṣur** URU^{KÍ} BE-ia ù **ib-luṭ** a-na-ku ù **u[r-r]a-[a]d** BE-ia ^{d}UTU KUR$^{\text{KI.ḪI.A}}$
> Moreover, *may* the king, my lord, *send* his commissioner who is strong, together [with troops] *to guard* the city of my lord, *so that I may live and serve* my lord, the Sun of all countries (EA 84.26–29—Byblos)

> uš-ši-ra-am-mi ^{LÚ}DUMU KIN-ka it-ti-ia a-na ma-ḫar LUGAL BE-ka ù lu-ú **li-di-na-ku** ERÍN^{MEŠ} ù ^{GIŠ}GIGIR^{MEŠ} i-zi-ir-tam a-na ka-tam ù **ti-ṣú-ru** URU

Send your messenger here to me before the king, you lord, *so that he may give* you troops and chariots as a help to you *to guard* the city (EA 87.9–14—Byblos)

3.4.1. Negative Jussives

In peripheral dialects of Akkadian, the two negative particles *ul* and *lā* occur interchangeably.[83] West Semitic influence is clear in the use of *ul* as a negative particle with volitives. This particle corresponds to the Hebrew particle of negation אַל, which normally occurs with jussives and cohortatives. In EA Canaanite, the *ul* negative particle is common with indicative verbs in interrogative sentences where no interrogative pronoun is used. According to Rainey, "[C]lauses having an interrogative pronoun or an interrogative adver(ial) are negated by *lā*; clauses without such elements, which are simply interrogative by nature, are negated by *ul*. There is practically no exception to this rule."[84] Huehnergard adds that this phenomenon not only is true in EA and in Mari texts but occurs in Old Babylonian texts in general.[85]

a-na mi-nim-mi la-a **tu-wa-ši-ra** ^{LÚ}DUMU ši-ip-ri-ka a-na maḫ-ri-ia
Why *did you not send* your messenger to me?
(EA 34.9–10; 34.46–48–*lā* with the interrogative particle)

[ú]-ul ta-aq-[bu a-n]a EN-ka ù yu-wa-ši-ru-n[a-k]a i-na pa-ní ERÍN^{MEŠ} pí-[ṭ]á-ti ù tu-ša-am-ri-ru LÚ^{MEŠ} GAZ
Will you not speak to your lord that he send you at the head of the archers to drive off the Apiru from the mayors
(EA 77.21—Byblos, *ul* with no interrogative particle)

Moran advocates that "there is no distinction made in the usage of *ul* and *lā*" at Byblos, but a close look at their distribution in the whole EA Canaanite corpus reveals the following features:

1. Some scribes use *both negative particles indiscriminately with the same verb*, in order to express the same idea. This indicates that, in the mind of those scribes, a distinction between the two particles was nonexistent. EA 68 provides a good example in which both negative particles appear with the verb *qâlu*, expressing the same idea in both passages:

ù **la a-a-qúl-me** LUGAL EN-ia iš-tu [^{UR}]^{U}Ṣu-mu-ur^{KI}
So, *may* the king my lord *not keep silent* regarding the city of Ṣumur
(EA 68.14–16)

83. Huehnergard, "Review of *A Grammar of Amarna Canaanite* by A. Rainey," 71.
84. Rainey, *Canaanite in the Amarna Tablets*, 3:214.
85. Huehnergard, "Review of *A Grammar of Amarna Canaanite* by A. Rainey," 75.

ù ú-ul **[a-a-q]úl-ma** LUGAL iš-t[u] [UR]U$^{\text{DIDLI.KI}}$-šu
So *may* the king *not keep silent* regarding his cities (EA 68.30–32)

2. Both *ul* and *la* occur *with jussives in main clauses*:

[ú]-ul yi-iš-me LUGAL kar$_5$-ṣí ÌR ki-ti-šu
May the king *not listen* to the slander of his loyal servant (EA 119.26–27)

la-a yi-iš-mé LUGAL be-li a-wa-teMEŠ ša-nu-ti
May the king, my lord, *not listen* to the words of other men (EA 126.62–63)

ú-ul ta-qa-al-mi ìš-tu [š]i-ip-ri an-nu-ú
Do not remain silent regarding this message (EA 76.46–47)

3. After a volitive in the main clause, *ul* occurs with the volitive in a negative purpose clause:

uš-ši-ru-na-ni NINNU ta-pal ANŠE.KUR.RA ù MIN me ERÍN^{MEŠ} GÌR^{MEŠ} ù **i-zi-za** i-na ^{URU}Ši-ga-ta i-na pa-ni-šu a-di a-ṣí ERÍN^{MEŠ} pí-ṭá-ti ú-ul **yu-pa-ḫi-ra** ka-li LÚ^{MEŠ} GAZ^{MEŠ} ù **[y]i-ìl-qa** ^{URU}Ši-ga-t[a]
Send 50 teams of horses and 200 foot soldiers so that I *may* be able to withstand him in Šigata until the archer host goes out, *lest he muster* all the Apiru and take Šigata (EA 71.23–30)

mi-lik-mi a-na UR[U-ka] [ú-u]l **yi-ìl-qé-ši** ^{m}ÌR-[A-ši-ir-ta]
Give thought to [your] city [*les*]*t* Abdi-Aširta *take it* (EA 90.11)

4. The volitive *yaqtula* is negated with the particle *ul* in independent and subordinate clauses:

ú-ul yi-ìš-ma ^{m}ÌR-a-ši-ir-[ta]
Do not let Abdi-Aširta *hear* (of it)! (EA 82.23)

ú-ul yi-ma-qú-ta ERÍN^{MEŠ} ka-ra-[š]i
May the campaigning troops *not attack me* (EA 83.43)

ù lu-wa-ši-ra be-li-ia LÚ^{MEŠ} ú ti-ìl-qú mi-im-mi^{MEŠ} ^{d}DA.MU-ia a-na ma-ḫar BE-ia ù ú-ul **ìl-ti-qa** mi-im-ma^{MEŠ} [š]a DINGIR^{MEŠ}-ka
So *may* my lord send men so that they can take the property of my Tammuz to my lord, *lest* the property that belongs to your gods *be taken* (EA 84.31)

3.5. The *yaqtula*

Moran was the first to propose the existence of a Canaanite (non–East Semitic) modal prefix conjugation with final short *-a* (*yaqtula*) in the NWSemitic corpus of the EA letters.[86] In his study of the morphosyntax of the indicative *yaqtulu* and the nonindicative *yaqtula* in the Byblos corpus, Moran stated,

> To prove that there is a subjunctive in these letters, we must show: 1) that *yaqtula* is reserved for the expression of a certain type of idea or for a certain syntactical situation, and this is in general accord with the use of the subjunctive in Arabic; 2) that *yaqtulu* and *yaqtula* are not used indiscriminately but that a shift from one to the other is significant. . . . The overall statistics on the *yaqtula* forms in the Byblos letters are the following: out of 75 occurrences, 18 are used as jussives, 30 are used to express purpose, or intended result, 14 are verbs of an apodosis or a protasis in a conditional sentence, 5 are doubtful because of a damaged context, 8 can only be called allatives. In themselves, apart from detailed analysis, these facts are significant, for they show that *yaqtula* found favor with the Byblian scribes only in a very restricted usage, that of a volitive.[87]

As mentioned above (see §2.2.4.2), Moran's study of the syntax of the *yaqtula* in purpose clauses led him to propose the rule of modal congruence. Rainey originally supported this view but, after examining the evidence closely, he concluded that the *yaqtula* in EA texts represents the Akkadian ventive.[88] Josef Tropper and Steven Fassberg also challenged Moran's conclusions. Tropper proposed that the EA *yaqtula* represents a Canaanite modal form in the first person, an Akkadian ventive in the second and third persons, and possibly a Canaanite *yaqtulanna* in verbal forms where a pronoun suffix is preceded by *-a(n)*.[89] Steven Fassberg highlighted the directional nature of the *yaqtula* and proposed that the basic function of the modal form indicates a verbal action that is directed toward the speaker or on his/her behalf.[90]

The following list shows the distribution of (1) *yaqtula* with verbs that rarely appear with the Akkadian ventive ending *-a(m)*, and (2) *yaqtula* with verbs that are commonly attested with the Akkadian ventive.[91]

---

86. W. L. Moran, "A Syntactical Study of the Dialect of Byblos as Reflected in the Amarna Tablets" in *Amarna Studies: Collected Writings* (ed. J. Huehnergard and S. Izre'el; HSS 54; Winona Lake, IN: Eisenbrauns, 2003) 84–95; "Early Canaanite *yaqtula*," in *Amarna Studies: Collected Writings* (ed. J. Huehnergard and S. Izre'el; HSS 54; Winona Lake, IN: Eisenbrauns, 2003) 179–95).

87. Moran, *Syntactical Study of the Dialect of Byblos*, 87.

88. Rainey, *Canaanite in the Amarna Tablets*, 2:202–11, 254–63.

89. Josef Tropper, "Ventiv oder *yaqtula*-Volitiv in den Amarnabriefen aus Syrien-Palästina?" in *Ana šadî Labnāni lū allik* (ed. B. Pongratz-Leisten et al.; *AOAT* 247; Neukirchen-Vluyn: Neukirchener Verlag, 1997) 402–3; *Ugaritische Grammatik* (AOAT 273; Münster: Ugarit-Verlag) 457.

90. Steven E. Fassberg, "The Lengthened Imperative *qōtlâ* in Biblical Hebrew," *HS* 40 (1999) 7–13.

91. The list of verbs is taken from the following corpus of Canaanite letters: EA 68–130 (Byblos), 267–271, 292, 297–300, 378 (Gezer), 286–290 (Jerusalem), and 362–367 (various rulers).

- Not commonly attested with the Akkadian ventive

First Person:

naṣāru (e.g., EA 74.56, 83.33, 90.47, 117.73, 123.26)
balāṭu (e.g., EA 117.92, 123.26)
dabābu (e.g., EA 119.23)
epēšu (e.g., EA 83.23)
maḫāṣu (e.g., EA 270.21)
dabāru (e.g., EA 85.68)
dakû (e.g., EA 131.28)
arādu ('to serve', e.g., EA 294.53, 300.20)[92]

Third Person:

šemû (e.g., EA 82.23)

- Commonly attested with the Akkadian ventive

First Person:

izuzzu (e.g., EA 71.25, 94.12, 107.34, 132.48)
ezēbu (e.g., EA 294.31)

Second Person:

šapāru (e.g., EA 77.7, 95.7, 102.14)
erēbu (e.g., EA 300.18)

Third Person:

leqû (e.g., EA 71.28, 81.32, 84.34, 91.6, 118.33)
nadānu (e.g., EA 74.54; 83.31; 85.19, 76; 93.11; 117.78; 118.16; 79.32; 85.38; 86.32)
wuššuru (e.g., EA 74.60; 83.34; 85.18; 117.25, 66, 72, 77)[93]
waṣû (e.g., EA 81.30, 82.30, 87.17)
paḫāru (e.g., EA 71.28, 85.77)
paṭāru (e.g., EA 118.34)
qabû (e.g., EA 129.52)
maqātu (e.g., EA 81.31, 83.43)
ḫamāṭu (e.g., EA 129.78)
ezēbu (e.g., EA 126.45)

1. The following examples belong to the first category (*not commonly attested with the Akkadian ventive*). The verbs appear either in

92. In Akkadian, the verb *arādu* means 'to come/go down', while the Canaanite verb *arādu* means 'to serve'. Izre'el suggests that the root of the latter is a *prima aleph* verb rather than a *prima waw* verb, consequently explaining the new meaning in the Canaanite texts (Izre'el, "The Gezer Letters of the El-Amarna Archive," 42 and n. 278b).

93. See also EA 104.14, 116.72, 118.42, 123.41, 131.12, 129.30.

independent clauses, in a sequence of injunctives, or in the apodosis of conditional sentences:[94]

*With **naṣāru:***[95]

yu-wa-ši-ra LUGAL^{ru} ANŠE.KUR.RA a-na ÌR-šu ù **a-na-ṣa-ra URU LUGAL**
May the king send horses to his servant *so that I may guard* the city of the king (EA 117.73)

*With **balāṭu:***

uš-ši-ra **[3]** LÚMEŠ ù **ib-lu-ṭa** ù **i-na-ṣi-ra URU a-na** LUGAL^{ri}
Send [3] men *so that I may live* and guard the city for the king (EA 123.26)

*With **dabābu:***

ù a-da-bu-ba ka-li ip-ši[-š]u-nu ù yi-di LUGAL^{ru} i-nu-ma ÌR ki-ti a-na-ku a-na ša-šu
So let me tell about all their deeds so that the king *may* know that I am a loyal servant of his (EA 119.23)

*With **epēšu:***

šu-te-ra a-wa-tam a-na ia-ši ù **i-pu-ša a-na-ku ki-ta it-ti** ^{m}ÌR-A-ši-ir-ta ki-ma ^{m}Ia-pa-^{d}IM ù ^{m}Zi-im-ri-[d]a
Send back word to me *or I will make* an alliance with Abdi-Aširta, like Iapa-Hadda and Zimrida (EA 83.23)

*With **maḫāṣu:***

id-na-m[i] DAM-ka ù DUMU^{MEŠ}-ka ù lu-ú **i-ma-ḫa-ṣa**
Give me your wife and your sons, *or I will smite* (you) (EA 270.21)

*With **dabāru:***

i-nu-ma DIŠ "a-za-nu SAG$_{4}^{bu}$-šu it-ti SAG$_{4}^{bi}$-ia ù **ú-da-bi-ra** ^{m}ÌR-A-ši-ir-ta iš-tu ^{KUR}A-mur-ri
If one mayor would ally himself with me, *then I would drive out* Abdi-Aširta from Amurru (EA 85.68)

94. These functions correspond to those of the Hebrew cohortative (see §2.4).
95. When *a-na-ṣa-ru* occurs (e.g., EA 296.21, 378.11), it does not express volition, while *a-na-ṣa-ra* always occurs in sequences of volitives. The Hebrew cognate נָצַר appears as a long imperative in Ps 141:3 and as a cohortative in Ps 119.33, 34, 115, 145 (in main and purpose clauses). This similarity in morphology and syntax between *naṣāru* and נָצַר shows that the EA scribes were familiar with the modal form and chose to add the *-a* ending to express modality.

With ***arādu:***

‘to serve’, e.g., EA 294.53, 300.20 (for text 300, see VAT 1606; for text 294, see BM 29854)

2. The following examples belong to the second category (*commonly attested with the Akkadian ventive*). The verbs with final *-a* can be interpreted either as jussives + ventive morpheme or as *yaqtula* volitives. As mentioned above, when motion is obvious, preference is given to the ventive, notwithstanding the possibility that the scribe may also have intended to include a modal nuance in the context. The verbs occur in main clauses or in purpose clauses according to the rule of “modal congruence.”

With ***leqû:***

ù lu-wa-ši-ra be-li-ia LÚ^{MEŠ} ú ti-ìl-qú mi-im-mi^{MEŠ} ^{d}DA.MU-ia a-na ma-ḫar BE-ia ù ú-ul **ìl-ti-qa** mi-im-ma^{MEŠ} [š]a DINGIR^{MEŠ}-ka
Now, *may* my lord send men so that they *may* take the property of my Tammuz to my lord, *lest* the property belonging to your gods *be taken* (EA 84.34)

With ***nadānu:***

yi-ìš-mé LUGAL^{ru} a-wa-te ÌR-šu [i]a-di-na LÚ^{MEŠ} a-na na-ṣa-ar [UR]U-šu
May the king hear the word of his servant (and) *give* men to guard his city (EA 85.76)

With ***wuššuru:***

yu-wa-ši-ra [LÚ]-šu ù yi-zi-iz i-na-an-na ù ad-šu-[ud] a-na-ku a-na ma-ḫar LUGAL^{ri} EN
May he send his man to stay this time so that I may come into the presence of the king (my) lord (EA 74.60)

With ***waṣû:***

uš-ši-ir-mi ^{GIŠ}MÁ a-na ^{KUR}Ia-ri-mu-ta ù **ú-ṣa-ka** KÙ.BABBAR^{MEŠ} lu-bu-ši ìš-tu ša-šu-⟨nu⟩
Send a ship to Iarimuta *so that* silver and garments *be sent to you* from them (EA 82.29)

With ***paṭāru:***

uš-ši-ru-na-ni NINNU ta-pal ANŠE.KUR.RA ù MIN me ERÍN^{MEŠ} GÌR^{MEŠ} ù i-zi-za i-na ^{URU}Ši-ga / ta / i-na pa-ni-šu a-di a-ṣi ERÍN^{MEŠ} pí-ṭá-ti ú-ul **yu-pa-ḫi-ra** ka-li LÚ^{MEŠ} GAZ^{MEŠ} ù [y]i-ìl-qa ^{URU}Ši-ga-t[a]

Send me 50 teams of horses and 200 foot soldiers so that I may stand in fiigata until the coming of the archer host, *lest he muster* all the Apiru and take Šigata (EA 71.28)

With ***paṭāru:***

Uš-ši-ra [amêlu]rabiṣa yi-íl-qa-šu-nu ú-ul i-ti-zi-ib URU ù **i-pa-ta-ra** a-na mu-ḫi-ka
Send the commissioner to take them, *lest* I abandon the city *and go off* to you (EA 118.34)

With ***qabû:***

la-a-mi yi-iq-ba LUGAL be-lí
May the king, my lord, *not say* (EA 129.52)

With ***maqātu:***

ú-ul yi-ma-qú-ta ERÍN[MEŠ] ka-ra-[š]i UGU-ia
May the troops on campaign *not fall* upon me (EA 83.43)

With ***ḫamāṭu:***

yu-ḫa-mi-ta uš-šar ERÍN[MEŠ] p[i-ṭa]-t[i] LUGAL[ru] ù yi-íl-qi-šu-nu
May the king *hasten* to send archer hosts to take them (EA 129.78)

Although most occurrences of third person with final *-a* appear with verbs of motion commonly used with the ventive in Akkadian, the possibility exists that some of these verbs also represent a volitive, since the Canaanite paradigm of prefix conjugations includes a volitive form with final *-a* used mainly with the first person.[96]

3.5.1. Theories about the Origin of the *yaqtula*

Scholars have long debated the origin of the Canaanite *yaqtula*. The main views that have been proposed are as follows:

(1) *Volitive/Subjunctive.* The *yaqtula* is a West Semitic volitive that is parallel in function to the Canaanite jussive and the Akkadian and Arabic subjunctive.[97] Moran is the primary proponent of this view and, in his dissertation, he states that five out of seven of all the Byblos examples of *yaqtula* function as clear volitives.[98] His conclusion is based on a comparative study of the

96. This conclusion is supported by the presence of a first-person volitive in Biblical Hebrew (cohortative).

97. W. L. Moran, "The Hebrew Language in Its Northwest Semitic Background," in *The Bible and the Ancient Near East: Essays in Honor of William Foxwell Albright* (ed. G. E. Wright; repr. Winona Lake, IN: Eisenbrauns, 1979) 64.

98. "The overall statistics on the *yaqtula* forms in the Byblos letters are the following: out of 75 occurrences, 18 are used as jussives, 30 are used to express purpose or intended

functions of the Canaanite *yaqtula*, the Arabic subjunctive, and the Biblical Hebrew cohortative.[99] In Moran's opinion, the Canaanite *yaqtula* compares with the Arabic subjunctive in that it expresses purpose (in Arabic, after specific particles) and appears in conditional sentences.[100] He advocates that the Canaanite *yaqtula* corresponds to the Hebrew cohortative when it expresses self-encouragement, a wish or request, purpose or result (especially after another volitive), and when it appears in conditional sentences.[101] Korchin finds Moran's theory the most convincing, stating that,

> the comparative Semitic evidence also supports Moran's theory. Moran convincingly demonstrates a diachronic morphosyntactic connection between CanAkk *yqtl-a* and BH *ʾeqtəlâ/niqtəlâ*. He points to the essentially identical nonindicative modal environments in which these forms typically occur: (1) in main clauses expressing wish, request, or command; (2) in subordinate clauses expressing purpose or intended result; and (3) in either the subordinate (protasis) or the main (apodosis) clauses of conditional sentences. Moran . . . concludes that the BH forms are the formal and functional direct descendants of CanAkk *yqtl-a*, thereby verifying the existence of a *yqtl-a* verb paradigm in NWS (or, at the very least, isolating a termainal *-a* morpheme in NWS which does not comport with the distributions and functions of the CoreAkk ventive). The absence of a uniform functional correspondence between EA *yqtl-a* and ES *-a(m)* argues against deriving both from the same source, as would appear to be implied by Fassberg's argument concerning BH.[102]

In addition, Korchin indicates that, in the structural opposition of *yqtl-a* : *yqtl-Ø*, differentiated by the presence or absence of the final short *-a* ending, the *yqtl-a* is (1) unmarked for deixis, temporal orientation (*Zeitbezug*), tense, and aspect; and is (2) marked for mood (nonindicative modality).[103]

(2) *Ventive.* In his article "Is There Really a *yaqtula* Conjugation Pattern in the Canaanite Amarna Tablets?"[104] as well as in *CAT*,[105] Rainey emphasizes

---

result, 14 are verbs of an apodosis or a protasis in a conditional sentence, 5 are doubtful because of a damaged context, 8 can only be called allatives" (Moran, *Syntactical Study of the Dialect of Byblos*, 92).

99. The Arabic subjunctive *yaqtula* only appears in subordinate clauses, while the Canaanite *yaqtula* and the Hebrew cohortative appear in main clauses and in subordinate clauses.

100. Moran, *Syntactical Study of the Dialect of Byblos*, 90.

101. Ibid., 91. As noted above, I disagree with Moran when he advocates that the Hebrew cohortative originates from the Canaanite *yaqtula*. I favor the view that the Hebrew cohortative is morphologically related to the Canaanite *yaqtula(n)na*, while the Canaanite *yaqtula* has become morphologically identical to the Hebrew imperfect *yiqtol* after the loss of the final short vowel.

102. Korchin, *Markedness in Canaanite and Hebrew Verbs*, 221.

103. Ibid., 246–49.

104. A. F. Rainey, "Is There Really a *yaqtula* Conjugation Pattern in the Canaanite Amarna Tablets?" *JCS* 43–45 (1991–93) 107–18.

105. Idem, *Canaanite in the Amarna Tablets*.

that most verbal forms with final *-a* are ventives, not volitives. He examines the verbs on which Moran based his conclusions and attempts to demonstrate that most of these verbs are commonly used in the ventive in Akkadian. Some of the verbs included in this category are: *(w)aṣû* (e.g., EA 73.9, 82.29, 104.51, 362.60), *leqû* (e.g., EA 20.10, 14; 71.30; 81.32; 84.34; 91.6; 95.37; 162.18; 362.23), *šapāru* (e.g., EA 1.10; 3.13; 6.13, 19; 7.23; 11.13; 15.7; 19.68; 40.28; 170.29, 33; 362.22), *wuššuru* (e.g., EA 35.25; 38.12; 70.17; 74.60; 90.45; 287.51, 52, 58), *babālu* (e.g., EA 9.12 [3×], 27.104, 88.35), *kašādu* (e.g., EA 3.11, 9.35, 10.39, 82.51, 86.6, 95.34, 102.30), *nadānu* (e.g., EA 1.12, 83.31, 93.11, 103.42), *maqātu* (e.g., EA 81.31, 83.43). According to Rainey,

> It is abundantly clear that the EA texts have not given us any conclusive evidence for the existence of a Canaanite *yaqtula* pattern. In spite of Moran's brilliant mustering of the evidence, it is still possible to argue that the *-a* suffix is merely the Akkadian ventive. Moran was not unaware of the problem. His main argument was the injunctive nature of all the various contexts in which he found this *-a* suffix in the Byblos letters. However, the *-a* suffix almost always was attached to verbs which tend to be employed with the ventive and in many of the examples cited, especially the purpose clauses, there were other, parallel verbs with the same syntactic function but with the -Ø suffix of the jussive. There are no glosses or strictly Canaanite verbal forms with the *-a* suffix (unlike the evidence for the WS imperfect and jussive). Furthermore, even in the Byblos corpus, there were some instances where the *-a* suffix appeared in past narrative and in some *inūma* clauses (topic clauses in complex sentences); those contexts were completely unsuitable for an injunctive and leave little doubt that the *-a(m)* suffix is the Akkadian ventive (Moran 1960: 16–17). . . . Further in support of Moran's theory is the unequivocal (albeit meager) evidence of *yqtl-a* in Ugaritic, a NWS language nearly contemporaneous with EA CanAkk.[106]

Although Rainey strongly advocated for his view on the ventive, he also stated that, "besides the volitives with -Ø [*yaqtul*], there are also the 'emphatic volitives' with *-a* (which are in fact interchangeable with the jussives by this time)."[107] Rainey adds that "the comparative evidence from Ugaritic, Hebrew and Arabic suggests that the Canaanite scribes had a *yaqtula* in their native repertoire which made them partial to Akkadian ventives."[108]

In his study of the long imperative *qotl-â*, the cohortative, and the Akkadian ventive with *-a(m)*, Fassberg concludes that the Canaanite *yaqtula* identifies an action that is directed toward or on behalf of the speaker.[109] John Huehnergard casts doubts on this view, stating that, in the case of *yaqtula*,

106. Ibid., 2:262.

107. Idem, "Morphology and the Prefix-Tenses of West Semitized El-ʾAmarna Tablets," *UF* 7 (1975) 414.

108. Idem, *Canaanite in the Amarna Tablets*, 2:263.

109. Fassberg, "The Lengthened Imperative *qōtlâ* in Biblical Hebrew." Fassberg makes the same distinction between the regular imperative and the long imperative with final *-â*, which seems to be marked to indicate direction toward the speaker.

If such forms are indeed ventive, we should expect at least a few examples of plural verbs with the ventive allomorph *-ni* (*iprusūni*), which the scribes would presumably have learned at the same time as the singular; yet such forms are lacking, the plural counterpart to singular *yaqtula* being, in fact, the expected *tiqtulū*, which is also the plural of the apocopate *yaqtul*, just as in Ugaritic and Arabic. In other words, we find injunctive singulars written both *yaqtul* and *yaqtula*, and injunctive plurals written *tiqtulū*; this is just what we expect if both *yaqtul* and *yaqtula* represent NWS modal forms, and contrary to what is expected if *yaqtula* forms are ventive, viz., plurals written *tiqtulūni*.[110]

(3) *Ventive and/or injunctive.* The loss of mimation on the Akkadian ventive marker for the singular (*-am*) resulted in the morphologically identical base form *yqtul-∅* for the jussive with ventive *-a(m)*, and the injunctive *yaqtula*. Consequently, one form can represent one of two unrelated functions (direction toward the speaker or modality) or a combination of both. Tropper holds this middle ground position. He distinguishes between the function of *yaqtula* in the first person (primarily modal; these verbs do not normally take ventive) and the function of *yaqtula* in second and third persons (primarily ventive; these verbs normally take the ventive).[111] In his view, the *yaqtula* represents both the ventive and the modal-subjunctive.

Although the ventive function is usually identified more easily than the modal function (since direction is more obvious than modality), we are left with the difficulty of assessing in which case we have one form over the other. As mentioned above, I advocate that verbs with final *-a* that do not typically take the Akkadian ventive (e.g., *naṣāru*, *balātu*, *arādu*) and express nuances similar to those of the Hebrew cohortative and the Arabic subjunctive, reveal the presence of a Canaanite volitive morpheme, *yaqtula*, which was familiar to the scribes of the EA texts. I also advocate that verbs commonly found in the ventive in Akkadian can represent direction and modality simultaneously, as the EA evidence seems to support.

3.5.2. Functions of the *yaqtula*

As mentioned above, Moran notes that the three most common uses of the Canaanite *yaqtula*[112] and the Biblical Hebrew cohortative are comparable. They are used in *wishes*, *purpose/result clauses*, and *conditional sentences*:

---

110. Huehnergard, "Review of *A Grammar of Amarna Canaanite* by A. Rainey," 71.

111. Tropper, "Ventiv oder *yaqtula*-Volitiv," 400–401. Tropper advocates for a first-person *yaqtula* in addition to a *yqtl-∅* jussive in Ugaritic. Tropper compares this dual modal representation with the two forms of the imperative—the regular imperative *qtl* and long imperative *qtla* (*Ugaritische Grammatik*, 455–57).

112. For comments on the word order, deixis, mood, *Zeibezug*, tense, and aspect of the *yqtl-a* in precative, purpose, volitive-asseverative, and volitive-result functions in EA Canaanite, see idem, *Markedness in Canaanite and Hebrew Verbs*, 223–45.

(1) *Wish, request, command.* In independent clauses, the *yaqtula* expresses a wish or indirect command:

> **yu-wa-š[i-ra]** EN^{li} LÚ^{MEŠ} ma-ṣa-ar-ta a-na MIN URU^{ni}-šu a-di a-ṣé ER[ÍN^{MEŠ}] pí-ṭá-ti
> *May my lord send* a garrison to his own towns until the coming of the archer host (EA 79.29)

> **ù a-da-bu-ba** ka-li ip-ši[-š]u-nu ù yi-de LUGAL^{ru} i-nu-ma Ì[R] ki-ti a-na-ku a-na ša-šu
> *So let me tell* about all their deeds so that the king may know that I am his loyal servant (EA 119.23)

(2) *Purpose clauses.* In the Byblos texts, the most common use of *yaqtula* is in purpose or result clauses. This phenomenon occurs when the *yaqtula* follows another volitive—namely, an imperative, a jussive, or another *yaqtula*. In his article on the "Early Canaanite *yaqtula*," Moran contrasts the use of the *yaqtulu* indicative and the *yaqtula* volitive and presents a rule that he calls "modal congruence":

> if the verb of the first clause states a fact (perfect, indicative), then in the purpose clause the verb is in the indicative; if the verb of the first clause is an imperative, a jussive or *yaqtula* expressing wish, etc., then in the purpose clause the verb is a jussive—or *yaqtula*.[113]

"Modal congruence" also appears in Akkadian when the verb of the main clauses is accompanied by the enclitic *-ma*, and the second clause expresses purpose. In these cases, the verbs of both clauses are in the same mood (indicative or injunctive) and are logically irreversible.[114] Non-Canaanite EA texts include numerous examples of this syntactical construction with *-ma*:

3.5.2.1. Non-Canaanite EA Letters[115]

> mâr ši-ip-ri-ka ḫa-mu-ut-ta ṭi-e-ma **šu-ku-un-ma li-i[l-li-ka]**
> *Inform* my messenger now *so that he may come to me* (EA 7.52–Babylonia)

> aḫi-ia li-gi-ib-bi-iz-zu i-na ḫa-di-e **li-miš-šer-šu-ma li-du-u-ra**
> May my brother honor her; *may he let her go* at his pleasure *so that she may come back* (EA 23.24—Mittani)

> ù ša ḫa[-*š*]*I*- ḫ[a-*tu*] i-na tuppi^{pi} **šu-ku-un-ma lu-še-bi-[l]u**

113. Moran, *Syntactical Study of the Dialect of Byblos*, 9.

114. The coordinator *u* does not have this restriction. See Huehnergard, *Grammar of Akkadian*, 49; Buccellati, *Structural Grammar of Babylonian*, 480.

115. See also EA 7.61, 64, 9.18, 19.72, 28.45.

So *put down* [ ] on a tablet *so that I may send* (it to you) (EA 37.17—Alašiya)

In addition to having a sequence of injunctives that follow the rule of "modal congruence," EA Canaanite letters include a syntactical construction for purpose clauses in which the enclitic *-mi* functions similarly to the Akkadian enclitic *-ma*. In these cases, the enclitic *-mi* appears on the verb of the main clause, followed by a purpose clause with a verb in the same mood (indicative or injunctive), and is logically irreversible.

3.5.2.1.1. Canaanite Letters with *-mi*

uš-ši-ir-mi ^{GIŠ}MA a-na ^{KUR}Ia-ri-mu-ta ù **ú-ṣa-ka** KU.BABBAR^{MEŠ} lu-bu-ši ìš-tu ša-šu-<nu>
Send a ship to Iarimuta *so that* the silver and clothing *may come out* to you from them (EA 82.28)

š]a-ni-tam **qí-ba-mi** a-na [LUGAL] ù **yu-da-na** a-n[a ^{URU}Gub-la] mu-ú-ṣa ša ^{KUR}Ia-r[i-mu-ta]
Moreover, *speak* to the [king] *in order that* the product of the land of Iarimuta *be given* to [the city of Byblos] (EA 86.31)

uš-ši-ra-am-mi ^{LÚ}DUMU KIN-ka it-ti-ia a-na ma-ḫar LUGAL BE-ka ù lu-ú **li-di-na-ku** ERÍN^{MEŠ} ù ^{GIŠ}GIGIR^{MEŠ}
Send your messenger to me before the king, *so that he may give you* troops and chariots (EA 87.9)

3.5.2.1.2. Canaanite Letters with "Modal Congruence" (without *-ma* or *-mi*)

ù uš-ši-ru-na-ni NINNU ta-pal ANŠE.KUR.RA ù MIN me ERÍN^{MEŠ} GÌR^{MEŠ} ù **i-zi-za** i-na ^{URU}Ši-ga-ta i-na pa-ni-šu a-di a-ṣi ERÍN^{MEŠ} pí-ṭá-ti
So send me 50 pairs of horses *so that I may resist* him in Šigata until the coming out of the archer host (EA 71.23—Byblos)

yi-eš-me a-wa-ti-ia ù **ia-di-na** kiti-[i]a
May he hear my message *so that he may give me* my right (EA 118.15—Byblos)

yu-wa-ši-ra LUGAL^{ru} ERÍN-šu pí-ṭá-ti ù **yu-ša-ap-ši-iḫ** KUR-šu
May the king send his archer host *to pacify* his land (EA 118.42—Byblos)

(3) *Conditional sentences.* The volitive *yaqtula* occasionally introduces the apodosis of conditional sentences:

ù šum-ma ki-a-ma i-ba-šu ù [l]a-a **ti-zi-za** URU ṣu-mu-ra
So if it continues as such, *then* the city of Ṣimyra *will not stand* (EA 107.32)

šum-ma i-na-na qa-la-ta ù [I]pi-ḫu-ra la-a **yi-zi-za** i-na URU ku-me-di
If now you are negligent, then Piḫura *will not stay* in Kumidu (EA 132.46)

3.5.3. *Yaqtulanna*

According to Moran, there is no strong evidence for an energic *yaqtulan(n)a* in EA-Byblos. The only potential example discussed by both Moran and Rainey is found in one of Rib-Haddi's letters (EA 77:36–37), in a negative purpose clause after a verb of fearing:

[p]al-ḫa-ti LÚ^{MEŠ} ḫu(!)-u[p-ši-ia] ul **ti-ma-ḫa-ṣa-na-n[i]**
I am afraid *that* the peasa[ntry] *will strike m*[*e*] *down* (Moran)
I [f]ear [my] tenant [farmers]. *Please do not smite m*[*e*]! (Youngblood)

Moran identifies the verb *ti-ma-ḫa-ṣa-na-ni* as an energic subjunctive and links its form to the Arabic modal form *yaqtulan*(*na*) and to the Hebrew cohortative followed by נָא.[116] Youngblood treats the two clauses independently and advocates that *ul ti-ma-ḫa-ṣa-na-n*[*i*] is "an emphatic reiteration of the plea ending line 12" that is expressed by *ul ti-ma-*[*ḫ*]*a-aṣ*.[117]

Rainey states that an energic volitive probably existed in EA Canaanite, since it is attested in Ugaritic (evidenced on III-*ʾalep* verbs)[118] and in Arabic. However, Rainey admits that this unique example could also be an Akkadian ventive, or the ending could reveal a third-feminine plural form with a third-masculine noun as the subject. The evidence is obviously too weak to draw a conclusion based on this one example.

3.5.4. Negative *yaqtula*

The negative *yaqtula* is discussed in §3.3.1 c with the negative jussives.

3.6. Verbal Sequences with Volitives

The possible "meaningful syntactical relationships" with volitives in EA texts are.

Imperative	*followed by*	(*ù*) Imperative
Imperative	*followed by*	(*ù*) Jussive
Imperative	*followed by*	(*ù*) Precative
Imperative	*followed by*	(*ù*) *Yaqtula*
Jussive	*followed by*	(*ù*) Imperative
Jussive	*followed by*	(*ù*) Jussive
Jussive	*followed by*	(*ù*) Precative
Jussive	*followed by*	(*ù*) *Yaqtula*
Precative	*followed by*	(*ù*) Imperative

116. Moran, *Syntactical Study of the Dialect of Byblos*, 56.
117. Youngblood, *Amarna Correspondence of Rib-Haddi*, 189–90.
118. For example, *iqran*, KTU 1.23:23.

Precative	*followed by*	(*ù*) Jussive
Precative	*followed by*	(*ù*) Precative
Precative	*followed by*	(*ù*) *Yaqtula*
Yaqtula	*followed by*	(*ù*) Imperative
Yaqtula	*followed by*	(*ù*) Jussive
Yaqtula	*followed by*	(*ù*) Precative
Yaqtula	*followed by*	(*ù*) *Yaqtula*

As discussed in §2.1, the syntactical function of a verb can be determined by its place in a verbal sequence. Izre'el states,

> While TMA [tense, mood, aspect] is marked morphologically, its implications go beyond the boundaries of a single sentence. There is interrelation in TMA usage between two or more sentences which are semantically related, i.e., where there is a sequential coherence in the message of the sentences. Thus, predicative complexes of a second or any following sentences within the discourse unit are dependent on the one in the opening sentence. This dependency may affect coordinated sentences with or without a conjunction.[119]

Where verbs occur in sequences, the first verb of the string functions as it does in independent clauses, while the remaining verbs express one of the following: (a) purpose/result, (b) parallel/hendiadys, (c) sequentiality, or (d) conjunctivity. Since the syntactical relationships of non-Canaanite verbal sequences differ from those of the Canaanite corpus, it is fitting that we first treat each group separately and then do a comparison of the data.

3.6.1. Non-Canaanite Corpus

The two most meaningful verbal sequences identified with the non-Canaanite corpus are: (1) precative *followed by* precative; and (2) imperative *followed by* precative.

Precative followed by precative. When a precative is followed by another precative, the sequence of verbs represents the following functions:

(1) *Conjunctivity.* The relationship is said to be conjunctive when the events can occur in any order without changing the logical outcome. Such events are reversible and therefore not marked for sequentiality.

> lu-ú a-na-ku-ma ŠEŠ-ia el a-bi-ia [*10-šu*] lu-ú ú-te-it-te-ra-an-ni ù KU.BABBAR ma-a-a[t-ta] ša ši-ip-ra la ip-šu li-še-e-bi-l[a-an-ni]
> Let my brother treat me [ten times] better than he did my father, and may he send much gold that has not been worked (EA 19:41–42)

> i-na ŠÀ ŠEŠ-ia lu-ú la-a im-mar-ra-a ù at-du-ia ŠÀ bi ŠEŠ-ia lu-ú la-a ú-ša-am-ra-a
> May it not be a distress to my brother, and may he not cause me distress (EA 19:65–66)

119. Izre'el, *Canaano-Akkadian*, 70–71.

ištar bêlit ša-me-e ŠEŠ-ia ù ia-ši li-iṣ-ṣur-an-na-ši I me li-im MU^{MEŠ} ù ḫe-du-ta ra-bi-ta NIN-ni$_5$ a-na ki-la-a-al-li-ni li-id-din-an-na-ši-ma
May Šauška, the lady of heaven, protect my brother and me 100,000 years, and may our mistress grant both of us great joy (EA 23.27–29)

MU^{kan} ù M[U^{kan} -ma DUMU ši-ip-ri-ia-ma [*a-na pa-ni-ka*] li-li-ki ù at-t[a-*ma*] DUMU ši-ip-ri-ka . . . pa-ni-i[a] li-li-ki-ma
Year after year let my messenger come before you and let your messenger come before me . . . (EA 33.29)

(2) *Sequentiality.* Events are sequential when the fulfillment of events must occur in the order in which the events are stated. In order to determine temporal and logical sequentiality, the clauses are tested for irreversibility. When the events are reversible, they are not sequential.[120]

[înā] ša a-ḫi-ia li-mu-ra-ma a-ḫu-ú-a li-ik-nu-uk-ma li-še-bi-la
Let my brother make a check, let him seal it, (and) let him send it to me (EA 7.68)

ša-am-mi ša ṣi-e-ri ša a-na a-ḫa-mi-iš ma-aš-lu ša ši-in-ni li-il-pu-tum ù li-i-ru-pu-ú-ma li-il-qu-ni
Matching plants of the countryside are to be carved, colored, and taken to me (EA 11:10–12)

a-na KUR mi-iṣ-ri-i i-na KUR ša a-ra-ʾa-a-mu lu-ul-lik-ma-me lu-uz-za-ḫe-ir-me
Let me go to Egypt, to the land that I love, then let me return (EA 23:15–16)

(3) *Purpose.*[121] The purpose or result stated in the subordinate clause (the *consequent*) depends on the fulfillment of the event of the main clause (the *antecedent*).[122] These verb sequences primarily indicate subordination of one event to another and are secondarily logically sequential (e.g., Go [*antecedent*] to the king in order to inform (*consequent*) him of the defeat of his armies). Sentences with purpose or result clauses are tested against a negative condition: IF the *antecedent* (main clause event) does not take place, THEN the *consequent* (the purpose or result) cannot occur.

ù mi-nu-ú ša a-ḫu-ú-a ḫa-aš-ḫu a-ḫu-ú-a li-iš-pu-ra-am-ma ul-tu bi-ti-šu-nu li-il-qu-ni-iš-šu

120. Li, *Expression of Sequence and Non-Sequence*, 10.

121. By default, purpose/result clauses are also sequential, since the events of the main clause must precede the events of the purpose/result clause.

122. J. E. Grimes, *The Thread of Discourse* (Janua Linguarum Series Minor 207; The Hague: Mouton, 1975) 223.

Let my brother write me about what he wants so that it may be taken to him from the house (EA 7.61–62)

a-ḫu-ú-a GUŠKIN ba-na-a ma-ʾa-da li-še-bi-la-am-ma a-na du-ul-li-ia lu-uš-ku-un (EA 7.64–65)
May my brother send me much fine gold so that I may use it on my work (EA 7.64–65)

(4) *Parallel/hendiadys.* Verbs function as parallels when they represent a single event. In these cases, the verbs are reversible and do not represent sequentiality.

um-ma lu-ú a-na-ku-ma a-na ma-a-du-ti ta-an-ni-is lu ni-ir-ta-na-ʾa-am ù i-na be-ri-ni lu-ú ta-a-pa-nu
Let us love each other very, very much and let there be friendship between us (EA 19.31–32)

3.6.2. Imperative Followed by Precative

The second most meaningful verbal sequence of the non-Canaanite corpus is where an imperative is followed by a precative. The sequence of verbs represents the following function:
(1) *Purpose/result*:

ša ḫa-aš-ḫa-ta i-na KUR-ia šu-u[p-ra-am-ma] li-il-qu-ni-ik-ku
Write about what you want from my house so that it may be taken to you (EA 6.13–14)

ù at-ta mi-im-ma ša ḫa-aš-ḫa-a-ta i-na KUR-ia šu-up-ra-am-ma li-il-qu-ni-ik-ku
And as for you, whatever you want from my land, write to me so that it may be taken to you (EA 9.18)

ù a-šar LÚ te-i-e AMA-ka ti-ša-ʾa-al-šu-nu-ti-ma li-id-bu-pa-ak-ku
So ask Teye your mother about them so that she may tell you (EA 28.45–46)

ù ša ḫa-[-*š*]*I*- ḫ[a-*t* [*ú*] i-na DUB^{bi} *šu*-ku-un-ma lu-še-bi-[*l*]*u*
So put down [ ] on a tablet so that I can send (it to you) (EA 37.17)

3.6.3. Canaanite Corpus

The following verbs express injunctions in EA Canaanite texts: the imperative, jussive, precative, and volitive *yaqtula*. As mentioned above (see §3.2.2), imperatives with final *-a* can be interpreted as long imperatives, as imperatives + ventive, or as a combination of both (it is possible that scribes may have intended to express both the sense of direction [ventive] and a modal nuance [volitive] in the same passage). The prefix conjugation with *-a* ending can also be interpreted in a number of ways: (1) as a jussive + ventive, especially with verbs of motion, (2) as an injunctive (*yaqtula*), or (3) as a combination of both, indicating both direction and modality.

When verbs with final *-a* indicate obvious direction toward the speaker or toward the addressee, they will first be treated as jussives + ventive. If they appear in sequences of injunctives, they will also be considered possible modals. When verbs that are not commonly attested with the ventive in Akkadian (1) include a final *-a* in Canaanite letters, (2) appear in sequences of injunctives, and (3) have modal functions, they will be treated as *yaqtula* volitives.

Since the EA Canaanite verbal paradigm includes modal forms not found in the Akkadian paradigm (e.g., *yaqtula*, jussive), the list of meaningful verbal sequences with injunctives is therefore longer than in the EA non-Canaanite correspondence. The Canaanite meaningful syntactical relationships include:

Imperative	*followed by*	*Imperative*
Imperative	*followed by*	*Jussive*
Imperative	*followed by*	*Yaqtula*
Jussive	*followed by*	*Jussive*
Jussive	*followed by*	*Yaqtula*
Precative	*followed by*	*Jussive*
Precative	*followed by*	*Precative*
Yaqtula	*followed by*	*Jussive*
Yaqtula	*followed by*	*Yaqtula*

In Canaanite texts, as in non-Canaanite letters, the relationships represented by the verbal sequences are one of the following: (a) purpose/result, (b) sequence, or (c) conjunctive.[123] The most common syntactical relationships with volitives appear in *purpose/result clauses*, when a volitive appears in the main clause, followed by another volitive in the purpose/result clause (with or without a connecting *ù*).

(1) *Purpose clauses.*[124] The purpose or result stated in the subordinate clause (the *consequent*) depends on the fulfillment of the event of the main clause (the *antecedent*).[125] These verb sequences primarily indicate subordination of one event to another and are secondarily logically sequential (e.g., *Go* (antecedent) *to the king in order to inform* (consequent) *him of the defeat of his armies*). Sentences with purpose or result clauses are tested against a negative condition: IF the *antecedent* (main clause event) does not take place, THEN the *consequent* (the purpose or result) cannot occur.

123. Although the description of each function is included above, I will also include it in this section in order to facilitate the reading.

124. By default, purpose/result clauses are also sequential, since the events of the main clause must precede the events of the purpose/result clause.

125. Grimes, *Thread of Discourse*, 223.

uš-ši-ra ERÍN^{MEŠ} pí-ṭá-ti ra-ba ù tu-da-bi-ir a-ia-bi LUGAL iš-tu ŠAG$_4^{\text{bi}}$ KUR-šu ù ti-né-ep-šu ka-li KUR.KUR^{MEŠ} a-na LUGAL^{ri}
Send me a large archer host so that it may drive out the enemies of the king from the midst of his land, that all the lands might turn themselves over to the king[126] (EA 76.38–43—*imperative + jussive*)

[uš]-ši-ra L[Ú]^{MEŠ} ma-ṣa-ar-ta [a-na na-ṣ]a-ar KU[R-k]a ú-ul tu-ṣa-bat [KUR]-ka
Send a garrison to protect you land lest your land be seized (EA 85.45–47—*imperative + negative jussive*)

mi-lik-mi a-na UR[U-ka] [ú-u]l yi-ìl-qé-ši ^{m}ÌR-[A-ši-ir-ta]
Give thought to [your l]and lest Abdi Aširta take it (EA 90.11–12—*imperative + negative jussive*)

ù uš-ši-ra ERÍN^{MEŠ} pi-ṭá-tí ù ti-íl-qi-šu ù ta-ap-šu-uḫ KUR LUGAL^{ri}
So send an archer host to take it then (as a result) the land of the king will be at peace (EA 107.29–31—*imperative + jussive*)

ù te-ra-ni a-wa-tú ù i-di ip-ša ša i-pu-šu
So send back a word so that I may know what I am to do (EA 114.25–26—*imperative + jussive*)

uš-ši-ru-na-ni NINNU ta-pal ANŠE.KUR.RA ù MIN me ERÍN^{MEŠ} GÌR ^{MEŠ} ù i-zi-za i-na ^{URU}Ši-ga-t[a] i-na pa-ni-šu a-di a-ṣi ERÍN^{MEŠ} pí-ṭá-ti ú-ul yu-pa-ḫi-ra ka-li LÚ^{MEŠ} GAZ^{MEŠ} ù [y]i-ìl-qa ^{URU}Ši-ga-t[a]
Send me 50 teams of horses and 200 foot soldiers so that I might withstand him in Šigata until the archer host goes out, lest he muster all the ʿApiru and[t]ake Šigat[a] (EA 71.23–30—*imperative + jussive/ ventive*)

ù qí-bi a-na LUGAL be-li-[ka] ù [t]u-wu-ša-<ra> til-la-tu [a-na] ia-ši ki-ma ar-ḫìš
So speak to the king, [your] lord that an auxiliary force be [s]ent to me without delay (EA 73.43–44—*imperative + jussive/ventive*)

uš-ši-ir-mi ^{GIŠ}MÁ a-na ^{KUR}Ia-ri-mu-ta ù ú-ṣa-ka KÙ.BABBAR^{MEŠ} lu-bu-ši ìš-tu ša-šu-<nu>
Send a ship to the land of Yarimuta so that silver and clothing may be sent out to you (EA 82.28–29—*imperative + jussive/ventive*)

ši-mé ia-ši [ù] qí-bi a-na LUGAL [ù t]u-da-na a-na ^{d}N[IN ù] . . . .
Listen to me and speak to the king so that it may be given to the Lady. . . . (EA 86.28–29—*imperative + jussive/ventive*)

126. Moran comments that either *ÉRIN.MESH pitati* is a feminine singular or the subject remains the king addressed by Rib Haddi in the second person, therefore translating: 'Send . . . so that you may drive out' (Moran, *Amarna Letters*, 147).

[š]a-ni-tam qí-ba-mi a-na [LUGAL] ù yu-da-na a-n[a ^{URU}Gub-la] mu-ú-ṣa ša ^{KUR}Ia-r[i-mu-ta]
Moreover, speak to the king that he may send the product of the land of Iarimuta to Byblos (EA 86.31–35—*imperative + jussive/ventive*)

ù yi-eš-mi LU[GAL]ru a-wa-te ÌR ki-ti-šu ù ia-di-en ba-la-ṭa a-na ÌR-šu ù GEME$_2$-šu URUgub-la
May the king heed the word of his servant and may he give provision to his servant and his maidservant Byblos (EA 116.44–46—*jussive + jussive*)

uš-ši-ra [3] LÚMEŠ ù ib-lu-ṭa ù i-na-ṣi-ra URU a-na LUGAL^{ri}
Send [3] men so that I may live and guard the city for the king (EA 123.26—*imperative + yaqtula*)

[t]a-din-ni i-na qa-at mIa-an-ḫa-mi ù ia-ti-na ŠE$^{\text{im-HI.A}}$ a-na a-ka-li-ia ù a-na-ṣa-ra URU LUGAL a-na ša-a-šu
May you place me in Yanhamu's charge so that he may give me grain to eat so that I may guard the city of the king for him (EA 83.30–33–*jussive + yaqtula*)

yu-wa-ši-ra LUGAL^{ru} ANŠE.KUR.RA a-na ÌR-šu ù a-na-ṣa-ra URU LUGAL
May the king send horses to his servant so that I may guard the city of the king (EA 117.73—*jussive + yaqtula*)

ù lu-wa-ši-ra be-li-ia LÚ^{MEŠ} ú ti-ìl-qú mi-im-mi^{MEŠ} ^{d}DA.MU-ia a-na ma-ḫar BE-ia ù ú-ul ìl-ti-qa mi-im-ma^{MEŠ} [š]a DINGIR^{MEŠ}-ka
May my lord send men so that they may take the belongings of . . . and so that the belongings of your god may not be taken (EA 84.31–34—*precative + jussive/ventive*)

li-iš-me LUGAL^{ri} a-na abdi-ḫi-ba ÌR-ka ù lu-ma-šar ERÎN^{MEŠ} pi-ṭá-tí ù lu-ti-ra KUR LUGAL^{ri} a-na LUGAL^{ri}
May the king give heed to Abdi-Heba, your servant and send archers that I might restore the land of the king to the king (EA 290.19–21—*precative + precative*)

[š]a-a yu-da-[n]u pa-na-nu i-na ^{URU}[ḫ]u-mu-ra [y]u-da-nam i-na-na i-na ^{URU}Gub-la [ù] n[u]-ba-li-iṭ a-di ti-š[a-a-l]u [a-n]a URU^{li}-ka
[Let that] which was giv[e]n formerly in [S]imyra [be g]iven to me now in Byblos [so th]at w[e] may preserve life until you can in[vestiga]te [concer]ning your city[127] (EA 85.36–39—*jussive/ventive + jussive*)

yu-wa-ši-ra [LÚ]-šu ù yi-zi-iz i-na-an-na ù ak-šu-[ud] a-na-ku a-na ma-ḫar LUGAL^{ri} EN

127. Moran: '[so that] we may have provisions until you gi[ve thou]ght to your city' (Moran, *Amarna Letters*, 157).

May he [the king] send his [man], and may he stay (here) now so that I might com[e] into the presence of the king, (my) lord (EA 74.60–62—*jussive/ventive + jussive*)

(2) *Conjunctive.* The relationship is said to be conjunctive when the events can occur in any order without changing the logical outcome. The events are reversible and, therefore, not marked for sequentiality.

ù yi-da-ga[l LUGAL] [KUR]-šu ù [LUGALru yi-im]-lik K[UR-šu] ù šu-u[p-ši-iḫ KUR-k]a-ma
So may the king survey his land, and may the king care for his land (EA 74.57—*jussive + jussive*)

(3) *Sequential.* Events are sequential when the fulfillment of events must occur in the order in which the events are stated. In order to determine temporal and logical sequentiality, the clauses are tested for irreversibility. When the events are reversible, they are not sequential.[128]

du-ku-mi EN-ku-nu ù in-né-ep-šu a-na LÚ^MEŠ
Kill your lord, then join the Apiru (EA 73.27–28—*imperative + imperative*)

AŠ É NIN.URTA pu-ḫu-ru-nim-mi ù ni-ma-qú-ut UGU ^URU gub-la
Assemble in the temple of Ninurta, and then, let us fall upon Gubla (EA 74.31—*imperative + jussive*)

[š]a-ni-tam k[u]-uš-da at-[t]a ki-ma ar-ḫi-ìš ù l[e-qa] gáb-ba ù tu-ur ù le-qa ERÍN^MEŠ pí-ṭá-[ti] ar-k[a]-nu
Moreover, come yourself quickly and take everything. Then return to take the archers later (EA 95.34–37—*imperative + imperative*)

li-ìš-me LUGAL^ru a-wa-te ÌR-šu ù ia-di-na ba-la-ṭa ÌR-šu
May the king listen to the word of his servant and grant life to his servant (EA 74.53—*precative + jussive/ventive*)

yu-wa-ši-ra [LÚ]-šu ù yi-zi-iz i-na-an-na
May he send his man, and may he stay this time (EA 74.60–61—*jussive/ventive + jussive*)

3.7. Additional Verbs with Modal Functions

3.7.1. Perfect – *qatala*

The suffix conjugation concerns us only where it expresses the optative mood, or where it is syntactically related to a volitive. In the EA correspondence, we find only a few cases where the perfect is governed by an impera-

128. Li, *Expression of Sequence and Non-Sequence*, 10.

tive. In each case, the perfect is preceded by *ù*, and speaks of a state or event that is sequential to the event of the imperative.[129] The first example occurs in the first-person singular. The event of the perfect is sequential (and consequential) to that of the imperative:

> 3 LÚ.MEŠ ša-a šu-ri-ib I bi-ḫu-ra uš-ši-ra ù bal-ta-ṭi
> Send the 3 men whom Pihura brought in, and then (consequently) I will survive (EA 123.35)
>
> (Compare lines 25–27 with *yaqtula* in purpose clauses:
> uš-ši-ra [3] LÚ.MEŠ ù ib-lu-ṭa ù i-na-ṣi-ra URU a-na LUGAL.ri
> Send the 3 men so that I may live and guard the city of the king)

The second two examples appear in the second-person singular. Both verbs are statives and express events sequential (and consequential) to the previous imperative:

> du-ku-mi [e]ṭ-la-ku-nu ù i-ba-ša-tu-nu ki-ma ia-ti-nu [ù] pa-aš-ḫa-tu-nu
> Kill your leader and then you will be like us and be at peace[130] (EA 74.26)

We should note here that this direct discourse is spoken by someone "greater" to someone "lesser" (Abdi-Aširta to the people of Ammiya). In Biblical Hebrew, the perfect consecutive after an imperative is typical of this sort of social dynamic. Since the EA correspondence mostly consists of communication from someone "lesser" to someone "greater," it comes as no surprise that the Canaanite syntagma "imperative + (*ù*) perfect" appears only rarely.

EA texts exhibit cases in which an imperative is followed by the optative/asseverative particle *l* + a perfect of the same verb as the imperative. Since in each case the utterance is spoken by Pharaoh and addresses the vassals, it cannot be treated as a Canaanite syntagma, yet it is worth noting that the social dynamics are again from "greater" to "lesser":

> ú-ṣur-mi lu-ú na-ṣir-ta
> Guard! Be on your guard! (EA 112.9; see also 117.84, 99.7–8, 367.4, 370.5)

3.7.2. Imperfect – *yaqtulu*

According to Moran's descriptive table, the common form *yaqtulu* is used in EA-Byblos primarily to express the present or future.[131] Rarely does it express past tense but, when it does, it usually refers to a customary or repeated

129. This feature corresponds to the Hebrew construction imperative + *weqatal*.

130. For a discussion about the use of *eṭlu* 'young adult male' rather than *bʿlu*, see Moran, *Amarna Letters*, 144 n. 7; and Youngblood, *Amarna Correspondence of Rib-Haddi*, 139.

131. A West Semitic counterpart of Akkadian *iparras*.

action in the past[132] or is found in a subordinate-circumstantial clause with past meaning. *Yaqtulu* is common in conditional sentences, both in the protasis and the apodosis, and in purpose clauses, when dependent on a verbal clause with either an indicative *yaqtulu* or a form of the suffix conjugation. *Yaqtulu* never expresses the jussive mood.

Since the equivalent Arabic and Hebrew forms of the prefix conjugation often express modality ("should, can, might, etc."), Moran acknowledges that the EA *yaqtulu* probably also included these modal nuances but states that "indicative remains an adequate and accurate designation of the form in so far as its modality is concerned."[133] Moran concludes that the Canaanite *yaqtulu* in EA-Byblos texts expresses "continuity of action" whether in the past, present, or future, rather than expressing mainly "tense."[134] The tense itself is derived from the context.

As is commonly attested with sequences of volitives, sequences of indicatives also produce purpose clauses (Moran's rule of "modal congruence"). In these cases, the verb of the main clause is either a perfect (*qatala*) or an indicative (*yaqtulu*).

> a-di yu-pa-ḫi-ru ka[-*l*]*ā* URU.MEŠ ù yi-ìl-qú-še
> He is again gathering together all the cities that he may capture it (EA 124.14–15)

> a-na mi-ni la-a tu-te-ru-[n]a a-wa-tam a-na ia-a-ši ù i-de ip-ša ša i-pu-š[u]
> Why do you not send back word to me that I may know what I should d[o]? (EA 83.7–9)

3.7.2.1. *Yaqtulun(na)*

The so-called energic form of the indicative is *yaqtulun(n)a*.[135] This verbal form could be confused with the third-masculine-plural morpheme *yaqtulna*, since no morphological distinction can be made in cuneiform writing between the indicative imperfect plural and the singular indicative energic.[136] The reader must identify, through the syntax of the sentence, which form is actually attested.

Although treated as an "energic" morpheme by many scholars,[137] the modal form with *-n(n)* ending reflects the writer's subjective approach to the message

132. As is common for the indicative prefix conjugation in Canaanite languages.

133. Moran, *Syntactical Study of the Dialect of Byblos*, 49.

134. Huehnergard labels this form a "durative" (*A Grammar of Akkadian*, 96). The present tense is natural for expressing a habitual action.

135. For examples with *āpušuna* (74.63, 90.22, 91.26, etc.), *inaṣ(ṣ)aruna* (112.10, 125.12), *tiliʾuna* (82.6), *tištapruna* (117.8).

136. In his list of verbs with *-una* ending, Ebeling did not distinguish between the modal form and the plural form (Ebeling, "Das Verbum der El-Amarna Briefe," 69–73).

137. Moran, *Syntactical Study of the Dialect of Byblos*, 53; Rainey, *Canaanite in the Amarna Tablets*, 2:234; Zewi, *Syntactical Study of Verbal Forms Affixed by* -n(n) *Endings*,

of the text, rather than an energizing of the verb.[138] In her study of Classical Arabic, Tamar Zewi speaks of the "energicus as a fourth mood" and then follows her statement with a short discussion on the difficulty of the term *energicus* or *emphatic*, noting that "it might be better to replace the emphasis explanation by that of a modal nuance added to the verbal forms."[139] Zewi recognizes that a modal element adds a subjective nuance to the verb, and does not "energize" or "emphasize" it. Since it appears in questions, doubts, uncertainty, and other such contexts, it naturally deviates from the idea of emphasis toward a nuance of uncertainty.

In Williams's opinion, long verbal forms with *-n(n)* are used purposely to extend the sound and add weight to the writer's message. Williams states that the "energic" form "is merely a stylistic variant which is employed when required for the natural rhythm of the sentence. It serves, in other words, to provide a longer and heavier form comparable to the English expressions 'to' and 'unto,' or 'I have' and 'I have got.'"[140]

Regarding the EA form *yaqtulun(n)a*, Moran states that, "essentially, it is an emphatic form of *yaqtulu*, with the precise nuance of emphasis determined by the context."[141] He notes that, "once *yaqtulu* is recognized as the normal indicative form in Byblian of the 14th century B.C., then there can be no reason for rejecting *yaqtuluna* as the indicative-energic in Byblian of the same time."[142]

Rainey attributes the presence of the *-na* ending on *yaqtulu* as "an optional means for strengthening the force of the verb."[143] Gottlieb notes that the verbal forms with *-na* endings are "applied especially in the following cases: as terms for order or wish, consequently in cases where in Hebrew you would apply jussive, voluntative or imperative."[144] As discussed in the previous chapter, in Semitic languages, the *-n(na)* ending adds a softening to the verb on which it is appended. In Ugaritic, it appears on imperatives and on prefix conjugations, sometimes as a part of the verb and, at other times, separated from the verb by

---

157; C. Brockelmann, *Grundriss der vergleichenden Grammatik der semitischen Sprachen* (2 vols.; Berlin: Reuther & Reichard, 1908–13) 1:557, 641; GKC, §58i; H. Bauer and P. Leander, *Historische Grammatik der hebraischen Sprache des Alten Testaments* (Halle: Olms, 1918–22) §48q–s; R. J. Williams, "Energic Verbal Forms in Hebrew," in *Studies on the Ancient Palestinian World Presented to Professor F. V. Winnett* (ed. J. W. Wevers and D. B. Redford; Toronto: University of Toronto Press, 1972) 80; G. Ryckmans, *Grammaire accadienne* (Louvain: Bureaux du Muséon, 1938) §§239–42; G. R. Castellino, *The Akkadian Personal Pronouns and Verbal System in the Light of Semitic and Hamitic* (Leiden: Brill, 1962) 79.

138. C. H. J. van der Merwe, "The Vague Term 'Emphasis'," *JSem* 1/1 (1989) 118–32.

139. Zewi, *Syntactical Study of Verbal Forms Affixed by* -n(n) *Endings*, 15–16.

140. Williams, "Energic Verbal Forms in Hebrew," 85.

141. Moran, "A Syntactical Study," 54.

142. Ibid., 53.

143. Rainey, *CAT* 2: 235.

144. Gottlieb, "The Hebrew Particle *nâ*," 49.

a word divider.[145] This particle of modality appears as an independent particle in Biblical Hebrew and is used to express politeness and respect.

Although the *yaqtulun(n)a* appears more often in main clauses, it is also found in "temporal, substantival, conditional, and relative clauses."[146] In his study of the Byblos corpus, Moran notes that of the 38 examples of *yaqtulun(n)a*, 22 occur in interrogative sentences (including rhetorical questions).[147] The distinction that exists between the indicative *yaqtulu* and the modal *yaqtulun(n)a* is not always clear. Verbs with *-na* and without *-na* appear in the same passage, with similar meanings, and sometimes with the same verb. Nevertheless, when languages use more than one form, I advocate that they express more than one type of nuance, although the distinction often eludes us:

i-nu-ma **yi-eš-ta-pa-ru** LUGAL^{ru} EN^{li} ú-ṣur-me ra-ma-an-ka
As for the king, my lord, *having written*: Guard yourself! (EA 119.8)

versus:

i-nu-ma **yi-eš-tap-ru-na** LUGAL^{ru} EN-ia a-na ia[š]i ú-ṣur-me [r]a-m[a-a]n-k[a]
As for the king, my lord, *having written* to me: Guard yourself! (EA 121.7)

mi-lik-mi a-na UR[U-ka] [ú-u]l yi-ìl-qé-ši ^{m}ÌR-[A-ši-ir-ta] [ù **l]a ti-ìš-me** a-na ia-š[i]
Give thought to [your] city lest'Abdi-Aširta take it. But *you do not listen* to me (EA 90.13)

versus:

a-nu-ma ki-a-ma aš-ta-pa-ar a-na É.GAL ù **ú-ul ti-eš-mu-na** a-wa-tu-ia
I have written like this to the palace, but *you do not listen to* my words[148] (EA 74.50)

---

145. See Ugaritic examples in §2.2.2.1 above.
146. Moran, "A Syntactical Study," 53.
147. Ibid., 53.
148. Emendations to the passive form of the verb (*tušmûna awâtuya*) have been suggested by Younglood, *Amarna Correspondence of Rib-Haddi*, 149; Rainey, *Canaanite in the Amarna Tablets*, 1:157; while Moran and Weisberg prefer the unemended active form of the verb, arguing that, in the intensity of the context and in order to appreciate Rib-Hadda's "anguished state of mind," an energic active form is preferable to a so-called passive polite form suggested by Youngblood (Moran, *Syntactical Study of the Dialect of Byblos*, 53; D. Weisberg, "Rib-Hadda's Urgent Tone," in *Assyriologica et Semitica* [AOAT 252; Münster: Ugarit-Verlag, 2000] 543).

3.8. Conclusion

Our study of the EA Canaanite modal system reveals three principal prefix conjugations: the *yaqtul* jussive, the volitive *yaqtula*, and the modal injunctive *yaqtulan(na)*. Related to each of these forms is an imperative. These modal forms express several nuances related to volition in independent and subordinate clauses.

3.8.1. Commands in EA Canaanite

- The EA texts use mainly the Akkadian imperative to express commands and requests, except for a few possible Canaanite forms: nu-pu-ul-mi (EA 252.25), *ku-na* (EA 137.35).
- In the EA introductory epistolary formula, the imperative of the verb *qabû* appears as *qí-bí-ma*, a well-known Akkadian form. In the body of the texts, both *qí-bí* (the regular imperative) and *qí-ba-mi* (with modal ending) appear. The form *qí-bí* is the unmarked form for commands, while *qí-ba-mi* indicates additional modality since it includes the modal affix *-a* and is always accompanied by a morpheme/syntagma used to express urgency (e.g., *ša-ni-tam*).
- The imperative often appears in rhetorical statements, which EA scribes use with consistency. The most common verbs used in these expressions are: *lamādu*, *naṣāru*, *malāku*, and *wuššuru*.
- In addition to expressing a regular command, the imperative of *amāru* is used as an interjection (e.g., EA 88.42, 106.16, 117.9). This feature with verbs related to the physical senses is not restricted to Semitic languages but occurs in a variety of language families (e.g., Indo-European, Romance languages).
- In some cases, the imperative of *alāku* ('to go, walk') functions adverbially, indicating motion, especially before another imperative (e.g., EA 102.15).
- When imperatives appear with a final *-a*, they indicate either a ventive morpheme or a modal ending. Verbs that commonly appear with the ventive in Akkadian are treated as such in EA texts (e.g., *uš-ši-ra*), while verbs with final *-a* that are typically Canaanite are treated as imperatives with modal ending (e.g., *ku-na*).
- The modal ending *-n(n)a* appears on several verbal forms: the indicative *yaqtulu*, the imperative, and the volitive *yaqtula*. Due to the nature of the script, it is impossible to know if *-n(na)* was always appended to the verb or if it also functioned as an independent particle of modality.
- Negative commands are expressed with the negative particle *ul* or *lā* before an indicative, jussive, or precative. The imperative does not occur with a negative particle.

3.8.2. *Yaqtul* Jussive

- The introductory epistolary formula of EA Canaanite letters often includes the jussive of *nadānu* in its various orthographic conventions (e.g., *ti-din*, *ti-di-in*$_4$, *ti-id-di-in*$_4$). Wishes found in these formulas are never expressed by the volitive *yaqtula*; they only occur with the jussive.
- The jussive and precative forms of several verbs occur in rhetorical statements (e.g., *lamādu*, *qâlu*, *malāku*).
- The jussive appears with both negative particles indiscriminately (with *ul* and with *lā*).

3.8.3. *Yaqtula*

- When a prefix conjugation appears with a final *-a* in EA Canaanite texts, the possibilities are as follows: (1) a jussive + ventive, (2) a volitive *yaqtula*.[149]
- The EA volitive *yaqtula* is more noticeable in the first person than in the second and third persons. The distribution of verbs with final *-a* shows that verbs not commonly attested with the ventive in Akkadian appear mostly in the first-person *yaqtula*, while verbs that are commonly attested with the ventive in Akkadian occur mostly in the third person (see list in §3.4). I conclude, therefore, that the third-person occurrences (common with the ventive) are probably jussives + ventive, while verbs with final *-a* in the first person are true *yaqtula* volitives. Since Canaanite already has a volitive form to express a third-person wish or desire (*yaqtul* jussive), a third-person *yaqtula* is not necessary. This does not, on the other hand, exclude the possibility that the volitive *yaqtula* exists in all three persons.
- The EA volitive *yaqtula* is used to express wishes, requests, and indirect commands. It appears in main clauses, in purpose clauses, and in conditional sentences.

3.8.4. *Yaqtulan(na)*

- Although there is very little evidence for a modal *yaqtulan(na)* in EA texts, its presence in Ugaritic and Arabic make it likely that it existed in the Canaanite paradigm of the modal system.

149. Neither the jussive nor the volitive *yaqtula* is present in non-Canaanite EA texts. These two injunctives are typical of the NWSemitic corpus and do not exist in Akkadian. The Akkadian precative serves to express wishes and indirect commands in non-Canaanite EA texts.

3.8.5. Syntax of EA Canaanite Volitives in Verbal Sequences

- Since the paradigm of the Canaanite modal system includes forms not found in Akkadian, the EA Canaanite texts include more verbal sequences with injunctives than the non-Canaanite texts.
- When injunctives (imperative, jussive, *yaqtula*, precative) appear in verbal sequences, they express one of the following syntactical relationships: purpose/result, parallel ideas, sequentiality, or conjunctivity.
- The most common meaningful verbal sequence with injunctives is that of purpose/result. Moran's rule of "modal congruence" is consistent in both Canaanite and non-Canaanite letters.

3.8.6. Perfect – *qatala*

- There are only a few instances in which a *qatala* is governed by a previous volitive. In both cases, the verb of the main clause is an imperative, and the clause with the *qatala* is introduced by *ù*.
- When the *qatala* is governed by an imperative, it expresses an event sequential to that expressed by the imperative.
- In the cases where a second-person *qatala* follows an imperative, the utterance is spoken by one of higher social status to one of lower social status.
- In the cases where a second-person *qatala* follows an imperative, the *qatala* is a stative verb (*bašû*, *balāṭu*).

3.8.7. *Yaqtulu*

- The indicative *yaqtulu* expresses obligation and possibility (e.g., "should, can, might"), but it never expresses the jussive mood in EA texts.

3.8.8. *Yaqtulun(na)*

- The *yaqtulun(na)* appears frequently in Canaanite and non-Canaanite EA texts, in independent, temporal, relative clauses, and in conditional sentences.
- Although the *-n(n)a* ending appears on the indicative *yaqtulu*, the different nuances expressed by the two forms is not always clear to the modern reader.

Chapter 4
Conclusion
Synopsis of the Modal System of the Northwest Semitic Languages

4.1. *Yaqtul* (Jussive)

In the *Biblical Hebrew* strong verb, there is no morphological difference between the indicative (*realis*) prefix conjugation and the jussive (*irrealis*). In certain weak verbs and in the Hiphil stem, on the other hand, the jussive is morphologically distinct. The Hebrew jussive appears in the first, second, and third persons (e.g., יָשֵׂם, נַשְׁאֵר, תְּהִי).

In *EA Canaanite*, the jussive also appears in the first, second, and third persons (e.g., *ni-pu-uš, ú-ul ta-qa-al-mi, yu-ba-li-iṭ*). Although the scribes show familiarity with the West Semitic form, preference is given to the Akkadian precative to express wishes and indirect requests.

4.1.1. Additional NWSemitic Evidence

In *Ugaritic*, the morphological features of the jussive can only be identified in the III-*yod* verbs and with the negative particle *ʾl* (e.g., *ybn, ʾl tkl*). In other types of verb, the jussive is identical to the indicative. In these cases, when

Author's note: The NWSemitic data discussed in this book are taken from Biblical Hebrew, EA Canaanite, Ugaritic, Phoenician, and inscriptions. For summary of modal forms in East, Central, South, and NWSemitic modal forms, see B. Kienast, *Historische Semitische Sprachwissenschaft* (Wiesbaden: Harrassowitz, 2001) 263–92; E. Lipiński, *Semitic Languages: Outline of a Comparative Grammar* (OLA; Leuven: Peeters, 2001) 359–86. For Ugaritic, see J. Tropper, *Ugaritische Grammatik* (AOAT 273; Münster: Ugarit-Verlag, 2000) 719–36; D. Sivan, *A Grammar of the Ugaritic Language* (Leiden: Brill 2001) 96–107; J. Huehnergard, *An Introduction to Ugaritic* (Peabody, MA: Hendrickson, 2012) 56–59; P. Bordreuil and D. Pardee, *A Manual of Ugaritic* (LSAWS 3; Winona Lake, IN: Eisenbrauns, 2009) 47–51. For Phoenician, see C. R. Krahmalkov, *Phoenician-Punic Grammar* (Leiden: Brill, 2001) 151–214; P. C. Schmitz, "Phoenician-Punic Grammar and Lexicography in the New Millennium," *JSOT* 124 (2004) 539–41; A. Schade, "A Text Linguistic Approach to the Syntax and Style of the Phoenician Inscription of Azatiwada," *JSS* 50 (Spring 2005) 50–53. For inscriptions, see S. Landis Gogel, *A Grammar of Epigraphic Hebrew* (SBL Resources for Biblical Study 23; Atlanta: Society of Biblical Literature, 1998); E. J. Bridge, "Polite Language in the Lachish Letters," *VT* 60 (2010) 518–34; J. Naveh, *Studies in West-Semitic Epigraphy* (Jerusalem: Magnes, 2009) 367–74.

the verb expresses a wish or indirect command and/or appears in sequences of injunctives, it is identified as a jussive.

In *Phoenician*, the jussive is attested in the second and third persons. Although the second-person occurrence is a strong verb and morphologically identical to an indicative, the negative particle אל that precedes it, reveals its identity as a jussive.

In *Hebrew inscriptions*, there is evidence of a jussive in the second and third persons. The second person is identified by the negative particle אל. The absence of vocalization requires us to focus on the syntax of the verb in order to identify its form and function in context.

4.2. *Yaqtula*

In *Biblical Hebrew*, the volitive *yaqtula* of a strong verb cannot be recognized morphologically. It can only be identified through an analysis of the *yiqtol* in contexts where a volitive is expected. When the Hebrew *yiqtol* expresses a wish or request, in independent clauses, subordinate clauses, and sequences of injunctives the verb represents a volitive *yiqtol* (< *yaqtula*). Due to the loss of final short vowels in Hebrew, the indicative *yiqtol* and the volitive *yiqtol* are morphologically identical in the strong verb and in most weak verbs. With strong verbs, the jussive and the indicative display the same features, but with III-*he* verbs, the jussive and indicative differ morphologically. When a III-*he* *yiqtol* expresses volition in contexts where an injunctive is expected, the verb is a volitive (*irrealis*) *yiqtol* (< *yaqtula*) and not an indicative (*realis*) *yiqtol* (< *yaqtulu*).

In the *EA Canaanite* correspondence, a modal prefix conjugation with final -*a* (*yaqtula*) appears frequently. In many cases, the verb is a jussive with a ventive ending (-*a*[*m*]), but in other cases, the verb is an identifiable West Semitic prefix-conjugation volitive. The majority of instances of jussive with ventive ending (-*a*[*m*]) appear in the third person in verbs that typically appear with the ventive in Akkadian. On the other hand, the majority of occurrences of *yaqtula* are in the first person and occur with verbs that do not typically take a ventive ending in Akkadian. Scribes of EA letters had three modal forms at their disposition to express wishes and requests—the jussive *yaqtul*, the precative *liprus*, and the volitive *yaqtula*. As noted in this study, they adopted the volitive *yaqtula* as the common injunctive form for the first person and used mostly the jussive and the precative as third-person injunctives.

4.2.1. Additional NWSemitic Evidence

In *Ugaritic*, a volitive form with modal ending -*a* appears in the first- and third-persons singular of some III-*ʾalep* verbs (e.g., *iqra, ymẓa*). The choice of the *a-ʾalep* sign as the final consonant of such verb reveals a volitive-prefix conjugation.

In *Phoenician*, there is no clear evidence of a volitive *yaqtula*. This is mainly due to the absence of vocalization in the written language. Nevertheless, a comparison with the other languages points to the possibility that Phoenician scribes used *yaqtula* alongside the jussive.

Due to the absence of vocalization in the texts, there is no concrete evidence of a volitive *yaqtula* in *Hebrew inscriptions*. This should not exclude the possibility that the communities that spoke Hebrew, Moabite, Edomite, and Ammonite were familiar with a modal form of this sort.

4.3. *Yaqtulan(na)*

In *Biblical Hebrew*, the Canaanite *yaqtulan(na)* modal form is preserved in the first, second, and third persons without the modal ending *-n(na)* and with a final *-ā*. The final *-ā* appears in the parallel Arabic form (*yaqtulan*) in pause (*yaqtulā*). The loss of a final *nun* is a phenomenon seen in Hebrew in the imperfect (*yaqtulun* [in pause] > *yaqtulū* [contextual]) and in the cohortative (*yaqtulan* > *yaqtulā*). The original ending of the modal form *yaqtulan(na)* eventually separated from the verb and became the independent morpheme נָא.

In *EA Canaanite* texts, there is only one clear example of a *yaqtulan(na)* modal form. In most cases where the modal ending *-n(na)* appears, the verb is an indicative (*yaqtulu*).

4.3.1. Additional NWSemitic Evidence

In *Ugaritic*, a prefix conjugation ending with *-n* (*yaqtulan*) or *-nn* (*yaqtulanna*) is depicted in the first, second, and third persons (e.g., *iqran, trḫṣ.nn, ystrn*). In some cases, the modal ending *-n(na)* is appended to the verb, while at other times, it is separated from the verb by a word divider and functions as an independent morpheme.

In *Phoenician*, prefix conjugations occasionally appear with a *nun* suffix. In these cases, the verbs appear in negative purpose clauses and in modal contexts, expressing negative commands. Since the *-(n)na* modal suffix is common on the *yaqtulu* of EA texts and also appears on a modal *yaqtula* in Ugaritic and EA texts, the Phoenician evidence is either *yaqtuluna* or *yaqtulana*. The lack of vocalization limits our ability to determine the exact form.

In *Hebrew inscriptions*, there is no evidence of a modal prefix conjugation with final *-n(na)*. There is also no evidence of a modal particle נָא. On the other hand, the presence of an imperative with *-ennu* pronominal suffix provides a clue that long modal forms were included in the paradigm of the modal system.

4.4. Regular Imperative

In *Biblical Hebrew*, the regular imperative is commonly used to express commands. In the strong verb, a regular imperative cannot be distinguished morphologically from a long imperative with a ָה ending. In some III-*he* verbs on the other hand, the regular imperative and the imperative with the additional modal הָ ending can be distinguished from each other (e.g., גַּל / גְּלֵה, צַו / צַוֵּה, מַן / מְנֵה).

In *EA Canaanite* texts, most of the imperatives are typical Akkadian forms. Only a few verb forms display strictly West Semitic features (e.g., *nu-pul, ku-na*).

4.4.1. Additional NWSemitic Evidence

In *Ugaritic*, the regular imperative can be identified in I-*yod*, I-*nun*, and III-*yod* verbs (e.g., *rd, lk, tn, ʿl*). In the strong verb on the other hand, the imperative and the infinitive absolute are morphologically identical and therefore difficult to distinguish from each other. In Hebrew, the imperatives of *yrd, hlk,* and *y/ntn* appear in the long imperative with final הָ, but based on the attested form of the same verbs in Ugaritic, these verbs appear only in their regular form, possibly with a final modal *-a* ending. Due to the lack of vocalization in Ugaritic, the imperative with modal *-a* ending cannot be identified, except with III-*ʾalep* and III-*yod* verbs.

In *Phoenician*, a number of verbs express commands, but due to the absence of vocalization, what seems to be imperative forms could also be interpreted as infinitives absolute (e.g., בדד, ברח, עבר). These appear in the incantations from Arslan Tash.

In *Hebrew inscriptions*, the regular imperative appears in verbs that are also frequently attested in Biblical Hebrew. There is no evidence of long imperatives. The same form appears in Biblical Hebrew and in the Hebrew inscriptions (e.g., תן, רד, לך).

4.5. Imperative with Modal *-a* Ending

As mentioned in the previous section, the *Biblical Hebrew* imperative of III-*he* verbs is manifest in two forms: a regular imperative and an imperative with an additional modal ending הָ. This phenomenon becomes apparent if one compares the Ugaritic III-*yod*'s two forms of imperative with the Hebrew III-*he*'s two forms of the imperative. In the imperative with modal ending הָ, the Ugaritic final *yod* is preserved, indicating a vocalic ending. In Hebrew, the final *he* is preserved on verbs the regular imperatives of which appear without the *he* (e.g., גַּל / גְּלֵה, צַו / צַוֵּה, מַן / מְנֵה).

- The first form is based on the jussive (e.g., גַּל, צַו, מַן). In these cases, the imperative is apocopated and loses its final *he*.
- The second form is based on the volitive with final *-a* (e.g., גְּלֵה, צַוֵּה, מְנֵה). In these cases, the imperative is not apocopated and preserves its final *he*.

In *EA Canaanite*, the verb *kânu* appears in the imperative with a final *-a*. Since the form *kuna* is not Akkadian and is not conducive to taking a ventive ending, it is identified as a West Semitic imperative with modal ending *-a*, as is found in Ugaritic.

4.5.1. Additional NWSemitic Evidence

In *Ugaritic*, there is evidence of imperatives with a modal *-a* ending in III-*ʾalep* verbs and III-*yod* verbs (e.g., *šа, šty, ṯny*). With III-*yod* verbs, the presence of the *yod* indicates that a final vowel was present. Where no vowel is expected, as in the regular imperative, the *yod* is absent (e.g., *ʿl, bn*).

In *Phoenician*, there is not enough evidence to confirm whether an imperative with modal *-a* ending existed. In *Hebrew inscriptions*, the evidence is not sufficient to confirm the presence or absence of imperatives with modal *-a* ending.

4.6. Long Imperative with *-n(na)* Ending

In *Biblical Hebrew*, the long imperative with final ָה is common. As mentioned above, the modal ending *-n(na)* has become an independent particle of modality in Hebrew (נָא). When this particle follows a long imperative, it always includes a *dagesh forte,* as with the cohortative.

In the *EA Canaanite* correspondence, there is no evidence of imperatives with modal *-n(na)* ending. This comes as no surprise since the prefix conjugation *yaqtulan(na)* is barely present in the corpus. Since scribes used primarily the Akkadian forms of the imperative, the Canaanite modal ending is unlikely to appear.

4.6.1. Additional NWSemitic Evidence

In *Ugaritic*, the imperative with the *-n* or *-nn* ending is attested and is either appended directly to the verb or is separated by a word divider (e.g., *qḥn, gr.nn*). These features allow for the possibility that imperatives appeared with both *-an* and *-anna* endings.

In *Phoenician*, there is no evidence of a long imperative with modal *-n(na)* ending. In *inscriptions*, the only evidence of a long imperative occurs with the verb שלח, on which the third-person-pronominal נו- suffix is appended (שלחנו).

In conclusion, the texts surveyed for this research reveal that a tripartite system of prefix conjugations forms the basis of the modal system of the NWSemitic corpus: the *yaqtul* jussive, the *yaqtula* volitive, and the *yaqtulan(na)* long modal form. Based on this tripartite system, I conclude that there are also three forms of imperative: *qtl* regular imperative, *qtl-a* modal imperative, and *qtl-an(na)* or *qtl-ā* long imperative. Traditional paradigms of Biblical Hebrew volitives have not shown a distinction between the two forms of III-*he* imperatives (*qtl* and *qtl-a* < *yaqtula*). This is understandable because the modal prefix conjugation with final *-a* (*yaqtula*) to which this second form of the imperative is connected has not been recognized by Hebrew grammarians.

Table 4.1. Volitives in Northwest Semitic Languages

	Biblial Hebrew	*EA Canaanite*	*Ugaritic*	*Phoenician*	*Inscriptional (Heb., Moab)*
Regular impv.	כְּתֹב מַן, צַו, גַּל	*nupul,* *limad*	*tn, rd, lk,* *mǵ*	בדד, ברח (possible inf. abs.)	לך, רד, תן
Impv. modal *-a* ending	גְּלֵה, צַוֵּה, מְנֵה	*kuna*	*šty, ša, ṯny*	?	?
Impv. + final *-n(n)*	קוּמָה, הִשָּׁבְעָה	?	*gr.nn, qḥn*		שלחנו
Negative command	אַל־אֶפֹּלָה, אַל־תָּשֵׁת, אַל־יַעַל	*ul ia-qá-ar-ri-ib, la-a yi-iš-mé*	*ʾal tqrb*	אל תשמע אל ישא	אל תאחר
Jussive 1st person	נַשְׁאֵר	*ni-pu-uš*	?	?	?
Jussive 2nd person	תְּהִי,	*ta-qal-mi*	*tkl*	תשמע	תאחר
Jussive 3rd person	יָשֵׂם	*ia-az-ku-ur*	*yšt, ymǵ*	ישא	יגע
Yaqtula 1st person	?	*a-na-ṣa-ra,* *i-pu-ša*	*ʾiqra*	?	?
Yaqtula 2nd person	?	?	?	?	?
Yaqtula 3rd person	יַעֲשֶׂה	*yi-ìš-ma*	*ymẓa*	?	?
Yaqtulan(na) 1st person	אֶשְׁלְחָה	?	*ʾanḫn,* *ʾašt.n,* *ʾiqrʾan* ?	?	?
Yaqtulan(na) 2nd person	תָּבוֹאָה	*ti-ma-ḫa-ṣa-na-ni*	*trḫṣ.nn*	תבאן? תדרכן?	?
Yaqtulan(na) 3rd person	יָחִישָׁה	?	*ystrn*	יסגרנם?	?

YAQTUL (jussive) ______	*QTL*	גַּל, כְּתֹב
YAQTULa ______	*QTLa*	גְלֵה, כְּתֹב
YAQTULan(na) ______	*QTLan(na)*	קוּמָה

The most revealing data for a tripartite system is found in Ugaritic and Biblical Hebrew, especially in III-*ʾalep* and III-*yod* verbs. Ugaritic clearly attests the three modal prefix conjugations *and* the three forms of the imperative. In Biblical Hebrew, the picture is not as clear, but the evidence points to the presence of three modal prefix conjugations *and* three forms of the imperative.

Table 4.1 provides examples of each form in the first, second, and third persons in the NWSemitic corpus.

4.7. The Volitives and Social Dynamics

In the introductory chapter, I showed that in many languages—Semitic and non-Semitic—social dynamics in direct discourse are marked with identifiable linguistic elements (e.g., Tagalog particle of politeness *po*, Korean prefixes and suffixes). Throughout the book, I noted instances in which NWSemitic volitives are marked for specific social contexts (e.g., lesser to greater, greater to lesser, equals). This phenomenon is more evident in Biblical Hebrew than in the other languages treated in this book, since the corpus is large, direct discourse occurs at all social levels, and the language includes a great variety of speakers and listeners (e.g., God, kings, rulers, leaders, officials, servants). In Hebrew, the most significant verb forms and verbal sequences marked for specific *social contexts* include the following:

- *Long imperative.* The long imperative is marked for expressing polite petitions from a "lesser to a greater" person in the direct discourse of prose texts. In judicial texts, the *long imperative* does not appear because a morpheme marked for mitigation is not compatible with the giving of laws. In these contexts, the imperative introduces a series of commands, and the *weqatal* (*irrealis*) and *yiqtol* (*irrealis*) continue the sequence.
- Weqatal. Whne the *weqatal* is governed by an imperative and expresses a command, it almost exclusively appears in discourse where someone "greater" is addressing someone "lesser." In the majority of cases, God is the speaker of the utterance. Since this is the case, I conclude that the *weqatal* is not only marked for sequentiality but is also marked for the social dynamic of "greater to lesser."
- *Infinitive absolute.* When an infinitive absolute expresses a command, the social dynamics are that of "greater to lesser." Commands given with the infinitive absolute are not conducive to expressing politeness and therefore never occur with the particle of entreaty נָא. On the contrary, commands expressed by an infinitive absolute are

strong and imply long-term effects. In the majority of cases where the infinitive absolute is in the imperative mood, the speaker addresses the whole community or a select group of leaders within the community.

- The *jussive* appears in all three possible types of social dynamics: "greater to lesser," "lesser to greater," and between "equals." The jussive with נָא, on the other hand, appears far more often when a "lesser" is addressing a "greater."
- The *cohortative* is well distributed among the three types of social dynamics. The cohortative with נָא reflects the use of the jussive with נָא and appears significantly more often from someone "lesser" to someone "greater" than from a "greater to a lesser."

I therefore conclude that, in Hebrew, verbal forms were marked for social dynamics. Scribes chose unmarked forms when no distinction needed to be made between the social status of the speaker and that of the listener. In contexts where the social dynamics were significant, scribes used marked forms and added the particle of politeness נָא for additional modality. The nature of the texts and the limited number of texts in the rest of the NWSemitic corpus (e.g., Moabite, Ammonite, and Phoenician) prevent us from showing that social dynamics were represented in other languages.

My research on volitives will hopefully serve as a platform for further study on the verbal systems of Semitic languages, both for the NWSemitic corpus and beyond. This book deals with a corpus with an approximate dating of 1500–500 B.C.E. A thorough examination of the modal forms in the languages that follow this period would certainly add to this study (e.g., the Dead Sea Scrolls and rabbinic literature). A diachronic analysis of the volitives in Biblical Hebrew could prove helpful in answering questions related to the dating of certain books and might help clarify some intertextual issues.

Finally, I am grateful to the scholars on whose shoulders I stand for having provided the scholarly world with a solid foundation for research in this area. To those who are yet to come, I wish to provide encouragement in their endeavors to understand the intricacies of the verbal systems of the Semitic languages.

Bibliography

Albright, W. F. "The Amarna Letters from Palestine." Pp. 98–116 in *The Cambridge Ancient History*, vol. 2/2: *History of the Middle East and the Aegean Region, 1380–1000 B.C.*, ed. I. E. S. Edwards et al. 3rd ed. 14 vols. Cambridge: Cambridge University Press, 1975.

Allan, K. "Mood, Clause Types, and Illocutionary Force." Pp. 267–71 in vol. 8 of *Encyclopedia of Language and Linguistics*, ed. K. Brown. 2nd ed. 14 vols. Oxford: Elsevier, 2006.

Andersen, Francis I., and A. Dean Forbes. *Biblical Hebrew Grammar Visualized.* LSAWS 6. Winona Lake, IN: Eisenbrauns, 2012.

Andrason, Alexander. "The Panchronic *Yiqtol*: Functionally Consistent and Cognitively Plausible." *JHS* 10 (2010) 2–63. http://www.jhsonline.org.

________. "The Biblical Hebrew Verbal System in Light of Grammaticalization." *HS* 52 (2011) 19–51.

________. "The BH *Weqatal:* A Homogenous Form with No Haphazard Functions (Part 1)." *JNSL* 372 (2011) 1–26.

________. "An Optative Indicative? A Real Factual Past? Toward a Cognitive-Typological Approach to the Precative Qatal." *JHS* 13 (2013) 1–41. http://www.jhsonline.org.

Anstey, Matthew P. "The Biblical Hebrew *qatal* Verb: A Functional Discourse Grammar Analysis." *Linguistics* 47 (2009) 825–44.

Austin, J. L. *How To Do Things with Words*. London: Oxford University Press, 1962.

Avanzini, A. "Origin and Classification of the Ancient South Arabian Languages." *JSS* 54 (2009) 205–20.

Baden, J. S. "The *weyiqtol* and the Volitive Sequence." *VT* 58 (2008) 147–58.

________. "The Morpho-Syntax of Genesis 12:1–3: Translation and Interpretation." *CBQ* 72 (2010) 223–37.

Bandstra, Barry L. "Word Order and Emphasis in Biblical Hebrew Narrative: Syntactic Observations on Genesis 22 from a Discourse Perspective." Pp. 109–23 in *Linguistics and Biblical Hebrew*, ed. Walter R. Bodine. Winona Lake, IN: Eisenbrauns, 1992.

Bar, Tali. "Optative Expressions." P. 716 in vol. 3 of *Encyclopedia of Hebrew Language and Linguistics*, ed. Geoffrey Kahn. Leiden: Brill, 2013.

Bar-Asher, Elitzur Avraham. "The Imperative Forms of Proto-Semitic and a New Perspective on Barth's Law." *JAOS* 128 (2008) 233–55.

Bar-Magen, M. "המלה 'נא' במקרא." *Beit Miqra* 25 (1980) 163–71.

Bartelt, Andrew H. "The Hebrew Infinitive." *Concordia Journal* (Winter 2010) 35–38.

________. "On the Subtleties of Hebrew Verbs." *Concordia Journal* (2008) 61–62.

________. "On the Subtleties of Hebrew Verbs, Part II." *Concordia Journal* (2008) 301–3.

Bauer, H., and Leander, P. *Historische Grammatik der Hebräischen Sprache des Alten Testaments*, vol. 1. Hildesheim: Olms, 1991.

Bavin, E. L. "Syntactic Development." Pp. 383–90 in vol. 12 of *Encyclopedia of Language and Linguistics*, ed. K. Brown. 2nd ed. 14 vols. Oxford: Elsevier, 2006.

Beeston, A. F. L. *A Descriptive Grammar of Epigraphic South Arabian*. London: Luzac, 1962.

Benveniste, Emile. *Problèmes de linguistique générale*. Paris: Gallimard, 1966.

Bezold, C., and Budge, E. W. *The Tell el-Amarna Tablets in the British Museum*. London: British Museum, 1892.

Blachère, R., and M. Gaudefroy-Demombynes. *Grammaire de l'arabe classique: Morphologie et syntaxe*. 3rd ed. Paris: Maisonneuve, 1952.

Blau, Joshua. "Studies in Hebrew Verb Formation." *HUCA* 42 (1971) 133–46.

________. *A Grammar of Biblical Hebrew*. 2nd ed. Porta Linguarum Orientalium n.s. 12. Wiesbaden: Harrassowitz, 1993.

Bloomfield, L. *Language*. New York: Holt, Rinehart and Winston, 1963.

Bodine, Walter R. "How Linguists Study Syntax." Pp. 89–107 in *Linguistics and Biblical Hebrew*, ed. W. R. Bodine. Winona Lake, IN: Eisenbrauns, 1992.

Böhl, Franz M. *Die Sprache der Amarnabriefe: Mit besonderer Berücksichtigung der Kanaanismen*. Leipziger semitistische Studien 5/2. Leipzig: Hinrich, 1909.

Bordreuil, P., and D. Pardee. *A Manual of Ugaritic*. LSAWS 3. Winona Lake, IN: Eisenbrauns, 2009.

Boyd, Steven. *A Synchronic Analysis of the Medio-Passive-Reflexive in Biblical Hebrew*. Ph.D. dissertation. Hebrew Union College–Jewish Institute of Religion, 1993.

Branden, A. van den. *Grammaire phénicienne*. Bibliothèque de l'Université Saint-Esprit 2. Beirut: Librairie du Liban, 1969.

Brent, J. F. "The Problem of the Placement of Ugaritic among the Semitic Languages." *WTJ* 41 (1978) 84–107.

Bridge, Edward J. "Polite Language in the Lachish Letters." *VT* 60 (2010) 518–34.

Bright, John. "Apodictic Prohibition: Some Observations." *JBL* 92 (1973) 185–204.

Brockelmann, Carl. *Grundriss der vergleichenden Grammatik der semitischen Sprachen*. 2 vols. Berlin: Reuther & Reichard, 1913.

Brown, R., and A. Gilman. The Pronouns of Power and Solidarity. Pp. 252–81 in *Style in Language*, ed. T. A. Sebeok. Cambridge, MA: MIT Press, 1960.

Brown, F., S. R. Driver, and C. A. Briggs, eds. *A Hebrew and English Lexicon of the Old Testament with an Appendix Containing the Biblical Aramaic*. Oxford: Clarendon, 1906.

Buccellati, G. *A Structural Grammar of Babylonian*. Wiesbaden: Harrassowitz, 1996.

Buth, Randall John. "Word Order Differences between Narrative and Non-narrative Material in Biblical Hebrew." Pp. 9–16 in *Proceedings of the Tenth World Congress of Jewish Studies, Jerusalem, August 16–24, 1985*, division D/1: *The Hebrew Language—Jewish Languages*. Jerusalem: World Union of Jewish Studies, 1990.

Bybee, Joan, and Suzanne Fleischman. "Modality in Grammar and Discourse: An Introductory Essay." Pp 1–14 in *Modality in Grammar and Discourse*, ed. J. Bybee and S. Fleischman. Typological Studies in Language 32. Amsterdam: John Benjamins, 1995.

Callahan, Scott N. *Modality and the Biblical Hebrew Infinitive Absolute*. Abhandlungen für die Kunde des Morgenlandes 71. Wiesbaden: Harrassowitz, 2010.

________. "Mood and Modality: Biblical Hebrew." Pp. 687–89 in vol. 2 of *Encyclopedia of Hebrew Language and Linguistics*, ed. Geoffrey Khan. Leiden: Brill, 2013.

Cantineau, J. "La langue de Ras Shamra." *Sem* 3 (1972) 21–34.

Castellino, G. R. *The Akkadian Personal Pronouns and Verbal System in the Light of Semitic and Hamitic*. Leiden: Brill, 1962.

Cazelles, H. "Précis de grammaire ugaritique." *BeO* 21 (1979) 253–65.

Chaine, Marius. *Grammaire éthiopienne*. Beirut: Imprimerie catholique, 1938.

Christiansen, B. "A Linguistic Analysis of the Biblical Hebrew Particle *na*ʾ: A Test Case." *VT* 59 (2009) 379–93.

Clem, Eldon. *Unmarked Subject-Verb Position*. M.A. Thesis. Trinity Evangelical Divinity School, 1987.

Cochavi-Rainey, Z. "Canaanite Influence in the Akkadian Texts Written by Egyptian Scribes in the 14th and 13th Centuries B.C.E." *UF* 21 (1989) 39–46.

________. "Amarna Canaanite and Hebrew." Pp. 96–98 in vol. 1 of *Encyclopedia of Hebrew Language and Linguistics*, ed. Geoffrey Khan. Leiden: Brill, 2013.

Cohen, E. *The Modal System of Old Babylonian*. HSS 56. Winona Lake, IN: Eisenbrauns, 2005.

Cohen, Ohad. *The Verbal Tense System in Late Biblical Hebrew Prose*. HSS 63. Winona Lake, IN: Eisenbrauns, 2013.

Comean, R. F., F. L. Bustin, and N. J. Lamoureux. *Grammaire: An Integrated Approach to French*. 3rd ed. New York: Holt, Rinehart and Winston, 1986.

Comrie, Bernard. *Aspect: An Introduction to the Study of Verbal Aspect and Related Problems*. Cambridge: Cambridge University Press, 1976.

________. *Language Universals and Linguistic Typology*. Chicago: University of Chicago Press, 1981.

Cook, John A. *The Biblical Hebrew Verbal System: A Grammaticalization Approach*. Ph.D. dissertation. University of Wisconsin, 2002.

________. "Detecting Development in Biblical Hebrew Using Diachronic Typology." Pp. 83–95 in *Diachrony in Biblical Hebrew*, ed. Cynthia L. Miller-Naudé and Ziony Zevit. LSAWS 8. Winona Lake, IN: Eisenbrauns, 2012.

________. "The Hebrew Verb: A Grammaticalization Approach." *ZA* 14 (2001) 117–43.

________. "The Semantics of Verbal Pragmatics: Clarifying the Roles of *Wayyiqtol* and *Weqatal* in Biblical Hebrew Prose." *JSS* 49 (2004) 247–73.

________. *Time and the Biblical Hebrew Verb: The Expression of Tense, Aspect, and Modality in Biblical Hebrew*. LSAWS 7. Winona Lake, IN: Eisenbrauns, 2012.

________. "The *Vav*-Prefixed Verb Forms in Elementary Hebrew Grammar." *JHS* 8 (2008) 1–16. http://www.jhsonline.org.

Couper-Kulhen, W. "Intonation and Discourse: Current Views from Within." Pp. 13–34 in *The Handbook of Discourse Analysis*, ed. D. Shriffrin, D. Tannen and H. E. Hamilton. Malden, MA: Blackwell, 2001.

Croft, W. "Typology and Grammar." Pp. 343–50 in *Concise Encyclopedia of Syntactic Theories*, ed. K. Brown and J. Miller. New York: Pergamon, 1996.

Davidson, A. B. *Hebrew Syntax*. 3rd ed. Edinburgh: T. & T. Clark, 1989.

Dawson, D. A. *Text-Linguistics and Biblical Hebrew*. JSOTSup 17. Sheffield: Sheffield Academic Press, 1994.

DeCaen, Vincent. "Ewald and Driver on BH 'Aspect': Anteriority and the Orientalist Framework." *ZAH* 9 (1996) 140–41.

________. *On the Placement and Interpretation of the Verbs in Standard Biblical Hebrew Prose*. Ph.D. dissertation, University of Toronto, 1995.

Delekat, L. "Zum ugaritischen Verbum." *UF* 4 (1972) 11–26.

Dhorme, P. E. "La langue de Canaan, part 1." *RB* n.s. 10 (1913) 369–93.

________. "La langue de Canaan, part 2." *RB* n.s. 11 (1914) 37–59, 334–72.

Di Giulio, Marco. "Discourse Marker: Biblical Hebrew." P. 757 in vol. 1 of *Encyclopedia of Hebrew Language and* Linguistics, ed. Geoffrey Khan. Leiden: Brill, 2013.

Dillman, August. *Ethiopic Grammar*, ed. Karl Bezold. Translated by James Chrichton. London: Williams & Norgate, 1907.

Dobbs-Allsopp, F. W. "Ingressive *qwm* in Biblical Hebrew." *ZAH* 8 (1995) 31–54.

Driver, G. R. *Problems of the Hebrew Verbal System*. Edinburgh: T. & T. Clark, 1936.

Driver, S. R. *A Treatise on the Use of the Tenses in Hebrew*. 3rd ed. Oxford: Clarendon, 1892.

________. *A Treatise on the Use of the Tenses in Hebrew and Some Other Syntactical Questions*. Repr., Elibron Classics. Chestnut Hill, MA: Adamant, 2004.

Ebeling, E. "Das Verbum der El-Amarna Briefe." *BASS* 8 (1910) 39–79.

Edzard, D. O. "Die Modi beim älteren akkadischen Verbum." *Or* 42 (*Festschrift I. J. Gelb*; 1973) 121–31.

Endo, Yoshinobu. *The Verbal System of Classical Hebrew in the Joseph Story: An Approach from Discourse Analysis*. Studia Semitica Neerlandica. Assen: Van Gorcum, 1996.

Ervin-Tripp, Susan M. "Interaction of Language, Topic and Listener." Pp. 192–211 in *Readings in the Sociology of Language*, ed. Joshua A. Fishman. New York: Mouton, 1977.

Faber, Alice. "Genetic Subgrouping of the Semitic Languages." Pp. 3–15 in *The Semitic Languages*, ed. R. Hetzron. New York: Routledge, 1997.

Fassberg, S. E. "Cohortative." P. 476 in vol. 1 of *Encyclopedia of Hebrew Language and Linguistics*, ed. Geoffrey Khan. Leiden: Brill, 2013.

________. "The Lengthened Imperative *qōtlâ* in Biblical Hebrew." *HS* 40 (1999) 7–13.

________. "Imperative and Prohibitive: Pre-Modern." Pp. 243–44 in vol. 2 of *Encyclopedia of Hebrew Language and Linguistics*, ed. Geoffrey Khan. Leiden: Brill, 2013.

________. *Studies in Biblical Syntax*. Jerusalem: Magnes, 1994. [Hebrew]

Fassberg, S. E., and Avi Hurvitz, eds. *Biblical Hebrew in Its Northwest Semitic Setting: Typology and Historical Perspectives*. Institute for Advanced Studies 1. Winona Lake, IN: Eisenbrauns / Jerusalem: Magnes, 2006.

________. "Sequences of Positive Commands in Biblical Hebrew: הָלוֹךְ וְאָמַרְתָּ, לֵךְ וְאָמַרְתָּ, לֵךְ אֱמֹר." Pp. 51–64 in *Biblical Hebrew in Its Northwest Semitic Setting: Typological and Historical* Perspectives, ed. S. E. Fassberg and A. Hurvitz. Winona Lake, IN: Eisenbrauns / Jerusalem: Magnes, 2006.

Fenton, T. L. "Commands and Fulfillment in Ugaritic: *tqtl : yqtl* and *qtl : qtl*." *JSS* 14 (1969) 34–38.

Finley, T. J. "The Proposal in Biblical Hebrew: Preliminary Studies Using a Deep Structure Model." *ZAH* 2 (1989) 1–13.

Fleisch, Henri. *L'Arabe classique: Esquisse d'une structure linguistique*. Beirut: Dar El-Machreq, 1968.

________. "*Yaqtula* cananéen et subjonctif arabe." Pp. 65–76 in *Studia Orientalia in Memoriam Caroli Brockelmann*, ed. Manfred Fleishhammer. Wissenschaftliche Zeitschrift der M. Luther Universität 17/2–3. Halle: Martin-Luther Universität, 1968.

________. "Sur le système verbal du sémitique commun." *MUSJ* 27 (1948) 39–60.

Fradkin, Robert. *Stalking the Wold Verb Phrase*. New York: University Press of America, 1991.

Friedrich, J., and W. Röllig. *Phönizisch-punische Grammatik* 3. *AnOr* 55. Rome: Pontifical Biblical Institute, 1999.

Garr, R. *Dialect Geography of Syria–Palestine, 1000–586 B.C.* Repr. Philadelphia: University of Pennsylvania, 2008.

Gee, James P. *How to Do Discourse Analysis: A Toolkit*. New York: Routledge, 2011.

Geertz, Clifford. "Linguistic Etiquette." Pp. 282–95 in *Readings in the Sociology of Language*, ed. Joshua A. Fishman. New York: Mouton, 1977.

Gentry, P. "The System of the Finite Verb in Classical Biblical Hebrew." *HS* 39 (1998) 7–41.

Gianto Kentjanaputra, Agustinus. *A Study of Word Order Variations in the Byblos Amarna Letters*. Ph.D. dissertation, Harvard University, 1987.

Glinert, L. *The Grammar of Modern Hebrew*. Cambridge: Cambridge University Press, 1989.

Goddard, Burton L. *The Origin of the Hebrew Infinitive Absolute in the Light of the Infinitive Uses in Related Languages and Its Use in the Old Testament*. Ph.D. dissertation, Harvard University, 1943.

Gogel, S. Landis. *A Grammar of Epigraphic Hebrew*. SBL Resources for Biblical Study 23. Atlanta: Scholars Press, 1999.

Gordon, Cyrus. *Ugaritic Textbook*. AnOr 38. Rome: Pontifical Biblical Institute, 1965.

Gottlieb, H. "The Hebrew Particle *na'*." *AcOr* (*Danica*) 3 (1971) 47–54.

Greenberg, J. H. *Language Universals*. The Hague: Mouton, 1966.

Greenfield. J. C. "The Periphrastic Imperative in Aramaic and Hebrew." *IEJ* 19 (1969) 199–210.

Grimes, Joseph E. *The Thread of Discourse*. Janua Linguarum Series Minor 207. The Hague: Mouton, 1975.

Gropp, D. "The Function of the Finite Verb in Classical Biblical Hebrew." *HAR* 13 (1991) 45–62.

Gzella, Holger. "Northwest Semitic Languages and Hebrew." Pp. 852–63 in vol. 2 of *Encyclopedia of Hebrew Language and Linguistics*, ed. Goeffrey Kahn. Leiden: Brill, 2013.

Hackett, Jo Ann, and N. Pat-El. "On Canaanite and Historical Linguistics: Rejoinder to Anson Rainey." *MAARAV* 17 (2010) 173–88.

Haiman, J. "Iconicity." Pp. 196–200 in *Concise Encyclopedia of Syntactic Theories*, ed. K. Brown and J. Miller. New York: Pergamon, 1996.

Hammershaimb, E. *Das Verbum im Dialekt von Ras Schamra: Eine morphologische und syntaktische Untersuchung des Verbums in den alphabetischen Keilschrifttexten aus dem alten Ugarit.* Copenhagen: Hammershaimb, 1941.

Harris, Z. H. *The Development of the Canaanite Dialects: An Investigation in Linguistic History*. Repr. New Haven, CT: Yale University Press, 1939.

________. *A Grammar of the Phoenician Language.* AOS 8. Repr., New Haven, CT: American Oriental Society, 1990.

Hasselbach, Rebecca. "Canaanite and Hebrew." P. 607 in vol. 1 of *Encyclopedia of Hebrew Language and Linguistics*, ed. Goeffrey Kahn. Leiden: Brill, 2013.

________. "The Verbal Endings *-u* and *-a*: A Note on Their Functional Derivation." Pp. 119–36 in *Language and Nature: Papers Presented to John Huehnergard on the Occasion of His 60th Birthday*, ed. R. Hasselbach and Naʿama Pat-El. Studies in Ancient Oriental Civilization 67. Chicago: University of Chicago Press, 2012.

Hatav, Galia. "The Deictic Nature of the Directives in Biblical Hebrew." *Studies in Language* 30 (2006) 733–75.

________. *The Semantics of Aspect and Modality: Evidence from English and Biblical Hebrew*. Amsterdam: John Benjamins, 1997.

Haupt, Paul. "The Hebrew Particle *-nâ*." *Johns Hopkins University Circulars* 13 (1894) 109.

Hawkins, J. A. "Explaining Language Universals." Pp. 3–28 in *Explaining Language Universals*, ed. J. A. Hawkins. New York: Blackwell, 1988.

Heintz, Jean-Georges. *Index Documentaire d'El-Amarna—I.D.E.A.*, vol. 2: *Bibliographie des textes babyloniens d'El-Amarna* [*1888 à 1993*] *et Concordance des sigles EA*. Wiesbaden: Harrassowitz, 1995.

Heller, M. Discourse and Interaction. Pp. 250–64 in *The Handbook of Discourse Analysis*, ed. D. Schiffrin, D. Tannen and H. E. Hamilton. Malden, MA: Blackwell, 2001.

Heller, Roy L. *Narrative Structure and Discourse Constellations: An Analysis of Clause Function in Biblical Hebrew Prose.* HSS 55. Winona Lake, IN: Eisenbrauns, 2004.

Hendel, R. S. "In the Margins of the Hebrew Verbal System: Situation, Tense, Aspect, Mood." *ZAH* 9 (1996) 152–81.

Hetzron, Robert. "La division des languages sémitiques." Pp. 181–94 in *Actes du premier congrès international de linguistique sémitique et chamito-sémitique*, ed. A. Caquot and D. Cohen. Berlin: de Gruyter, 1974.

________. "The Evidence for a Perfect *yáqtul and Jussive *yaqtúl in Proto-Semitic." *JSS* 14 (1969) 1–21.

Hetzron, Robert, ed. *The Semitic Languages*. New York: Routledge, 1997.

Hewett, J. A. *New Testament Greek: A Beginning and Intermediate Grammar*. Peabody, MA: Hendrickson, 1986.

Hijirida, K., and M. Yoshikawa. *Japanese Language and Culture for Business and Travel*. Honolulu: University of Hawaii Press, 1987.

Hoftijzer, J. *The Function and Use of the Imperfect Forms with* Nun Paragogicum *in Classical Hebrew*. Studia Semitica Neerlandica 21. Assen: Van Gorcum, 1985.

Holmstedt, Robert D. *The Relative Clause in Biblical Hebrew: A Linguistic Analysis*. Ph.D. Dissertation. University of Wisconsin–Madison, 2002.

________. "The Typological Classification of the Hebrew of Genesis: Subject-Verb or Verb-Subject?" *JHS* 11 (2011) 2–39. http://www.jhsonline.org.

Hospers, J. H. "Some Remarks about the So-Called Imperative Use of the Infinitive Absolute (*Infinitivus pro Imperativo*) in Classical Hebrew." Pp. 97–102 in *Studies in Hebrew and Aramaic Syntax*, ed. K. Jongeling, H. L. Murre van den Berg and L. van Rompay. Leiden: Brill, 1991.

Huehnergard, John. *The Akkadian of Ugarit*. HSS 34. Atlanta: Scholars Press, 1989.

________. "The Early Hebrew Prefix-Conjugation." *HS* 29 (1988) 19–23.

________. "Features of Central Semitic." Pp. 155–203 in *Biblical and Oriental Essays in Memory of William L. Moran*, ed. A. Gianto Kentjanaputra. Rome: Pontifical Biblical Institute, 2005.

________. *A Grammar of Akkadian*. 3rd ed. HSS 45. Winona Lake, IN: Eisenbrauns, 2011.

________. *An Introduction to Ugaritic*. Peabody, MA: Hendrickson, 2012.

________. "Remarks on the Classification of the Northwest Semitic Languages." Pp. 282–93 in *The Balaam Text from Deir ʿAlla Re-evaluated: Proceedings of the International Symposium Held at Leiden, 21–24 August 1989*, ed. J. Hoftijzer and G. van der Kooij. Leiden: Brill, 1991.

________. "Review of *A Grammar of Amarna Canaanite* by A. Rainey." *BASOR* 310 (1998) 59–77.

Huehnergard, John, and Aaron D. Rubin. "Phyla and Waves: Models of Classification of the Semitic Languages." Pp. 259–78 in *The Semitic Languages: An International Handbook*, ed. S. Weninger. Handbooks of Linguistics and Communication Science 36. Berlin: de Gruyter, 2011.

Humphries, T., C. Padden, and T. J. O'Rourke. *A Basic Course in American Sign Language*. Silver Spring, MD: T. J. Publishers, 1982.

Huntley, Martin. "The Semantics of English Imperatives." *Linguistics and Philosophy* 7 (1984) 103–33.

Izre'el, S. *Amurru Akkadian: A Linguistic Study*, vol. 1. HSS 40. Atlanta: Scholars Press, 1991.

________. *Canaano-Akkadian*. Languages of the World / Materials 82. Munich: Lincom Europa, 1998.

________. "Canaano-Akkadian: Linguistics and Sociolinguistics." Pp. 171–218 in *Language and Nature: Papers Presented to John Huehnergard on the Occasion of his 60th Birthday*, ed. R. Hasselbach and Naʿama Pat-El. Studies in Ancient Oriental Civilization 67. Chicago: University of Chicago Press, 2012.

________. "The Gezer Letters of the El-Amarna Archive: Linguistic Analysis." *IOS* 8 (1978) 13–90.

Izre'el, S, ed. "The Amarna Letters from Canaan." Pp. 2411–19 in *Civilizations of the Ancient Near East*, ed. Jack M. Sasson. New York: Scribners, 1995.

________. *The Amarna Scholarly Tablets*. Cuneiform Monograph 9. Groningen: Styx, 1997.

________. *Semitic Linguistics: The State of the Art at the Turn of the Twenty-First Century*. IOS 20. Winona Lake, IN: Eisenbrauns, 2002.

Joosten, Jan. "Biblical Hebrew *w^{e}qatal* and Syriac *hwā qātel*: Expressing Repetition in the Past." *ZAH* 5 (1992) 1–14.

________. "The Disappearance of Iterative *Weqatal* in the Biblical Hebrew Verbal System." Pp. 135–53 in *Biblical Hebrew in Its Northwest Semitic Setting: Typology and Historical Perspectives*, ed. Steven E. Fassberg and Avi Hurvitz. Institute for Advanced Studies 1. Jerusalem: Magnes / Winona Lake, IN: Eisenbrauns, 2006.

________. "The Distinction between Classical and Late Biblical Hebrew as Reflected in Syntax." *HS* 46 (2005) 327–39.

________. "The Function of the So-Called *Dativus Ethicus* in Classical Syriac." *Or* 58 (1989) 473–92.

________. "The Indicative System of the Biblical Hebrew Verb and Its Literary Exploitation." Pp. 51–71 in *Narrative Syntax and the Hebrew Bible*, ed. Ellen van Wolde. Leiden: Brill, 1997.

________. "The Long Form of the Prefix Conjugation Referring to the Past in Biblical Hebrew Prose." *HS* 40 (1999) 15–26.

________. "Short Note: A Note on *weyiqtol* and Volitive Sequences." *VT* 59 (2009) 495–98.

________. *The Verbal System of Biblical Hebrew: A New Synthesis Elaborated on the Basis of Classical Prose*. Jerusalem Biblical Studies 10. Jerusalem: Simor, 2012.

Joüon, Paul. *A Grammar of Biblical Hebrew*, trans. and rev. T. Muraoka. 2 vols. Subsidia Biblica 14. Rome: Pontifical Biblical Institute, 2006.

Kaufman, Stephen A. "The Classification of the North West Semitic Dialects of the Biblical Period and Some Implications Thereof." Pp. 41–57 in *Proceedings of the Ninth World Congress of Jewish Studies*, Panel Sessions: *Hebrew and Aramaic Languages*, ed. M. Goshen-Gottstein. Jerusalem: Magnes, 1988.

________. "An Emphatic Plea for Please." *MAARAV* 7 (1991) 195–98.

________. "Of Beginnings, Ends, and Computers in Targumic Studies." Pp. 52–66 in *To Touch the Text: Biblical and Related Studies in Honor of Joseph A. Fitzmyer, S.J*, ed. M. P. Horgan and P. J. Kobelski. New York: Crossroad, 1989.

________. "Paragogic *nun* in Biblical Hebrew: Hypercorrection as a Clue to a Lost Scribal Practice." Pp. 95–99 in *Solving Riddles and Untying Knots: Biblical, Epigraphic, and Semitic Studies in Honor of Jonas C. Greenfield*, ed. Z. Zevit, S. Gitin, and M. Sokoloff. Winona Lake, IN: Eisenbrauns, 1995.

________. "Review of *A Scholar's Dictionary of Jewish Palestinian Aramaic*, by M. Sokoloff." *JAOS* 114 (1994) 245.

Kautzsch, Emil, ed. *Gesenius' Hebrew Grammar*, ed. and rev. E. Kautzsch. Trans. A. E. Cowley. Repr., Mineola, NY: Dover, 2006.

Kawashima, Robert S. "'Orphaned' Converted Tense Forms in Classical Biblical Hebrew Prose." *JSS* 55 (Spring 2010) 11–35.

Kaye, A. S. "Does Ugaritic Go with Arabic in Semitic Genealogical Sub-Classification?" *FO* 28 (1991) 115–28.

Kelly, Fred T. "The Imperfect with Simple *Waw* in Hebrew." *JBL* 39 (1920) 1–23.

Kiefer, F. "On Defining Modality." *Folia Linguistica; Acta Societatis Linguisticae Europaeae* 21 (1987) 67–94.

Kienast, B. *Historische Semitische Sprachwissenschaft*. Wiesbaden: Harrassowitz, 2001.

Kim, Dong-Hyuk. *Early Biblical Hebrew, Late Biblical Hebrew, and Linguistic Variability: A Sociolinguistic Evaluation of the Linguistic Dating of Biblical Texts*. VTSup 156. Leiden: Brill, 2012.

König, E. *Historisch-komparative Syntax der hebräischen Sprache*. Leipzig: Hinrichs, 1897.

Koenig, J.-P. Syntax-Semantics Interface. Pp. 427–38 in vol. 12 of *Encyclopedia of Language and Linguistics*, ed. K. Brown. 14 vols. 2nd ed. Oxford: Elsevier, 2006.

Knudtzon, J. A. *Die El-Amarna Tafeln*. 2 vols. Leipzig: Hinrichs, 1915.

Korchin, Paul. Grammaticalization and the Biblical Hebrew Pseudo-Cohortative. Pp. 269–84 in *Language and Nature: Papers Presented to John Huehnergard on the Occasion of his 60th Birthday*, ed. R. Hasselbach and Naᶜama Pat-El. Studies in Ancient Oriental Civilization 67. Chicago: University of Chicago Press, 2012.

________. *Markedness in Canaanite and Hebrew Verbs*. HSS 58. Winona Lake, IN: Eisenbrauns, 2008.

Krahmalkov, C. R. *A Phoenician-Punic Grammar*. Handbook of Oriental Studies: The Near and Middle East 54. Leiden: Brill, 2001.

Kretschmer, Richard. Interview, Professor of Special Education. University of Cincinnati, College of Education, September 28, 1999.

Lambert, M. *Traité de grammaire hébraïque*. Paris: Presses universitaires de France, 1946.

Lambdin, T. O. *Introduction to Biblical Hebrew*. London: Darton, Longman & Todd, 1991.

________. *Introduction to Classical Ethiopic (Geᶜez)*. HSS 24. Missoula, MT: Scholars Press, 1978.

________. "The Junctural Origin of the West Semitic Definite Article." Pp. 315–33 in *Near Eastern Studies in Honor of William Foxwell Albright*, ed. Hans Goedicke. Baltimore: Johns Hopkins University Press, 1971.

Lee, H. H. B. *Korean Grammar*. Oxford: Oxford University Press, 1994.

Lee, M. "Language, Perception and the World." Pp. 211–46 in *Explaining Language Universals*, ed. J. A. Hawkins. New York: Blackwell, 1988.

Li, Tarsee. *The Expression of Sequence and Non-Sequence in Northwest Semitic Narrative Prose*. Ph.D. dissertation. Hebrew Union College–Jewish Institute of Religion, 1999.

Lieberman, S. J. "Word Order in the Afro-Asiatic Languages." Pp. 1–8 in *Proceedings of the Ninth World Congress of Jewish Studies*, Panel Sessions: *Hebrew and Aramaic Languages*, ed. M. Goshen-Gottstein. Jerusalem: Magnes, 1986.

Lillo-Martin, Diane. Where Are All the Modality Effects? Pp. 241–62 in *Modality and Structure in Signed and Spoken Languages*, ed. R. P. Meier, K. Cormier, and D. Quinto-Pozos. Cambridge: Cambridge University Press, 2009.

Lipiński, Edward. *Semitic Languages: Outline of a Comparative Grammar*. OLA 80. Louvain: Peeters & Department of Oriental Studies, 2001.

Longacre, Robert. "Building for the Worship of God: Exodus 25:1–30:10." Pp. 21–50 in *Discourse Analysis of Biblical Literature: What It Is and What It Offers*, ed. W. R. Bodine. SBL Semeia Studies. Atlanta: Scholars Press, 1995.

________. "Discourse Perspective on the Hebrew Verb: Affirmation and Restatement." Pp. 177–89 in *Linguistics and Biblical Hebrew*, ed. W. R. Bodine. Winona Lake, IN: Eisenbrauns, 1992.

________. "The Discourse Structure of the Flood Narrative." *JAAR* Sup 47 (1979) 89–133.

________. "Interpreting Biblical Stories." Pp. 169–85 in *Discourse and Literature*, ed. T. A. van Dijk. Amsterdam: Benjamins, 1985.

________. *Joseph: A Story of Divine Providence—A Text Theoretical and Textlinguistic Analysis of Genesis 37 and 39–48*. Winona Lake, IN: Eisenbrauns, 1989.

________. "A Textlinguistic Approach to the Biblical Hebrew Narrative of Jonah." Pp. 336–58 in *Biblical Hebrew and Discourse Linguistics*, ed. R. D. Bergen. Dallas: Summer Institute of Linguistics / Winona Lake, IN: Eisenbrauns, 1994.

________. "Verb Ranking and the Constituent Structure of Discourse." *Journal of the Linguistic Association of the Southwest* 5 (1982) 177–202.

________. "*Weqatal* Forms in Biblical Hebrew Prose: A Discourse-Modular Approach." Pp. 50–98 in *Biblical Hebrew and Discourse Linguistics*, ed. R. D. Bergen. Dallas: Summer Institute of Linguistics / Winona Lake, IN: Eisenbrauns, 1994.

Lounsbury, Floyd G. "Linguistics and Psychology." Pp. 38–67 in in *Readings in the Sociology of Language*, ed. Joshua A. Fishman. New York: Mouton, 1977.

Lyons, J. *Semantics*. Vol. 2. Cambridge: Cambridge University Press, 1977.

Mallon, E. D. *The Ugaritic Verb in the Letters and Administrative Documents*. Ph.D. dissertation. Catholic University of America, 1982.

Mangano, Mark J. *Rhetorical Content in the Amarna Correspondence from the Levant*. Ph.D. dissertation. Hebrew Union College–Jewish Institute of Religion, 1990.

Martinet, André. *La linguistique synchronique, études et recherches*. 3rd ed. Paris: Presses universitaires de France, 1970.

McFall, Leslie. *The Enigma of the Hebrew Verbal System: Solutions from Ewald to the Present Day*. Historic Texts and Interpreters in Biblical Scholarship 2. Sheffield: Almond, 1982.

Meek, T. H. "Result and Purpose Clauses in Hebrew." *JQR* 46 (1955) 40–43.

Merwe, Christo H. J. van der. "The Vague Term 'Emphasis.'" *JSem* 1 (1989) 118–32.

Merwe, Christo H. J. van der, Jackie A. Naudé, and Jan H. Kroeze. *A Biblical Hebrew Reference Grammar*. Biblical Languages: Hebrew 3. Sheffield: Sheffield Academic Press, 1999.

Miller, Patrick. "Syntax and Theology in Genesis XII 3a." *VT* 34 (1984) 472–75.

Miller-Naudé, Cynthia L. *Diachrony in Biblical Hebrew*. LSAWS 8. Winona Lake, IN: Eisenbrauns, 2012.

———. "Direct and Indirect Speech: Biblical Hebrew." Pp. 740–42 in vol. 1 of *Encyclopedia of Hebrew Language and Linguistics*, ed. Geoffrey Khan. Leiden: Brill, 2013.

———. "Introducing Direct Discourse in Biblical Hebrew Narrative." Pp. 199–241 in *Biblical Hebrew and Discourse Linguistics*, ed. R. D. Bergen. Dallas: Summer Institute of Linguistics / Winona Lake, IN: Eisenbrauns, 1994.

———. *The Representation of Speech in Biblical Hebrew Narrative: A Linguistic Analysis*, ed. P. Machinist. HSM 55. Atlanta: Scholars Press, 1996.

———. *The Verbless Clause in Biblical Hebrew: Linguistic Approaches*. LSAWS 1. Winona Lake, IN: Eisenbrauns, 1999.

Mithun, M. *The Languages of Native North America*. Cambridge: Cambridge University Press, 1999.

Moscati, Sabatino, Anton Spitaler, Edward Ullendorff, and Wolfram von Soden. *An Introduction to the Comparative Grammar of the Semitic Languages: Phonology and Morphology*, ed. S. Moscati. Porta Linguarum n.s. 6. Wiesbaden: Harrassowitz, 1980.

Moran, William L., ed. and trans. *The Amarna Letters*. Baltimore: Johns Hopkins University Press, 1992.

———. "Amarna *shumma* in Main Clauses." *JCS* 7 (1953) 78–80.

———. "Does Amarna Bear on Karatepe? An Answer." *JCS* 6 (1952) 76–80.

———. "Early Canaanite *yaqtula*." *Or* 29 (1960) 1–19.

———. "Early Canaanite *yaqtula*." Pp. 179–95 in *Amarna Studies: Collected Writings*, by W. L. Moran, ed. J. Huehnergard and S. Izre'el. HSS 54. Winona Lake, IN: Eisenbrauns, 2003.

———. "The Hebrew Language in Its Northwest Semitic Background." Pp. 54–72 in *The Bible and the Ancient Near East. Essays in Honor of William Foxwell Albright*, ed. G. E. Wright. Repr., Winona Lake, IN: Eisenbrauns, 1979. [original, 1961]

———. "New Evidence on Canaanite *taqtul(na)*." *JCS* 5 (1951) 33–35.

———. *A Syntactical Study of the Dialect of Byblos*. Ph.D. dissertation. Johns Hopkins University Press, 1950.

———. "A Syntactical Study of the Dialect of Byblos as Reflected in the Amarna Tablets." Pp. 84–95 in *Amarna Studies: Collected Writings*, by W. L. Moran, ed. J. Huehnergard and S. Izre'el. HSS 54. Winona Lake, IN: Eisenbrauns, 2003.

———. "An Unexplained Passage in an Amarna Letter from Byblos." *JNES* 8 (1949) 124–25.

———. "The Use of the Canaanite Infinitive Absolute as a Finite Verb in the Amarna Letters from Byblos." *JCS* 4 (1950) 169–72.

Morrison, Craig E. "Courtesy Expressions: Biblical Hebrew." P. 911 in vol. 2 of *Encyclopedia of Hebrew Language and Linguistics*, ed. Geoffrey Khan. Leiden: Brill, 2013.

———. "Infinitive: Biblical Hebrew." Pp. 693–94 in vol. 3 of *Encyclopedia of Hebrew Language and Linguistics*, ed. Geoffrey Khan. Leiden: Brill, 2013.

Moshavi, Adina. *Word Order in the Biblical Hebrew Finite Clause: A Syntactic and Pragmatic Analysis of Preposing*. LSAWS 4. Winona Lake, IN: Eisenbrauns, 2010.

Muraoka, T. "The Alleged Final Function of the Biblical Hebrew Syntagm '*WAW* + A Volitive Verb Form.'" Pp. 229–41 in *Narrative Syntax and the Hebrew Bible*, ed. Ellen van Wolde. Leiden: Brill, 1997.

________. *Emphatic Words and Structures in Biblical Hebrew*. Jerusalem: Magnes, 1985.

________. "On the So-Called *Dativus Ethicus* in Hebrew." *JTS* 29 (1978) 495–98.

________. "On Verb Complementation in Biblical Hebrew." *VT* 29 (1979) 425–35.

Muraoka, T., and B. Porten. *A Grammar of Egyptian Aramaic*. Leiden: Brill, 1998.

Naudé, Jacobus A. "David: Biblical Hebrew." Pp. 274–75 in vol. 3 of *Encyclopedia of Hebrew Language and Linguistics*, ed. Goeffrey Kahn; Leiden: Brill, 2013.

Naveh, Joseph. *Studies in West-Semitic Epigraphy*. Jerusalem: Magnes, 2009.

Niccacci, Alviero. "Analysis of Biblical Narrative." Pp. 175–98 in *Biblical Hebrew and Discourse Linguistics*, ed. R. D. Bergen. Winona Lake, IN: Eisenbrauns / Dallas: Summer Institute of Linguistics, 1994.

________. "Basic Facts and Theory of the Biblical Hebrew Verb System in Prose." Pp. 168–202 in *Narrative Syntax and the Hebrew Bible: Papers of the Tilburg Conference 1996*. Biblical Interpretation Series 29. Leiden: Brill, 1997.

________. "Consecutive *Waw*." Pp. 569–70 in vol. 1 of *Encyclopedia of Hebrew Language and Linguistics*, ed. Geoffrey Khan. Leiden: Brill, 2013.

________. "Lettura Sintattica della Prosa Ebraico-biblica: Principie Applicazioni." *SBFLA* 31. Jerusalem: Franciscan Printing Press, 1990.

________. "A Neglected Point of Hebrew Syntax: *yiqtol* and Position in the Sentence." *LASBF* 37 (1987) 7–19.

________. "On the Hebrew Verbal System." Pp. 117–37 in *Biblical Hebrew and Discourse Linguistics*, ed. R.D. Bergen. Winona Lake, IN: Eisenbrauns / Dallas: Summer Institute of Linguistics, 1994.

________. "An Outline of the Hebrew Verbal System in Prose." *LASBF* 39 (1989) 7–26.

________. *The Syntax of the Verb in Classical Hebrew Prose*, trans. W. G. E. Watson. JSOTSup 86. Sheffield: JSOT Press, 1990.

Notarius, Tania. "Prospective *weqatal* in Biblical Hebrew: Dubious Cases or Unindentified Category?" *JNSL* 34 (2008) 39–55.

O'Connor, M. "Discourse Linguistics and the Study of Biblical Hebrew." Pp. 17–42 in *Congress Volume: Basel 2001*, ed. A. Lemaire. VTSup 92. Leiden: Brill, 2002.

________. *Hebrew Verse Structure*. Winona Lake, IN: Eisenbrauns, 1980.

O'Leary, D. D. De Lacy. *Colloquial Arabic*. London: Routledge & Kegan Paul, 1963.

Orlinsky, H. M. "On the Cohortative and Jussive after an Imperative or Interjection in Biblical Hebrew." *JQR* 31 (1940) 371–82; 32 (1942) 191–205, 273–77.

Palmer, F. R. *Mood and Modality*. Cambridge: Cambridge University Press, 1986.

________. *Mood and Modality*. 2nd ed. Cambridge Textbooks in Linguistics. Cambridge: Cambridge University Press, 2001.

________. *Semantics*. Cambridge: Cambridge University Press, 1981.

Pardee, Dennis. "Canaanite Dialects." Pp. 103–7 in *The Ancient Languages of Syria–Palestine and Arabia*, ed. R. D. Woodard. Cambridge: Cambridge University Press, 2008.

________. "Epistolary Formulae: Biblical Period." P. 852 in vol. 1 of *Encyclopedia of Hebrew Language and Linguistics*, ed. Goeffrey Kahn. Leiden: Brill, 2013.

———. "Further Studies in Ugaritic Epistolography." *AfO* 31 (1984) 213–30.

———. "Remarks on the Classification of the Northwest Semitic Languages." Pp. 100–105 in *The Balaam Text from Deir ʿAlla Re-evaluated: Proceedings of the International Symposium Held at Leiden, 21–24 August 1989*, ed. J. Hoftijzer and G. van der Kooij. Leiden: Brill, 1991.

———. "Three Ugaritic Tablet Joins." *JNES* 43 (1984) 243–45.

———. "Ugaritic." Pp. 131–44 in *The Semitic Languages*, ed. R. Hetzron. New York: Routledge, 1997.

———. "Ugaritic." Pp. 288–318 in *The Cambridge Encyclopedia of the World's Ancient Languages*, ed. Roger D. Woodard. Cambridge: Cambridge University Press, 2004.

———. "Ugaritic." Pp. 5–35 in *The Ancient Languages of Syria–Palestine and Arabia*, ed. R. D. Woodard. Cambridge: Cambridge University Press, 2008.

Pardee, Dennis, and R. M. Whiting. "Aspects of Epistolary Verbal Usage in Ugaritic and Akkadian." *BSOAS* 50 (1987) 1–31.

Petersson, Lina. "The Syntactic Pattern Imperfect *w-yiqtol* and the Expression of Indirect Command in Biblical Hebrew." Paper presented at the World Congress of Jewish Studies, Jerusalem, 28 July 2013.

Portner, Paul. *Modality*. Oxford: Oxford University Press 2009.

Pritchard, J. B. *The Ancient Near East in Pictures*. Vol. 1. Princeton: Princeton University Press, 1958.

Quinto-Pozos, David. "Deictic Points in the Visual-Gestural and Tactile-Gestural Modalities." Pp. 442–67 in *Modality and Structure in Signed and Spoken Languages*, ed. R. P. Meier, K. Cormier, and D. Quinto-Pozos. Cambridge: Cambridge University Press, 2009.

Rainey, A. F. "The Ancient Hebrew Prefix Conjugation in the Light of Amarnah Canaanite." *HS* 27 (1986) 4–19.

———. *Canaanite in the Amarna Tablets: A Linguistic Analysis of the Mixed Dialect Used by the Scribes from Canaan*. 4 vols. Leiden: Brill, 1996.

———. *El Amarna Tablets 359–379; Supplement to T. A. Knudtzon, Die El Amarna Tafeln*. AOAT 8. Kevelaer: Butzon & Bercker / Neukirchen-Vluyn: Neukirchener Verlag, 1970.

———. "Further Remarks on the Hebrew Verbal System." *HS* 29 (1988) 35–42.

———. "The Imperative 'See' as an Introductory Particle, an Egyptian–West Semitic Calque." Pp. 309–16 in *Go to the Land I Will Show You: Studies in Honor of Dwight W. Young*, ed. J. E. Coleson and V. H. Matthews. Winona Lake, IN: Eisenbrauns, 1996.

———. "Is There Really a *yaqtula* Conjugation Pattern in the Canaanite Amarna Tablets?" *JCS* 43–45 (1991–93) 107–18.

———. "Morphology of the Prefix-Tenses of West Semitized El Amarna Tablets." *UF* 7 (1975) 395–426.

———. "The Northwest Semitic Literary Repertoire and Its Acquaintance by Judean Writers." *MAARAV* 15.2 (2008) 193–205.

———. "Redefining Hebrew: A Transjordanian Language." *MAARAV* 14.2 (2007) 67–81.

________. "The Suffix Conjugation Pattern in Ancient Hebrew: Tense and Modal Functions." *Ancient Near Eastern Studies* 40 (2003) 3–42.

________. "The Use of the Precative by Canaanite Scribes in the Amarna Letters." Pp. 331–41 in *Mesopotamica–Ugaritica–Biblica*, ed. M. Dietrich and O. Loretz. AOAT 232. Kevelaer: Butzon & Bercker / Neukirchen–Vluyn: Neukirchener Verlag, 1993.

________. Whence Came the Israelites and Their Language? *IEJ* 57 (2007) 41–64.

________. "The *Yaqtul* Preterite in Northwest Semitic." Pp. 395–407 in *Hamlet on a Hill: Semitic and Greek Studies Presented to Professor T. Muraoka on the Occasion of His Sixty-Fifth Birthday*," ed. M. F. J. Baasten and W. T. van Peursen. Orientalia Lovaniensia Analecta 118. Leuven: Peeters, 2003.

Ramos, T. V. *Conversational Tagalog*. Honolulu: University of Hawaii Press, 1985.

________. *Tagalog Dictionary*. Honolulu: University of Hawaii Press, 1971.

Ramos, T. V., and R. M. Cena. *Modern Tagalog*. Honolulu: University of Hawaii Press, 1990.

Revell, E. J. "Address, Forms of." Pp. 32–33 in vol. 1 of *Encyclopedia of Hebrew Language and Linguistics*, ed. Goeffrey Kahn. Leiden: Brill, 2013.

________. "The Battle with Benjamin (Judges XX 29–48) and Hebrew Narrative Techniques." *VT* 35 (1985) 417–33.

________. *The Designation of the Individual: Expressive Usage in Biblical Narrative*. Kampen: Kok Pharos, 1996.

________. "The System of the Verb in Standard Biblical Prose." *HUCA* 60 (1989) 1–37.

Richardson, M. E. J. "Tense, Aspect and Mood in Ugaritic *YQTL*." Pp. 283–89 in *Proceedings of the Fifth International Hamito-Semitic Congress 1987*, vol. 2, ed. Hans G. Mukarovsky. Beiträge zur Afrikanistik 40–41. Vienna: Afro-Pub., 1991.

Robar, Elizabeth. Nunation. P. 909 in vol. 2 of *Encyclopedia of Hebrew Language and Linguistics*, ed. Geoffrey Khan. Leiden: Brill, 2013.

Rogland, Max. "Abram's Persistent Faith: Hebrew Verb Semantics in Genesis 15:6." *WTJ* 70 (2008) 239–44.

Rubin, A. "The Subgrouping of the Semitic Languages." *Language and Linguistics Compass* 2 (2008) 79–102.

Ryckmans, G. *Grammaire accadienne*. Louvain: Bureaux du Muséon, 1938.

Schade, Aaron. "A Text Linguistic Approach to the Syntax and Style of the Phoenician Inscription of Azatiwada." *JSS* 50 (2005) 35–58.

Schmitz, Philip C. "Phoenician-Punic Grammar and Lexicography in the New Millennium." *JAOS* 124 (2004) 533–47.

Schniedewind, W. M. "Prolegomena for the Sociolinguistics of Classical Hebrew." *JHS* 5 (2004). http://www.jhsonline.org.

Schroeder, Otto. *Die Tontaffeln von El-Amarna*. Leipzig: Hinrichs, 1915.

Segert, S. *A Basic Grammar of the Ugaritic Language*. Los Angeles: University of California Press, 1984.

Seow, C. L. *Grammar for Biblical Hebrew*. Nashville: Abingdon, 1987.

Shopen, T. *Language Typology and Syntactic Description: Clause Structure*. Vol. 1. Cambridge: Cambridge University Press, 1987.

Shulman, A." The Function of the 'Jussive' and 'Indicative' Imperfect Forms in Biblical Hebrew Prose." *ZAH* 13 (2000) 168–80.

________. "Imperative and Second Person Indicative Forms in Biblical Hebrew Prose." *HS* 42 (2001) 271–87.

________. "Jussive." Pp. 437–40 in vol. 2 of *Encyclopedia of Hebrew Language and Linguistics*, ed. Geoffrey Kahn. Leiden: Brill, 2013.

________. "The Particle נָא in Biblical Hebrew Prose." *HS* 40 (1999) 57–82.

________. *The Use of Modal Verb Forms in Biblical Hebrew Prose*. Ph.D. dissertation. University of Toronto, 1996.

Sivan, Daniel. *A Grammar of the Ugaritic Language*. Handbuch der Orientalistik: Der nahe und mittlere Osten 28. Leiden: Brill, 1997.

________. *A Grammar of the Ugaritic Language*. Leiden: Brill, 2001.

________. The Use of *QTL* and *YQTL* Forms in the Ugaritic Verbal System. Pp. 89–103 in *Past Links: Studies in the Languages and Cultures of the Ancient Near East Dedicated to Professor Anson F. Rainey*, ed. S. Izre'el, I. Singer, and R. Zadok. IOS 18. Winona Lake, IN: Eisenbrauns, 1998.

Smyth, H. W. *Greek Grammar*. Repr., Cambridge: Harvard University Press, 1956.

Sokoloff, M. "The Hebrew of *Bereshit Rabba* according to MS. Vat. Ebr. 30." *Leshonénu* 38 (1968–69) 270–79. [Hebrew].

Soden, W. von. "Des Akkadische Subordinativ-Subjunctiv." *ZA* 63 (1973) 56–58.

________. *Grundriss der Akkadischen Grammatik*. AnOr 32. Rome: Pontifical Biblical Institute, 1952.

________. "Tempus und Modus im älteren Semitsche." Pp. 463–93 in *Babylonien und Israel: Historische, religiöse une sprachliche Biezhungen*, ed. H. P. Müller. Darmstadt: Wissenschaftliche Buchgesellschaft, 1991.

Solá-Solé, J. M. *L'infinitif sémitique: Contribution à l'étude des formes et des fonctions des noms d'action et des infinitifs sémitiques*. Bibliothèque de l'École Pratique des Hautes Études. Paris: Ancienne Honoré Champion, 1961.

Stabnow, D. K. *A Discourse Analysis Perspective on the Syntax of Clauses Negated by* לא *in the Primary History*. Ph.D. dissertation. Westminster Theological Seminary, 2000.

Steele, Susan. "Word Order Variation: A Typological Study." Pp. 585–623 in vol. 4 of *Universals of Human Language: Syntax*, ed. J. H. Greenberg. Stanford: Stanford University Press, 1978.

Talstra, E. "Tense, Mood, Aspect and Clause Connections in the Biblical Hebrew: A Textual Approach." *JNSL* 23 (1997) 81–103.

________. "Text Grammar and Hebrew Bible II: Syntax and Semantics." *BiOr* 39 (1982) 26–38.

Tropper, Josef. "Das altkanaanäische und ugaritische Verbalsystem." Pp. 159–70 in *Ugarit: Ein ostmeditarranes Kulturzentrum im Alten Orient*, ed. M. Dietrich and O. Loretz. Abhandlungen zur Literatur Alt-Syrien-Palästinas 7. Münster: Ugarit-Verlag, 1995.

________. "Kanaanäisches in dem Amarnabriefen: Review of *Canaanite in the Amarna Tablets*, by Anson Rainey." *AfO* 44–45 (1997–98) 134–45.

________. *Ugaritische Grammatik*. AOAT 273. Münster: Ugarit-Verlag, 2000.

________. "Das ugaritische Verbalsystem." *UF* 24 (1992) 313–37.

________. "Ventiv oder *yaqtula*-Volitiv in den Amarnabriefen aus Syrien-Palästina?" Pp. 397–205 in *Ana šadî Labnāni lū allik*, ed. B. Pongratz-Leisten et al. AOAT

247. Neukirchen-Vluyn: Neukirchener-Verlag / Kevelaer: Butzon & Bercker, 1997.

Trubetzkoy, Nikolai S. "Die phonologischen Systeme." *Travaux du Cercle Linguistique de Prague* 4 (1931) 96–116.

Tsevat, M. *A Study of the Language of the Biblical Psalms*. JBL Monograph Series 9. Philadelphia: Society of Biblical Literature, 1955.

Ungnad, A. *Akkadian Grammar*, trans. H. A. Hoffner Jr. and rev. L. Matouš. Atlanta: Scholars Press, 1992.

Vereet, E. *Modi ugaritici: Eine morpho-syntaktische Abhandlung über das Modal-system im Ugaritischen.* Leuven: Peeters, 1988.

Verstraete, Jean-Christophe. "Subjective and Objective Modality: Interprersonal and Ideational Functions in the English Modal Auxiliary System." *Journal of Pragmatics* 33 (2001) 1505–28.

Voigt, Rainer M. "The Classification of Central Semitic." *JSS* 32 (1987) 1–21.

Waltke, Bruce K., and M. O'Connor. *An Introduction to Biblical Hebrew Syntax*. Winona Lake, IN: Eisenbrauns, 1990.

Watts, J. D. W. "Infinitive Absolute as Imperative and the Interpretation of Exodus 20:8." *ZAW* 74 (1962) 141–47.

________. *Survey of Syntax in the Hebrew Old Testament*. Grand Rapids, MI: Eerdmans, 1964.

Weisberg, David B. "Rib-Hadda's Urgent Tone." Pp. 539–544 in *Assyriologica et Semitica*. AOAT 252. Münster: Ugarit-Verlag, 2000.

Wierzbicka, Anna. "The Semantics of Modality." *Folia linguistica; acta Societatis Linguisticae Europaeae* 21 (1987) 25–43.

Williams, Ronald J. "Energic Verbal Forms in Hebrew." Pp. 75–85 in *Studies on the Ancient Palestinian World Presented to Professor F. V. Winnett*, ed. J. W. Wevers and D. B. Redford. Toronto: University of Toronto Press, 1972.

________. *Hebrew Syntax: An Outline*. Rev. 2nd ed. Toronto: University of Toronto Press, 1976.

Wilt, T. L. "A Sociolinguistic Analysis of *naʾ*." *VT* 46 (1996) 237–55.

Wright, W. *A Grammar of the Arabic Language*. 2 vols. 3rd ed. Cambridge: Cambridge University Press, 1991.

Yishai, T. "Markedness." Pp. 578–79 in vol. 2 of *Encyclopedia of Hebrew Language and Linguistics*, ed. Goeffrey Kahn. Leiden: Brill, 2013.

Young, Ian, and R. Rezetko. *Linguistic Dating of Biblical Texts*. 2 vols.; London: Equinox, 2008.

Youngblood, Ronald Fred. *The Amarna Correspondence of Rib-Haddi, Prince of Byblos (EA 68–96)*. Ph.D. dissertation, Dropsie College, 1961.

Zewi, Tamar. *Parenthesis in Biblical Hebrew*. Leiden: Brill, 2007.

________. *A Syntactical Study of Verbal Forms Affixed by* -n(n) *Endings in Classical Arabic, Biblical Hebrew, El-Amarna Akkadian and Ugaritic*. AOAT 260. Münster: Ugarit-Verlag, 1999

Ziegeler, D. P. "Mood and Modality in Grammar." Pp. 259–67 in vol. 8 of *Encyclopedia of Language and Linguistics*, ed. K. Brown. 14 vols. 2nd edition. Oxford: Elsevier, 2006.

Index of Authors

Index of Scripture

Hebrew Bible

New Testament